MISS BEECHER'S

HOUSEKEEPER

AND

HEALTHKEEPER:

CONTAINING

FIVE HUNDRED RECIPES

FOR

ECONOMICAL AND HEALTHFUL COOKING;

ALSO,

MANY DIRECTIONS FOR SECURING HEALTH AND HAPPINESS.

APPROVED BY PHYSICIANS OF ALL CLASSES.

NEW YORK:
HARPER & BROTHERS, PUBLISHERS,
FRANKLIN SQUARE.
1873.

CONTENTS.

PART FIRST.

CHAPTER I.

HEALTH, ECONOMY, AND PLEASURE IN FOOD.

CHAPTER II.

MARKETING AND THE CARE OF MEATS.

CHAPTER III.

STEWS AND SOUPS.

CHAPTER IV.

SOUPS.

CHAPTER V.

HASHES.

CHAPTER VI.

BOILED MEATS.

CHAPTER VII.

ROAST AND BAKED MEATS.

CHAPTER VIII.

BROILED AND FRIED MEATS AND RELISHES.

CHAPTER IX.

PICKLES.

CHAPTER X.

SAUCES AND SALADS.

CHAPTER XI.

FISH.

CHAPTER XII.

VEGETABLES.

CHAPTER XIII.

FAMILY BREAD.

CHAPTER XIV.

BREAKFAST AND SUPPER.

CHAPTER XV.

PUDDINGS AND PIES.

CHAPTER XVI.

CAKE.

CHAPTER XVII.

PRESERVES AND JELLIES.

CHAPTER XVIII.

DESSERTS AND EVENING PARTIES.

CHAPTER XIX.

DRINKS AND ARTICLES FOR THE SICK AND YOUNG CHILDREN.

PART SECOND.

CHAPTER I.

NEEDFUL SCIENCE AND TRAINING FOR THE FAMILY STATE.

CHAPTER II.

A HEALTHFUL AND ECONOMICAL HOME.

CHAPTER III.

ON HOME VENTILATION.

CHAPTER IV.

ON WARMING A HOUSE.

CHAPTER V.

ON STOVES AND CHIMNEYS.

CHAPTER VI.

ECONOMIC MODES OF BEAUTIFYING A HOME.

CHAPTER VII.

ON THE CARE OF HEALTH.

CHAPTER VIII.

DOMESTIC EXERCISE.

CHAPTER IX.

HEALTHFUL FOOD AND DRINKS.

CHAPTER X.

ON CLEANLINESS.

CHAPTER XI.

CLOTHING.

CHAPTER XII.

EARLY RISING.

CHAPTER XIII.

DOMESTIC MANNERS.

CHAPTER XIV.

THE PRESERVATION OF GOOD TEMPER IN THE HOUSEKEEPER.

CHAPTER XV.

HABITS OF SYSTEM AND ORDER.

CHAPTER XVI.

HEALTH OF MIND.

CHAPTER XVII.

CARE OF THE AGED.

CHAPTER XXII.

CARE OF YARDS AND GARDENS.

CHAPTER XXIII.

SEWING, CUTTING, AND FITTING.

CHAPTER XXIV.

ACCIDENTS AND ANTIDOTES.

CHAPTER XXV.

RIGHT USE OF TIME AND PROPERTY.

CHAPTER XXVI.

CARE OF INFANTS.

CHAPTER XXVII.

MANAGEMENT OF YOUNG CHILDREN.

CHAPTER XXVIII.

FAMILY RELIGIOUS TRAINING.

THE

HOUSEKEEPER AND HEALTHKEEPER.

PART FIRST.

CHAPTER I.

ADDRESS OF THE AUTHOR TO AMERICAN HOUSEKEEPERS.

My dear Friends,—This volume embraces, in a concise form, many valuable portions of my other works on Domestic Economy, both those published by Harper and Brothers and those published by J. B. Ford and Co., together with other new and interesting matter. It is designed to be a complete encyclopædia of all that relates to a woman's duties as housekeeper, wife, mother, and nurse.

The First Part embraces a large variety of recipes for food that is both healthful and economical, put in clear, concise language, with many methods for saving labor, time, and money, not found in any other works of the kind. It also gives more specific directions as to *seasonings* and *flavors* than the common one of "Season to the Taste," which leaves all to the judgment of the careless or ignorant. The recipes have been tested by some of the best housekeepers, and all relating to health has been approved by distinguished physicians of all schools.

The Second Part contains interesting information as to the construction of the body, in a concise form, omitting all details, except such as have an immediate connection with a housekeeper's practical duties. These are so simplified and illustrated, that by aid of this, both servants and children can be made so to understand the *reasons* for the laws of health, as to render that willing and intelligent obedience which can be gained in no other way.

It is my most earnest desire to save you and your household from the sad consequences I have suffered from ignorance of the *laws of health*, especially those which women peculiarly need to understand and obey.

God made woman to do the work of the family, and to train those under her care to the same labor. And her body is so formed that family labor and care tend not only to good health, but to the *highest culture of mind.* Read all that is included in our "profession," as detailed in the Second Part of this work, and see how much there is to cultivate every mental faculty, as well as our higher moral powers. Domestic labor with the muscles of the arms and trunk, with intervals of sedentary work, are exactly what keep all the functions of the body in perfect order, especially those which, at the present day, are most out of order in our sex. And so the women of a former generation, while they read and studied books far less than women of the present time, were better developed both in mind and body.

It was my good fortune to be trained by poverty and good mothers and aunts to do every kind of domestic labor, and so, until one-and-twenty, I was in full enjoyment of health and happiness. Then I gave up all domestic employments for study and teaching, and in ten years I ruined my health, while my younger sisters and friends suffered in the same mistaken course. And my experience has been repeated all over the land, until there is such decay of female constitutions and health, as alarms, and justly alarms, every well-informed person.

After twenty years of invalidism, I have been restored to perfect health of body and mind, and *wholly* by a strict obedience to the *laws of health and happiness*, which I now commend to your especial attention, with the hope and prayer that by obedience to them you may save yourselves and households from unspeakable future miseries.

I wish I could give you all the evidence that I have gained to prove that woman's work in the household *might* be so conducted as to be agreeable, tasteful, and promotive of both grace and beauty of person. But this never can be generally credited till women of high culture set the example of training their sons and daughters, instead of hired servants alone, to be their domestic helpers.

According to the present tendency of wealth and culture, it is women of moderate or humble means who will train their own children to health and happiness, and rear prosperous families. Meantime, the rich women will have large houses, many servants, poor health, and little domestic comfort, while they train the children of foreigners to do family work, and in a way that will satisfy neither mistress nor servant; for a woman who does not work herself is rarely able to properly teach others. Choose wisely, then, O youthful mother and housekeeper! train yourself to wholesome labor and intelligent direction, and be prepared to educate a cheerful and healthful flock of your own children.

Your friend and well-wisher,

CATHARINE E. BEECHER.

NEW YORK, *April* 2, 1873.

CHAPTER II.

MARKETING AND THE CARE OF MEATS.

EVERY young woman, at some period of her life, may need the instructions of this chapter. Thousands will have the immediate care of buying meats for the family; and even those who are not themselves obliged to go to market, should have the knowledge which will enable them to direct their servants what and how to buy, and to judge whether the household, under their management, is properly served or not. Nothing so thoroughly insures the intelligent obedience of orders, as evidence that the person ordering knows exactly what is wanted.

The directions given in this and the ensuing chapters on meats, were carefully written, first in Cincinnati, with the counsel and advice of business men practically engaged in such matters. They have been recently rewritten in Hartford, Conn., after consultation with intelligent butchers and grocers.

MARKETING.

BEEF.

The animal, when slaughtered, should be bled very thoroughly. The care taken by the Jews in this and other points draws custom from other sects to their markets. The skin is tanned for leather, and the fat is used for candles and other purposes. The tail is used for soups, and the liver, heart, and tripe are also used for cooking. The body is split into two parts, through the back-bone, and each half is divided as marked in the drawing on following page. There are diverse modes of cutting and naming the parts, butchers in New England, in New York, in the South, and in the West, all making some slight differences; but the following is the most common method.

Fig. 1.

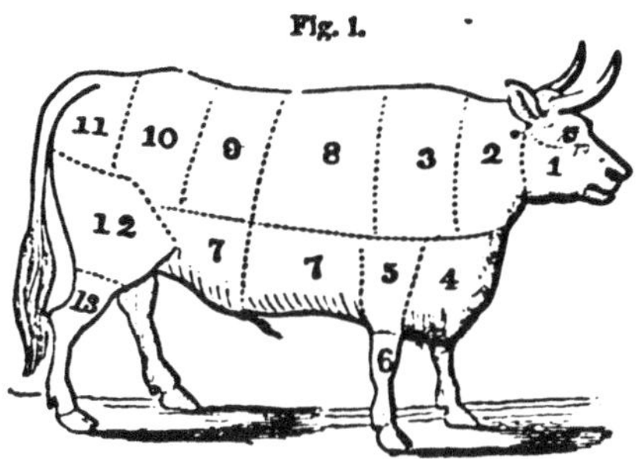

1. The *head:* frequently used for mince-pies; sometimes it is tried out for oil, and then the bones are used for fertilizers. The horns are used to make buttons and combs, and various other things. 2. The *neck;* used for soups and stews. 3. The *chuck-rib*, or *shoulder*, having four ribs. It is used for corning, stews, and soup, and some say the best steaks are from this piece. 4. The *front of the shoulder*, or the *shoulder-clod*, which is sometimes called the *brisket*, 5. The *back of the shoulder;* used for corning, soups, and stews. 6. The *fore-shin*, or *leg;* used for soups. 7, 7. The *plate-pieces;* the front one is called the brisket, (as is also 4,) and is used for corning, soups, and stews. The back plate-piece is called the *flank*, and is divided into the *thick flank*, or upper *sirloin*, and the *lower flank*. These are for roasting and corning. 8. The *standing ribs*, divided into *first*, *second*, and *third cuts;* used for roasting. The second cut is the best of the three. 9. The *sirloin*, which is the best roasting piece. 10. The *sirloin steak* and the *porter-house steak;* used for broiling. 11. The *rump*, or *aitch-bone;* used for soup or corning, or to cook *à la mode*. 12. The *round*, or *buttock;* used for corning, or for *à la mode;* also for dried beef. 13. The *hock*, or *hind shank;* used for soups.

In selecting *Beef*, choose that which has a loose grain, easily yielding to pressure, of a clear red, with whitish fat. If the lean is purplish, and the fat yellow, it is poor beef. Beef long kept turns a darker color than fresh killed. Stall-fed beef has a lighter color than grass-fed.

Ox beef is the best, and next, that of a heifer.

In cold weather, it is economical to buy a hind quarter; have it cut up, and what is not wanted immediately, pack with snow in a barrel. All meats grow tender by keeping. Do not let meats freeze; if they do, thaw them in cold water, and do not cook them till fully thawed. A piece weighing ten pounds requires ten or twelve hours to thaw.

Fig. 2.

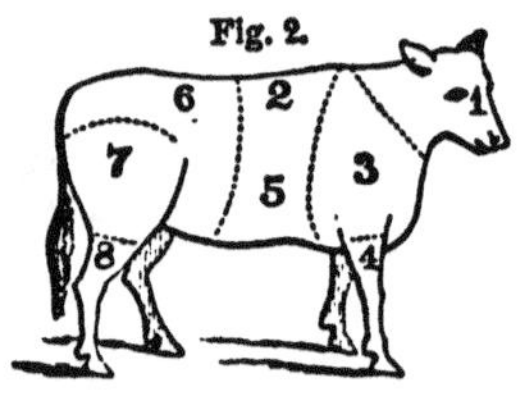

VEAL.

The calf should not be slaughtered until it is six weeks old. Spring is the best time for veal. It is divided as marked in the drawing.

1. The *head*, sold with the *pluck*, which includes the *heart*, *liver*, and *sweet-breads*. 2. The *rack*, including the neck; used for stews, pot-pies, and broths; also for chops and roasting. 3. The *shoulder*. This, and also half the rack and ribs of the fore-quarter, are sometimes roasted, and sometimes used for stews, broths, and cutlets. 4. The *fore-shank*, or *knuckle;* used for broths. 5. The *breast;* used for stews and soups; also to stuff and bake. 6. The *loin;* used for roasting. 7. The *fillet*, or *leg*, including the hind flank; used for cutlets, or to stuff and boil, or to stuff and roast, or bake. 8. The *hind shank*, or *hock*, or *knuckle;* used for soups. The *feet* are used for jelly.

In selecting *Veal*, take that which is firm and dry, and the joints stiff, having the lean a delicate red, the kidney covered with fat, and the fat very white. If you buy the head, see that the eyes are plump and lively, and not dull and sunk in the head. If you buy the legs, get those which are not skinned, as the skin is good for jelly or soup.

Fig. 3.

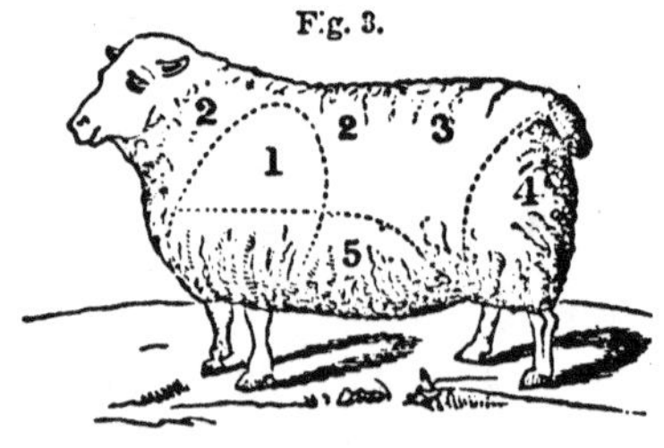

MUTTON.

1. The *shoulder;* for boiling or corning. 2, 2. The *neck* and *rack;* for

boiling or corning. 3. The *loin*; is roasted, or broiled as chops. 4. The *leg*; is boiled, or broiled, or stuffed and roasted. Many salt and smoke the leg, and call it smoked venison. 5. The *breast*; for boiling or corning.

In choosing *Mutton*, take that which is bright red and close-grained, with firm and white fat. The meat should feel tender and springy on pressure. Notice the vein on the neck of the fore-quarter, which should be a fine blue.

Fig. 4.

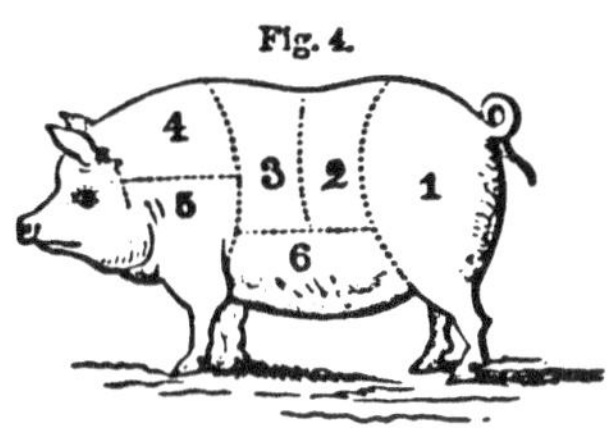

PORK.

1. The *leg*, or *ham*; used for smoking. 2. The *hind loin*. 3. The *fore loin*. 4. The *spare-rib*; for roasting; sometimes including all the ribs. 5. The *hand*, or *shoulder*; sometimes smoked, and sometimes corned and boiled. 6. The *belly*, or *spring*, for corning or salting down. The *feet* are used for jelly, head-cheese, and souse.

In selecting *Pork*, if young, the lean can easily be broken when pinched, and the skin can be indented by nipping with the fingers. The fat also will be white and soft. *Thin* rind is best.

In selecting *Hams*, run a knife along the bone, and if it comes out clean, the ham is good; but if it comes out smeared, it is spoiled. Good bacon has white fat, and the lean adheres closely to the bone. If the bacon has yellow streaks, it is rusty, and not fit to use.

In selecting *Poultry*, choose those that are full grown, but not old. When young and fresh-killed, the skin is thin and tender, the joints not very stiff, and the eyes full and bright. The breast-bone shows the age, as it easily yields to pressure if young, and is tough when old. If young, you can with a pin easily tear the skin. A goose, when old, has red and hairy legs; but when young, they are yellow, and have few hairs. The pin-feathers are the roots of feathers, which break off and remain in the skin, and always indicate a *young* bird. When very neatly dressed, they are pulled out.

Poultry and birds ought to be killed by having the head cut off, and then hung up by the legs to bleed freely. This makes the flesh white and more healthful.

In selecting *Fish*, take those that are firm and thick, having stiff fins and bright scales, the gills bright red, and the eyes full and prominent. When fish are long out of water, they grow soft, the fins bend easily, the scales are dim, the gills grow dark, and the eyes sink and shrink away. Be sure and have them dressed immediately; sprinkle them with salt, and use them, if possible, the same day. In warm weather, put them in ice, or corning, for the next day.

Shell-fish can be decided upon only by the smell. Lobsters are not good unless alive, or else boiled before offered for sale. They are black when alive, and red when boiled. When to be boiled, they are to be put alive into boiling water, which is the quickest and least cruel way to end their life.

THE CARE OF MEATS.

In hot weather, if there is no refrigerator, then wipe meat dry, sprinkle on a little salt and pepper, and hang in the cellar. Or, still better, wrap it, thus prepared, in a dry cloth, and cover it with charcoal or with wood-ashes. Mutton, wrapped in a cloth wet with vinegar, and laid on the ground of a *dry* cellar, keeps well and improves in tenderness.

Hang meat a day or two after it is killed before corning it.

In winter, meat is kept finely if well packed in snow, without salting; but some say it lessens the sweetness.

Frozen meat must be thawed in cold water, and not cooked till entirely thawed.

Beef and mutton are improved by keeping as long as they remain sweet. If meat begins to taint, wash it, and rub it with powdered charcoal, which often removes the taint.

Sometimes rubbing with salt will cure it. Soda water is good also.

Take all the kernels out that you will find in the round and thick end of the flank of beef, and in the fat, and fill the holes with salt. This will preserve it longer.

Salt your meat, in summer, as soon as you receive it.

A pound and a half of salt rubbed into twenty-five pounds of beef, will corn it so as to last several days in ordinary warm weather; or put it in strong brine.

In most books of recipes there are several different ones for corning, for curing pork hams, and for other uses, while an inexperienced person is at a loss to know which is best. The recipes here given are decided to be *the best*, after an examination of quite a variety, by the writer, who has resided where they were used; and she knows that the very best results are secured by these directions. These also are pronounced the best by business men of large experience.

To Salt down Beef to keep the Year round.—One hundred pounds of beef; four quarts of rock-salt, pounded fine; four ounces of saltpetre, pounded fine; four pounds of brown sugar. Mix well. Put a layer of meat on the bottom of the barrel, with a thin layer of this mixture under it. Pack the meat in layers, and between each put equal proportions of this mixture, allowing a little more to the top layers. Then pour in brine till the barrel is full.

To cleanse Calf's Head and Feet.—Wash clean, and sprinkle pounded resin over the hair; dip in boiling water and take out immediately, and then scrape them clean; then soak them in water for four days, changing the water every day.

To prepare Rennet.—Take the stomach of a new-killed calf, and do not wash it, as it weakens the gastric juice. Hang it in a cool and dry place five days or so; then turn the inside out, and slip off the curds with the hand. Then fill it with salt, with a little saltpetre mixed in, and lay it in a stone pot, pouring on a tea-spoonful of vinegar, and sprinkling on a handful of salt. Cover it closely, and keep for use. After six weeks, take a piece four inches square and put it in a bottle with five gills of cold water and two gills of rose brandy; stop it close, and shake it when you use it. A table-spoonful is enough for a quart of milk.

To Salt down Fish.—Scale, cut off the heads, open down the back, and remove most of the spine, to have them keep better. Lay them in salt water two hours, to extract blood. Sprinkle with fine salt, and let them lie over night. Then mix one peck of coarse and fine salt, one ounce of saltpetre, (or half an ounce of saltpetre and half an ounce of saleratus,) and one pound of sugar. Then pack in a firkin. Begin with a layer of salt, then a layer of fish, skin downward. A peck of salt will answer for twenty-five shad, and other fish in proportion.

As in most country families, when meat is salted for the year's use, pork is the meat most generally and most largely relied upon, considerable space is devoted to its proper preparation. Special attention is given to various modes of curing and preserving it.

To try out Lard.—Take what is called *the leaves*, and take off all the skin, cut it into pieces an inch square, put it into a clean pot over a slow fire, and try it till the scraps look a reddish-brown; take great care not to let it burn, which would spoil the whole. Then strain it through a strong cloth, into a stone pot, and set it away for use.

Take the fat to which the smaller intestines are attached, (not the large ones,) and the flabby pieces of pork not fit for salting, try these in the same way, and set the fat thus obtained where it will freeze, and by spring the strong taste will be gone, and then it can be used for frying. A tea-cup of water prevents burning while trying.

Corn-fed pork is best. Pork made by still-house slops is almost poisonous, and hogs that live on offal never furnish healthful food. If hogs are properly fed, the pork is not unhealthful.

Pork with kernels in it is measly, and is unwholesome.

A thick skin shows that the pork is old, and that it requires more time to boil. If bought pork is very salt, soak it some hours. Do not let pork freeze, if you intend to salt it.

The gentleman who uses the following recipe for curing pork hams, says it has these advantages over all others he has tried or heard of, namely, the hams thus cured are sweeter than by any other method; they are more solid and tender, and are cured in less than half the time. Moreover, they do not attract flies so much as other methods:

Recipe for Molasses-cured Hams.—Moisten every part of the ham with molasses, and then for every hundred pounds use one quart of fine salt, and four ounces of saltpetre, rubbing them in very thoroughly at every point. Put the hams thus prepared in a tight cask for four days. Then rub again with molasses and one quart of salt, and return the hams to the cask for four days. Repeat this the third and the fourth time, and then smoke the hams. This process takes only sixteen days, while other methods require five or six weeks.

The following is the best recipe for the ordinary mode of curing hams; and the brine or pickle thus prepared is equally good for corning and all other purposes for which brine is used. Some persons use saleratus instead of the saltpetre, and others use half and half of each, and say it is an improvement:

Brine or Pickle for corning Hams, Beef, Pork, and Hung Beef.—Four gallons of water; two pounds of rock-salt, and a little more of common salt; two ounces of saltpetre; one quart of molasses. Mix, but do not boil. Put the hams in a barrel and pour this over them, and keep them covered with it for six weeks. If more brine is needed, make it in the same proportions.

Brine for Beef, Pork, Tongues, and Hung Beef.—Four gallons of water; one and a half pounds of sugar; one ounce of saltpetre; one ounce of saleratus. Add salt; and if it is for use only a month or two, use six pounds of salt; if for all the year, use *nine* pounds. In hot weather, rub the meat with salt before putting it in, and let it lie for three hours, to extract the blood. When tongues and hung beef are taken out, wash the pieces, and, when smoked, put them in paper bags, and hang in a dry place.

Brine by Measure, easily made.—One gallon of cold water; one quart of rock-salt; and two of blown salt; one heaping table-spoonful of saltpetre, (or half as much of saleratus, with half a table-spoonful of saltpetre;) six heaping table-spoonfuls of brown sugar. Mix, but not boil. Keep it as long as salt remains undissolved at bottom. When scum rises, add more salt, sugar, saltpetre, and soda.

To Salt down Pork.—Allow a peck of salt for sixty pounds. Cover the bottom of the barrel with salt an inch deep. Put down one layer of pork, and cover that with salt half an inch thick. Continue thus till the barrel is full. Then pour in as much strong brine as the barrel will receive. Keep coarse salt between all pieces, so that the brine can circulate. When a white scum or bloody-looking matter rises on the top, scald the brine and add more salt. Leave out bloody and lean pieces for sausages. Pack as tight as possible, the rind next the barrel; and let it be *always* kept *under* the brine. Some use a stone for this purpose. In salting down a new supply, take the old brine, boil it down and remove all the scum, and then use it to pour over the pork. The pork may be used in six weeks after salting.

To prepare Cases for Sausages.—Empty the cases, taking care not to tear them. Wash them thoroughly, and cut into lengths of two yards each. Then take a candle-rod, and fastening one end of a case to the top of it, turn the case inside outward. When all are turned, wash very thoroughly, and scrape them with a scraper made for the purpose, keeping them in warm water till ready to scrape. Throw them into salt and water to soak till used. It is a very difficult job to scrape them clean without tearing them. When finished, they look transparent and very thin.

Sausage-Meat.—Take one third fat and two thirds lean pork, and chop it; and then to every twelve pounds of meat add twelve large even spoonfuls of pounded salt, nine of sifted sage, and six of sifted black pepper. Some like a little summer-savory. Keep it in a cool and dry place.

Another Recipe.—To twenty-five pounds of chopped meat, which should be one third fat and two thirds lean, put twenty spoonfuls of sage, twenty-five of salt, ten of pepper, and four of summer-savory.

Bologna Sausages.—Take equal portions of veal, pork, and ham; chop them fine; season with sweet herbs *and* pepper; put them in cases; boil them till tender, and then dry them.

To smoke Hams.—Make a small building of boards, nailing strips over the cracks to confine the smoke. Have within cross-sticks, on which to hang the hams. Have only one opening at top, at the end farthest from the fire. Set it up so high that a small stove can be set under or very near it, with the smoke-pipe entering the floor at the opposite end from the slide. These di-

Fig. 5.

rections are for a wooden house, and it is better thus than to have a fire *within* a brick house, because too much warmth lessens the flavor and tenderness of the hams. Change the position of the hams once or twice, that all may be treated alike. When this can not be done, use an inverted barrel or hogshead, with a hole for the smoke to escape, and resting on stones; and keep a small, smouldering fire. Cobs are best, as giving a better flavor; and brands or chips of walnut wood are next best. Keeping a small fire a longer time is better than quicker smoking, as too much heat gives the hams a strong taste, and they are less sweet.

The house and barrel are shown in Fig. 5, on preceding page.

CHAPTER III.

STEWS AND SOUPS.

IN using salt and pepper, diversities of strength make a difficulty in giving very exact directions; so also do inequalities in the size of spoons and tumblers. But so much can be done, that a housekeeper, after one trial, can give exact directions to her cook, or with a pencil alter the recipe.

It is a great convenience to have recipes that employ measures which all families have on hand, so as not to use steelyards and balances. The following will be found the most convenient:

A medium size tea-spoon, even full, equals 60 drops, or one eighth of an ounce.

A medium size table-spoon, even full, equals two tea-spoonfuls.

One ounce equals eight even tea-spoonfuls, or four table-spoonfuls.

One gill equals eight even table-spoonfuls.

Half a gill equals four even table-spoonfuls.

Two gills equal half a pint, and four gills equal one pint.

One common size tumbler equals half a pint, or two gills.

One pint equals two tumblerfuls, or four gills.

One quart equals four tumblerfuls, or eight gills.

Four quarts equal one gallon.

Four gallons equal one peck.

Four pecks equal one bushel.

A quart of sifted flour, heaped, a sifted quart of sugar, and a softened quart of butter each weigh about a pound, and so nearly that measuring is as good as weighing.

Water is heavier, and a pint of water weighs nearly a pound.

Ten eggs weigh about one pound.

The most economical modes of cooking, as to *time*, *care*, and *labor*, are stews, soups, and hashes; and when properly seasoned, they are great favorites, especially with children.

Below is a drawing of a stew and soup-kettle that any tinman can easily make. Its advantages are, that, after the meat is put in, there is no danger of scorching, and no watching is required, except to keep up the fire aright, so as to have a steady simmering. Another advantage is, that, by the tight cover, the steam and flavors are confined, and the cooking thus improved. Then, in taking up the stew, it offers several conveniences, as will be found on trial.

Fig. 6.

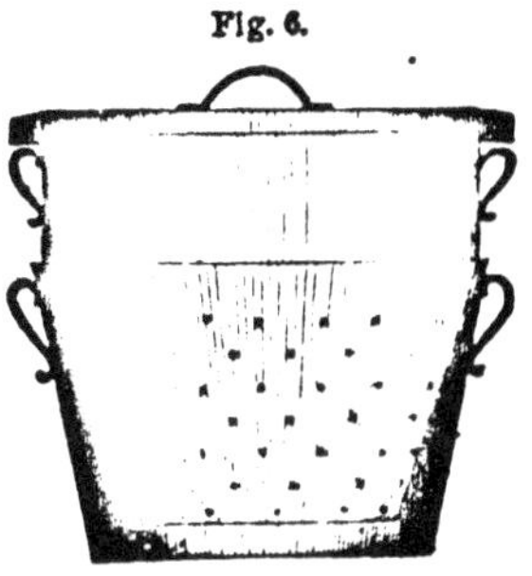

This stew-kettle consists of two pans, the inner one not fastened; but fitting tight to the outer, with holes the size of a large pin-head commencing half an inch from the bottom and continuing to within two inches of the top of the under pan. It has a flat lid, on which may be placed a weight, to confine steam and flavors. The holes may be an inch apart. The size of the kettle must depend on the size of the family: it may be of any desired size.

General Directions.

Generally, in making stews, use soft water; but when only hard is at hand, put in half a tea-spoonful of soda to every two quarts of water. Put in all the bones and gristle first, breaking the bones thoroughly.

Rub fresh meat with salt, and put it in *cold* water, for soups, as this extracts the juices.

As soon as water begins to boil, skim repeatedly till no more scum rises.

Never let water boil hard for soups or stews; for

"Meat fast boiled
Is meat half spoiled."

Let the water *simmer gently* and not stop simmering long, as this injures both looks and flavor.

Keep in water enough to cover the meat, or it becomes hard and dark.

In preparing for soups, it is best to make a good deal of broth at one time; cool it slowly, first removing sediment by straining through a colander. When cold, remove the fat from the top, and keep the liquor for soups and gravies. This is called *stock*, and as such should have no other seasoning than salt. The other seasoning is to be put in when heated and combined with other material for soup.

In hot weather, stock will keep only a day or two; but in cool weather, three or four days. If vegetables were boiled in it, it would turn sour sooner.

Remnants of cooked meats may be used together for soup; but take care that none is tainted, thus spoiling all. Liquor in which corned beef is boiled should be saved to mix with stock of fresh meat, and then little or no salt is needed. The recipes for stews that follow will make good soups by adding more water.

Beef and Potato Stew.—Cut up four pounds of beef into strips three inches by two, and put them into two quarts of water, with one onion sliced very fine. Let this *simmer* four hours. Add in half a cup of warm water six even tea-spoonfuls of salt, three of sugar, three of vinegar, a tea-spoonful of black pepper, and six heaping tea-spoonfuls of flower, lumps rubbed out. Pour these upon the meat; cut up, slice, and add six potatoes, and let all stew till the meat is very tender, and the potatoes are soft. If potatoes are omitted, leave out half a tea-spoonful of salt and a pinch of the pepper.

Be sure and skim very thoroughly when boiling commences, and do not allow hard boiling, but only a gentle simmer.

French Mutton and Turnip Stew.—Cut up two pounds of mutton, with a little of the fat, into two-inch squares. Rub two heaping table-spoonfuls of butter into two table-spoonfuls of flour, and stir it into the meat, with water just enough to cover it. Add three *even* tea-spoonfuls of salt, half a one of pepper, four of sugar, a sprig of parsley, and a small onion, sliced very fine. Skim as soon as it begins to boil, and then add thirty pieces of turnips, each an inch square, that have been fried brown. Let all stew till meat and turnips are tender; throw out the parsley, and serve with the turnips in the centre, and the meat around it.

A Simple Mutton Stew.—Cut four pounds of mutton into two-inch squares, add four *even* tea-spoonfuls of salt, four of sugar, half a one of pepper, and a small onion, sliced fine. Stew three hours, in two quarts of water, and then thicken with five tea-spoonfuls of flour, lumps rubbed out. Six tomatoes, or some tomato catsup, improves this.

A Beef Stew, with Vegetable Flavors.—Cut up four pounds of beef into two-inch squares, and add two quarts of water. Let it stew one hour. Then add one sliced onion, two sliced turnips, two sliced carrots, four sliced tomatoes, four heaping tea-spoonfuls of salt, one small tea-spoonful of pepper, four tea-spoonfuls of sugar, and five cloves. Let it stew till there is only about a tea-cupful of gravy, and thicken this with a little flour.

The above may be cooked without cutting up the meat, and it is good eaten cold. Pressing it under a weight improves it, and so does putting it in an oven for half an hour.

A Stew of Chicken, Duck, or Turkey, with Celery or Tomatoes.—Take a quart of lukewarm water, and add two heaping tea-spoonfuls of salt, two of sugar, and a salt-spoonful of pepper. Cut up a large head of celery, or four large tomatoes. Cut the fowl into eight or more pieces, and let all simmer together two hours, or till the meat is very tender. Then add two table-spoonfuls of butter, worked into as much flour, and let it simmer fifteen minutes.

A Favorite Irish Stew.—Cut two pounds of mutton into pieces two inches square; add a little of the chopped fat, three tea-spoonfuls of salt, half a one of black pepper, two of sugar, two sliced onions, and a quart of water. Let them simmer half an hour, and then add six peeled potatoes, cut in quarters, that have soaked in cold water an hour. Let the whole stew an hour longer, or rather till the meat is very tender. Skim it at first and just before taking up.

Veal Stew.—Put a knuckle of veal into two quarts of boiling water, with three tea-spoonfuls of salt and half a tea-spoonful of ground pepper. Then chop fine and tie in a muslin rag one carrot, two small onions, a small bunch of summer savory, and another of parsley; put them in the water, and let them stew three or four hours, till the meat is very tender. There should only be about half a pint of gravy at the bottom. Pour in *boiling* water, if needed. Strain the gravy, and thicken with four spoonfuls of flour or potato-starch, and let it boil up a minute only. This is improved by adding at first half a pound of salt pork or ham, cut in strips. When this is done, no salt is to be used, or only one tea-spoonful. Tomatoes improve it.

Another.—Cut four pounds of veal into strips one inch thick and three inches long, and peel and soak twelve potatoes cut into slices half an inch thick. Then put a layer of pork at the bottom, and alternate layers of potatoes and veal, with a layer of salt pork on the top. Put three tea-spoonfuls of salt, half a one of pepper, four of sugar, and six tea-spoonfuls of flour, with lumps rubbed out, into two quarts of water. Pour all upon the veal and potatoes, and let them stew till the veal is very tender. Add twelve peeled and sliced tomatoes, which will improve this.

A Favorite Turkish Stew, (called Pilaff.)—Take some rich broth, seasoned to the taste with pepper, salt, and tomato catsup. Add two tea-cups of rice, and let it simmer till the rice absorbs as much as it will take up without losing its form—say about fifteen minutes. Cut up a chicken, and season it with salt and pepper, and fry it in sweet butter or cream. Then put the chicken in the centre of the rice, and cover it entirely with rice. Then pour on half a pound of melted butter, and let it stand where it is hot, and yet will not fry, for fifteen minutes. To be served hot.

A Rice or Hominy Stew.—Take four pounds of any kind of fresh meat, cut into pieces two inches square, and put in the stew-pan with one pint of hominy. Then put into two quarts of warm water five heaping tea-spoonfuls of salt, four of sugar, half a one of pepper, and three of vinegar. Let them simmer four or five hours, till the meat is very tender. A tea-cup of rice may be used instead of hominy. A little salt pork improves this, as well as all other stews.

A Favorite English Beef Stew.—Simmer a shank or hock of beef in four quarts of water, with four heaping table-spoonfuls of salt, until the beef is soft and the water reduced to about two quarts. Then add peeled and soaked potatoes cut into thick slices, two tea-spoonfuls of pepper, two of sweet marjoram, and two of either thyme or summer savory. Stew till the potatoes are soft, add bread-crumbs and more salt if needful. One or two onions cut fine, and put in at first, improve it for most persons.

French Stew, or Pot au Feu.—Put three pounds of fresh meat into three quarts of cold water, with two tea-spoonfuls of salt. When it begins to simmer, add a gill of cold water, and skim thoroughly. Then add a quarter of a pound of liver, a medium-sized carrot sliced, two small turnips, two middle-sized leeks, half a head of celery, one sprig of parsley, a bay leaf, one onion with two cloves stuck in it, and two cloves of garlic. Simmer five hours. Strain the broth into a soup-dish, and serve the meat and vegetables on a platter. If more water is needed, add that which is boiling.

When the dish is served all together, it is called *Pot au Feu*, and the vessel in which it is cooked has the same name. It is the common dish of the French peasantry.

The following is the receipe for the favorite Spanish dish. A superior housekeeper tried it, and it was so much liked that several of her family were harmed *by eating too much:*

Spanish Olla Podrida.—Fry four ounces of salt pork in the pot, and, when partly done, add two pounds of fresh beef and a quarter of a pound of ham. Add two tea-spoonfuls of salt in cold water, and only enough just to cover the meat. Skim carefully the first half-hour, and then add a gill of peas, (if dried, soak them an hour first,) half a head of cabbage, one carrot, one turnip, two leeks, three stalks of celery, three stalks of parsley, two stalks of thyme, two cloves, two onions sliced, two cloves of garlic, ten pepper-corns, and a pinch of powdered mace or nutmeg. Simmer steadily for five hours. When the water is too low, add that which is boiling. Put the meat on a platter, and the vegetables around it. Strain the liquor on to toasted bread in a soup-dish.

All these articles can be obtained at grocers' or markets in our large cities, and of course can be procured in the country.

French Mutton Stew.—Take a leg of mutton and remove the large bone, leaving the bone at the small end as a handle; cut off also the bone below the knuckle, and fix it with skewers.

Put it in a stew-pan with a pinch of allspice, four onions, two cloves, two carrots, each cut in four pieces, a small bunch of parsley, two bay leaves, three sprigs of thyme, and *salt and pepper to the taste*. Add two ounces of bacon cut in slices, a quarter of a pint of broth, and cold water enough to cover it. After one hour of simmering, add a wine-glass of French brandy.

Let them simmer five hours longer, and then dish it; strain the sauce on it, and serve.

The American housekeeper by experiments can modify these foreign recipes to meet the taste of her family, and will find them *economical* modes of cooking, as well as healthful to most persons.

FRENCH MODES OF COOKING SOUPS AND STEWS.

The writer has examined the recipes of Gouffee, the chief French cook of the Queen of England, set forth in the expensive Royal Cook-Book; also those of Soyer and Professor Blot. She and her friends also have tested many of their recipes.

The following are most of the flavors used by them in cooking soups, stews, hashes, etc. Combination of these is recommended by those authors in these proportions:

One fourth of an ounce of thyme.
One fourth of an ounce of bay leaf.
One eighth of an ounce of marjoram.
One eighth of an ounce of rosemary.
Dry the above when fresh, mix in a mortar, and keep them corked tight in glass bottle.

Also the following in these proportions:

Half an ounce of nutmeg.
Half an ounce of cloves.
One fourth of an ounce of black pepper.
One eighth of an ounce of Cayenne pepper.

Pound, mix, and keep corked tight in glass. In using these with salt, put one ounce of the last recipe to four ounces of salt. In making force-meat and hashes, use at the rate of one ounce of this spiced salt to three pounds of meat.

Soup Powder.—Two ounces of parsley.
Two ounces of winter savory.
Two ounces of sweet marjoram.
Two ounces of lemon-thyme.
One ounce of lemon-peel.
One ounce of sweet basil.
Dry, pound, sift, and keep in a tight-corked bottle.

Let the housekeeper add these flavors so that they will *not be strong*, but quite delicate, and then *make a rule for the cook*.

The peculiar excellence of French cooking is the combination of flavors, so that no one is predominant, and all are delicate in force and quantity.

CHAPTER IV.

SOUPS.

General Directions.

Most of the preceding stews will serve also fairly as soups, by adding more water. Rub salt into meat for soups, but not for stews, as the salt extracts the juices; and in stews the meat is to be eaten, while in soups properly so called it is only the liquor that is served. Put meat into cold water for soups, as *slowly* heating also extracts the juices. For this same reason, meat that is boiled for eating should be put into boiling water to keep the juices in it.

Always *skim often*, as soon as the water begins to simmer; and do not add the salt and other seasoning till the scum ceases to rise.

Do not boil after the juices are extracted, as too much boiling injures the flavor.

Never cool soup in metal, as there may be poison in the soldering or other parts.

If you flavor your soup by vegetables, do not boil them in the soup, but in *very little* water, which is to be added to the soup with them, as it contains much of their flavor.

When onion is used for flavor, slice and fry it, and dredge on a little flour; add the water in which the vegetables for soup were boiled, or some meat broth, and then pour it into the soup. If you flavor with wine, soy, or catsup, put them into the tureen, and pour the soup upon them, as the flavor is lessened by putting them into the soup-kettle. Bread-crumbs, toast, or crackers also must be put in the tureen. Keep soup covered tight while boiling, to keep in flavors. If water is added, it must be boiling. The rule to guide in using salt and pepper is a heaping tea-spoonful of salt to a quart of water, and one-sixth as much pepper. But as tastes are different, and the salt and pepper vary in strength, the housekeeper can, on trial, change the recipe with a pencil.

Soup stock is broth of any kind of meat prepared in large quantity, to keep on hand for gravies and soups. Beef and veal make the best stock. One hind shin of beef makes five quarts of stock, and one hind shin of veal makes three quarts. Wash and put into twice as much water as you wish to, to have soup, and simmer five or six hours.

All kinds of bones should be mashed and boiled five or six hours, to take out all the nutriment, the liquor then strained, and kept in earthenware or stone, not in tin. Take off the fat when cool.

Cool broth quickly, and it keeps longer.

Use a flat-bottom kettle, as less likely to scorch.

Soft water is best for soups; a little soda improves hard water.

Stock will keep three or four days in cool weather; not so long in warm. Keep it in a cool place. When used, heat to boiling point, and then take up and flavor.

Put in the salt and pepper when the meat is thoroughly done.

Meat soups are best the second day, if warmed slowly and taken up as soon as heated. If heated too long, they become insipid.

Thin soups must be strained. If to be made very clear, stir in one or two well beaten eggs, with the shells, and let it boil half an hour.

Use the meat of the soup for a hash, warmed together with a little fat, and well seasoned.

Be *very* careful, in using bones and cold meats for soups, that none is *tainted*, for the soup may be ruined by a single bit of tainted meat or bone.

Potato Soup.—Take six large mealy potatoes, sliced and soaked an hour. Add one onion, sliced and tied in a rag, a quart of milk, and a quarter of a pound of salt pork cut in slices. Boil three quarters of an hour, and then add a table-spoonful of melted butter and a well-beaten egg, mixed in a cup of milk. This is a favorite soup with many, and easily made. Some omit the pork, and use salt and pepper to flavor it, and add one well beaten egg.

Green Corn Soup.—This is very nice made with sweet corn put into seasoned soup stock.

Plain Beef Soup.—Put three pounds of beef and one chopped onion, tied in a rag, to three quarts of cold water. Simmer till the meat is very soft—say four hours; then add three tea-spoonfuls of salt, as much sugar, and half a tea-spoonful of pepper. Any other flavors may be added to suit the taste. Strain the soup, and save the meat for mince-meat or hash. Half a dozen sliced tomatoes will much improve this. Some would thicken with three or four tea-spoonfuls of potato-starch or flour.

Rich Beef Soup.—The following is a specimen of soups that are most stylish, rich, and demand most care in preparation:

Simmer six pounds of beef for six hours in six quarts of water, using the bones, broken in small pieces. Cool it, and take off the fat. Next day, an hour before dinner, take out the meat to use for hash or mince-meat, heat the liquor, throw in some salt to raise the scum, and skim it well. Then slice small, and boil in very little water, these vegetables: two turnips, two carrots, one head of celery, one quart of tomatoes, half a head of small white cabbage, one pint of green corn or Shaker corn, soaked over night. Cook the cabbage in two waters, throwing away the first. Boil the soup half an hour after these are put in. Season with salt, pepper, mace, and wine to suit the taste.

Green Pea Soup.—Boil the pods an hour in a gallon of water. Strain the liquor, and put into it four pounds of beef or mutton, and simmer one hour. Then add half the peas contained in half a peck of pods, and boil half an hour; then thicken with two great spoonfuls of flour, and season with salt and pepper. Three tomatoes, sliced, improve this.

Dried Bean Soup or Pea Soup.—Soak the beans, if dry, over night, and then boil till soft. Then strain them through a colander; and to each quart of liquor add a tea-spoonful of sugar, a tea-spoonful of salt, and a salt-spoonful of pepper. Add a beaten egg, a tea-cup of milk, and two spoonfuls of butter. A sliced onion improves it for some, and not for others; also, half the juice of a lemon when taken up. Canned sweet-corn, or common corn with sugar added, makes good *succotash* for winter.

Clam Soup.—Wash and boil the clams till they come out of their shells easily; then chop them, and put them back into the liquor, which should first be strained. Add a tea-cup of milk for each quart of soup; thicken with a little flour, into which has been worked as much butter as it will hold, and season with salt and pepper to suit the taste.

A Vegetable and Meat Soup for Summer.—Take three quarts of stock that is duly seasoned with sugar, salt, and pepper. Add two small onions, chopped fine, three small carrots, three small turnips, one stalk of celery, and a pint of green peas—all chopped fine. Let it simmer two hours, and then serve it.

Dried Pea Soup with Salt Pork.—Soak a quart of split peas over night in soft water. Next morning wash them and put them in four quarts of water, with a tea-spoonful of sugar, two carrots, two small onions, and one stalk of celery—all cut in small pieces. Let them boil three hours. Boil a pound of salt pork in another pot for one hour; take off the skin, and put the pork in the soup, and then boil one hour longer.

Dried Bean or Pea Soup with Meat Stock.—Soak a pint of beans or split peas over night in soft water. Then boil them in three quarts of soup-stock, duly seasoned with salt and pepper, with one small onion, one turnip, one stalk of celery, and six cloves—all cut in small pieces. Let it boil four or five hours. Strain through a colander.

Mutton Soup.—Boil four pounds of mutton in four quarts of water, with four heaping tea-spoonfuls of salt, one even tea-spoonful of pepper, two tea-spoonfuls of sugar, one small onion, two carrots, and two turnips—all cut fine—and one tea-cup of rice or broken macaroni. Boil the meat alone two hours; then add the rest, and boil one hour and a half longer.

French Vegetable Soup.—Take a leg of lamb, of moderate size, and four quarts of water. Of potatoes, carrots, cabbage, tomatoes, and turnips, take a tea-cupful of each, chopped fine. Salt and black pepper at the rate of one heaping tea-spoonful of salt to each quart of water, and one sixth as much black pepper.

Wash the lamb, and put it into the four quarts of cold water. When the scum rises, take it off carefully with a skimmer. After having pared and chopped the vegetables, put them into the soup. Carrots require the most boiling, and should be put in first. This soup requires about three hours to boil.

Plain Calf's Head Soup.—Boil the head and feet in just water enough to cover them; when tender, take out the bones, cut in small pieces, and season with marjoram, thyme, cloves, salt, and pepper.

Put all into a pot, with the liquor, and four spoonfuls of butter; stew gently an hour; then, just as you take it up, add two or three glasses of port-wine, and the yelks of three eggs boiled hard.

An Excellent Simple Mutton Soup.—Put a piece of the fore-quarter of mutton into salted water, enough to more than cover it, and simmer it slowly two hours. Then peel a dozen turnips, and six tomatoes, and quarter them, and boil them with the mutton till just tender enough to eat. Thicken the soup with pearl barley. Some use, instead of tomatoes, the juice and rind of a lemon. Use half a tea-cup of rice, if you have no pearl barley.

CHAPTER V.

HASHES.

These are the common ways of spoiling hashes: 1. by frying, instead of merely heating them. Melted butter and oils are good and healthful when only heated, but are unhealthful when fried. 2. Dredging in flour, which, not being well cooked, imparts a raw taste of dough. 3. Using too much water, making them vapid; or too much fat or gravy, making them gross. 4. Using too much or too little salt and other seasoning. The following recipes will save from these mistakes, if exactly followed. When water is recommended in these recipes, *cold gravy* will be better, in which case the *butter* may be omitted:

A Seasoned Hash of any Fresh Meats.—Chop, but not very fine, any kinds of fresh meat, but be sure not to put in any that is tainted. To a common tumblerful of chopped meat put three table-spoonfuls of water, a tea-spoonful of sugar, a heaping tea-spoonful of salt, a salt-spoonful of pepper, and butter the size of half an egg. Warm, but do not fry; and when hot, break in three eggs, and stir till they are hardened a little; then serve. Bread-crumbs may be added. This may be put on buttered toast or served alone. This and all the following hashes may be varied in flavor, by adding, in delicate proportions, the mixed flavors on another page.

A Hash of Cold Fresh Meats and Potatoes.—Take two tumblerfuls of meat of any kind, chopped. Add as much cold potatoes, also chopped, two table-spoonfuls of sweet butter in six table-spoonfuls of hot water, and two tea-spoonfuls of salt. Sprinkle half a tea-spoonful of pepper over the meat, and also a spoonful of sugar; mix all, and warm about twenty minutes, but not so as to boil or fry. Tomatoes improve this.

Meat Hash with Eggs, (very nice.)—To a tumblerful of fresh cold meat cut in pieces about the size of peas, put three table-spoonfuls of hot water, two spoonfuls of butter, a tea-spoonful of sugar, two tea-spoonfuls of salt, and a salt-spoonful of pepper. Mix all, warm but not fry; and when hot, break in four eggs, and stir till they are hardened. Spread on buttered toast or serve alone. When eggs are used, the meat should not be chopped fine.

A Meat Hash with Tomatoes.—Cut up a pint of tomatoes into a saucepan, and when boiling-hot, add the cold meat in thin slices, with a table-spoonful of sugar, and salt and pepper, at the rate of a tea-spoonful of salt and half a tea-spoonful of pepper to each tumblerful of meat.

A Nice Beef Hash.—Make a gravy of melted butter, or take cold gravy; season with salt, pepper, and currant jelly or vinegar. Cut cold roast beef or the remnants of cold steak into mouthfuls, and put into the gravy till heated, but not to fry.

Or, season this gravy with the crushed juice of fresh tomatoes or tomato catsup.

A Simple and Excellent Veal Hash.—Chop cold veal very fine; butter a pudding-dish, and make alternate layers of veal and powdered crackers till the dish is full, the first layer of meat being at the bottom. Then beat up two eggs, and add a pint or less of milk, seasoned well with salt and pepper, and two or three spoonfuls of melted butter. Pour this over the meat and crackers; cover with a plate, and bake about half an hour. Remove the plate awhile, and let the top brown a little. This is the best way to cook veal, and children are very fond of it.

Rice and Cold Meats.—Chop remnants of fresh meats with salt pork, or cold ham. Season with salt and pepper and a little sugar; add two eggs and a little butter. Then make alternate layers with this and slices of cold boiled rice, and bake it half an hour.

Bread-Crumbs and Cold Meats.—Take any remnants of cooked fresh meats, and chop them fine with bits of ham or salt pork. Season with salt and pepper; add three eggs and a little milk, and then thicken with pounded bread-crumbs. Bake it as a pudding, or warm it for a hash, or cook it in flat cakes on a griddle.

A Meat Hash with Bread-Crumbs.—One tea-spoonful of flour, (or potato or corn-starch,) wet in four tea-spoonfuls of cold water. Stir it into a tea-cupful of boiling water, and put in a salt-spoonful of pepper, two tea-spoonfuls of salt, a tea-spoonful of sugar, and two table-spoonfuls of sweet butter. Use cold gravy instead of butter, if you have it. Set this in a stew-pan where it will be kept hot, but not fry. Chop the meat very fine, and mix with it while chopping half as much dried bread-crumbs. Put this into the gravy, and let it heat only ten minutes, and then serve it on buttered toast. Tomatoes, one or two, improve this.

A Hash of Cold Beefsteak alone or with Potatoes and Turnips.—Make a paste with a heaping tea-spoonful of flour in two tea-spoonfuls of water. Stir it into a tea-cup and a half of boiling water, with a salt-spoonful of black pepper, a half tea-spoonful of sugar, and two tea-spoonfuls of salt. Let it stand where it will be hot but not boil. Cut the beef into mouthfuls, and also as much cold boiled potatoes and half as much boiled turnips. Mix all, and then add two table-spoonfuls of butter, (or some cold gravy,) and a table-spoonful of tomato catsup, or two sliced tomatoes. Warm, but do not fry, for ten minutes.

When beef gravy is used, take less salt and pepper.

This is a good recipe for cold beef without vegetables.

A Hash of Cold Mutton (or Venison) and Vegetables.—Prepare as in the preceding recipe, but add one onion sliced fine, to hide the strong mutton taste. If onion is left out, put in a wine-glass of grape or currant jelly. If the vegetables are left out, put in a little less pepper and salt.

A Hash of Corned Beef.—Chop the meat very fine, fat and lean together; add twice as much cold potatoes chopped fine. For each tumblerful of this add butter half the size of a hen's egg melted in half a tea-cup of hot water, a salt-spoonful of pepper and another of salt. Heat very hot, but do not let it fry. Some would add parsley or other sweet herb.

A Hash of Cold Ham.—Chop, not very fine, fat and lean together. Add twice the quantity of bread-crumbs chopped, but not fine. Heat it hot, then break in two eggs for every tumblerful of the hash. A tea-spoonful of sugar improves it, and a salt-spoonful of pepper.

Meats warmed over.—Veal is best made into hashes. If it is liked more simply cooked, chop it fine, put in water just enough to moisten it, butter, salt, pepper, and a little juice of a lemon. Some like a little lemon-rind grated in. Heat it through, but do not let it fry. Put it on buttered toast, and garnish it with slices of lemon.

Cold salted or fresh beef is good chopped fine with pepper, salt, and catsup, and water enough to moisten a little. Add some butter just before taking it up, and do not let it fry, only heat it hot. It injures cooked meat to cook it again. Cold fowls make a nice dish to have them cut up in mouthfuls; add some of the gravy and giblet sauce, a little butter and pepper, and then heat them through.

A nice Way of Cooking Cold Meats.—Chop the meat fine, add salt, pepper, a little onion, or else tomato catsup; fill a tin bread-pan one third full, cover it over with boiled potatoes salted and mashed with cream or milk, lay bits of butter on the top, and set it into a Dutch or stove oven for fifteen or twenty minutes.

A Hash of Cold Meat for Dinner, (very good.)—Peel six large tomatoes and one onion, and slice them. Add a spoonful of sugar, salt and pepper, and a bit of butter the size of a hen's egg, and half a pint of cold water. Shave up the meat into small bits, as thin as thick pasteboard. Dredge flour over it, say two tea-spoonfuls, or a little less. Simmer the meat with all the rest for *half an hour* and then serve it, and it is very fine.

Dried tomatoes can be used. When you have no tomatoes, make a gravy with water, pepper, salt, and butter, or cold gravy; slice an onion in it, add tomato catsup, (two or three spoonfuls,) and then prepare the meat as above, and simmer it in this gravy *half an hour.*

Souse.—Cleanse pigs' ears and feet and soak them a week in salt and water, changing the water every other day. Boil eight or ten hours till tender. When cold, put on salt, and pour on hot spiced vinegar. Warm them in lard or butter.

Tripe.—Scrape and scour it thoroughly, soak it in salt and water a week, changing it every other day. Boil it eight or ten hours, till tender; then pour on spiced hot vinegar and broil it.

CHAPTER VI.

BOILED MEATS.

An Excellent Way to cook Tough Beef.—To eight pounds of beef put four quarts of water, two table-spoonfuls of salt, half a tea-spoonful of pepper, three tea-spoonfuls of vinegar, and four tea-spoonfuls of sugar. Put it on at eight in the morning, and let it simmer slowly till the water is more than half gone; then skim off the grease, and set it in the stove-oven till the water is all gone but about a tea-cupful, which is for gravy, and may be thickened a little. Add *boiling* water, if it goes too fast, (for in some kinds of weather it will evaporate much faster than in other days). This dish should be *very* tender, and is excellent cold, especially if it is pressed under a heavy weight. This was a favorite soldier's dish; and tough meat is as good as it is tender, when thus cooked.

Boiled Ham.—The best way to cook a ham is first to wash it; then take off the skin and bake it in a pan, with a little water in it, in a stove or brick oven, till tender, which is found by a fork piercing easily. Allow twenty minutes for each pound.

To boil a ham, soak it over night; then wash in two waters, using a brush. Boil slowly, and allow fifteen minutes for each pound. When cold, take off the skin, and ornament with dots of pepper and fringed paper tied around the shank.

A nice way to treat a cold boiled ham is, after removing the skin, to rub it over with beaten egg, and then spread over powdered cracker, wet with milk, and let it brown in the oven. Boiled ham is much improved by setting it in the oven half an hour, making it sweeter, while the fat that tries out is useful for cooking.

Boiled Beef.—Put it in salted water, (a tea-spoonful for each quart;) have enough to cover it. Skim well just before it begins to boil, and as long as the scum rises. Allow about fifteen minutes to each pound, or more for beef. Drain well, and serve with vegetables boiled separately.

Boiled Fowls.—Wash the inside carefully with soda water, to remove any taint. Stuff with seasoned bread-crumbs, or cracker, wet up with eggs, and sew up the openings. Put them in *boiling* water, enough to cover, and let them simmer gently till tender. It is a good plan to wrap in a cloth dredged with flour.

Fricasseed Fowls.—Cut them up, and put in a pot, with cold water enough to cover. Put some salt pork over, and let them simmer slowly till very tender and the water mostly gone. When done, stir in a cup of milk, mixed with two well-beaten eggs, first mixing slowly some of the hot liquor with the milk and eggs.

Some fry the pork first, thus increasing the flavor, and others leave it out.

To Boil a Leg or Shoulder of Veal, or Mutton, or Lamb.—Mutton should be cooked more rare than any other meat. Make a stuffing of chopped bread, seasoned with pepper and salt, and mixed with one or two eggs. Make deep gashes in the meat, (or, better, take out the bone;) fill the openings with stuffing and sew them up. Wrap it tight in a cloth, and put it so as to be covered with water, salted at the rate of a tea-spoonful to each quart. Let it simmer slowly about two or three hours. Skim thoroughly just before it comes to boiling heat. If needful, add *boiling* water. Save the water for broth for next day. If you pour cold water on the cloth before removing it, and let it stand two minutes, it improves the looks.

Calf's Feet.—Wash and scrape till very clean. Boil three hours in four quarts of water salted with four even tea-spoonfuls of salt. Take out the bones, and put the rest into a saucepan, with three table-spoonfuls of butter, two table-spoonfuls of vinegar, a great-spoonful of sugar, and a salt-spoonful of pepper. Add three tea-cups of the liquor in which the feet were boiled; dredge in some flour, and simmer for fifteen minutes. Garnish with sliced lemon. (Save the liquor to make calf's-foot jelly.)

Calf's Liver and Sweetbreads.—These are best split open, boiled, and then dressed with pepper, salt, and butter.

To cook Kidneys.—Wash them clean, and split them. Heat them half an hour in a saucepan, without water. Then wash them again, and cover them with a pint of water, having in it a tea-spoonful of salt and a salt-spoonful of pepper. Boil one hour, and then take off the skin. Cut them in mouthfuls; add two great-spoonfuls of butter, more salt and hot water, if needed, and let them simmer fifteen minutes.

Pillau, a Favorite Dish in the South.—Fricassee a chicken with slices of salt pork, or with sweet butter or sweet cream. Put the chicken, when cooked, in a bake-dish, and cover it with boiled rice, seasoned with salt, pepper, and one dozen allspice. Pile the rice, pour on some melted butter, smooth it, and cover with yelk of an egg. Bake half an hour.

To boil Smoked Tongues.—Soak in cold water only two hours, as long soaking lessens sweetness. Wash them, and boil four or five hours, according to the size. When done, take off the skin and garnish with parsley. A table-spoonful of sugar for each tongue, put in the water, improves them.

To boil Corned Beef.—Do not soak it, but wash it, and put it in *hot* water, to keep in the juices; allow a pint for each pound. Skim just before it begins to boil. Let it simmer slowly, and allow twenty-five minutes for every pound. Keep it covered with water, adding boiling hot water, if needed. It is much improved for eating cold by pressing it with a board and heavy stone. It is an excellent piece of economy to save the water to use for soup.

Some think it an improvement to put on a little sugar, and pour a little vinegar on before boiling. Some like to boil turnips, potatoes, and cabbage with it. In that case, they must be peeled, and the potatoes soaked two hours.

To boil Partridges or Pigeons.—Cleanse and rinse the insides with soda-water, and then with pure water. Wrap them in a damp floured cloth; put them into boiling water which is salted at the rate of a heaping tea-spoonful to a quart; also, two tea-spoonfuls of sugar and a salt-spoonful of pepper. Simmer them twenty minutes to half an hour. When done, make a sauce of butter rubbed into flour and half a cup of milk; put the birds into a dish and pour on this sauce. Some would add cut parsley, or other flavors.

To boil Ducks.—Let them lie in hot water two hours. Then wrap in a cloth dredged with flour; put them in cold water, salted at the rate of half a tea-spoonful for each pint. Add a tea-spoonful of sugar for each pint. Let them simmer half an hour; then take them up, and pour over them a sauce made of melted butter rubbed into flour, and seasoned with lemon-juice, salt, and pepper, and thinned with gravy or hot water.

Wild ducks must be soaked in salt and water the night previous, to remove the fishy taste, and then in the morning put in fresh water, which should be changed once or twice.

To boil a Turkey.—Make a stuffing for the craw of chopped bread and butter, cream, oysters, and the yelks of eggs. Sew it in, and dredge flour over the turkey, and put it in hot water to boil, with a spoonful of salt in it, and enough water to cover it well. Let it simmer for two hours and a half, or, if small, less time. Skim it while boiling. It will look nicer if wrapped in a cloth dredged with flour while cooking.

Serve it with drawn butter, in which are put some oysters.

CHAPTER VII.

ROAST AND BAKED MEATS.

THE beef of an ox is best, and the next best is that of a heifer. The best pieces for roasting are the second cut of the sirloin, the second cut of the ribs, and the back part of the rump.

The art of roasting well consists in turning the meat often, to prevent burning, and basting often, to make it juicy.

Never dredge flour into gravies, as it makes lumps. Strain all gravies.

Brown Flour for Meat Gravies.—This is used to thicken meat gravies, to give a good color. It is prepared by putting flour on a tin plate in a hot oven, stirring it often until well browned; it must be kept, corked, in a jar, and shaken occasionally.

Roast Beef.—A piece of beef weighing ten pounds requires about two hours to roast in a tin oven before a fire. Allow ten minutes for each pound over or under this weight. Have the spit and oven clean and bright. They should have been washed before they grew cold from the last roasting.

Put the meat on the spit so that it will be evenly balanced; set the bony side toward the fire; let it roast slowly at first, turning it often; and when all sides are partly cooked, move it nearer the fire. If allowed to scorch at first, it will not cook in the middle without burning the outside.

Baste often with the drippings and with salted water, (about half a pint of water with half a tea-spoonful of salt,) which has been put in the oven bottom. Just before taking up, dredge on some flour, mixed with a little salt; then baste and set it near the fire, turning it so as to brown it all over alike. Half an hour before it is done, pour off the gravy, season it with salt and pepper, and thicken with corn or potato-starch, or flour.

To roast in a Cook Stove.—Put the meat in an iron pan, with three or four gills of water, and a tea-spoonful of salt. Turn it occasionally, that it may cook evenly, and baste often. When done, dredge on some salted flour, baste again, and set it back till browned.

Roast Pork.—Cover a spare-rib with greased paper, till half done; then dredge with flour, and baste with the gravy. Just before taking it up, cover the surface with cracker or bread-crumbs, wet up with pepper, salt, and powdered sage; let it cook ten minutes longer, and then baste again. Skim the gravy, thicken it with brown flour, season with a little powdered sage and lemon-juice, or vinegar; strain it, and pour over the meat. Pork must be cooked slowly and very thoroughly, and served with apple-sauce. Tomato catsup improves the gravy.

Roast Mutton.—The leg of mutton may be boiled. The shoulder and loin should always be roasted.

Put the meat in the oven or roaster, and then pour boiling hot water over it, to keep in the juices. Baste often with salt and water at first and then with the gravy. With a hot fire, allow ten minutes for each pound. If there is danger of burning, cover the outside with oiled white paper. Skim the gravy; strain it and thicken with brown flour. Serve with acid jelly. Lamb requires less time in roasting; but mutton should be rare. Make a brown gravy, and serve with currant jelly.

Roast Veal.—Follow the above directions for roasting mutton, except to allow more time, as veal should be cooked more than mutton. Allow twenty minutes to each pound, and baste often. Too much roasting and little basting spoils veal. To be served with apple-sauce. It much improves roast veal to cut slits in it, and insert bits of salt pork.

Roast Poultry.—No fowl should be bought when the entrails are not drawn; and the insides should always be washed with soda-water—a tea-spoonful of soda to a pint of water. Rinse out with fair water. Stuff with seasoned bread-crumbs, wet up with eggs. Sew and tie the stuffing in thoroughly. Allow about ten minutes' cooking for each pound, more or less, according to the fire and size of the fowl.

Put a grate in the bake-pan, with a tea-cup of salted water. Dredge the fowl with flour at first, and baste often. Strain the gravy, and add the giblets, chopped fine. Many dislike the liver, and so leave it out. If fowls are bought with the intestines in, or if they have been kept too long, the use of soda-water, and then rinsing with pure water, will often prevent the tainted taste; so it is well to do this, except when it is certain that the fowl is just killed. Put a tea-spoonful of soda to a pint of water.

Pot-Pie, of Beef, Veal, or Chicken.—The best way to make the crust is as follows: Peel, boil, and mash a dozen potatoes; add a tea-spoonful of salt, two table-spoonfuls of butter, and half a cup of milk, or cream. Then stiffen it with flour, till you can roll it. Be sure to get all the lumps out of the potatoes. Some persons leave out the butter.

Some roll butter into the dough of bread; others make a raised biscuit, with but little shortening; others make a plain soda pie-crust. But none are so good and healthful as the potato crust; so choose what is best for all.

To prepare the meat, first fry half a dozen slices of salt pork, and then cut up the meat and pork, and boil them in just water enough to cover them, till the meat is nearly cooked. Then peel a dozen potatoes, and slice them thin.

Roll the crust half an inch thick, and cut it into oblong pieces. Then put alternate layers of crust, potatoes, and meat, till all is used. The top and bottom layer must be crust. Divide the pork so as to have some in each layer.

Lastly, pour on the liquor in which the meat was boiled, until it just covers the whole, and let it simmer till the top crust is well cooked—say half or three quarters of an hour. Season the liquor with salt, at the rate of a tea-spoonful for each quart, and one sixth as much pepper. If you have occasion to add more liquor, or water, it must be *boiling hot*, or the crust will be spoiled.

The excellence of this pie depends on having light crust, and therefore the meat must first be *nearly cooked* before putting it in the pie; and the crust must be in only just long enough to cook, or it will be clammy and hard.

Mutton and Beef Pie.—Line a dish with a crust made of potatoes, as directed in the Chicken Pot-Pie. Broil the meat ten minutes, after pounding it till the fibres are broken. Cut the meat thin, and put it in layers, with thin slices of broiled salt pork; season with butter, the size of a hen's egg, salt, pepper, (and either wine or catsup, if liked;) put in water till it nearly covers the meat, and dredge in considerable flour; cover it with the paste, and bake it an hour and a half, if quite thick. Cold meats are good cooked over in this way. Cut a slit in the centre of the cover.

Chicken-Pie.—Joint and boil two chickens in salted water, just enough to cover them, and simmer slowly for half an hour. Line a dish with potato crust, as directed in the recipe for pot-pie; then, when cold, put the chicken in layers, with thin slices of broiled pork, butter, the size of a goose egg, cut in small pieces. Put in enough of liquor, in which the meat was boiled, to reach the surface; salt and pepper each layer; dredge in a little flour, and cover all with a light, thick crust. Ornament the top with the crust, and bake about one hour in a hot oven. Make a small slit in the centre of the crust. If it begins to scorch, lay a paper over a short time.

Rice Chicken-Pie.—Line a pudding-dish with slices of broiled ham; cut up a boiled chicken, and nearly fill the dish, filling in with gravy or melted butter; add minced onions, if you like, or a little curry powder.

Then pile boiled rice to fill all interstices, and cover the top quite thick. Bake it for half or three quarters of an hour.

Potato-Pie.—Take mashed potatoes, seasoned with salt, butter, and milk, and line a baking-dish. Lay upon it slices of cold meats of any kind, with salt, pepper, catsup, and butter or gravy. Put on another layer of potatoes, and then another of cold meat, as before. Lastly, on the top put a cover of potatoes.

Bake it till it is thoroughly warmed through, and serve it in the dish in which it is baked, setting it in or upon another.

Calf's Head.—Take out the brains and boil the head, feet, and lights in salted water, just enough to cover them, about two hours. When they have boiled nearly an hour and a half, tie the brains in a cloth and put them in to boil with the rest. They should be skinned, and soaked half an hour in cold water. When the two hours have expired, take up the whole, mash the brains fine, and season them with bread-crumbs, pepper, salt, and a glass of port or claret, and use them for sauce. Let the liquor remain for a soup the next day. It serves more handsomely to remove all the bones. Serve with a gravy of drawn butter.

3

CHAPTER VIII.

BROILED AND FRIED MEATS AND RELISHES.

Broiled Mutton or Lamb Chops.—Cut off the skinny part, which only turns black and can not be eaten. Put a little pepper and salt on each one, and broil by a quick fire. Mutton chops should be rare.

Broiled Beefsteak.—Have the steak cut three quarters of an inch to an inch in thickness. The sirloin and porter-house are the best. The art of cooking steak will depend on a good fire and turning often after it begins to drip. When done, lay it on a hot platter, season with butter, pepper, and salt; cover with another hot platter, and send to the table. Use beef-tongs, as pricking lets out the juices. *Slow* cooking and *much* cooking spoils a steak.

Broiled Fresh Pork.—Cut in thin slices, broil quickly and very thoroughly; then season with salt, pepper, and powdered sage.

Broiled Ham.—Cut in *thin* slices, and soak fifteen minutes in hot water. Pour off this and soak again as long. Wipe dry and broil over a quick fire, and then pepper it. Ham that is already cooked rare is best for broiling.

Broiled Sweetbreads.—The best way to cook sweetbreads is to broil them thus: Parboil them, and then put them on a clean gridiron for broiling. When delicately browned, take them off and roll in melted butter on a plate, to prevent their being dry and hard. Some cook them on a griddle well buttered, turning frequently; and some put narrow strips of fat salt pork on them while cooking.

Broiled Veal.—Cut it thin, and put thin slices of salt pork on the top after it is laid on the gridiron, and broil both together. When turning, put the pork again on the top. When the veal is thoroughly cooked, brown the pork a little by itself, while the veal stands on a hot dish.

A good Pork Relish.—Broil thin slices of fresh pork, first pouring on boiling water to lessen saltness. Cut them in small mouthfuls, and add butter, pepper, and salt.

FRIED MEATS AND RELISHES.

The most slovenly and unhealthful mode of cooking is frying, as it usually is done. If the fat is very hot, and the articles are put in and taken out exactly at the right time, it is well enough. But fried fat is hard to digest, and most fried food is soaked with it, so that only a strong stomach can digest it. Almost every thing that is fried might be better cooked on a griddle slightly oiled. A griddle should always be oiled only just enough to keep from sticking. It is best to fry in lard not salted, and this is better than butter. Mutton and beef suet are good for frying. When the lard seems hot, try it by throwing in a bit of bread. When taking up fried articles, drain off the fat on a wire sieve.

A nice Way of Cooking Calf's or Pig's Liver.—Cut in slices half an inch thick, pour on boiling water, and then pour if off *entirely;* then let the liver brown in its own juices, turning it till it looks brown on both sides. Take it up, and pour into the frying-pan enough cold water to make as much gravy as you wish; then sliver in a *very* little onion; add a little salt and nutmeg, and a bit of butter to season it; let it boil up once, then put back the liver for a minute longer.

Beef Liver.—Cut it in slices half an inch thick, pour boiling water on it, broil it with thin slices of pork dipped in flour, cut it in mouthfuls, and heat it with butter, pepper, and salt for three or four minutes.

Egg Omelet.—Beat the yelks of six eggs, and add a cup of milk, half a teaspoonful of salt, and a pinch of pepper. Pour into hot fat, and cook till just stiffened. Turn it on to a platter brown side uppermost. Some add minced cooked ham, or cold meat chopped and salted. Others put in chopped cauliflower or asparagus cooked and cold.

Frizzled Beef.—Sliver smoked beef, pour on boiling water to freshen it, then pour off the water, and frizzle the beef in butter.

Veal Cheese.—Prepare equal quantities of sliced boiled veal and boiled smoked tongue, or ham sliced. Pound each separately in a mortar, moistening with butter as you proceed. Then take a stone jar, or tin can, and mix them in it, so that it will, when cut, look mottled and variegated. Press it hard, and pour on melted butter. Keep it covered in a dry place. To be used at tea in slices.

A Codfish Relish.—Take thin slivers of codfish, lay them on hot coals, and when done to a yellowish brown, set them on the table.

Another Way.—Sliver the codfish fine, pour on boiling water, drain it off, and add butter and a very little pepper, and heat them three or four minutes, but do not let them fry.

Salt Herrings.—Heat them on a gridiron, remove the skin, and then set them on the table.

CHAPTER IX.

PICKLES.

Do not keep pickles in common earthenware, as the glazing contains lead, and combines with the vinegar.

Vinegar for pickling should be sharp, but not the sharpest kind, as it injures the pickles. Wine or cider vinegar is reliable. Much manufactured vinegar is sold that ruins pickles and is unhealthful. If you use copper, bell-metal, or brass vessels for pickling, never allow the vinegar to cool in them, as it then is poisonous. Add a table-spoonful of alum and a tea-cup of salt to each three gallons of vinegar, and tie up a bag with pepper, ginger-root, and spices of all sorts in it, and you have vinegar prepared for any kind of common pickling, and in many cases all that is needed is to throw the fruit in and keep it in till wanted.

Keep pickles only in wood or stone ware.

Any thing that has held grease will spoil pickles.

Stir pickles occasionally, and if there are soft ones, take them out, scald the vinegar, and pour it hot over the pickles. Keep enough vinegar to cover them well. If it is weak, take fresh vinegar, and pour on hot. Do not boil vinegar or spice over five minutes.

Sweet Pickles, (a great favorite.)—One pound of sugar, one quart of vinegar, two pounds of fruit. Boil fifteen minutes, skim well, put in the fruit and let it boil till half cooked. For peaches, flavor with cinnamon and mace; for plums and all dark fruit, use allspice and cloves.

To pickle Tomatoes.—As you gather them, leave an inch or more of stem; throw them into cold vinegar. When you have enough, take them out, and scald some spices, tied in a bag, in good vinegar; add a little sugar, and pour it hot over them.

To pickle Peaches.—Take ripe but hard peaches, wipe off the down, stick a few cloves into them, and lay them in *cold* spiced vinegar. In three months they will be sufficiently pickled, and also retain much of their natural flavor.

To pickle Peppers.—Take green peppers, take the seeds out carefully so as not to mangle them, soak them nine days in salt and water, changing it every day, and keep them in a warm place. Stuff them with chopped cabbage, seasoned with cloves, cinnamon, and mace; put them in cold spiced vinegar.

To pickle Nasturtions.—Soak them three days in salt and water as you collect them, changing it once in three days; and when you have enough, pour off the brine, and pour on scalding hot vinegar.

To pickle Onions.—Peel, and boil in milk and water ten minutes, drain off the milk and water, and pour scalding spiced vinegar on to them.

To pickle Gherkins.—Keep them in strong brine till they are yellow, then take them out and turn on hot spiced vinegar, and keep them in it, in a warm place, till they turn green. Then turn off the vinegar, and add a fresh supply of hot spiced vinegar.

To pickle Mushrooms.—Stew them in salted water, just enough to keep them from sticking. When tender, pour off the water, and pour on hot spiced vinegar. Then cork them tight, if you wish to keep them long. Poison ones will turn black if an onion is stewed with them, and then all must be thrown away.

To pickle Cucumbers.—Wash the cucumbers in cold water, being careful not to bruise or break them. Make a brine of rock or blown salt (rock is the best), strong enough to bear up an egg or potato, and of sufficient quantity to cover the cucumbers.

Put them into an oaken tub, or stone-ware jar, and pour the brine over them. In twenty-four hours, they should be stirred up from the bottom with the hand. The third day pour off the brine, scald it, and pour it over the cucumbers. Let them stand in the brine nine days, scalding it every third day, as described above. Then take the cucumbers into a tub, rinse them in cold water, and if they are too salt, let them stand in it a few hours. Drain them from the water, put them back into the tub or jar, which must be washed clean from the brine. Scald vinegar sufficient to cover them, and pour it upon them. Cover them tight, and in a week they will be ready for use. If spice is wanted, it may be tied in a linen cloth and put into the jar with the pickles, or scalded with the vinegar, and the bag thrown into the pickle-jar. If a white scum rises, take it off and scald the vinegar, and pour it back. A small lump of alum added to the vinegar improves the hardness of the cucumbers.

Pickled Walnuts.—Take a hundred nuts, an ounce of cloves, an ounce of allspice, an ounce of nutmeg, an ounce of whole pepper, an ounce of race ginger, an ounce of horse-radish, half pint of mustard-seed, and four cloves of garlic, tied in a bag.

Wipe the nuts, prick with a pin, and put them in a pot, sprinkling the spice as you lay them in; then add two table-spoonfuls of salt; boil sufficient vinegar to fill the pot, and pour it over the nuts and spice. Cover the jar close, and keep it for a year, when the pickles will be ready for use.

Butternuts may be made in the same manner, if they are taken when green, and soft enough to be stuck through with the head of a pin. Put them for a week or two in weak brine, changing it occasionally. Before putting in the brine, rub them about with a broom in brine, to cleanse the skins. Then proceed as for the walnuts.

The vinegar makes an excellent catsup.

Mangoes.—Take the latest growth of young musk-melons, cut out a small piece from one side and empty them. Scrape the outside smooth, and soak them four days in strong salt and water. If you wish to green them, put vine leaves over and under, with bits of alum, and steam them awhile. Then powder cloves, pepper, and nutmeg in equal portions, and sprinkle on the inside, and fill them with strips of horse-radish, small bits of calamus, bits of cinnamon and mace, a clove or two, a very small onion, nasturtions, and then American mustard-seed to fill the crevices. Put back the piece cut out, and sew it on, and then sew the mango in cotton cloth. Lay all in a stone jar, the cut side upward.

Boil sharp vinegar a few minutes with half a tea-cup of salt, and a table-spoonful of alum to three gallons of vinegar, and turn it on to the melons. Keep dried barberries for garnishes, and when you use them, turn a little of the above vinegar of the mangoes heated boiling hot on to them, and let them swell a few hours. Sliced and salted cabbage with this vinegar poured on hot is very good.

Fine pickled Cabbage.—Shred red and white cabbage, spread it in layers in a stone jar, with salt over each layer. Put two spoonfuls of whole black pepper, and the same quantity of allspice, cloves, and cinnamon, in a bag, and scald them in two quarts of vinegar, and pour the vinegar over the cabbage, and cover it tight. Use it in two days after.

An excellent Way of preparing Tomatoes to eat with Meat.—Peel and slice ripe tomatoes, sprinkling on a little salt as you proceed. Drain off the juice, and pour on hot spiced vinegar.

To pickle Martinoes.—Gather them when you can run a pin-head into them, and after wiping them, keep them ten days in weak brine, changing it every other day. Then wipe them, and pour over boiling spiced vinegar. In four weeks they will be ready for use. It is a fine pickle.

A convenient Way to pickle Cucumbers.—Put some spiced vinegar in a jar, with a little salt in it. Every time you gather a mess, pour boiling vinegar on them, with a little alum in it. Then put them in the spiced vinegar. Keep the same vinegar for scalding all. When you have enough, take all from the spiced vinegar, and scald in the alum vinegar two or three minutes, till green, and then put them back in the spiced vinegar.

Indiana Pickles.—Take green tomatoes, and slice them. Put them in a basket to drain in layers, with salt scattered over them, say a tea-cupful to each gallon. Next day, slice one quarter the quantity of onions, and lay the onions and tomatoes in alternate layers in a jar, with spice intervening. Then fill the jar with cold vinegar. Tomatoes picked as they ripen, and just thrown into cold spiced vinegar, are a fine pickle, and made with very little trouble.

To pickle Cauliflower, or Broccoli.—Keep them twenty-four hours in strong brine, and then take them out and heat the brine, and pour it on scalding hot, and let them stand till next day. Drain them, and throw them into spiced vinegar.

CHAPTER X.

SAUCES AND SALADS.

SUCCESS in preparing savory meats and salads depends greatly on the different sauces, and these demand extra care in preparation and in flavoring. The following is a sauce that is a great favorite, and serves for some meats, for fish, for macaroni, and for some salads:

Milk and Egg Sauce, (excellent.)—Take eight table-spoonfuls of butter and mix it with a table-spoonful of flour, add a pint of milk and heat it, stirring constantly till it thickens a little. Then beat the yelk of an egg in a table-spoonful of water and mix it well with the sauce, taking care that it does not boil, but only be very hot. For fish, add to the above a table-spoonful of vinegar or lemon-juice and a little of the peel grated. Some add parsley chopped; and for boiled fowls, add chopped oysters. Fine bread-crumbs are better than flour for thickening. For macaroni, make in the dish alternate layers with that and grated cheese, and then pour on this sauce before baking, and it is very fine. Some omit the cheese.

Drawn Butter.—Take six table-spoonfuls of butter, half a tea-spoonful of salt, two tea-spoonfuls of flour or of fine bread-crumbs worked into the butter, and one tea-cup of hot water. Heat very hot, but do not let it boil. Two hard-boiled and chopped eggs improve it much. For fish, add a table-spoonful of vinegar and chopped capers or green nasturtion seeds.

Mint Sauce for Roast Lamb.—Chop three table-spoonfuls of green mint, and add a heaping table-spoonful of sugar and half a coffee-cup of vinegar. Stir them while heating, and cool before using.

Cranberry Sauce.—Wash well and put a tea-cup of water to every quart of cranberries. Let them stew about an hour and a half, then take up and sweeten abundantly. Some strain them through a colander, then sweeten largely and then put into moulds. To be eaten with fowls.

Apple Sauce.—Core and slice the best apples you can get, cook till soft, then add sugar and a little butter. Serve it with fresh pork and veal.

Walnut or Butternut Catsup.—Gather the nuts when they can be pierced with a pin. Beat them to a soft pulp and let them lie for two weeks in quite salt water, say a small handful of salt to every twenty, and water enough to cover them. Drain off this liquor, and pour on a pint of boiling vinegar and mix with the nuts, and then strain it out. To each quart of this liquor put three table-spoonfuls of pepper, one of ginger, two spoonfuls of powdered cloves, and three spoonfuls of grated nutmeg. Boil an hour, and bottle when cold. See that the spice is equally mixed. Do not use mushroom catsup, as the above is as good and not so dangerous.

Mock Capers.—Dry the green but full-grown nasturtion seeds for a day in the sun, then put them in jars and pour on spiced vinegar. These are good for fish sauce, in drawn butter.

Salad Dressing.—Mash fine two boiled potatoes, and add a tea-spoonful of mustard, two of salt, four of sweet-oil, three of sharp vinegar, and the yelks of two well-boiled eggs rubbed fine. Mix first the egg and potatoes, add the mustard and salt, and gradually mix in the oil, stirring vigorously the while. Stir in the vinegar last. Melted butter may be used in place of sweet-oil. The more a salad dressing is stirred, the better it will be.

Turkey or Chicken Salad, also a Lettuce Salad.—Take one quarter chopped meat (the white meat of the fowl is the best for this purpose) and three quarters chopped celery, well mixed, and pour over it a sauce containing the yelks of two hard-boiled eggs chopped, a tea-spoonful of salt, half a salt-spoonful of black pepper, half a tea-spoonful of mustard, three tea-spoonfuls of sugar, half a tea-cupful of vinegar, and three tea-spoonfuls of sweet-oil or of melted butter. Mix the salt, pepper, sugar, and mustard thoroughly, whip a raw egg and add slowly, stir in the sweet-oil or melted butter, mixing it well and very slowly, and lastly add the vinegar. Garnish with rings of whites of eggs boiled hard. Chopped pickles may be added, and white cabbage in place of the celery.

Tomato Catsup.—Boil a peck of tomatoes, strain through a colander, and then add four great-spoonfuls of salt, one of pounded mace, half a table-spoonful of black pepper, a table-spoonful of powdered cloves, two table-spoonfuls of ground mustard, and a table-spoonful of celery seed tied in a muslin rag. Mix all and boil five or six hours, stirring frequently and constantly the last hour. Let it cool in a stone jar, take out the celery seed, add a pint of vinegar, bottle it, and keep it in a dark, cool place.

3*

CHAPTER XI.

FISH.

Stewed Oysters.—Strain off all the oyster liquor, and then add half as much water as you have oysters. Some of the best housekeepers say this is better than using the liquor. Add a salt-spoonful of salt for each pint of oysters, and half as much pepper; and when they begin to simmer, add half a small tea-cup of milk for each pint of oysters. When the edges begin to "ruffle," add some butter, and do not let them stand, but serve immediately. Oysters should not simmer more than five minutes in the whole. When cooked too long, they become hard, dark, and tasteless.

Fried Oysters.—Lay them on a cloth to absorb the liquor; then dip first in beaten egg, and afterward in powdered cracker, and fry in hot lard or butter to a light brown. If fresh lard is used, put in a little salt. Cook quickly in very hot fat, or they will absorb too much grease.

Oyster Fritters.—Drain off the liquor, and to each pint of oysters take a pint of milk, a salt-spoonful of salt, half as much pepper, and flour enough for a thin batter. Chop the oysters and stir in, and then fry in hot lard, a little salted, or in butter. Drop in one spoonful at a time. Some make the batter thicker, so as to put in one oyster at a time surrounded by the batter.

Scalloped Oysters.—Make alternate layers of oysters and crushed crackers wet with oyster liquor, and milk warmed. Sprinkle each layer with salt and pepper, (some add a *very* little nutmeg or cloves;) let the top and bottom layer be crackers. Put bits of butter on the top, pour on some milk with a beaten egg in it, and bake half an hour.

Broiled Oysters.—Dip in fine cracker crumbs, broil very quick, and put a small bit of butter on each when ready to serve.

Oyster Omelet, (very fine.)—Take twelve large oysters chopped fine. Mix the beaten yelks of six eggs into a tea-cupful of milk, and add the oysters. Then put in a spoonful of melted butter, and lastly add the whites of the eggs beaten to a stiff froth. Fry this in hot butter or salted lard, and do not stir it while cooking. Slip a knife around the edges while cooking, that the centre may cook equally, and turn it out so that the brown side be uppermost.

Pickled Oysters.—Take for fifty large oysters half a pint of vinegar, six blades of mace, twelve black pepper-corns, and twelve whole cloves. Heat the oysters with the liquor, but not to boil; take out the oysters, and then put the vinegar and spices into the liquor, boil it, and when the oysters are nearly cold, pour on the mixture scalding hot. Next day cork the oysters tight in glass jars, and keep them in a dark and cool place. Vinegar is sometimes made of sulphuric or pyroligneous acid, and this destroys the pickles. Use cider or wine vinegar.

Roast Oysters.—Put oysters in the shell, after washing them, upon the coals so that the flat side is uppermost, to save the liquor; and take them up when they begin to gape a little.

Scallops.—Dip them in beaten egg and cracker crumbs, and fry or stew them like oysters.

Clams.—Wash them and roast them; or stew or fry them like oysters; or make omelets or fritters by the recipe for oysters.

Clam Chowder.—Make alternate layers of crackers wet in milk, and clams with their liquor, and thin slices of fried salt pork. Season with black pepper and salt. Boil three quarters of an hour. Put this into a tureen, having drained off some liquor which is to be thickened with flour or pounded crackers, seasoned with catsup and wine, and then poured into the tureen. Serve with pickles.

Boiled Fish.—Wrap in a cloth wet with vinegar, floured inside. Boil in cold salted water till the bones will slip out easily; drain and serve with egg sauce, or drawn butter, or a sauce of milk, butter, and egg. Try boiling fish with a fork, and if that goes in easily, it probably is done.

Broiled Fish.—Split so that the backbone is in the middle; sprinkle with salt; lay the inside down at first till it begins to brown, then turn and broil the other side. Dress with butter, pepper, and salt. It is best to take out the backbone.

Baked Fish.—Wash and wipe, and rub with salt and pepper outside and inside. Set it on a grate over a baking-pan, and baste with butter and the drippings; if it browns too fast, cover with white paper. Thicken the gravy, and season to the taste, using lemon-juice or tomato catsup. Some put in wine.

Pickle for cold Fish.—To two quarts of vinegar add a pint of the liquor in which the fish was boiled, a dozen black pepper-corns, a dozen cloves, three sticks of cinnamon, and a tea-spoonful of mustard. Let them boil up, and then skim so as not to take out the spice.

Cut the fish into inch squares, and when the liquor boils, put them into it till just heated through. Pack tight in a glass jar, and then pour on the pickle; cook it till air-tight. This will keep a long time. It is a great convenience for a supper relish.

CHAPTER XII.

VEGETABLES.

FRESH-GATHERED vegetables are much the best. Soaking in cold water improves all. Always boil in *salted* water, a tea-spoonful for each quart of water. Do not let them stop boiling, or they will thus become watery.

POTATOES.

The excellence of potatoes depends greatly on the *species* and on the *age*. Much also depends on the cooking, and here there are diversities of modes and opinions. Peeling potatoes before cooking saves labor at the time of taking up dinner, which is a matter of consequence. They should, after peeling, soak an hour in cold water; then boil them in salted water, putting them in when the water boils. Have them equal in size, that all may be done alike. Try with a fork, and when tender drain off the water, sprinkle on a little fine salt, and set them in the oven, or keep them hot in the pot till wanted.

Some boil with skins on; in this case, pare off a small ring, or cut off a little at each end for the water within to escape, as this makes them more mealy.

Some make a wire basket and put in the potatoes peeled and of equal size; and when done, take them up and set in the oven a short time. This is the surest and easiest method.

Old potatoes should be boiled in salted water, then mashed with salt, pepper, and cream or butter.

New potatoes boil in salted water, and rub off the tender skins with a coarse towel.

A good Way for old Potatoes.—Peel and soak in cold water half an hour, then slice them into salted water that is boiling; when soft, pour off the water, add cream, or milk and butter, with salt and pepper, also dredge in a very little flour.

Another way is to chop the cold boiled potatoes, and then mix in milk, butter, salt, and pepper.

Some cold potatoes are nice cooked on a gridiron. A favorite relish for supper is cold potatoes sliced and dressed with a salad dressing of boiled eggs, salt, mustard, oil, and vinegar.

Cold Potato Puffs.—Take cold mashed or chopped potatoes and stir in milk and melted butter. Beat two eggs and mix, and then bake till browned. It is very nice, and the children love it as well as their elders. This may be baked in patties for a pretty variety.

To cook Sweet Potatoes.—The best way is to parboil with the skins on, and then bake in a stove oven.

Green Corn.—Husk it; boil in salted water, and eat from the cob; or cut off the corn and season it with butter or cream and salt and pepper. If green corn is to be roasted, open it and take off the silk, and then cook it with husks on, buried in hot ashes; or if before the fire, turn it often.

Succotash.—Boil white beans by themselves. Cut the corn from the cob and let the cobs boil ten minutes, then take them out and put in the corn. Have only just water enough to cover the corn when cut. If there is more than a tea-cupful when the corn is boiled about half an hour, lessen it to that quantity, and add as much milk, and let the boiling continue till, on trial, the corn is soft, and then stir in a table-spoonful of flour wet in cold water. Then let it boil three or four minutes, take up the corn, and add the beans, with butter, pepper, and salt. Have twice as much corn as beans. Some use string-beans cut up.

If you have boiled corn left on the cob, cut it off for breakfast, and add milk and eggs, salt and pepper, and bake it. Some say this is the best way of all to cook sweet corn.

Salsify, or Oyster Plant.—Scrape, cut into inch pieces, and throw into cold water awhile; put into salted boiling water, just enough to cover them, and when tender turn off the water and add milk, butter, salt, and pepper, and thicken with a very little flour; then serve. Or, mash fine, and add a beaten egg and a little flour; make round, flat cakes, and cook on a griddle.

Egg Plant.—Cut into slices an inch thick and peel. Lay these in salted water an hour; then dip into egg, and rub in bread or cracker-crumbs, and cook on a griddle.

Carrots.—Boil in salted water till tender, take off the skin, slice and butter them. They are improved by cooking in broth. Some add chopped onion and parsley.

Beets.—Wash, but do not cut them before boiling; boil till tender, take off the skin, slice and season with salt, pepper, vinegar, and melted butter. If any are left, slice them into vinegar, for a pickle.

Parsnips.—Boil in salted water, take off the skins, cut in slices lengthwise, and season with salt, pepper, and butter. When cold, chop fine, add salt, pepper, egg, and flour, make small cakes, and cook on a griddle.

Pumpkin and Squash.—Cut in slices, boil in salted water till tender, drain, and season with salt, pepper, and butter. Baked pumpkin, cut in slices, is very good.

Celery.—Cut off the roots and green leaves, wash, and keep in cold water till wanted.

Radishes.—Wash, cut off tops, and lay in cold water till wanted.

Onions.—Many can not eat onions without consequent discomfort; though to most others they are a healthful and desirable vegetable. The disagreeable effect on the breath, it is said, may be prevented by afterward chewing and swallowing three or four roasted coffee-beans. Those who indulge in this vegetable should, as a matter of politeness and benevolence, try this precaution.

The best way to cook onions is to peel, cut off top and tail, put in cold water for awhile, and then into boiling salted water. When nearly done, pour off the water, except a little, then add milk, butter, pepper, and salt. When onions are old and strong, boil in two or three waters; have each time *boiling* water.

Tomatoes.—Pour on scalding water, then remove the skins, cut them up, and boil about half an hour. Add salt, butter or cream, and sugar. Adding green corn cut from the cob is a good variety. Some use pounded or grated stale bread-crumbs to thicken. Some slice without peeling, broil on a gridiron, and then season with pepper, salt, and butter. Some peel, slice, and put in layers, with seasoning and bread-crumbs between, and bake in an oven. If eaten raw, the skins should be removed by a knife, as scalding lessens flavor and crispness. Ice improves them much. The acid is so sharp that many are injured by eating too many.

Cucumbers.—Peel and slice into cold water, and in half an hour drain and season with salt, pepper, and vinegar. Some slice them quarter of an inch thick into boiling water, enough to cover them, and in fifteen minutes drain through a colander, and season with butter, salt, pepper, and vinegar.

Cabbage and Cauliflower.—Take off the outer leaves and look for any insects to be removed, and let it stand in cold water awhile. It should be cut twice transversely through the hardest part, that all may cook alike. It is more delicate if boiled awhile in one water, then changed to another boiling hot water, in the same or another vessel. If you are cooking corned beef, use for the second water some of the meat liquor, and it improves the flavor. Drain it through a colander. Some chop the cabbage before serving, and add butter, salt, pepper, and vinegar. Others omit the vinegar, and add two beaten eggs and a little milk, then bake it like a pudding. This is the favorite mode in some families. Cauliflower is to be treated like cabbage.

Asparagus.—The best way to cook it is to cut it into inch pieces, leave out the hardest parts, boil in salted water, drain with a colander, and add pepper, salt, melted butter or cream, when taken up. Some beat up eggs and add to this; stir till hardened a little, and then serve.

Macaroni.—Break into inch pieces and put into salted boiling water, and stew till soft—say twenty minutes. Drain it and put it in layers in a pudding-dish, with grated cheese between each layer. Add a little salted milk or cream, and bake about half an hour. Many can not eat this with cheese. In this case it is better to pour cold soup or gravy upon it, and bake without cheese.

Various Ways of cooking Eggs.—Put eggs into boiling water from three to five minutes, according to taste. A hard-boiled egg is perfectly healthy if well masticated. Another way is to put them in a bowl or an egg-boiler, and pour on boiling water for two or three minutes, then pour off the water and add boiling water, and in five or six minutes the eggs will be cooked enough.

To make a *plain omelet*, beat the yelks of six eggs, add a cup of milk, season with salt and pepper, and then stir in the whites cut to a stiff froth. Cook in a frying-pan or griddle, with as little butter or fat as possible. Let it cook about ten minutes, and then take up with a spad, or lay a hot dish over and turn the omelet on to it. This is improved by mixing in chopped ham or fowl. Some put sugar in, but it is more apt to burn.

A *bread omelet* is made as above, with bread-crumbs added, and is very good.

An *apple omelet* is made as above, with mashed apple-sauce added, and this also is very good. Jelly may be used instead of apple.

CHAPTER XIII.

FAMILY BREAD.

The most important article of food is good family bread, and the most healthful kind of bread is that made of coarse flour and raised with yeast. All that is written against the healthfulness of yeast is owing to sheer ignorance, as the most learned physicians and chemists will affirm.

Certain recent writers on hygiene are ultra and indiscriminating in regard to the use of unbolted flour. The simple facts about it are these: Every kernel of wheat contains nutriment for different parts of the body, and in about the right proportions. Thus, the outside part contains that which nourishes the bones, teeth, hair, nails, and the muscles. The germ, or eye, contains what nourishes the brain and nerves; and the central part (of which fine flour is chiefly made) consists of that which forms fat, and furnishes fuel to produce animal heat, while in gentle combustion it unites with oxygen in the capillaries. When first ground, the flour contains all the ingredients as in the kernel. The first bolting alters the proportions but very little, forming what is called *middlings*. The second bolting increases the carbonaceous proportion, making *fine* flour. The third bolting makes the superfine flour, and removes nearly all except the carbonaceous portion, which is fitted only to form fat and generate animal heat. No animal could live on superfine flour alone but for a short time, as has been proved by experiments on dogs.

But meats, vegetables, fruit, eggs, milk, and several other articles in family diet contain the same elements as wheat, though in different proportions; so that it is only an *exclusive* use of fine flour that is positively dangerous. Still there is no doubt that a large portion of young children using white bread for common food, especially if butter, sugar, and molasses are added, have their teeth, bones, and muscles not properly nourished. And it is a most unwise, uneconomical, and unhealthful practice to use flour deprived of its most important elements because it is white and is fashionable. It would be much cheaper, as well as more healthful, to use the *middlings*, instead of fine or superfine flour. It would be still better to use unbolted flour, except where delicate stomachs can not bear it, and in that case the middlings would serve nearly as well for nutrition and give no trouble.

Some suppose that bread wet with milk is better than if wet with water, in the making. Many experienced housekeepers say that a little butter or lard in warm water makes bread that looks and tastes exactly like that wet with milk, and that it does not spoil so soon.

Experienced housekeepers say also that bread, *if thoroughly kneaded*, may be put in the pans, and then baked as soon as light enough, without the second or third kneading, which is often practiced. This saves care and trouble, especially in training new cooks, who thus have only one chance to make mistakes, instead of two or three.

It is not well to use yeast powders instead of yeast, because it is a daily taking of medicinal articles not needed, and often injurious. Cream tartar is supertartrate of potash, and soda is a supercarbonate of soda. These two, when united in dough, form tartrate of potash, tartrate of soda, and carbonate of soda; while some one of the three tends to act chemically and injuriously on the digestive fluids. Professor Hosford's method is objectionable for the same reason, especially when his medical articles are mixed with flour; for thus poor flour is sold more readily than in ordinary cases. These statements the best-informed medical men and chemists will verify.

Flour loses its sweetness by keeping, and this is the reason why sugar is put in the recipes for bread. The best kind of flour, when new and fresh ground, has eight per cent. of sugar; and when such flour is used, the sugar may be omitted.

Some people make bread by mixing it so that it can be stirred with a spoon. But the nicest kind of bread can be made only with a good deal of kneading.

RECIPES FOR YEAST AND BREAD.

The best yeast is brewers' or distillery, as this raises bread much sooner than home-brewed. The following is the best kind of home-made yeast, and will keep good two or three weeks:

Hop and Potato Yeast.—Pare and slice five large potatoes, and boil them in one quart of water with a large handful of common hops (or a square inch of pressed hops), tied in a muslin rag. When soft, take out the hops and press the potatoes through a colander, and add a small cup of white sugar, a tea-spoonful of ginger, two tea-spoonfuls of salt, and two tea-cups of common yeast, or half as much distillery. Add the yeast when the rest is only blood-warm. White sugar keeps better than brown, and the salt and ginger help to preserve the yeast.

Do not boil in iron or use an iron spoon, as it colors the yeast. Keep yeast in a stone or earthenware jar, with a plate fitting well to the rim. This is better than a jug, as easier to fill and to cleanse. Scald the jar before making new yeast.

The rule for *quantity* is, one table-spoonful of brewers' or distillery yeast to every quart of flour; or twice as much home-made yeast.

Potato Yeast is made by the above rule, omitting the hops. It can be used in large quantities without giving a bitter taste, and so raises bread sooner. But it has to be renewed much oftener than hop yeast, and the bread loses the flavor of hop yeast.

Hard Yeast is made with home-brewed yeast (not brewers' or distillery), thickened with Indian meal and fine flour in equal parts, and then made into cakes an inch thick and three inches by two in size, dried in the wind but not in the sun. Keep them tied in a bag in a dry, cool place, where they will not freeze. One cake soaked in a pint of warm water (not hot) is enough for four quarts of flour. It is a good plan to work in mashed potatoes into this yeast, and let it rise well before using it. This makes the nicest bread. Some housekeepers say pour boiling water on one third of the flour, and then mix the rest in immediately, and it has the same effect as using potatoes.

When there is no yeast to start with, it can be made with one pint of new milk, one tea-spoonful of fine salt, and a table-spoonful of flour. When it is worked, use twice as much as common yeast. This is called Milk Yeast or Salt Risings, and bread made of it is poor, and soon spoils.

When yeast ceases to look foamy, and becomes watery, with sediment at the bottom, it must be renewed. When good, the smell is pungent, but not sour. If sour, nothing can restore it.

Bread of Fine Flour.—Take four quarts of sifted flour, one quart of lukewarm water, in which are dissolved two tea-spoonfuls of salt, two tea-spoonfuls of sugar, a table-spoonful of melted butter, and one cup of yeast. Mix and knead *very thoroughly*, and have it as soft as can be molded, using as little flour as possible. Make it into small loaves, put it in buttered pans, prick it with a fork, and when light enough to crack on the top, bake it. Nothing but experience will show when bread is just at the right point of lightness.

If bread rises too long, it becomes sour. This is discovered by making a sudden opening and applying the nose, and the sourness will be noticed as different from the odor of proper lightness. Practice is needed in this. If bread is light too soon for the oven, knead it awhile, and set it in a cool place. Sour bread can be remedied somewhat by working in soda dissolved in water—about half a tea-spoonful for each quart of flour. Many spoil bread by too much flour, others by not kneading enough, and others by allowing it to rise too much.

The goodness of bread depends on the quality of the flour. Some flour will not make good bread in any way. New and good flour has a yellowish tinge, and when pressed in the hand is adhesive. Poor flour is dry, and will not retain form when pressed. Poor flour is bad economy, for it does not make as nutritious bread as does good flour.

Bread made with milk sometimes causes indigestion to invalids and to children with weak digestion.

Take loaves out of the pans, and set them sidewise, and not flat, on a table. Wrapping in a cloth makes the bread clammy.

Bread is better in small loaves. Let your pans be of tin (or better, of iron), eight inches long, three inches high, three inches wide at the bottom, and flaring so as to be four inches wide at the top. This size makes more tender crust, and cuts more neatly than larger loaves.

Oil the pans with a swab and sweet butter or lard. They should be well washed and dried, or black and rancid oil will gather.

All these kinds of bread can be baked in biscuit-form; and, by adding water and eggs, made into griddle-cakes. Bread having potatoes in it keeps moist longest, but turns sour soonest.

Bread of Middlings or Unbolted Flour.—Take four quarts of coarse flour, one quart of warm water, one cup of yeast, two tea-spoonfuls of salt, one spoonful of melted lard or butter, two cups of sugar or molasses, and half a tea-spoonful of soda. Mix thoroughly, and bake in pans the same as the bread of fine flour. It is better to be kneaded rather than made soft with a spoon.

Bread raised with Water only.—Many persons like bread made either of fine or coarse flour, and raised with water only. Success in making this kind depends on the proper quantity of water, quick beating, the heating of very small pans, and very quick baking. There are cast-iron patties made for this purpose, and also small, coarse earthen cups. The following is the rule, but it must be modified by trying:

Recipe.—To one quart of unbolted flour put about one quart, or a little less, of *hot* water. Beat it very quickly, put it in hot pans, and bake in a hot oven. White flour may be used in place of coarse, and the quantity ascertained by trial. When right, there is after baking little except a crust, which is sweet and crisp.

Rye and Indian Bread.—The Boston or Eastern Brown Bread is made thus: One quart of rye, one quart of corn-meal, one cup of molasses, half a cup of distillery yeast, or twice as much home-brewed; one tea-spoonful of soda, and one tea-spoonful of salt. Wet with hot water till it is stiff as can be stirred with a spoon. This is put in a large brown pan and baked four or five hours. It is good toasted, and improved by adding boiled squash.

Third Bread.—This is made with equal parts of rye, corn-meal, and unbolted flour. To one quart of warm water add one tea-spoonful of salt, half a cup of distillery or twice as much home-brewed yeast, and half a cup of molasses, and thicken with equal parts of these three kinds of flour. It is very good for a variety.

Rye Bread.—Take a quart of warm water, a tea-spoonful of salt, half a cup of molasses, and a cup of home-brewed yeast, or half as much of distillery. Add flour till you can knead it, and do it very thoroughly.

Oat-Meal Bread.—Oat-meal is sometimes bitter from want of care in preparing. When good, it makes excellent and healthful bread.

Take one pint of boiling water, one great-spoonful of sweet lard or butter, two great-spoonfuls of sugar; melt them together, and thicken with two-thirds oat-meal and one-third fine flour. When blood-warm, add half a cup of home-brewed yeast and two well-beaten eggs. Mold into small cakes, and bake on buttered tins, or make two loaves.

Pumpkin Bread and Apple Bread.—These are very good for a variety. Stew and strain pumpkins or apples, and then work in either corn-meal or unbolted flour, or both. To each quart of the fruit add two table-spoonfuls of sugar, a pinch of salt, and a cup of home-brewed yeast. If the apples are quite sour, add more sugar. Make it as stiff as can be stirred with a spoon, and bake in patties or small loaves. Children like it for a change.

Corn-Meal Bread.—Always scald corn-meal. Melt two table-spoonfuls of butter or sweet lard in one quart of hot water; add a tea-spoonful of salt and a tea-cup of sugar. Thicken with corn-meal, and one-third as much fine flour, or unbolted flour, or middlings. Two well-beaten eggs improve it. Make it as stiff as can be easily stirred with a spoon, or, as some would advise, knead it like bread of white flour.

If raised with yeast, put in a tea-cup of home-brewed yeast, or half as much of distillery. If raised with powders, mix two tea-spoonfuls of cream tartar *thoroughly* with the meal, and one tea-spoonful of soda in the water.

Sweet Rolls of Corn-Meal.—Mix half corn-meal and half fine or unbolted flour; add a little salt, and then wet it up with sweetened water, raise it with yeast, and bake in small patties or cups in a very quick oven.

Soda Biscuit.—In one quart of flour mix *very thoroughly* two tea-spoonfuls of cream tartar, and a tea-spoonful of salt. Dissolve in a pint of warm water one tea-spoonful of soda and one table-spoonful of melted butter or lard. *Mix quickly*; add flour till you can roll, but let it be as soft as possible. Bake in a quick oven, and as soon as possible after mixing.

Yeast Biscuit.—Take a pint of raised dough of fine flour: pick it in small pieces; add one well-beaten egg, two great-spoonfuls of butter or lard, and two great-spoonfuls of sugar. Work thoroughly for ten minutes; add flour to roll, and then cut in round cakes and bake on tins, or mold into biscuits. Let them stand till light, and then bake in a quick oven.

If you have no dough raised, make biscuit as you would bread, except adding more shortening.

Potato Biscuit.—Boil and press through a colander twelve *mealy* potatoes; any others are not good. While warm, add one cup of butter, one tea-spoonful of salt, four great-spoonfuls of sugar, and half a cup of yeast. Mix in white or coarse flour till it can be well kneaded. Mold into small cakes; let them stand till light, and bake in a quick oven. These are the best kind, especially if made of coarse floor.

Buns.—These are best made by the rule for potato biscuit, adding twice as much sugar. When done, rub over a mixture of half milk and half molasses, and it improves looks and taste.

CHAPTER XIV.

BREAKFAST AND SUPPER.

WHAT shall we have for breakfast to-morrow? is the constant question of trial to a housekeeper, and it is the aim of the present chapter to meet this want by presenting a good and successive variety of articles healthful, economical, and easily prepared.

Some of the best housekeepers have taken this method: they provide a good supply of the following articles, to be used in succession—rice, corn-meal, rye flour, wheat grits, unbolted wheat, cracked wheat, pearl wheat, oat grits, oatmeal, and hominy, with which they make a new article for every day in the week. Some one of these is selected for either a dinner vegetable or dessert, or for a dish at tea, and the remainder used for the next morning's breakfast.

The following will indicate the methods:

Corn-Meal.—Take four large cups of corn-meal, and scald it. In *all* cases, scald corn-meal before using it. Add half a cup of fine flour, three table-spoonfuls of sugar or molasses, one tea-spoonful of soda, and one of salt. Make a batter, and boil an hour or more, stirring often; or, better, cook in a tin pail set in boiling water. Use it as mush, with butter, sugar, and milk for supper. Next morning, thin it with hot water: add two or three eggs, and bake either as muffins or griddle-cakes.

Hominy.—Soak and then boil a quart of hominy with two heaping tea-spoonfuls of salt. Use it for dinner as a vegetable, or for supper with sugar and milk or cream. Next morning use the remainder, soaked in water or milk, with two eggs and a salt-spoonful of salt. Bake as muffins or griddle-cakes, or cut in slices, dipped in flour and fried. Farina may be used in the same way.

Rice.—Pick over one pint of rice; add two tea-spoonfuls of salt and three quarts of *boiling* water. Then boil fifteen minutes; then uncover; let it steam fifteen minutes. This to be used for a vegetable at dinner, or for a tea-dish, with butter and sugar. At night, soak the remainder in as much milk or water, and next morning add as much fine or unbolted flour as there was rice, three eggs, a tea-spoonful of salt, and half a tea-spoonful of soda. Thin with water or milk, and bake as muffins or griddle-cakes.

The most economical Breakfast Dish, (healthful also).—Keep a jar for remnants of bread, both coarse and fine, for potatoes, remnants of hominy, rice, grits, cracked wheat, oat-meal, and all other articles used on table. Add all remnants of milk, whether sour or sweet, and water enough to soak all, so as to be soft, but not thin. When enough is collected, add enough water to make a batter for griddle-cakes, and put in enough soda to sweeten it. Add two spoonfuls of sugar, and half a tea-spoonful of salt, and two eggs for each quart, and you make an excellent dish of material, most of it usually wasted. Thicken it a little with fine flour, and it makes fine waffles.

Biscuits of sour Milk and white or unbolted Flour.—One pint unbolted flour.

One spoonful of sugar.

One tea-spoonful of salt.

Melt a spoonful of butter in a little of the sour milk; then mix all, and just before setting in the oven, add very *quickly* and very *thoroughly* a tea-spoonful of soda dissolved in half a tea-cup of water. This should be done last and quickly, so that the carbonic acid gas produced by the union of the soda and the acid of the milk (lactic) may not escape. Use half a tea-cup of fine flour when molding into biscuits.

Pearl Wheat or Cracked Wheat.—Boil one pint in a pail set in boiling water till quite soft, but so as not to lose its form. Add a tea-spoonful of sugar, and as much salt; also water, when needed. It must boil a long time. Eat a part for supper, with sugar and cream, and next morning add two eggs, a great-spoonful of sugar, and fine flour enough to make it suitable for muffin-rings or drop-cakes.

Rye and Corn-Meal.—Put into a pint and a half of boiling water one tea-spoonful of salt, two great-spoonfuls of sugar, two well-beaten eggs, three great-spoonfuls of corn-meal or unbolted wheat. Thicken with rye flour, and then add two well-beaten eggs. Bake in muffin-rings or as drop-cakes.

Oat-Meal.—Take one pint of boiling water, and pour it on to one pint of oat-meal. Add a great-spoonful of butter, half a tea-spoonful of salt, and two great-spoonfuls of sugar. Stir fast and thoroughly; then add two well-beaten eggs, and boil twenty minutes. To be eaten as mush for supper; and next morning thin it, and bake in muffin-rings.

Several of the above articles are good with only salt and water; and many persons would like them better with the butter, sugar, and eggs omitted.

Wheat Muffins.—One pint of milk, and two eggs.

One table-spoonful of yeast, and a salt-spoonful of salt. One table-spoonful of butter.

Mix these ingredients with sufficient flour to make a thick batter. Let it rise four or five hours, and bake in muffin-rings. This can be made of unbolted flour or grits, adding two great-spoonfuls of molasses, and it is very fine. Make it so thick that a table-spoon will stand erect in it.

Sally Lunn, improved.—Seven tea-cups of unbolted flour, or fine flour.

One pint of water.

Half a cup of melted butter, and half a cup of sugar.

One pinch of salt.

Three well-beaten eggs.

Two table-spoonfuls of brewers' yeast, or twice as much of home-brewed.

Pour into square buttered pans, and let it rise two or three hours with brewers' yeast; with home-brewed, five hours are required. It is still better baked in patties.

Cream Griddle-Cakes.—One pint of thick cream.

One tea-spoonful of salt.

One table-spoonful of sugar.

Three well-beaten eggs.

Make a thin batter of unbolted or of fine flour, and bake on a griddle.

Royal Crumpets.—Three tea-cups of raised dongh.

Two table-spoonfuls of melted butter.

Half a tea-cup of white sugar, mixed with three well-beaten eggs.

Bake in two buttered pans for half an hour.

Muffins of fine Flour or unbolted Flour.—One pint of milk or water.

One pinch of salt.

Two well-beaten eggs.

One table-spoonful of yeast.

Make a thick batter of fine flour or unbolted flour, and let it rise four or five hours. Bake in muffin-rings.

Unbolted Flour Waffles.—One pint of unbolted flour.

One pint of sour milk, or buttermilk, or water.

Half a tea-spoonful of soda, or more if needed, to sweeten the milk.

Three well-beaten eggs.

Two table-spoonfuls of sugar.

Drop-Cakes of fine Wheat or of Rye.—One pint of milk or water.

One pinch of salt.

Two table-spoonfuls of sugar.

Three well-beaten eggs.

Stir in rye, or fine or unbolted flour to a thick batter, and bake in cups or patties halt an hour.

Sachem's Head Corn-Cake.—One quart of sifted corn-meal, scalded.
One tea-spoonful of salt.
Three pints of scalded sweet milk or water.
Half a tea-spoonful of soda in two great-spoonfuls of warm water.
Half a tea-cup of sugar.
Eight eggs, the whites beaten separately, and added the last thing.
Make the cakes an inch thick in buttered pans before baking, and, if baked right, they will puff up to double the thickness, like sponge-cake, and are very fine.

Rice Waffles.—One pint of milk. Half a tea-cup of solid boiled rice, soaked three hours in the milk.
Two cups of wheat flour or rice flour.
Three well-beaten eggs. Bake in waffle-irons.
The rice must be salted enough when boiled.

Another Rice Dish.—One pint of rice, well cleaned.
Three quarts of cold water.
Three tea-spoonfuls of salt.
Boil it twenty minutes; then pour off the water, add milk or cream, and let it boil ten minutes longer, till quite soft. Let it stand till cold, and then cut it in slices and fry it on a griddle. It can also be made into griddle-cakes or muffins by the preceding recipe.

A good and easy Way to use cold Rice.—Heat a pint of boiled rice in milk; add two well-beaten eggs, a little salt, butter, and sugar; let it boil up once, and then grate on nutmeg.

Buckwheat-Cakes.—One quart of buckwheat.
One tea-spoonful of salt.
Two table-spoonfuls of distillery yeast, or four of home-brewed.
Two table-spoonfuls of molasses.
Wet the flour with warm water, and then add the other articles. Keep this warm through the night. If it sours, add half a tea-spoonful of soda in warm water. These cakes have a handsomer brown if wet with milk or part milk.

Fine Cottage Cheese.—Let the milk be turned by rennet, or by setting it in a warm place. It must not be *heated*, as the oily parts will then pass off, and the richness is lost. When fully turned, put in a coarse linen bag, and hang it to drain several hours, till all the whey is out. Then mash it fine, salt it to the taste, and thin it with good cream, or add but little cream, and roll it into balls. When thin, it is very fine with preserves or sugared fruit.

It also makes a fine pudding, by thinning it with milk, and adding eggs and sugar, and spice to the taste, and baking it. Many persons use milk when turned to *bonny-clabber* for a dessert, putting on sugar and spice. Children are fond of it.

CHAPTER XV.

PUDDINGS AND PIES.

WHERE sugar is made by slaves, the little children feed constantly on it, and grow fat and healthy. But they are nearly naked, live out-of-doors, exercise constantly, and have nothing to do but play. Thus their lungs and skin gain the healthful and purifying action of the air and the sun, and the excess of carbonaceous food is rendered harmless. But for those whose skin never meets the sun, rarely meets the air, and only now and then some water, a very different regimen is needful. Sugar, molasses, butter, and fats are chiefly carbonaceous, and therefore demand a large supply of oxygen through lungs and skin. And yet our custom is to use fine flour, which is chiefly carbon; butter and cream, chiefly carbon; sweet cakes, chiefly carbon; sweetmeats and candy, chiefly carbon; and worst of all, pie-crusts, chiefly carbon, and the most difficult of all food for digestion.

But the love for sweet food is common to all, and demands gratification. All that is required is moderation and temperance. For these reasons, a large supply is here provided of cakes and puddings, which are not rich, and yet are as highly relished as richer food. As pies are the most unhealthful of all food, some instruction and but few recipes are given, lest, if entirely omitted, the book would not be read so widely, and other more unhealthful ones be used.

The puddings here offered afford a great variety for desserts, are made with far less labor than pies, and are both more economical and more healthful. They also can be made more ornamental and attractive in appearance, and equally good to the taste. It is hoped, therefore, that the conscientious housekeeper will not tempt her family to eat unhealthful food when such an abundance is offered that is at once economical of labor, time, expense, and health. The first recipe for pudding can be varied in many ways, and has the advantage which heretofore has recommended pies, namely, that several can be made at once, and kept on hand as equally good either cold or warmed over. It is also economical and convenient, as not requiring eggs or milk.

The Queen of all Puddings.—Soak a tea-cup of tapioca and a tea-spoonful of salt in three tumblerfuls of warm, not hot, water for an hour or two, till softened. Take away the skins and cores of apples without dividing them, put them in the dish with sugar in the holes, and spice if the apples are without flavor: not otherwise. Add a cup of water, and bake till the apples are softened, turning them to prevent drying, and then pour over the tapioca, and bake *a long time*, till all looks A BROWNISH YELLOW. Eat with a hard sauce. Do not fail to bake a long time.

This can be extensively varied by mixing chopped apples, or quinces, or oranges, or peaches, or any kind of berries with the tapioca; and then sugar must be added according to the acid of the fruit, though some would prefer it omitted when the sauce is used.

The beauty may be increased by a cover of sugar beaten into the whites of eggs, and then turned to a yellow in the oven. Several such puddings can be made at once, kept in a cool place, and when wanted warmed over; many relish it better when very cold. Sago can be used instead of tapioca. When no sago or tapioca are at hand, the following recipe for flour pudding may be used, baking a long time:

Flour Puddings.—Take four table-spoonfuls of flour, half a tea-spoonful of salt, a pint of water or milk, three eggs, and a salt-spoonful of soda. Mix and beat very thoroughly, and bake as soon as done, or it will not be light. It must bake till the middle is not lower than the rest. Eat with liquid sauce. This can be cooked in a covered tin pan set in boiling water. This is enough for a family of five. Change the quantity according to the family.

This may be made richer by a spoonful of butter, more sugar, and some flavoring.

It will be lighter not to beat the eggs separately. If a bag is used to boil, rub flour or butter on the inside, to prevent sticking.

Flour and Fruit Puddings.—Add to the above, chopped apples or any kind of berries. Chopped apples and quinces together are fine when dried. When berries are used, a third more flour is needed for those very juicy, and less for cherries. Put in fruit the last thing.

Rusk and Milk.—Keep all bits of bread, dry in the oven, and pound them, putting half a salt-spoonful of salt to a pint. This eaten with good milk is what is especially relished by children, and named "rusk and milk."

Rusk Puddings.—Mix equal quantities of rusk-crumbs with stewed fruit or berries, then add a *very sweet* custard, made with four or five eggs to a quart of milk. Eaten with sweet sauce. This may be made without fruit, and is good with sauce.

Meat and Rusk Puddings.—Chop any kind of cold meat with salt pork or ham, season it well with butter, pepper, and salt, and add two or three beaten eggs. Then make alternate layers of wet rusk-crumbs, with milk or cold boiled hominy or rice, and bake half or three quarters of an hour. Let the upper layer be crumbs, and cover with a plate while baking, and, when nearly done, take it off to brown the top.

A handsome and good Pudding easily made.—Put a pint of scalded milk (water will do as well) to a pint of bread-crumbs, and add the yelks of four eggs, well beaten, a tea-cup of sugar, butter the size of an egg, and the grated rind of one lemon. Bake, and, when cool, cover with stewed fruit of any kind. Then beat the whites of the eggs into five table-spoonfuls of powdered sugar and the juice of one lemon. Cover the pudding with it, and set in the oven till it is a brownish yellow. Puddings covered with sugar and eggs in this way are called Meringue Puddings.

Pan Dowdy.—Put apples pared and sliced into a large pan, and put in an abundance of molasses or sugar, and some spice if the apples have little flavor; not otherwise. Cover with bread-dough, rolled thin, or a potato pie-crust. Bake a long time, and then break the crust into the fruit in small pieces. Children are very fond of this, especially if well sweetened and baked a long time.

Corn-Meal Pop-overs.—Two tumblers of scalded corn-meal fresh ground, three well-beaten eggs, a cup of milk or water, a tea-spoonful of salt, and three of sugar, two spoonfuls of melted butter. Bake in hot patties, and eat with sweet sauce.

Best Apple-Pie.—Take a deep dish, the size of a soup-plate, fill it heaping with peeled tart apples, cored and quartered; pour over it one tea-cup of molasses, and three great-spoonfuls of sugar, dredge over this a considerable quantity of flour, enough to thicken the sirup a good deal. Cover it with a crust made of cream, if you have it; if not, common dough, with butter worked in, or plain pie-crust, lapping the edge over the dish, and pinching it down tight, to keep the sirup from running out. Bake about an hour and a half. Make several at once, as they keep well.

Rice Pudding.—One tea-cup of rice.
One tea-cup of sugar.
One half tea-cup of butter.
One quart of milk.
Nutmeg, cinnamon, and salt to the taste.

Put the butter in melted, mix all in a pudding-dish, and bake it two hours, stirring it frequently, until the rice is swollen. It is good made without butter.

Bread and Fruit Pudding.—Butter a deep dish, and lay in slices of bread and butter, wet with milk, and upon these sliced tart apples, sweetened and spiced. Then lay on another layer of bread and butter and apples, and continue thus till the dish is filled. Let the top layer be bread and butter, and dip it in milk, turning the buttered side down. Any other kind of fruit will answer as well. Put a plate on the top, and bake two hours, then take it off and bake another hour.

Boiled Fruit Pudding.—Take light dough and work in a little butter, roll it out into a very thin large layer, not a quarter of an inch thick. Cover it thick with berries or stewed fruit, and put on sugar, roll it up tight, double it once or twice, and fasten up the ends. Tie it up in a bag, giving it room to swell. Eat it with butter, or sauce not very sweet.

Blackberries, whortleberries, raspberries, apples, and peaches, all make excellent puddings in the same way.

English Curd Pudding.—One quart of milk.

A bit of rennet to curdle it.

Press out the whey, and put into the curds three eggs, a nutmeg, and a table-spoonful of brandy. Bake it like custard.

Common Apple-Pie.—Pare your apples, and cut them from the core. Line your dishes with paste, and put in the apple; cover and bake until the fruit is tender. Then take them from the oven, remove the upper crust, and put in sugar and nutmeg, cinnamon or rose-water, to your taste. A bit of sweet butter improves them. Also, to put in a little orange-peel before they are baked, makes a pleasant variety. Common apple-pies are very good, to stew, sweeten, and flavor the apple before they are put into the oven. Many prefer the seasoning baked in. All apple-pies are much nicer if the apple is grated and then seasoned.

Plain Custard.—Boil half a dozen peach-leaves, or the rind of a lemon, or a vanilla bean in a quart of milk; when it is flavored, pour into it a paste made by a table-spoonful of rice flour, or common flour, wet up with two spoonfuls of cold milk and a half tea-spoonful of salt, and stir it till it boils again. Then beat up four eggs and put in, and sweeten it to your taste, and pour it out for pies or pudding. More eggs make it a rich custard.

Bake as pudding, or boil in a tin pail set in boiling water, stirring often, and pour into cups.

Another Custard.—Boil six peach-leaves, or a lemon-peel, in a quart of milk, till it is flavored; cool it, add three spoonfuls of sugar, a tea-spoonful of salt, and five eggs beaten to a froth. Put the custard into a tin pail, set it in boiling water, and stir it till cooked enough. Then turn it into cups; if preferred, it can be baked.

Mush, or Hasty Pudding.—Wet up the Indian-meal in cold water, till there are no lumps, stir it gradually into boiling water which has a little sugar and more salt added; boil till so thick that the stick will stand in it. Boil slowly, and so as not to burn, stirring often. Two or three hours' boiling is needed. Pour it into a broad, deep dish, let it grow cold, cut it into slices half an inch thick, flour them, and fry them on a griddle with a little lard, or bake them in a stove oven.

Stale Bread Pudding, (fine.)—Cut stale bread in thick slices, and put it to soak for several hours in cold milk.

Then cook on a griddle, with some salt, and eat it with sugar, or molasses, or a sweet sauce. To make it more delicate, take off the crusts. It is still better to soak it in uncooked custard. Baker's bread is best.

To prepare Rennet Wine.—Put three inches square of calf's rennet to a pint of wine, and set it away for use. Three table-spoonfuls will serve to curdle a quart of milk.

Rennet Custard.—Put three table-spoonfuls of rennet wine to a quart of milk, and add four or five great-spoonfuls of white sugar and a salt-spoonful of salt. Flavor it with wine, or lemon, or rose-water. It must be eaten in an hour, or it will turn to curds.

Bird'snest Pudding.—Pare tart, well-flavored apples, scoop out the cores without dividing the apple, put them in a deep dish with a small bit of mace, and a spoonful of sugar in the opening of each apple. Pour in water enough to cook them. When soft, pour over them an unbaked custard, so as just to cover them, and bake till the custard is done.

A Minute Pudding of Potato Starch.—Take four heaped table-spoonfuls of potato flour, three eggs, and a tea-spoonful of salt, and one quart of milk. Boil the milk, reserving a little to moisten the flour. Stir the flour to a paste, perfectly smooth, with the reserved milk, and put it into the boiling milk. Add the eggs well beaten, let it boil till very thick, which will be in two or three minutes, then pour into a dish and serve with liquid sauce. After the milk boils, the pudding must be stirred every moment till done.

Tapioca Pudding.—Soak eight table-spoonfuls of tapioca in a quart of warm milk and tea-spoonful of sugar, till soft, then add two table-spoonfuls of melted sweet lard or butter, five eggs well beaten, spice, sugar, and wine to your taste. Bake in a buttered dish, without any lining. Sago may be used in place of tapioca.

Cocoa-Nut Pudding (plain).—Take one quart of milk, five eggs, and one cocoa-nut, grated. The eggs and sugar are beaten together, and stirred into the milk when hot. Strain the milk and eggs, and add the cocoa-nut, with nutmeg to the taste. Bake about twenty minutes like puddings.

New-England Squash or Pumpkin-Pie.—Take a pumpkin or winter-squash, cut in pieces, take off the rind and remove the seeds, and boil it until tender, then rub it through a sieve. When cold, add to it milk to thin it, and to each quart of milk five well-beaten eggs. Sugar, cinnamon, and ginger to your taste. The quantity of milk must depend upon the size and quality of the squash.

These pies require a moderate heat, and must be baked until the centre is firm.

Ripe Fruit Pies—Peach, Cherry, Plum, Currant, and Strawberry.—Line your dish with paste. After picking over and washing the fruit carefully (peaches must be pared, and the rest picked from the stem), place a layer of fruit and a layer of sugar in your dish, until it is well filled, then cover it with paste, and trim the edge neatly, and prick the cover. Fruit-pies require about an hour to bake in a thoroughly-heated oven.

Mock Cream.—Beat three eggs well, and add three heaping tea-spoonfuls of sifted flour. Stir it into a pint and a half of boiling milk, add a salt-spoon of salt, and sugar to your taste. Flavor with rose-water or essence of lemon.

This can be used for cream-cakes or pastry.

A Pudding of Fruit and Bread Crumbs.—Mix a pint of dried and pounded bread-crumbs with an equal quantity of any kind of berries, or of dried and chopped sour apples. Add three eggs, half a pint of milk, three spoonfuls of fine flour, and half a tea-spoonful of salt. Bake on a griddle or in an oven in muffin-rings, or, when made thinner, as griddle-cakes. If dried fruit is used, more milk is needed than for fresh berries.

This may also be boiled for a pudding. Flour the pudding-cloth and tie tight, as it will not swell in cooking.

Bread and Apple Dumplings.—Mix half a pint of dried bread-crumbs and half a pint of fine flour. Wet it with water and two eggs thick enough to roll. Then put it around large apples peeled and cored whole, and boil for dumplings in several small floured cloths, or put all into one large floured cloth, tied tight, as they will not swell. Try with a fork, and when the apples are soft, take up and serve with a sweet sauce.

An excellent Indian Pudding without Eggs.—Take seven heaping spoonfuls of scalded Indian meal, half a tea-spoonful of salt, two spoonfuls of butter or sweet lard, a tea-cup of molasses, and two tea-spoonfuls of ginger or cinnamon, to the taste. Pour into these a quart of milk while boiling hot. Mix well and put in a buttered dish. Just as you set in the oven, stir in a tea-cup of cold water, which will produce the same effect as eggs. Bake three-quarters of an hour in a dish that will not spread it out thin.

Boiled Indian and Suet Pudding.—Three pints of milk, ten heaping table-spoonfuls of sifted Indian meal, a tumblerful of molasses, two eggs. Scald the meal with the milk, add the molasses and a tea-spoonful of salt. Put in the eggs when it is cool enough not to scald them. Put in a table-spoonful of ginger. Tie the bag so that it will be about two-thirds full of the pudding in order to give room to swell. The longer it is boiled the better. Some like a little chopped suet with the above.

A Dessert of Rice and Fruit.—Pick over and wash the rice, and boil it fifteen minutes in water, with salt at the rate of a heaping tea-spoonful to a quart. Rice is much improved by having the salt put in while cooking. Pour out the water in fifteen minutes after it begins to boil. Then pour in rich milk and boil till of a pudding thickness. Then pour it into cups to harden, when it is to be turned out inverted upon a platter in small mounds. Make an opening on the top of each, and put in a pile of jelly or fruit. Lastly, pour over all a custard made of three eggs, a pint of milk, and a tea-spoonful of salt boiled in a tin pail set in boiling water. This looks very prettily. Sweet cream with a little salt can be used instead of custard. This can be modified by having the whole put in a bowl and hardened, and then inverted and several openings made for the fruit.

Another Dessert of Rice and Fruit.—Boil the rice in salt and water, a tea-spoonful to a quart of water. When cooked to a pudding consistency, cool it, and then cut it in slices. Then put a thin layer of rice at the bottom of a pudding-dish, cover it with a thin layer of jelly or stewed fruit half an inch thick. Continue to add alternate layers of rice and jelly or fruit, smooth it at top, grate on sugar, and then cut the edges to show stripes of fruit and rice. Help it in saucers, and have cream or a thin custard to pour on it. Make the custard with two eggs, half a pint of milk, and half a tea-spoonful of salt. Boil it in a pail set in boiling water.

Dessert of cold Rice and stewed or grated Apple.—Cut cold boiled rice in slices, and then lay in a buttered pudding-dish alternate layers of rice and grated or stewed apples. Add sugar and spice to each layer of apples. Cover with the rice, smooth with a spoon dipped in cold water or milk, and bake three-quarters of an hour if the apples are raw. To be served with a sweet sauce.

A rich Flour Pudding.—Six eggs.
Three spoonfuls of flour.
One pint of milk.
A tea-spoonful of salt.

Beat the yelks well and mix them smoothly with the flour, then add the milk. Lastly, whip the whites to a stiff froth; work them in, and bake immediately.

To be eaten with a liquid sauce.

Apple-Pie.—Take fair apples; pare, core, and quarter them.

Take four table-spoonfuls of powdered sugar to a pie.

Put into a preserving-pan, with the sugar; water enough to make a thin sirup; throw in a few blades of mace; boil the apple in the sirup until tender, a little at a time, so as not to break the pieces. Take them out with care, and lay them in soup-dishes.

When you have preserved apple enough for your number of pies, add to the remainder of the sirup cinnamon and rose-water, or any other spice, enough to flavor it well, and divide it among the pies. Make a good paste, and line the rim of the dishes, and then cover them, leaving the pies without an under crust. Bake them a light brown.

Spiced Apple Tarts.—Rub stewed or baked apples through a sieve; sweeten them, and add powdered mace and cinnamon enough to flavor them. If the apples are not very tart, squeeze in the juice of a lemon. Some persons like the peel of the lemon grated into it. Line soup-dishes with a light crust, double on the rim, and fill them and bake them until the crust is done. Little bars of crust, a quarter of an inch in width, crossed on the top of the tart before it is baked, are ornamental.

Baked Indian Pudding.—Three pints of milk.

Ten heaping table-spoonfuls of Indian meal.

Three gills of molasses.

A piece of butter as large as a hen's egg.

Scald the meal with the milk, and stir in the butter and molasses, and bake four or five hours. Some add a little chopped suet in place of the butter. This can be boiled.

Apple Custard.—Take half a dozen very tart apples, and take off the skin and cores. Cook them till they begin to be soft, in half a tea-cup of water. Then put them in a pudding-dish, and sugar them. Then beat six eggs with four spoonfuls of sugar; mix it with three pints of milk, and two tea-spoonfuls of salt; pour it over the apples, and bake for about half an hour.

Plain Macaroni or Vermicelli Puddings.—Put two ounces of macaroni or vermicelli into a pint of milk, and simmer until tender. Flavor it by putting in two or three sticks of cinnamon while boiling, or some other spice when done. Then beat up three eggs, mix in an ounce of sugar, half a pint of milk, a tea-spoonful of salt, and a glass of wine. Add these to the broken macaroni or vermicelli, and bake in a slow oven.

Green Corn Pudding.—Twelve ears of corn, grated. Sweet-corn is best. One pint and a half of milk. Four well-beaten eggs. One tea-cup and a half of sugar.

Mix the above, and bake it three hours in a buttered dish. More sugar is needed if common corn is used.

Bread Pudding for Invalids or young Children.—Grate half a pound of stale bread; add a pinch of salt, and pour on a pint of hot milk, and let it soak half an hour. Add two well-beaten eggs, put it in a covered basin just large enough to hold it, tie it in a pudding-cloth, and boil it half an hour; or put it in a buttered pan in an oven, and bake it that time. Make a sauce of thin sweet cream, sweetened with sugar, and flavored with rose-water or nutmeg.

A good Pudding.—Line a buttered dish with slices of wheat bread, first dipped in milk. Fill the dish with sliced apple, and add sugar and spice. Cover with slices of bread soaked in milk; cover close with a plate, and bake three hours.

Loaf Pudding.—When bread is too stale, put a loaf in a pudding-bag and boil it in salted water an hour and a half, and eat it with hard pudding-sauce.

A Lemon Pudding.—Nine spoonfuls of grated apple, one grated lemon, (peel and pulp,) one spoonful of butter, and three eggs. Mix and bake, with or without a crust, about an hour. Cream improves it.

Green Corn Patties, (like oysters.)—Twelve ears of sweet-corn grated. (Yellow corn will do, but not so well.)

One tea-spoonful of salt, and one of pepper.

One egg beaten into two table-spoonfuls of flour.

Mix, make into small cakes, and cook on a griddle.

Cracker Plum Pudding, (excellent.)—Make a very sweet custard, and put into it a tea-spoonful of salt.

Take soda crackers, split them, and butter them very thick.

Put a layer of raisins on the bottom of a large pudding-dish, and then a layer of crackers, and pour on a little of the custard when warm, and after soaking a little, put on a thick layer of raisins, pressing them into the crackers with a knife. Then put on another layer of crackers, custard and fruit, and proceed thus till you have four layers. Then pour over the whole enough custard to rise even with the crackers. It is best made over night, so that the crackers may soak. Bake from an hour and a half to two hours. During the first half-hour, pour on, at three different times, a little of the custard, thinned with milk, to prevent the top from being hard and dry. If it browns fast, cover with paper.

Bread and butter pudding is made in a similar manner.

SAUCES FOR PUDDINGS.

Liquid Sauce.—Six table-spoonfuls of sugar. Ten table-spoonfuls of water. Four table-spoonfuls of butter. Two table-spoonfuls of wine. Nutmeg, or lemon, or orange-peel, or rose-water, to flavor.

Heat the water and sugar very hot. Stir in the butter till it is melted, but be careful not to let it boil. Add the wine and nutmeg, just before it is used.

Hard Sauce.—Two table-spoonfuls of butter.

Ten table-spoonfuls of sugar.

Work this till white, then add wine or grated lemon-peel, and spice to your taste.

Another Hard Sauce.—Mix half as much butter as sugar, and heat it fifteen minutes in a bowl set in hot water. Stir till it foams. Flavor with wine or grated lemon-peel.

A Healthful Pudding Sauce.—Boil, in half a pint of water, some orange or lemon-peel, or peach-leaves. Take them out and pour in a thin paste, made with two spoonfuls of flour, and boil five minutes. Then put in a pint of sugar, and let it boil. Then put in two spoonfuls of butter, add a glass of wine, and take it up before it boils.

An excellent Sauce for any Kind of Pudding.—Beat the yelks of three eggs into sugar enough to make it quite sweet. Add a tea-cup of cream, or milk, and a little butter, and the grated peel and juice of two lemons. When lemons can not be had, use dried lemon-peel, and a little tartatic acid. This is a good sauce for puddings, especially for the Starch Minute Pudding. Good cider in place of wine is sometimes used.

PASTE FOR PUDDINGS AND PIES.

This is an article which, if the laws of health were obeyed, would be banished from every table; for it unites the three evils—animal fat, *cooked* animal fat, and heavy bread. Nothing in the whole range of cooking is more indigestible than rich pie-crust, especially when, as bottom crust, it is made still worse by being soaked, or slack-baked. Still, as this work does not profess to leave out unwholesome dishes, but only to set forth an abundance of healthful ones, and the reasons for preferring them, the best directions will be given for making the best kinds of paste.

Pie-Crusts without Fats.—Good crusts for plain pies are made by wetting up the crust with rich milk turned sour, and sweetened with saleratus. Still better crusts are made of sour cream, sweetened with saleratus.

Mealy potatoes boiled in salt water and mixed with the same quantity of flour, and wet with sour milk sweetened with saleratus, make a good crust.

Good light bread rolled thin makes a good crust for Pan-Dowdy, or pan-pie, and also for the upper crust of fruit-pies, to be made without bottom crusts.

Pie-Crust made with Butter.—Very plain paste is made by taking a quarter of a pound of butter for every pound of flour. Still richer, allow three quarters of a pound of butter to a pound of flour.

Directions for making rich Pie-Crust.—Take a quarter of the butter to be used, rub it thoroughly into the flour, and wet it with *cold* water to a stiff paste.

Next dredge the board thick with flour, cut up the remainder of the butter into thin slices, lay them upon the flour, dredge flour over thick, and then roll out the butter into thin sheets, and lay it aside.

Then roll out the paste thin, cover it with a sheet of this rolled butter; dredge on more flour, fold it up and roll it out, and repeat the process till all the butter is used up.

Paste should be made as quick and as cold as possible. Some use a marble table in order to keep it cold. Roll *from* you every time.

CHAPTER XVI.

CAKE.

THE multiplication of recipes for cakes, pies, puddings, and desserts is troublesome and needless, inasmuch as a little generalization will reduce them to a comparatively small compass, and yet afford a large variety.

Cake is of three classes, as raised either by eggs, or by yeast, or by powders; and different proportions of flour, sugar, shortening, and wetting make the variety, as it appears in what follows.

General Directions.

Sift flour, roll sugar, sift spices, and prepare fruit beforehand. Break eggs that are to be whipped, one at a time, in a cup, and let none of the yelk go in. Have them *cold*, and you will get on faster.

Excepting dough-cake, never use the hand in making cake, but a wooden spoon, and in an earthen vessel.

The goodness of cake depends greatly on baking. If too hot at bottom, set the pan on a brick; if too hot at top, cover with paper. If top-crust is formed suddenly, it prevents what is below from rising properly; and so, when the oven is very hot, cover with paper.

When fruit is used, sprinkle the fruit with a little flour to keep it from sinking when baking. Some put fruit in in layers, one in the middle and another near the top, as this spreads it evenly. Put in the flour just before baking.

When using whites beaten to a froth separately, put in the last thing, so that the bubbles of air which make the lightness may be retained more perfectly. Bake as soon as the cake is ready.

Water is as good as milk for most cakes as well as for bread; a mixture of new and stale milk injures the cake.

Streaks in cake are made either by imperfect mixing, or

unequal baking, or by sudden decrease of heat before the cake is done. Try when cake is done, by inserting a splinter or straw; if it comes out clean, the cake is done.

The best way to keep cake is in a tin box or stone jar.

Do not wrap cake or bread in a cloth.

In baking, move cake *gently* if you change its place, or it will fall in streaks. Cake is more nicely baked when the pan is lined with oiled paper, especially in old pans, which often give a bad taste to the bottom and sides of the cake.

CAKE RAISED WITH POWDERS.

Although it is unhealthful to use powders in bread for daily food, the small quantity used for cake will do no harm.

The cake most easily made is raised with soda and cream tartar or other baking powders, and many varieties can be made by the following recipes:

One, Two, Three, Four Cake.—Take one cup of butter, (half a cup is better,) two cups of sugar, three cups of flour, and four eggs. Mix butter, sugar, and yelks. Then add the flour very thoroughly, and lastly the whites in a stiff froth. Bake immediately, and the cake will be light, with nothing added. But it is equally light to omit the eggs and work two tea-spoonfuls of cream tartar into the flour, and then mix well first the butter and sugar, and then the flour. When ready to bake, mix very thoroughly and quickly a tea-spoonful of soda, or a bit of sal volatile dissolved in a cup of warm (not hot) water. This makes two loaves. The following are varieties made by this recipe, using raising either with eggs or powders:

Chocolate-Cake.—Bake the above in thin layers, only a little thicker than carpeting. When nearly cool, spread over the cake a paste made of equal parts of scraped chocolate and sugar wet with water. Place the cake in layers one over another, frost the top, and then cut in oblong pieces for the cake-basket.

Jelly-Cake.—Proceed as above, only using jelly instead of chocolate.

Orange-Cake.—Proceed as for jelly-cake, having flavored the cake when making with a little grated orange-peel. The oranges must be peeled, chopped fine, and sweetened.

Almond and Cocoa-nut Cake.—Blanch three ounces of almonds, (that is, pour on boiling water and take off the skins.) Chop or pound them with an equal quantity of sugar, make a thin paste with water, and use this instead of the jelly. Cocoa-nut, chopped fine, can be used instead of almonds. *Straw-*

berries, *Peaches*, *Cranberries*, and *Quinces*, and any other fruit, mashed or cooked, can be used in place of the jelly, being first sweetened.

This cake can be made richer by adding spices and fruit before baking. Cream can be used in place of butter. Chopped almonds, citron, or cocoa-nut may be put *in* the cake for baking, making still another variety.

CAKES RAISED WITH EGGS.

Pound-Cake, (very rich.)—One pound of flour, one pound of sugar, half a pound of butter, nine eggs, a glass of brandy, one nutmeg, one tea-spoonful of pounded cinnamon. Mix half the flour with the butter, brandy, and spice; add the yelks of eggs beaten well into the sugar. Beat the whites to a stiff froth, and add them in alternate spoonfuls with the rest of the flour: then beat a long time, and bake as soon as done.

Plain Cake raised with Eggs.—Take a pound or quart of flour, half as much sugar, half as much butter as sugar, four or five eggs, one nutmeg, and a tea-spoonful of cinnamon. Mix well the sugar, butter, yelks, and spice; then the flour, and last the whites as stiff froth.

These two cakes are varied by adding citron, fruit, or other spices, making them more or less rich.

Fruit-Cake.—This to be made either like pound-cake, with fruit added; or like plain cake, raised with eggs or yeast, adding fruit.

Walnut-meats or *Almonds* may be chopped and put in the cake instead of fruit, making another variety.

Huckleberry-Cake.—One quart of huckleberries, three cups of sugar, three cups of flour, six eggs, one cup of sweet milk, and one tea-spoonful of soda dissolved in a little hot water. Cream the butter and sugar, and add the beaten yelks. Then add the milk, flour, and two grated nutmegs. Then add the whites, whipped to a stiff froth, and the berries, gently, so as not to mash them. An excellent cake.

Currants and other berries may be used in the same way. If very sour, add more sugar. If doubtful of raising it enough, add a tea-spoonful of soda; or, more surely, a bit of sal volatile the size of a hickory-nut.

Gold and Silver Cake.—This makes a pretty variety when cut and placed together in a cake-dish. For each, take one cup of sugar (for the silver, white; and for the gold, brown), half a cup of butter, half a cup of milk, two cups of flour, one tea-spoonful of cream tartar, and half as much soda. For the one, use the yelk of three eggs; and the white, as stiff froth, for the other. Mix the cream tartar very thoroughly in the flour, and put in the soda last. Bake immediately. This makes one loaf of each kind, in flat pans, and is to be frosted. If more is wanted, double the quantity of each ingredient.

Rich Sponge-Cake.—Take twelve eggs, and the weight of ten in sugar, and six in flour. Beat the sugar into the yelks, add the juice and grated peel of one lemon, then the flour, and then the whites cut to a stiff froth, and bake as soon as possible. Bake in brick-shaped pans, and line them with buttered paper.

Plain Sponge-Cake, (easily made.)—Mix thoroughly two cups of sifted flour and two cups of white sugar with one tea-spoonful of cream tartar. Beat four eggs to a froth, not separating the whites, and add some grated lemon-peel, or nutmeg, or rose-water. Just before baking, add half a tea-spoonful of soda dissolved in three great-spoonfuls of warm water. Beat quick, and set in the oven immediately.

GINGERBREAD, FRIED CAKES, COOKIES, AND OTHER CAKES.

Aunt Esther's Gingerbread.—Take half a pint of molasses, a small cup of soft butter, a gill and a half of water, a heaping tea-spoonful of soda dissolved in a table-spoonful of hot water, and one even table-spoonful of strong ginger, or two if weak. Rub butter and ginger into the flour, add the water, soda, and molasses, and while doing it, put in two table-spoonfuls of vinegar. Roll it in cards an inch thick, and bake half an hour in a quick oven.

Sponge Gingerbread.—Add to the above two beaten eggs, and water to make it thin as pound-cake, and bake as soon as well mixed.

Ginger-Snaps and Seed-Cookies.—One cup of butter, two cups of sugar or molasses, one cup of water, one table-spoonful of ginger, one heaping tea-spoonful of cinnamon and one of cloves, one tea-spoonful of soda dissolved in a small cup of hot water. Mix and add flour for a stiff dough, roll and cut in small round cakes. Omit the spices, and put in four or five table-spoonfuls of caraway seeds, and you have *seed-cakes.* Leave out all spice and seeds, and you have plain cookies.

Fried Cakes.—For *Doughnuts,* use the recipe for Plain Sponge-Cake, adding flour enough to roll. Or take Plain Cake raised with eggs, and add flour enough to roll. Or take Dough-Cake, or Plain Loaf-Cake, and thicken so as to roll. Roll about half an inch thick and cut into oblong pieces. For *Crullers,* take plain cake raised with eggs, and thicken stiff with flour; roll it thin, and cut into strips, and form twisted cakes. More sugar and butter make it richer, but less healthful.

Have plenty of lard, or, better, strained beef-fat, quite hot; try with a small piece first, and, if right, there will be a bubbling. Turn two or three times to cook all alike, break open one to try if done, and when done, take up with a skimmer and drain well. If the fat is too hot, it will brown too quick; if not hot enough, the fat will soak into the cake. Remember that frying is the most unhealthful mode of cooking food, and the one most likely to be done amiss.

CAKE RAISED WITH YEAST.

Plain Loaf-Cake.—Two pounds of dried and sifted flour, a pint of warm water in which is melted a quarter of a pound of butter, half a tea-spoonful of salt, three eggs without beating, and three quarters of a pound of sugar, well mixed; and then add two nutmegs, two tea-spoonfuls of cinnamon, and two gills of home-brewed or half as much distillery yeast. When light, add two or three pounds of fruit, and let it stand half an hour.

Rich Loaf-Cake is made like the above, only adding more butter and sugar. The following are specimens of the diverse proportions: Four pounds of flour, three of sugar, two of butter, a quart of water or milk, ten unbeaten eggs, half a pint of wine, three nutmegs, three tea-spoonfuls of cinnamon, and two cloves; two gills of distillery yeast, or twice as much home-brewed. This is what in New-England would be called Election or Commencement-Cake. Two or three risings used to be practiced, but one is as good if the mixing is thorough.

Dough-Cake.—Three cups of raised dough, half a cup of butter, two cups of sugar, two eggs, fruit and spice to the taste. When light, bake in loaves. This can be made more or less sweet, and shortened by lessening or increasing the quantity of dough. It must be mixed with the hands.

Icing for Cake.—Put the whites of eggs into a dish, and for each egg use about a quarter of a pound of sugar. Beat the whites, slowly adding the sugar. This is better than beating the whites first, and then adding sugar. A little lemon-juice or tartaric acid makes it whiter and better. Spread the icing, after pouring it upon the centre, with a knife dipped in water. If you can, dry in an open, sunny window. Otherwise, harden it in the oven. It improves it by mixing, when adding sugar, some almonds pounded to a thin paste.

CHAPTER XVII.

PRESERVES AND JELLIES.

General Directions.

GATHER fruit when it is dry.

Long boiling hardens the fruit.

Pour boiling water over the sieves used, and wring out jelly-bags in hot water the moment you are to use them.

Do not squeeze while straining through jelly-bags.

Let the pots and jars containing sweetmeats just made remain uncovered three days.

For permanent covering, lay brandy papers over the top, cover them tight, and seal them; or, what is best of all, soak a split bladder and tie it tight over them. In drying, it will shrink so as to be perfectly air-tight.

Keep them in a dry but not warm place.

A thick, leathery mold helps to preserve fruit, but when mold appears in specks, the preserves must be scalded in a warm oven, or the jars containing them are to be set into hot water, which must then boil till the preserves are scalded.

Always keep watch of preserves which are not sealed, especially in warm and damp weather. The only sure way to keep them without risk or care is to make them with enough sugar and seal them or tie bladder covers over.

The best kettle is iron lined with porcelain. If brass is used, it must be bright, or acids will make a poison.

The chief art is to boil continuously, slowly, and gently, and take up as soon as done; too long boiling makes the fruit hard and dark. Jellies will not harden well if the boiling stops for some minutes. Try jellies with a spoon, and as soon as they harden around the edge quickly, they are done. In making, the sugar should be heated, and not added till the juice boils.

Keep preserves in small glass jars, as frequent opening injures them.

Canned Fruit.—This is far more economical than to preserve in sugar. Some can be canned without any sugar, and very nice sugar demands only one fourth sugar to three fourths fruit. The best cans are glass with metal tops. Those of Wilcox are the best known to the author. The W. L. Imlay's, of Philadelphia, are recommended as best of any.

Directions.—Set the jars in a large boiler, and then fill it with cold water and heat to boiling. Having filled the jars to within an inch of the top with alternate layers of fruit and sugar, (in proportion of one half or one fourth of a pound of sugar to a pound of fruit, according as it is more or less acid,) set them in cold water. As soon as the fruit has risen to the top of the jar, screw on the cover and take from the water. Peaches and pears may be canned without sugar.

To clarify Sirup for Sweetmeats.—For each pound of sugar allow half a pint of water. For every three pounds of sugar allow the white of one egg. Mix when cold, boil a few minutes, and skim it. Let it stand ten minutes and skim it again, then strain it.

Brandy Peaches.—Prick the peaches with a needle, put them into a kettle with cold water, heat the water, scald them until sufficiently soft to be penetrated with a straw. Take half a pound of sugar to every pound of peaches; make the sirup with the sugar, and while it is a little warm mix two thirds as much of white brandy with it, put the fruit into jars and pour the sirup over it. The late white clingstones are the best to use.

Peaches, (not very rich.)—To six pounds of fruit put five of sugar. Make the sirup. Boil the fruit in the sirup till it is clear. If the fruit is ripe, half an hour will cook it sufficiently.

Peaches, (very elegant.)—First take out the stones, then pare them. To every pound of peaches allow one third of a pound of sugar. Make a thin sirup, boil the peaches in the sirup till tender, but not till they break. Put them into a bowl and pour the sirup over them. Put them in a dry, cool place, and let them stand two days. Then make a new, rich sirup, allowing three quarters of a pound of sugar to one of fruit. Drain the peaches from the first sirup, and boil them until they are clear in the last sirup. The first sirup must not be added, but may be used for any other purpose you please, as it is somewhat bitter. The large white clingstones are the best.

To preserve Quinces whole.—Select the largest and fairest quinces, (as the poorer ones will answer for jelly.) Take out the cores and pare them. Boil the quinces in water till tender. Take them out separately on a platter. To each pound of quince allow a pound of sugar. Make the sirup, then boil the quinces in the sirup until clear.

Quince Jelly.—Rub the quinces with a cloth until perfectly smooth. Remove the cores, cut them into small pieces, pack them tight in your kettle, pour cold water on them until it is on a level with the fruit, but not to cover it; boil till very soft, but not till they break. Dip off all the liquor you can, then put the fruit into a sieve and press it, and drain off all the remaining liquor. Then to a pint of the liquor add a pound of sugar and boil it fifteen minutes. Pour it, as soon as cool, into small jars or tumblers. Let it stand in the sun a few days, till it begins to dry on the top. It will continue to harden after it is put up.

Calf's-Foot Jelly.—To four nicely cleaned calf's feet put four quarts of water; let it simmer gently till reduced to two quarts, then strain it and let it stand all night. Then take off all the fat and sediment, melt it, add the juice, and put in the peel of three lemons and a pint of wine, the whites of four eggs, three sticks of cinnamon, and sugar to your taste. Boil ten minutes, then skim out the spice and lemon-peel and strain it.

The American gelatine, now very common, makes a good jelly, with far less trouble; and in using it, you only need to dissolve it in hot water, and then sweeten and flavor it.

To preserve Apples.—Take only tart and well-flavored apples; peel and take out the cores without dividing them, and then parboil them. Make the sirup with the apple water, allowing three quarters of a pound of white sugar to every pound of apples, and boil some lemon-peel and juice in the sirup. Pour the sirup, while boiling, upon the apples, turn them gently while cooking, and only let the sirup simmer, as hard boiling breaks the fruit. Take it out when the apple is tender through. At the end of a week, boil them once more in the sirup.

Pears.—Take out the cores, cut off the stems, and pare them. Boil the pears in water till they are tender. Watch them that they do not break. Lay them separately on a platter as you take them out. To each pound of fruit take a pound of sugar. Make the sirup, and boil the fruit in the sirup till clear.

Pine-Apples, (very fine.)—Pare and *grate* the pine-apple. Take an equal quantity of fruit and sugar. Boil them slowly in a saucepan for half an hour.

Purple Plums, No. 1.—Make a rich sirup. Boil the plums in the sirup very gently till they begin to crack open. Then take them from the sirup into a jar, and pour the sirup over them. Let them stand a few days, and then boil them a second time very gently.

Purple Plums, No. 2.—Take an equal weight of fruit and nice brown sugar. Take a clean stone jar, put in a layer of fruit and a layer of sugar till all is in. Cover them tightly with dough, or other tight cover, and put them in a brick oven after you have baked in it. If you bake in the morning, put the plums in the oven at evening, and let them remain till the next morning. When you bake again, set them in the oven as before. Uncover them and stir them carefully with a spoon, and so as not to break them. Set them in the oven thus *the third* time, and they will be sufficiently cooked.

White or Green Plums.—Put each one into boiling water and rub off the skin. Allow a pound of fruit to a pound of sugar. Make a sirup of sugar and water. Boil the fruit in the sirup until clear—about twenty minutes. Let the sirup be cold before you pour it over the fruit. They can be preserved without taking off the skins by pricking them. Some of the kernels of the stones boiled in give a pleasant flavor.

Citron Melons.—Two fresh lemons to a pound of melon. Let the sugar be equal in weight to the lemon and melon. Take out the pulp of the melon and cut it in thin slices, and boil it in fair water till tender. Take it out and boil the lemon in the same water about twenty minutes. Take out the lemon, add the sugar, and, if necessary, a little more water. Let it boil. When clear, add the melon and let it boil a few minutes.

Strawberries.—Look over them with care. Weigh a pound of sugar to each pound of fruit. Put a layer of fruit on the bottom of the preserving-kettle, then a layer of sugar, and so on till all is in the pan. Boil them about fifteen minutes. Put them in bottles, hot, and seal them. Then put them in a box and fill it in with dry sand. The flavor of the fruit is preserved more perfectly by simply packing the fruit and sugar in alternate layers, and sealing the jar, without cooking; but the preserves do not look so well.

Blackberry Jam.—Allow three quarters of a pound of brown sugar to a pound of fruit. Boil the fruit half an hour, then add the sugar and boil all together ten minutes.

To preserve Currants to eat with Meat.—Strip them from the stem. Boil them an hour, and then to a pound of the fruit add a pound of brown sugar. Boil all together fifteen or twenty minutes.

Cherries.—Take out the stones. To a pound of fruit allow a pound of sugar. Put a layer of fruit on the bottom of the preserving-kettle, then a layer of sugar, and continue thus till all are put in. Boil till clear. Put them in bottles hot and seal them. Keep them in dry sand.

Currants.—Strip them from the stems. Allow a pound of sugar to a pound of currants. Boil them together ten minutes. Take them from the sirup and let the sirup boil twenty minutes, and pour it on the fruit. Put them in small jars or tumblers, and let them stand in the sun a few days.

Raspberry Jam, No, 1.—Allow a pound of sugar to a pound of fruit. Press them with a spoon in an earthen dish. Add the sugar, and boil all together fifteen minutes.

Raspberry Jam, No. 2.—Allow a pound of sugar to a pound of fruit. Boil the fruit half an hour, or till the seeds are soft. Strain one quarter of the fruit, and throw away the seeds. Add the sugar, and boil the whole ten minutes. A little currant-juice gives it a pleasant flavor, and when that is used, an equal quantity of sugar must be added.

Currant Jelly.—Pick over the currants with care. Put them in a stone jar, and set it into a kettle of boiling water. Let it boil till the fruit is very soft. Strain it through a sieve. Then run the juice through a jelly-bag. Put a pound of sugar to a pint of juice, and boil it together five minutes. Set it in the sun a few days. If it stops boiling, it is less likely to turn to jelly.

Quince Marmalade.—Rub the quinces with a cloth, cut them in quarters. Put them on the fire with a little water, and stew them till they are sufficiently tender to rub them through a sieve. When strained, put a pound of sugar to a pound of the pulp. Set it on the fire, and let it cook slowly. To ascertain when it is done, take out a little and let it get cold, and if it cuts smoothly, it is done.

Crab-apple marmalade is made in the same way.

Crab-apple jelly is made like quince jelly.

Most other fruits are preserved so much like the preceding that it is needless to give any more particular directions than to say that a pound of sugar to a pound of fruit is the general rule for all preserves that are to be kept through warm weather and a long time.

Preserved Watermelon Rinds.—This a fine article to keep well without trouble for a long time. Peel the melon, and boil it in just enough water to cover it till it is soft, trying with a fork. (If you wish it green, put green vine-leaves above and below each layer, and scatter powdered alum, less than half a tea-spoonful to each pound.)

Allow a pound of sugar to each pound of rind, and clarify it as directed previously.

Simmer the rinds two hours in this sirup, and flavor it with lemon-peel grated and tied in a bag. Then put the melon in a tureen, and boil the sirup till it looks thick, and pour it over. Next day, give the sirup another boiling, and put the juice of one lemon to each quart of sirup. Take care not to make it bitter by too much of the peel.

Citrons are preserved in the same manner. Both these keep through hot weather with very little care in sealing and keeping.

Preserved Pumpkin.—Cut a thick yellow pumpkin, peeled, into strips two inches wide and five or six long.

Take a pound of white sugar for each pound of fruit, and scatter it over the fruit, and pour on two wine-glasses of lemon-juice for each pound of pumpkin.

Next day, put the parings of one or two lemons with the fruit and sugar, and boil the whole three quarters of an hour, or long enough to make it tender and clear without breaking. Lay the pumpkin to cool, strain the sirup, and then pour it on to the pumpkin.

If there is too much lemon-peel, it will be bitter.

CHAPTER XVIII.

DESSERTS AND EVENING PARTIES.

Ice-Cream.—One quart of milk. One and a half table-spoonfuls of arrow-root. The grated peel of two lemons. One quart of thick cream.

Wet the arrow-root with a little cold milk, and add it to the quart of milk when boiling hot; sweeten it very sweet with white sugar, put in the grated lemon-peel, boil the whole, and strain it into the quart of cream. When partly frozen, add the juice of the two lemons. Twice this quantity is enough for thirty-five persons. Find the quantity of sugar that suits you by measure, and then you can use this every time, without tasting. Some add whites of eggs; others think it just as good without. It must be made *very* sweet, as it loses much by freezing.

If you have no apparatus for freezing, (which is *almost* indispensable), put the cream into a tin pail with a very tight cover, mix equal quantities of snow and blown salt, (not the coarse salt), or of pounded ice and salt, in a tub, and put it *as high as the pail, or freezer;* turn the pail or freezer half round and back again with one hand, for half an hour, or longer, if you want it very nice. Three quarters of an hour steadily will make it good enough. While doing this, stop four or five times, and mix the frozen part with the rest, the last time very thoroughly, and then the lemon-juice must be put in. Then cover the freezer tight with snow and salt till it is wanted. The mixture must be perfectly cool before being put in the freezer. Renew the snow and salt while shaking, so as to have it kept tight to the sides of the freezer. A hole in the tub holding the freezing mixture, to let off the water, is a great advantage. In a tin pail it would take much longer to freeze than in the freezer, probably nearly twice as long. A long stick, like a coffee-stick, should be used in scraping the ice from the sides. Iron spoons will be affected by the lemon-juice, and give a bad taste.

In taking it out for use, first wipe off every particle of the freezing mixture dry, then with a knife loosen the sides, then invert the freezer upon the dish in which the ice is to be served, and apply two towels wrung out of hot water to the bottom part, and the whole will slide out in the shape of a cylinder. Freezers are now sold quite cheap, and such as freeze in a short time.

Strawberry Ice-Cream.—Rub a pint of ripe strawberries through a sieve, add a pint of cream, and four ounces of powdered sugar, and freeze it. Other fruits may be used thus.

Ice-Cream without Cream.—A vanilla bean or a lemon rind is first boiled in a quart of milk. Take out the bean or peel, and add the yelks of four eggs, beaten well. Heat it scalding hot, but do not boil it, stirring in white sugar till *very* sweet. When cold, freeze it.

Fruit Ice-Cream.—Make rich boiled custard, and mash into it the soft ripe fruit, or the grated or cooked hard fruit, or grated pine-apples. Rub all through a sieve, sweeten it very sweet, and freeze it. Quince, apple, pear, peach, strawberry, and raspberry are all very good for this purpose.

A Cream for stewed Fruit.—Boil two or three peach leaves, or a vanilla bean, in a quart of cream, or milk, till flavored. Strain and sweeten it, mix it with the yelks of four eggs, well beaten; then, while heating it, add the whites cut to a froth. When it thickens take it up. When cool, pour it over the fruit or preserves.

Currant, Raspberry, or Strawberry Whisk.—Put three gills of the juice of the fruit to ten ounces of crushed sugar, add the juice of a lemon, and a pint and a half of cream. Whisk it till quite thick, and serve it in jelly-glasses or a glass dish.

Lemonade Ice, and other Ices.—To a quart of lemonade, add the whites of six eggs, cut to a froth, and freeze it. The juices of any fruit, sweetened and watered, may be prepared in the same way, and are very fine.

Charlotte Russe.—One ounce of gelatine simmered in half a pint of milk or water, four ounces of sugar beat into the yelks of four eggs, and added to the gelatine when dissolved. Then add a pint of cream or new milk. Lastly, add the whites beat to a stiff froth, and beat all together. Line a mold with slices of sponge-cake and set it on ice, and when the cream is a little thickened, fill the mold; let it stand five or six hours, and then turn it into a dish.

Flummery.—Cut sponge-cake into thin slices, and line a deep dish. Make it moist with white wine; make a rich custard, using only the yelks of the eggs. When cool, turn it into the dish, and cut the whites to a stiff froth, and put on the top.

Chicken Salad.—Cut the white meat of chickens into small bits the size of peas. Chop the white parts of celery nearly as small.

Prepare a dressing thus: rub the yelks of hard-boiled eggs smooth, to each yelk put half a tea-spoonful of liquid mustard, the same quantity of salt, a table-spoonful of oil mixed in very slowly and thoroughly, and half a wine-glass of vinegar. Mix the chicken and celery in a large bowl, and pour over this dressing.

The dressing must not be put on till just before it is used. Bread and butter and crackers are served with it.

Wine Jelly.—Two ounces of American isinglass or gelatine. One quart of boiling water. A pint and a half of white wine. The whites of three eggs.

Soak the gelatine in cold water half an hour. Then take it from the water, and pour on the quart of boiling water. When cooled, add the grated rind of one lemon, and the juice of two, and a pound and a half of loaf-sugar. Then beat the whites of the eggs to a stiff froth, and stir them in, and let the whole boil till the egg is well mixed, but do not stir while it boils. Strain through a jelly-bag, and then add the wine.

In cold weather, a pint more of water may be added. This jelly can be colored by beet-juice, saffron, or indigo, for fancy dishes.

An Apple Lemon Pudding.—Six spoonfuls of grated, or of cooked and strained, apple. Three lemons, pulp, rind, and juice, all grated. Half a pound of melted butter. Sugar to the taste. Seven eggs well beaten.

Mix, and bake with or without paste. It can be made still plainer by using nine spoonfuls of apple, one lemon, two thirds of a cup full of butter, and three eggs.

Wheat Flour Blanc-Mange.—Wet up six table-spoonfuls of flour to a thin paste with cold milk, and stir it into a pint of boiling milk. Flavor with lemon-peel or peach-leaves boiled in the milk. Add a pinch of salt, cool it in a mold, and eat with sweetened cream and sweetmeats.

Orange Marmalade.—Take two lemons and a dozen oranges; grate the yellow rinds of all the oranges but five, and set it aside. Make a clear sirup of an equal weight of sugar. Clear the oranges of rind and seeds, put them with the grated rinds into the sirup, and boil about twenty minutes till it is a transparent mass.

A simple Lemon Jelly, (easily made.)—One ounce of gelatine. A pound and a half of loaf-sugar. Three lemons, pulp, skin, and juice, grated.

Pour a quart of boiling water upon the isinglass, add the rest, mix and strain it, then add a glass of wine, and pour it to cool in some regular form. If the lemons are not fresh, add a little cream of tartar or tartaric acid.

Cranberry.—Pour boiling water on them, and then you can easily separate the good and the bad. Boil them in a very little water till soft, then sweeten to your taste. If you wish a jelly, take a portion and strain through a fine sieve.

Apple Ice, (very fine.)—Take finely-flavored apples, grate them fine, and then make them *very* sweet, and freeze them. It is very delicious.

Pears, peaches, or quinces also are nice, either grated fine or stewed and run through a sieve, then sweetened *very* sweet, and frozen. The flavor is much better preserved when grated than when cooked.

Whip Syllabub.—One pint of cream. Sifted white sugar to your taste. Half a tumbler of white wine. The grated rind and juice of one lemon. Beat all to a stiff froth.

Apple Snow.—Put six very tart apples in cold water over a slow fire. When soft, take away the skins and cores and mix in a pint of sifted white sugar; beat the whites of six eggs to a stiff froth, and then add them to the apples and sugar. Put it in a dessert-dish and ornament with myrtle and box.

Iced Fruit.—Take fine bunches of currants on the stalk, dip them in well-beaten whites of eggs, lay them on a sieve and sift white sugar over them, and set them in a warm place to dry.

Ornamental Froth.—The whites of four eggs in a stiff froth, put into the sirup of preserved raspberries or strawberries, beaten well together, and turned over ice-cream or blanc-mange. Make white froth to combine with the colored in fanciful ways. It can be put on the top of boiling milk, and hardened to keep its form.

To clarify Isinglass.—Dissolve an ounce of isinglass in a cup of boiling water, take off the scum, and drain through a coarse cloth. Jellies, candies, and blanc-mange should be done in brass and stirred with silver.

Blanc-Mange.—Two and a half sheets of gelatine broken into one quart of milk; put in a warm place and stir till it dissolves. An ounce and a half of clarified isinglass stirred into the milk. Sugar to your taste. A tea-spoonful of fine salt. Flavor with lemon, or orange, or rose-water. Let it boil, stirring it well, then strain it into molds.

Three ounces of almonds pounded to a paste and added while boiling is an improvement. Or filberts or hickory-nuts can be skinned and used thus. It can be flavored by boiling in it a vanilla bean or a stick of cinnamon. (Save the bean to use again.)

Apple Jelly.—Boil tart peeled apples in a little water till glutinous; strain out the juice, and put a pound of white sugar to a pint of the juice. Flavor to your taste, boil till a good jelly, and then put it into molds.

Orange Jelly.—The juice of nine oranges and three lemons. The grated rind of one lemon, and one orange, pared thin. Two quarts of water, and four ounces of gelatine broken up and boiled in it to a jelly. Add the above, and sweeten to your taste. Then add the whites of eight eggs, well beaten to a stiff froth, and boil ten minutes; strain and put into molds, first dipped in cold water. When perfectly cold, dip the mold in warm water, and turn on to a glass dish.

Floating Island.—Beat the yelks of six eggs with the juice of four lemons, sweeten it to your taste, and stir it into a quart of boiling milk till it thickens, then pour it into a dish. Whip the whites of the eggs to a stiff froth, and put it on the top of the cream.

A Dish of Snow.—Grate the white part of cocoa-nut, put it in a glass dish, and serve with oranges sliced and sugared, or with currant or cranberry jellies.

To clarify Sugar.—Take four pounds of sugar, and break it up. Whisk the white of an egg, and put it with a tumblerful of water into a preserving-pan, and add water gradually till you have two quarts, stirring well. When there is a good frothing, throw in the sugar, boil moderately, and skim it. If the sugar rises to run over, throw in a little cold water, and then skim it, as it is then still. Repeat this, and when no more scum rises, strain the sugar for use.

Candied Fruits.—Preserve the fruit, then dip it in sugar boiled to candy thickness, and then dry it. Grapes and some other fruits may be dipped in uncooked, and then dried, and they are fine.

Another Way.—Take it from the sirup, when preserved, dip it in powdered sugar, and set it on a sieve in an oven to dry.

To make an Ornamental Pyramid for a Table.—Boil loaf-sugar as for candy, and rub it over a stiff form made for the purpose, of stiff paper or pasteboard, which must be well buttered. Set it on a table, and begin at the bottom, and stick on to this frame with the sugar, a row of macaroons, kisses, or other ornamental articles, and continue till the whole is covered. When cold, draw out the pasteboard form, and set the pyramid in the centre of the table with a small bit of wax-candle burning with it, and it looks very beautifully.

CHAPTER XIX.

DRINKS AND ARTICLES FOR THE SICK AND YOUNG CHILDREN.

DRINKS made of the juice of fruits and water are good for all who are in health. Various preparations of cocoa-nuts are so also. Tea is often made or adulterated with unhealthful articles. Coffee is usually drank so strong as to injure children and grown persons of delicate constitution. All alcoholic drinks are dangerous, because they are so generally mixed with harmful matter, and because they so often lead to excess, and then to ruin. The common-sense maxim is, when there is danger, choose the safest course. The Christian maxim is, "We that are strong ought to bear the infirmities of the weak, and not to please ourselves."

Obedience to these two maxims would save thousands of young children and delicate persons from following the dangerous example of those "that are strong."

To make Tea.—The safest tea is the black, as less stimulating than green; both excite the brain and nerves when strong. The chief direction is to have water *boiling* hot. First soak the tea in a very little hot water, and then add boiling water.

To make Coffee.—Roast it slowly in a tight vessel, and so it can be stirred often. To roast all equally a dark brown and have none burned, is the main thing. Keep it in a tight box, or, better, grind it fresh when used. Clear it by putting into it, when making, a fresh egg-shell crushed, or the white of an egg, or a small bit of fish-skin. Some filter, and some boil; and there are coffee-pots made for each method, and some that require nothing put in to clear the coffee. The aroma is retained just in proportion as the coffee is confined, both before making and also while making.

Fish-skin for Coffee.—Take it from codfish before cooking; have it nice and dry. Cut in inch squares, and take one for two quarts of coffee.

Cocoa.—The cracked is best. Put two table-spoonfuls of it into three pints of cold water. Boil an hour for first use, save the remnants and boil it again, as it is very strong. Do this several times. For ground cocoa use two table-spoonfuls to a quart, and boil half an hour. Boil the milk by itself, and add it liberally when taken up. For the *shells* of cocoa, use a heaping tea-cupful for a quart of water. Put them in over night and boil a long time.

Cream for Coffee and Tea.—Heat new milk, and let it stand till cool and all the cream rises; this is the best way for common use. To every pint of this add a pound and a quarter of loaf-sugar, and it will keep good a month or more, if corked tight in glass.

Chocolate.—Put three table-spoonfuls when scraped to each pint, boil half an hour, and add boiled milk when used.

Delicious Milk-Lemonade.—Half a pint of sherry wine and as much lemon-juice, six ounces loaf-sugar, and a pint of water poured in when boiling. Add not quite a pint of cold milk, and strain the whole.

Strawberry and Raspberry Vinegar.—Mix four pounds of the fruit with three quarts of cider or wine vinegar, and let them stand three days. Drain the vinegar through a jelly-bag and add four more pounds of fruit, and in three days do the same. Then strain out the vinegar for summer drinks, effervescing with soda or only with water.

White Tea, and Boys' Coffee for Children.—Children never love tea and coffee till they are trained to it. They always like these drinks. Put two tea-spoonfuls of sugar to half a cup of hot water, and add as much good milk. Or crumb toast or dry bread into a bowl with plenty of sugar, and add half milk to half boiling water.

Dangerous Use of Milk.—Milk is not only drink, but rich food. It therefore should not be used as drink with other food, as is water or tea and coffee. Persons often cause bilious difficulties by using milk in addition to ordinary food as the chief drink. It is a well-established fact that some grown persons as well as young children can not drink milk, and in some cases can not eat bread wet with milk, without trouble from it.

Simple Drinks.—Pour boiling water on mashed cranberries, or grated apples, or tamarinds, or mashed currants or raspberries, pour off the water, sweeten, and in summer cool with ice.

Pour boiling water on to bread toasted quite brown, or on to pounded parched corn, boil a minute, strain, and add sugar and cream, or milk.

Simple Wine Whey.—Mix equal quantities of milk and boiling water, add wine and sweeten.

Toast and Cider.—Take one third brisk cider and two thirds cold water, sweeten it, crumb in toasted bread, and grate on a little nutmeg. Acid jelly will do when cider is not at hand.

Panada.—Toast two or three crackers, pour on boiling water and let it simmer two or three minutes, add a well-beaten egg, sweeten and flavor with nutmeg.

Water-Gruel.—Scald half a tumblerful of fresh ground corn-meal, add a table-spoonful of flour made into a paste, boil twenty minutes or more, and add salt, sugar, and nutmeg. Oat-meal gruel is excellent made thus.

Beef-Tea.—Pepper and salt some good beef cut into small pieces, pour on boiling water and steep half an hour. A better way is to put the meat thus prepared into a bottle kept in boiling water for four or five hours.

Tomato Sirup.—Put a pound of sugar to a quart of juice, bottle it, and use for a beverage with water.

Sassafras Jelly.—Soak the pith of sassafras till a jelly, and add a little sugar.

Egg Tea, Egg Coffee, and Egg Milk.—Beat the yelk of an egg in some sugar and a little salt; add either cold tea or coffee or milk. Then beat the whites to a stiff froth and add. Flavor the milk with wine. Some do not like the taste of raw egg, and so the other articles may first be made boiling hot before the white is put in.

Oat-Meal Gruel.—Four table-spoonfuls of *grits*, (unbolted oat-meal,) a pinch of salt and a pint of boiling water. Skim, sweeten, and flavor. Or make a thin batter of fine oat-meal, and pour into boiling water; then sweeten and flavor it.

Pearl Barley-Water.—Boil two and a half ounces of pearl barley ten minutes in half a pint of water, strain it, add a quart of boiling water, boil it down to half the quantity, strain, sweeten, and flavor with sliced lemon or nutmeg.

Cream Tartar Beverage.—Put two even tea-spoonfuls cream tartar to a pint of boiling water, sweeten and flavor with lemon-peel.

Rennet Whey, (good for a weak stomach after severe illness.)—Soak rennet two inches square one hour, add half a gill of water and a pinch of salt; then pour it into a pint of warm (not hot) milk. Let it stand half an hour, then cut it, and after an hour drain off the liquid. Let it stand awhile, and drain off more whey.

Refreshing Drink for a Fever.—Mix sprigs of sage, balm, and sorrel with half a sliced lemon, the skin on. Pour on boiling water, sweeten and cork it.

CHAPTER XX.

THE PROVIDING AND CARE OF FAMILY STORES.

The art of keeping a good table consists not in loading on a variety at each meal, but rather in securing a *successive* variety, a table neatly and tastefully set, and every thing that is on it cooked in the best manner.

There are some families who provide an abundance of the most expensive and choice articles, and spare no expense in any respect, yet who have every thing cooked in such a miserable way, and a table set in so slovenly a manner, that a person accustomed to a *really* good table can scarcely taste a morsel with any enjoyment.

On the contrary, there are many tables where the closest economy is practiced; and yet the table-cloth is so white and smooth, the dishes, silver, glass, and other table articles so bright, and arranged with such propriety; the bread so light and sweet; the butter so beautiful, and every other article of food so well cooked, and so neatly and tastefully served, that every thing seems good, and pleases both the eye and the palate.

A habit of *doing every thing in the best manner* is of unspeakable importance to a housekeeper, and every woman ought to *aim* at it, however great the difficulties she may have to meet. If a young housekeeper commences with a determination to *try* to do *every thing* in the best manner, and perseveres in the effort, meeting all obstacles with patient cheerfulness, not only the moral but the intellectual tone of her mind is elevated by the attempt. Although she may meet many insuperable difficulties, and may never reach the standard at which she aims, the simple effort, *persevered* in, will have an elevating influence on her character; while, at the same time, she actually will reach a point of excellence far ahead of those who, discouraged by many obstacles, give up in despair, and resolve to make no more efforts, and let things go as they will. The grand distinction between a noble and an ignoble mind is, that one *will* control circumstances; the other yields, and allows circumstances to control her.

It should be borne in mind that the constitution of man demands *a variety* of food, and that it is just as cheap to keep on hand a good variety of materials in the store-closet, so as to make a frequent change, as it is to buy one or two articles at once, and live on them exclusively, till every person is tired of them, and then buy two or three more of another kind.

It is too frequently the case that families fall into a very limited round of articles, and continue the same course from one year to another, when there is a much greater variety within reach of articles which are just as cheap and as easily obtained, and yet remain unthought of and untouched.

A thrifty and generous provider will see that her store-closet is furnished with such a variety of articles that successive changes can be made, and for a good length of time. To aid in this, a slight sketch of a well-provided store-closet will be given, with a description of the manner in which each article should be stored and kept, in order to avoid waste and injury. To this will be added modes of securing a *successive variety* within the reach of all in moderate circumstances.

It is best to have a store-closet open from the kitchen, because the kitchen fire keeps the atmosphere dry, and this prevents the articles stored from molding, and other injury from dampness. Yet it must not be kept warm, as there are many articles which are injured by warmth.

A *cool* and *dry* place is indispensable for a store-room, and a small window over the door, and another opening out-doors, give a great advantage, by securing coolness and circulation of fresh air.

Flour should be kept in a barrel, with a flour-scoop to dip it, a sieve to sift it, and a pan to hold the sifted flour, either in the barrel or close at hand. The barrel should have a tight cover to keep out mice and vermin. It is best to find, by trial, a lot of first-rate flour, and then buy a year's supply. But this should not be done unless there are accommodations for keeping it dry and cool, and protecting it from vermin.

Unbolted flour should be stored in kegs or covered tubs, and always be kept on hand as regularly as fine flour. It should be bought only when freshly ground, and only in moderate quantities, as it loses sweetness by keeping.

Indian meal should be purchased in small quantities, say fifteen or twenty pounds at a time, and be kept in a covered tub or keg. It is always improved by scalding. It must be kept very cool and dry, and if occasionally stirred, is preserved more surely from growing sour or musty. Fresh ground is best.

Rye should be bought in small quantities, say forty or fifty pounds at a time, and be kept in a keg or half-barrel, with a cover.

Buckwheat, Rice, Hominy, and *Ground Rice* must be purchased in small quantities, and kept in covered kegs or tubs. Several of these articles are infested with small black insects, and examination must occasionally be made for them.

Arrowroot, Tapioca, Sago, Pearl Barley, Pearl Wheat, Cracked Wheat, American Isinglass, Macaroni, Vermicelli, and *Oat-meal* are all articles which help to make an agreeable variety, and it is just as cheap to buy a small quantity of each as it is to buy a larger quantity of two or three articles. Eight or ten pounds of each of these articles of food can be stored in covered jars or covered wood boxes, and then they are always at hand to help to make a variety. All of them are very healthful food, and help to form many delightful dishes for desserts. Some of the most healthful puddings are those made of rice, tapioca, sago, and macaroni; while isinglass, or American gelatine, forms elegant articles for desserts, and is also excellent for the sick.

Sugars should not be bought by the barrel, as the brown is apt to turn to molasses, and run out on to the floor. Refined loaf for tea, crushed sugar for the nicest preserves and to use with fruit, nice brown sugar for coffee, and common brown for more common use. The loaf can be stored in the paper, on a shelf. The others should be kept in close covered kegs, or covered wooden articles made for the purpose.

Butter must be kept in the dryest and coldest place you can find, in vessels of either stone, earthen, or wood, and never in tin.

Lard and Drippings must be kept in a dry, cold place, and should not be salted. Usually the cellar is the best place for them. Earthen or stone jars are the best to store them in.

Salt must be kept in the *dryest* place that can be found. *Rock salt* is the best for table-salt. It should be washed, dried, pounded, sifted, and stored in a glass jar, and covered close. It is common to find it growing damp in the *salt-stands* for the table. It should then be set by the fire to dry, and afterward be reduced to fine powder again. Few things are more disagreeable than coarse or damp salt on a table.

Vinegar is best made of wine or cider. Buy a keg or half-barrel of it, set and it in the cellar, and then keep a supply for the casters in a bottle in the kitchen. If too strong, it *eats* the pickles. Much manufactured vinegar is sold that ruins pickles, and is unhealthful.

Pickles never must be kept in glazed ware, as the vinegar forms a poisonous compound with the glazing.

Oil must be kept in the cellar. *Winter-strained* must be got in cold weather, as the *summer-strained* will not burn except in warm weather. Those who use kerosene oil should never trust it with heedless servants or children. Never fill lamps with it at night, nor allow servants to kindle fire with it, or to fill a lamp with it when lighted. Inquire for the safest pattern of lamps, and learn all the dangers to be avoided, and the cautions needful in the use of this most dangerous explosive oil. Neglect this caution, and you probably will be a sorrowful mourner all your life for the sufferings or death of some dear friend.

Molasses, if bought by the barrel or half-barrel, should be kept in the cellar. If bought in small quantities, it should be kept in a demijohn. No vessel should be corked or bunged, if filled with molasses, as it will swell and burst the vessel, or run over.

Hard Soap should be bought by large quantity, and laid to harden on a shelf in a very dry place. It is much more economical to buy hard than soft soap, as those who use soft soap are very apt to waste it in using it, as they can not do with hard soap.

Starch it is best to buy by a large quantity. It comes very nicely put up in papers, a pound or two in each paper, and packed in a box. The high-priced starch is cheapest in the end.

Indigo is not always good. When a good lot is found by trial, it is best to get enough for a year or two, and store it in a tight tin box.

Coffee it is best to buy by the bag, as it improves by keeping. Let it hang in the bag in a dry place, and it loses its rank smell and taste. It is poor economy to buy ground coffee, as it often has other articles mixed, and loses flavor by keeping after it is ground.

Tea, if bought by the box, is several cents a pound cheaper than by small quantities. If well put up in boxes lined with lead, it keeps perfectly; but put up in paper, it soon loses its flavor. It therefore should, if in small quantities, be put up in glass or tin, and shut tight.

Soda should be bought in small quantities, then powdered, sifted, and kept tight corked in a large-mouth glass bottle. It grows damp if exposed to the air, and then can not be used properly.

Raisins should not be bought in large quantities, as they are injured by time. It is best to buy the small boxes.

Currants for cake should be prepared, and set by for use in a jar.

Lemon and *Orange Peel* should be dried, pounded, and set up in corked glass jars.

Nutmeg, *Cinnamon*, *Cloves*, *Mace*, and *Allspice* should be pounded fine, and corked tight in small glass bottles, with mouths large enough for a junk-bottle cork, and then put in a tight tin box, made for the purpose. Or they can be put in small tin boxes with tight covers. Essences are as good as spices.

Sweet Herbs should be dried, the stalks thrown away, and

the rest be kept in corked large-mouth bottles, or small tin boxes.

Cream Tartar, *Citric* and *Tartaric Acids*, *Bicarbonate of Soda*, and *Essences* should be kept in corked glass jars. *Sal volatile* must be kept in a large-mouth bottle, with a ground-glass stopper to make it air-tight. Use cold water in dissolving it. It must be powdered.

Preserves and *Jellies* should be kept in glass or stone, in a cool, dry place, well sealed, or tied with bladder covers. If properly made and thus put up, they never will ferment. If it is difficult to find a cool, dry place, pack the jars in a box, and fill the interstices with sand, very thoroughly dried. It is best to put jellies in tumblers, or small glass jars, so as to open only a small quantity at a time.

The most easy way of keeping *Hams* perfectly is to wrap and tie them in paper, and pack them in boxes or barrels with ashes. The ashes must fill all interstices, but must not touch the hams, as it absorbs the fat. It keeps them sweet, and protects from all kinds of insects.

After smoked beef or hams are cut, hang them in a coarse linen bag in the cellar, and tie it up to keep out flies.

Keep *Cheese* in a cool, dry place, and after it is cut, wrap it in a linen cloth, and keep it in a tight tin box.

Keep *Bread* in a tin covered box, and it will keep fresh and good longer than if left exposed to the air.

Cake also should be kept in a tight tin box. Tin boxes made with covers like trunks, with handles at the ends, are best for bread and cake.

Smoked herring keep in the cellar.

Codfish is improved by changing it, once in a while, back and forth from garret to cellar. Some dislike to have it in the house anywhere.

All *salted provision* must be watched, and kept under the brine. When the brine looks bloody, or smells badly, it must be scalded, and more salt put to it, and poured over the meat.

CHAPTER XXI.

ON SETTING TABLES, AND PREPARING VARIOUS ARTICLES OF FOOD FOR THE TABLE.

To a person accustomed to a good table, the manner in which the table is set, and the mode in which food is prepared and set on, has a great influence, not only on the eye, but the appetite. A housekeeper ought, therefore, to attend carefully to these particulars.

The table-cloth should always be *white*, and well washed and ironed. When taken from the table, it should be folded in the ironed creases, and some heavy article laid on it. A heavy bit of plank, smoothed and kept for the purpose, is useful. By this method, the table-cloth looks tidy much longer than when it is less carefully laid aside.

When table-napkins are used, care should be taken to keep the same one to each person; and in laying them aside, they should be folded so as to hide the soiled places, and laid under pressure. It is best to use napkin-rings.

The table-cloth should always be put on *square*, and right side upward. The articles of table furniture should be placed with order and symmetry.

The bread for breakfast and tea should be cut in even, regular slices, not over a fourth of an inch thick, and all crumbs removed from the bread-plate. They should be piled in a regular form, and if the slices are large they should be divided.

The butter should be cooled in cold water, if not already hard, and then cut into a smooth and regular form, and a butter-knife be laid by the plate, to be used for no other purpose but to help the butter.

A small plate should be placed at each plate for butter, and a small salt-cup set by each breakfast or dinner-plate. This saves butter and salt.

All the flour should be wiped from small cakes, and the crumbs be kept from the bread-plate.

In preparing dishes for the dinner-table, all water should be carefully drained from the vegetables, and the edges of the platters and dishes should be made perfectly clean and neat.

All soiled spots should be removed from the outside of pitchers, gravy-boats, and every article used on the table; the handles of the knives and forks must be clean, and the knives bright and sharp.

In winter, the plates and all the dishes used, both for meat and vegetables, should be set to the fire to warm, when the table is being set, as cold plates and dishes cool the vegetables, gravy, and meats, which by many is deemed a great injury.

Cucumbers, when prepared for table, should be laid in cold water for an hour or two to cool, and then be peeled and cut into fresh cold water. Then they should be drained, and brought to the table, and seasoned the last thing.

The water should be drained thoroughly from all greens and salads.

There are certain articles which are usually set on together, because it is *the fashion*, or because they are *suited* to each other.

Thus, with *strong-flavored meats*, like mutton, goose, and duck, it is customary to serve the strong-flavored vegetables, such as onions and turnips. Thus, turnips are put in mutton broth, and served with mutton, and onions are used to stuff geese and ducks. But onions are usually banished from the table and from cooking on account of the disagreeable flavor they impart to the atmosphere and breath.

Boiled Poultry should be accompanied with boiled ham or tongue.

Boiled Rice is served with poultry as a vegetable.

Jelly is served with mutton, venison, and roasted meats, and is used in the gravies for hashes.

Fresh Pork requires some acid sauce, such as cranberry, or tart apple-sauce.

Drawn Butter, prepared as in the recipe, with eggs in it, is used with boiled fowls and boiled fish.

Pickles are served especially with fish, and *Soy* is a fashionable sauce for fish, which is mixed on the plate with drawn butter.

There are modes of *garnishing dishes*, and preparing them for table, which give an air of taste and refinement that pleases the eye. Thus, in preparing a dish of fricasseed fowls, or stewed fowls, or cold fowls warmed over, small cups of boiled rice can be laid inverted around the edge of the platter, to eat with the meat.

On *Broiled Ham* or *Veal*, eggs boiled or fried, and laid one on each piece, look well.

Greens and *Asparagus* should be well drained, and laid on buttered toast, and then slices of boiled eggs be laid on the top and around.

Hashes and preparations of pigs' and calves' head and feet should be laid on toast, and garnished with round slices of lemon.

Curled Parsley, or *Common Parsley*, is a pretty garnish, to be fastened to the shank of a ham, to conceal the bone, and laid around the dish holding it. It looks well laid around any dish of cold slices of tongue, ham, or meat of any kind.

In setting a tea-table, small-sized plates are set around, with a knife, napkin, and butter-plate laid by each in a regular manner, while the articles of food are to be set, also, in regular order. On the waiter are placed tea-cups and saucers, sugar-bowl, slop-bowl, cream-cup, and two or three articles for tea, coffee, and hot water, as the case may be. On the dinner-table, by each plate, is a knife, fork, napkin, and tumbler; and a small butter-plate and salt-cup should also be placed by each plate.

CHAPTER XXII.

WASHING, IRONING, AND CLEANSING.

MANY a woman without servants, or with those untrained, must do her own washing and ironing, or train others to do it, and this is the most trying department of housekeeping. The following may aid in lessening labor and care.

It saves washing and is more healthful to use flannel shirts. Farmers, sailors, and soldiers have found by experience that they are more comfortable than cotton or linen, even in the hottest days. Many gentlemen use them for common wear, changing to a cotton-flannel night-gown for sleeping. So young children can have a flannel jacket and flannel drawers sewed to the jacket in front, and buttoned behind, and change them at night for cotton-flannel made in the same way. The under-garments for women may be made of the same material and pattern, and this will save washing and promote health.

Some ladies economize time and labor by wearing three-cornered lace articles for the neck, trimmed with imitation Valenciennes lace, wash them in their wash-bowl, whiten in soap-suds in a tumbler or bowl in their window, stiffen with gum-arabic, and after stretching, press under weights between clean papers. This is a happy contrivance when on a journey or without servants. Those who wish to save all needless labor in washes should have under-garments and night-gowns made in sack forms or other fashions that save in both material and labor. They also should omit ruffles and other trimmings that increase the labor of ironing.

There is nothing which tends more effectually to secure good washing than a full supply of all conveniences. A plenty of soft water is a very important item. When this can not be had, lye or soda can be put in hard water, to soften it. Borax is safer than soda, which turns white clothes yellow, and injures texture. Buy crude borax, and for a common washing use half an ounce. A *borax soap* is thus made: To a pound of bar-soap, cut in small pieces, put a quart of hot water and an ounce of powdered borax. Heat and mix, but do not boil, cool and cut into cakes, and use like hard soap. Soak the white clothes in a suds made of this soap over night, and it saves much rubbing. Two wash-forms are needed; one for the two tubs in which to put the suds, and the other for bluing and starching-tubs. Four tubs, of different sizes, are necessary; also, a large *wooden* dipper, (as metal is apt to rust;) two or three pails; a grooved washboard; a clothes-line, (sea-grass or horse-hair is best;) a wash-stick to move clothes when boiling, and a wooden fork to take them out. Soap-dishes, made to hook on the tubs, save soap and time. Provide, also, a clothes-bag, in which to boil clothes; an indigo-bag, of double flannel; a starch-strainer, of coarse linen; a bottle of ox-gall for calicoes; a supply of starch, neither sour nor musty; several dozens of clothes-pins, which are cleft sticks, used to fasten clothes on the line; a bottle of dissolved gum-arabic; two clothes-baskets; and a brass or copper kettle, for boiling clothes, as iron is apt to rust. A closet for keeping all these things is a great convenience. Tubs, pails, and all hooped wooden ware, should be kept out of the sun, and in a cool place, or they will fall to pieces.

COMMON MODE OF WASHING.

Assort the clothes, and put those most soiled in soak the night before. Never pour hot water on them, as it sets the dirt. In assorting clothes, put the flannels in one lot, the colored clothes in another, the coarse white ones in a third, and the fine clothes in a fourth lot. Wash the fine clothes in one tub of suds. When clothes are very much soiled, a second suds is needful, turning them wrong side out. Put them in the boiling-bag, and boil them in strong suds for half an hour, and not much more. Move them, while boiling, with the clothes-stick. Take them out of the boiling-bag, and put them into a tub of water, and rub the dirtiest places again, if need be. Throw them into the rinsing-water, and then wring them out, and put them into the bluing-water. Put the articles to be stiffened into a clothes-basket by themselves, and, just before hanging out, dip them in starch, clapping it in, so as to have them equally stiff in all parts. Hang white clothes in the sun, and colored ones (wrong side out) in the shade. Fasten them with clothes-pins. Then wash the coarser white articles in the same manner. Then wash the colored clothes. These must not be soaked, nor have lye or soda put in the water, and they ought not to lie wet long before hanging out, as it injures their colors. Beef's-gall, one spoonful to two pailfuls of suds, improves calicoes. Lastly, wash the flannels in suds as hot as the hand can bear. Never rub on soap, as this shrinks them in spots. Wring them out of the first suds, and throw them into another tub of hot suds, turning them wrong side out. Then throw them into hot bluing-water. Do not put bluing into suds, as it makes specks in the flannel. Never leave flannels long in water, nor put them in cold or luke-warm water. Before hanging them out, shake and stretch them. Some housekeepers have a close closet, made with slats across the top. On these slats, they put their flannels, when ready to hang out, and then burn brimstone under them, for ten minutes. It is but little trouble, and keeps the flannels as white as new. Wash the colored flannels and hose after the white, adding more hot water. Some persons dry woolen hose on stocking-boards, shaped like a foot and leg, with strings to tie them on the line. This keeps them from shrinking, and makes them look better than if ironed. It is also less work than to iron them properly.

Bedding should be washed in long days, and in hot weather. Empty straw beds once a year.

The following cautions in regard to calicoes are useful. Never wash them in very warm water; and change the water when it appears dingy, or the light parts will look dirty. Never rub on soap; but remove grease with French chalk, starch, magnesia, or Wilmington clay. Make starch for black calicoes with coffee-water, to prevent any whitish appearance. Glue is good for stiffening calicoes. When laid aside, not to be used, all stiffening should be washed out, or they will often be injured. Never let calicoes freeze in drying. Some persons use bran-water (four quarts of wheat-bran to two pails of water), and no soap, for calicoes; washing and rinsing in the bran-water. Potato-water is equally good. Take eight peeled and grated potatoes to one gallon of water.

To cleanse Gentlemen's Broadcloths.—The best way, which the writer has repeatedly tried with unfailing success, is the following: Take one beef's-gall, half a pound of saleratus, and four gallons of warm water. Lay the article on a table, and scour it thoroughly, in every part, with a clothes-brush dipped in this mixture. The collar of a coat, and the grease-spots, (previously marked by stitches of white thread,) must be repeatedly brushed. Then take the article and rinse it up and down in the mixture. Then rinse it up and down in a tub of soft cold water. Then, without wringing or pressing, hang it to drain and dry. Fasten a coat up by the collar. When perfectly dry, it is sometimes the case, with coats, that nothing more is needed. In other cases, it is necessary to dampen with a sponge the parts which look wrinkled, and either pull them smooth with the fingers, or press them with an iron, having a piece of bombazine or thin woollen cloth between the iron and the article.

TO MANUFACTURE LYE, SOAP, STARCH, AND OTHER ARTICLES USED IN WASHING.

To make Lye.—Provide a large tub, made of pine or ash, and set it on a form, so high that a tub can stand under it. Make a hole, an inch in diameter, near the bottom, on one side. Lay bricks inside about this hole, and straw over them. To every seven bushels of ashes add two gallons of unslacked lime, and throw in the ashes and lime in alternate layers. While putting in the ashes and lime, pour on boiling water, using three or four pailfuls. After this, add a pailful of cold soft water once an hour, till all the ashes appear to be well soaked. Catch the drippings in a tub and try its strength with an egg. If the egg rise so as to show a circle as large as a ten-cent piece, the strength is right; if it rise higher, the lye must be weakened by water; if not so high, the ashes are not good, and the whole process must be repeated, putting in fresh ashes, and running the weak lye through the new ashes, with some additional water. *Quick-lye* is made by pouring one gallon of boiling soft water on three quarts of ashes, and straining it. Oak ashes are best.

To make Soft Soap.—Save all drippings and fat, melt them, and set them away in cakes. Some persons keep, for soap-grease, a half-barrel, with weak lye in it, and a cover over it. To make soft soap, take the proportion of one pailful of lye to three pounds of fat. Melt the fat, and pour in the lye, by degrees. Boil it steadily, through the day, till it is ropy. If not boiled enough, on cooling it will turn to lye and sediment. While boiling, there should always be a little oil on the surface. If this does not appear, add more grease. If there is too much grease, on cooling, it will rise, and can be skimmed off. Try it, by cooling a small quantity. When it appears like jelly on becoming cold, it is done. It must then be put in a cool place and often stirred.

To make cold Soft Soap, melt thirty pounds of grease, put it in a barrel, add four pailfuls of strong lye, and stir it up thoroughly. Then gradually add more lye, till the barrel is nearly full, and the soap looks *about right.*

To make Potash-Soap, melt thirty-nine pounds of grease, and put it in a barrel. Take twenty-nine pounds of light ash-colored potash, (the *reddish*-colored will spoil the soap,) and pour hot water on it; then pour it off into the grease, stirring it well. Continue thus till all the potash is melted. Add one pailful of cold water, stirring it a great deal every day, till the barrel be full, and then it is done. This is the cheapest and best kind of soap. It is best to sell ashes and buy potash. The soap is better, if it stand a year before it is used; therefore make two barrels at once.

To prepare Starch.—Take four table-spoonfuls of starch; put in as much water, and rub it, till all lumps are removed. Then add half a cup of cold water. Pour this into a quart of boiling water, and boil it for half an hour, adding a piece of spermaceti, or a lump of salt or sugar, as large as a hazelnut. Strain it, and put in a very little bluing. Thin it with hot water.

Beef's-Gall.—Send a junk-bottle to the butcher, and have several gall-bladders emptied into it. Keep it salted, and in a cool place. Some persons perfume it; but fresh air removes the unpleasant smell which it gives, when used for clothes.

DIRECTIONS FOR STARCHING MUSLINS AND LACES.

Many ladies clap muslins, then dry them, and afterward sprinkle them. This saves time. Others clap them till nearly dry, then fold and cover, and then iron them. Iron wrought muslins on soft flannel, and on the wrong side.

To do up Laces nicely, sew a clean piece of muslin around a long bottle, and roll the lace on it; pulling out the edge, and rolling it so that the edge will turn in, and be covered as you roll. Fill the bottle with water, and then boil it for an hour in a suds made with white soap. Rinse it in fair water, a little blue; dry it in the sun; and, if any stiffening is wished, use thin starch or gum-arabic. When dry, fold and press it between white papers in a large book. It improves the lace to wet it with sweet-oil, after it is rolled on the bottle, and before boiling in the suds. *Blonde laces* can be whitened by rolling them on a bottle in this way, and then setting the bottle in the sun, in a dish of cold suds made with white soap, wetting it thoroughly, and changing the suds every day. Do this for a week or more; then rinse in fair water; dry it on the bottle in the sun, and stiffen it with white gum-arabic. Lay it away in loose folds. *Lace vails* can be whitened by laying them in flat dishes, in suds made with white soap; then rinsing, and stiffening them with gum-arabic, stretching them, and pinning them on a sheet to dry.

ARTICLES TO BE PROVIDED FOR IRONING.

Provide the following articles: A woolen ironing-blanket, and a linen or cotton sheet to spread over it; a large fire, of charcoal and hard wood, (unless furnaces or stoves are used;) a hearth free from cinders and ashes, a piece of sheet-iron in front of the fire, on which to set the irons while heating; (this last saves many black spots from careless ironers;) three or four holders, made of woolen, and covered with old silk, as these do not easily take fire; two iron-rings or iron-stands, on which to set the irons, and small pieces of board to put under them, to prevent scorching the sheet; linen or cotton wipers; and a piece of bees-wax, to rub on the irons when they are smoked. There should be at least three irons for each person ironing, and a small and large clothes-frame, on which to air the fine and coarse clothes. It is a great saving of space as well as labor to have a clothes-frame made with a large number of slats, on which to hang clothes. Then have it fastened to the wall, and, when not used, pushed flat against the wall. Any carpenter can understand how to make this.

A bosom-board, on which to iron shirt-bosoms, should be made, one foot and a half long and nine inches wide, and covered with white flannel. A skirt-board, on which to iron frock-skirts, should be made, five feet long and two feet wide at one end, tapering to one foot and three inches wide at the other end. This should be covered with flannel, and will save much trouble in ironing nice dresses. The large end may be put on the table, and the other on the back of a chair. Both these boards should have cotton covers made to fit them, and these should be changed and washed when dirty. These boards are often useful when articles are to be ironed or pressed in a chamber or parlor, and where economy of space is needful, they may be hung to a wall or door by loops on the covers. Provide, also, a press-board, for broadcloth, two feet long and four inches wide at one end, tapering to three inches wide at the other.

If the lady of the house will provide all these articles, see that the fires are properly made, the ironing-sheets evenly put on and properly pinned, the clothes-frames dusted, and all articles kept in their places, she will do much toward securing good ironing.

ON SPRINKLING, FOLDING, AND IRONING.

Wipe the dust from the ironing-board, and lay it down, to receive the clothes, which should be sprinkled with clear and warm water, and laid in separate piles, one of colored, one of common, and one of fine articles, and one of flannels. Fold the fine things, and roll them in a towel, and then fold the rest, turning them all right side outward. The colored clothes should be laid separate from the rest, and ought not to lie long damp, as it injures the colors. The sheets and table-linen should be shaken, stretched, and folded by two persons.

Iron lace and needle work on the wrong side, and carry them away as soon as dry. Iron calicoes with irons which are not very hot, and generally on the right side, as they thus keep clean for a longer time. In ironing a frock, first do the waist, then the sleeves, then the skirt. Keep the skirt rolled while ironing the other parts, and set a chair, to hold the sleeves while ironing the skirt, unless a skirt-board be used. In ironing a shirt, first do the back, then the sleeves, then the collar and bosom, and then the front. Iron silk on the wrong side, when quite damp, with an iron which is not very hot, as light colors are apt to change and fade. Iron velvet by turning up the face of the iron, and after dampening the wrong side of the velvet, draw it over the face of the iron, holding it straight and not biased.

TO WHITEN ARTICLES, AND REMOVE STAINS FROM THEM.

Wet white clothes in suds, and lay them on the grass, in the sun. It will save from grass stain, to have a clean white cloth under the articles to be whitened. Lay muslins in suds made with white soap, in a flat dish; set this in the sun, changing the suds every day. Whiten tow-cloth or brown linen by keeping it in lye through the night, laying it out in the sun, and wetting it with fair water, as fast as it dries.

Scorched articles can often be whitened again by laying them in the sun, wet with suds. Where this does not answer, put a pound of white soap in a gallon of milk, and boil the article in it. Another method is, to chop and extract the juice from two onions, and boil this with half a pint of vinegar, an ounce of white soap, and two ounces of fuller's earth. Spread this, when cool, on the scorched part, and, when dry, wash it off in fair water. *Mildew* may be removed by dipping the article in sour buttermilk, laying it in the sun, and, after it is white, rinsing it in fair water. Soap and chalk are also good; also, soap and starch, adding half as much salt as there is starch, together with the juice of a lemon. Stains in linen can often be removed by rubbing on soft soap, then putting on a starch paste and drying in the sun, renewing it several times. Wash off all the soap and starch in cold fair water.

MIXTURES FOR REMOVING STAINS AND GREASE.

Stain Mixture.—Half an ounce of oxalic acid in a pint of soft water. This can be kept in a corked bottle and is infallible in removing iron-rust and ink-stains. It is very poisonous. The article must be spread with this mixture over the steam of hot water, and wet several times. This will also remove indelible ink. The article must be washed, or the mixture will injure it.

Another Stain-Mixture is made by mixing one ounce of sal ammoniac, one ounce of salt of tartar, and one pint of soft water.

To remove Grease.—Mix four ounces of fuller's earth, half an ounce of pearlash, and lemon-juice enough to make a stiff paste, which can be dried in balls, and kept for use. Wet the greased spot with cold water, rub it with the ball, dry it, and then rinse it with fair cold water. This is for *white* articles. For silks and worsteds use French chalk, which can be procured of the apothecaries. That which is soft and white is best. Scrape it on the greased spot, under side, and let it lie for a day and night. Then brush off that used, and renew it till the spot disappears. Wilmington clay-balls are equally good. Ink-spots can often be removed from white clothes by rubbing on common tallow, leaving it for a day or two, and then washing as usual. Grease can be taken out of wall-paper by making a paste of potter's clay, water, and ox-gall, and spreading it on the paper. When dry, renew it, till the spot disappears.

Stains on floors, from *soot* or *stove-pipes*, can be removed by washing the spot in sulphuric acid and water. Stains in colored silk dresses can often be removed by pure water. Those made by acids, tea, wine, and fruits can often be removed by spirits of hartshorn, diluted with an equal quantity of water. Sometimes it must be repeated several times.

Tar, Pitch, and **Turpentine** can be removed by putting the spot in sweet-oil, or by spreading tallow on it, and letting it remain for twenty-four hours. Then, if the article be linen or cotton, wash it as usual; if it be silk or worsted, rub it with ether or spirits of wine.

Lamp-Oil can be removed from floors, carpets, and other articles by spreading upon the stain a paste made of fuller's earth or potter's clay, brushing off and renewing it, when dry, till the stain is removed. If gall be put into the paste, it will preserve the colors from injury. When the stain has been removed, carefully brush off the paste with a soft brush.

Oil-Paint can be removed by rubbing it with *very pure* spirits of turpentine. The impure spirits leave a grease-spot. *Wax* can be removed by scraping it off, and then holding a red hot poker near the spot. *Spermaceti* may be removed by scraping it off, then putting a paper over the spot, and applying a warm iron. If this does not answer, rub on spirits of wine.

Ink-Stains in carpets and woolen table-covers can be removed by washing the spot in a liquid composed of one tea-spoonful of oxalic acid dissolved in a tea-cupful of warm (not hot) water, and then rinsing in cold water. When ink is first spilled on a woolen carpet, pour on water immediately, and sop it up several times, and no stain will be made. Often on other articles, a stream of cold water poured on the *under side* of the ink-spot will so dilute the ink that it can be rubbed out in cold water.

Stains on Varnished Articles, which are caused by cups of hot water, can be removed by rubbing them with lamp-oil, and then with alcohol. **Ink-stains** can be taken out of mahogany by one tea-spoonful of oil of vitriol mixed with one table-spoonful of water, or by oxalic acid and water. These must be brushed over quickly, and then washed off with milk.

Silk Handkerchiefs and **Ribbons** can be cleansed by using French chalk to take out the grease, and then sponging them on both sides with lukewarm fair water. Stiffen them with gum-arabic, and press them between white paper, with an iron not very hot. A table-spoonful of spirits of wine to three quarts of water improves it.

Silk Hose or **Silk Gloves** should be washed in warm suds made with white soap, and rinsed in cold water; they should then be stretched and rubbed with a hard-rolled flannel, till they are quite dry. Ironing them very much injures their looks. *Wash-leather* articles should have the grease removed from them by French chalk or magnesia; they should then be washed in warm suds, and rinsed in cold water. *Light Kid Gloves* should have the grease removed from them, and then wash them on the hands with borax water and soft flannel—a tea-spoonful to a tumbler of water. Then stretch and press them. Dark Kid Gloves wash in the same way.

6

CHAPTER XXIII.

MISCELLANEOUS ADVICE AND RECIPES.

How to keep cool in Hot Weather.—Sit in a room covered with matting or without any carpet, and keep the floor wet with pure water and a watering-pot. In hot nights, place a double wet sheet on the bed and a woolen blanket over it, and it will cool the bed which is heated through the day, and does not cool as fast as the evening air. A hot bed is often the cause of sleeplessness. Wear wristlets and anklets of wet flannel. Shut all doors and windows early in the morning to keep in cool air, and let in air only through windows that are on the shady side of the house. If chambers open upon the hot roofs of piazzas or porticoes, cover them with clean straw or hay, and wet them with a watering-pot. In all these cases, the heat is taken from the air and from all surrounding things by the absorption of heat as the water changes to vapor.

Indelible Ink.—Put six cents' worth of lunar caustic in a small phial, and fill with rain-water. To prepare the cloth, put a great-spoonful of gum-arabic into a larger bottle, with a drachm of salt of tartar, fill with water, and, when dissolved, wet the cloth, and press it smooth with a warm (not hot) iron. Put the articles, when marked, in the sun.

To preserve Eggs.—Pack eggs in a jar small end downward, and then pour in a mixture of four quarts of slacked lime, two table-spoonfuls of cream tartar, and two of salt. This will cover about nine dozen for several months.

To prevent Earthen, Glass, and Iron Ware from being easily broken.—Put them in cold water, and heat till boiling, and cool gradually.

A good Cement for broken Earthen and Glass.—Mix Russian isinglass in white brandy, forming a thick jelly when cool. Strain and cork. When using it, rub it on the broken edges, and hold them together three or four minutes.

To keep Knives from Rust and other Injury.—Rub bright, and wrap in thick brown paper. Never let knife-handles lie in water, and do not let their blades stay in *very hot* water, as the heat expands the iron, and makes handles crack.

To cleanse or renovate Furniture.—White spots on furniture remove by camphene, or sometimes by oil or spirits of turpentine. Remove mortar-spots with warm vinegar, and paint-spots with camphene or burning-fluid. Powdered pumice-stone is better than sand to clean paint. To polish *unvarnished* furniture, rub on two ounces of bees-wax, half an ounce of alconet root, melted together, and, when cooled, two ounces of spirits of wine, and half a pint of spirits of turpentine.

To clean Silver.—Wet whiting with liquid hartshorn, and this will remove black spots. Or boil half an ounce of pulverized hartshorn in a pint of water, and pour it into rags, dry them, and use to cleanse silver. Polish with wash-leather.

To cleanse Wall-Paper.—Wipe with a clean pillow-case on a broom, and brush gently. Rub bad spots with soft bread-crumbs gently.

To Purify a Well.—Get out the water, and then put in three or four quarts of quick-lime. Any well long unused should be thus cleansed.

How to treat Roses and other Plants.—Water them daily with water steeped in wood-ashes. To destroy slugs, scatter ashes over the plant at night before the dew falls, or before a coming shower. Water all plants with washing-day suds, and it makes them flourish. Scatter salt in gravel-walks to get out grass and weeds. Use old brine for this purpose. Use saw-dust to manure plants; also wood-ashes; even that used to make lye is good.

Easy Way to keep Grapes.—When not dead ripe, have them free from dampness, take out the decayed, and wrap each bunch in cotton, putting only two layers in a box. Keep in a dry, cool room, where they will not freeze.

Snow for Eggs.—Two table-spoonfuls of snow strewed in quickly, and baked immediately, is equal to one egg in puddings or pan-cakes.

Paper to keep Preserves.—Soft paper dipped in the white of an egg is the best cover for jellies and pickles. Turn it over the rim.

To make Butter cool in hot Weather.—Set it on a bit of brick, cover with a flower-pot, and wrap a wet cloth around the pot. The evaporation cools it as well as ice.

To stop Cracks in Iron.—Mix ashes and common salt and a little water, and fill the cracks.

To stop Creaking Hinges.—Put on oil.

To stop Creaking Doors and make Drawers slide easily.—Rub on hard soap.

To renovate Black Silk.—Wash in cold tea or coffee, with a little sugar in them. Put in a little ink if very rusty. Drain and do not wring, and iron on the wrong side.

Another Way to clean Kid Gloves.—Rub them lightly with benzine, and, as they dry, with pearl-powder. Expose to the air to remove the smell.

To remove Grease-Spots.—Put an ounce of powdered borax to a quart of boiling water. Wash with this, and keep it corked for further use.

To get rid of Rats and Mice.—A cat is the best remedy. Another is to half fill a tub with water, and sprinkle oats and meal on the top. For a while they will be deceived, jump in, and be drowned or caught.

ODDS AND ENDS.

There are certain *odds and ends* where every housekeeper will gain much by having a *regular time* to attend them. Let this time be the last Saturday forenoon in every month, or any other time more agreeable; but let there be a *regular fixed time* once a month in which the housekeeper will attend to the following things:

First. Go around to every room, drawer, and closet in the house, and see what is out of order, and what needs to be done, and make arrangements as to time and manner of doing it.

Second. Examine the store-closet, and see if there is a proper supply of all articles needed there.

Third. Go to the cellar, and see if the salted provision, vegetables, pickles, vinegar, and all other articles stored in the cellar are in proper order, and examine all the preserves and jellies.

Fourth. Examine the trunk or closet of family linen, and see what needs to be repaired and renewed.

Fifth. See if there is a supply of dish-towels, dish-cloths, bags, holders, floor-cloths, dust-cloths, wrapping-paper, twine, lamp-wicks, and all other articles needed in kitchen work.

Sixth. Count over the spoons, knives, and forks, and examine all the various household utensils, to see what need replacing, and what should be repaired.

Seventh. Have in a box a hammer, tacks, pincers, gimlets, nails, screws, screw-driver, small saw, and two sizes of chisels for emergencies when no regular workman is at hand. Also be prepared to set glass. Every lady should be able in emergency to do such jobs herself.

A housekeeper who will have *a regular time* for attending to these particulars will find her whole family machinery moving easily and well; but one who does not will constantly be finding something out of joint, and an unquiet, secret apprehension of duties left undone or forgotten, which no other method will so effectually remove.

A housekeeper will often be much annoyed by the accumulation of articles not immediately needed, that must be saved for future use. The following method, adopted by a thrifty housekeeper, may be imitated with advantage. She bought some cheap calico, and made bags of various sizes, and wrote the following labels with indelible ink on a bit of broad tape, and sewed them on one side of the bags: *Old Linens, Old Cottons, Old black Silks, Old colored Silks, Old Stockings, Old colored Woolens, Old Flannels, New Linen, New Cotton, New Woolens, New Silks, Pieces of Dresses, Pieces of Boys' Clothes*, etc. These bags were hung around a closet, and filled with the above articles, and then it was known where to look for each, and where to put each when not in use.

Another excellent plan, for the table, is for a housekeeper once a month to make out *a bill of fare* for the four weeks to come. To do this, let her look over this book, and find out what kind of dishes the season of the year and her own stores will enable her to provide, and then make out a list of the dishes she will provide through the month, so as to have an agreeable variety for breakfast, dinners, and suppers. Some systematic arrangement of this kind at regular periods will secure great comfort and enjoyment to a family, and prevent that monotonous round so common in many families.

PART SECOND.

CHAPTER I.

NEEDFUL SCIENCE AND TRAINING FOR THE FAMILY STATE.

THAT women need as much and even more scientific and practical training for their appropriate business than men, arises from the fact that they must perform duties quite as difficult and important, and a much greater variety of them. A man usually selects only one branch of business for a profession, and, after his school education, secures an apprenticeship of years to perfect his practical skill; and thus a success is attained which would be impossible were he to practice various trades and professions.

Now let us notice what science and training are needed for the various and difficult duties that are demanded of woman in her ordinary relations as wife, mother, housekeeper, and the mistress of servants.

First, the department of a housekeeper demands some knowledge of all the arts and sciences connected with the proper *construction* of a family dwelling.

In communities destitute of intelligent artisans, a widow, or a woman whose husband has not time or ability to direct, on building a house, would need for guidance the leading principles of architecture, pneumatics, hydrostatics, calorification, and several other connected sciences, in order to secure architectural beauty, healthful heating and ventilation, and the economical and convenient arrangements for labor and comfort. A housekeeper properly instructed in these principles would know how to secure chimneys that will not smoke, the most economical furnaces and stoves, and those that will be sure to "draw." She would know how dampers and air-boxes should be placed and regulated, how to prevent or remedy gas escapes, leaking water-pipes, poisonous recession of sewers, slamming shutters, bells that will not ring, blinds that will not fasten, and doors that will not lock or catch. She will understand about ball-cocks, and high and low pressure on water-pipes and boilers, and many other mysteries which make a woman the helpless victim of plumbers and other jobbers often as blundering and ignorant as herself. She would know what kind of wood-work saves labor, how to prevent its shrinkage, when to use paint, and what kind is best, and many other details of knowledge needed in circumstances to which any daughter of wealth is liable: knowledge which could be gained with less time and labor than is now given in public schools to geometry and algebra.

On supposition of a *yard* and *garden*, with young boys and domestic animals under her care, she would need the first principles of landscape gardening, floriculture, horticulture, fruit culture, and agriculture; also, the fitting and furnishing of accommodations and provision for domestic animals. And to gain this knowledge would demand less time than young girls often give to picking pretty flowers to pieces and saying hard names over them, or storing them in herbariums never used. And yet botany might be so taught as to be practically useful.

Next, in *selecting furniture*, a woman so instructed would know when glue and nails are improperly used instead of the needed dovetailing and mortising. She would know when drawers, tables, and chairs were properly made, and when brooms, pots, saucepans, and coal-scuttles would last well and do proper service. She would know the best colors and materials for carpets, curtains, bed and house linen, and numerous other practical details as easily learned as the construction of "bivalves" and "multivalves," and other particulars in natural history now studied, and, being of no practical use, speedily forgotten.

Next, in the *ornamentation* of a house, she will need the general principles that guide in the making or selection of pictures, statuary, in drawing, painting, music, and all the fine arts that render a home so beautiful and attractive.

Next comes all involved in the *cleansing*, *neatness*, and

order of houses filled with sofas, ottomans, curtains, pictures, musical instruments, and all the varied collection of beautiful and frail ornaments or curiosities so common. Every girl should be taught to know the right and the wrong way of protecting or cleansing every article, from the rich picture-frames and frescoes to the humblest crockery and stew-pan. And this would include much scientific knowledge as well as practical training.

Next comes the selection of *healthful food*, the proper care of it, and the most economical and suitable modes of cooking. Here are demanded the first principles of physiology, animal chemistry, and domestic hygiene, with the practical applications. Thus instructed, the housekeeper will know the good or bad condition of meats, milk, bread, butter, and all groceries. And a class could be taken to a market or grocery for illustration, as easily as to a museum or the field for illustrations of mineralogy or botany. All this should be done before a young girl has the heavy responsibilities of housekeeper, wife, mother, and nurse. The art of cookery, in all its departments, has received more attention than any other domestic duty in former days; but at the present time no systematic mode is devised for training a young girl to superintend and instruct servants in this complicated duty, on which the health and comfort of a family so much depend.

Next, in providing *family clothing* and in the care of household stuffs, she will know how to do and to teach in the best manner plain sewing, hemming, darning, mending, and the use of a sewing-machine, thus cultivating ingenuity, dexterity, and common sense in judging the best way of doing things and deciding what is worth doing and what is not. She will exercise good taste and good judgment in dress for herself and family, in the selection of materials, in the adaptation of colors and fashion to age, shape, and employments, and in the avoidance of unhealthful and absurd fashions; and she will have such knowledge of domestic chemistry as is needed in the cleansing, dyeing, and preservation of household clothing and stuffs.

Next comes all involved in the *care of health*. This again involves the first principles of animal and domestic chemistry, hydrostatics, pneumatics, caloric, light, electricity, and especially hygiene and therapeutics. A housekeeper instructed in these will have pure water, pure air, much sunlight, beds and clothes well cleansed, every arrangement for cleanliness and comfort, and all that tends to prevent disease or retard its first approaches. And her knowledge and skill she will transmit to the children and servants under her care, while the dumb animals of her establishment will share in the blessings secured by her scientific knowledge and trained skill.

Next comes the care of *family expenses* in all departments of economy, and in which science and training are also demanded: to this add the enforcement of system and order, hospitalities to relatives, friends, and the homeless, the claims of society as to calls, social gatherings, the sick, the poor, benevolent associations, school and religious duties.

Not the least of the onerous duties of a housekeeper is the training and government of *servants* of all kinds of dispositions, habits, nationalities, and religions.

All these multiplied and diverse duties are demanded of every woman, whether married or single, who becomes mistress of a house.

The distinctive duties of *wife and mother* are such that both science and training are of the greatest consequence, and a dreadful amount of suffering has resulted from want of such proper instruction. One of the most important of these duties is the care of new-born infants and their mothers. Thousands of young infants perish and young mothers are made sufferers for life for want of science and training in the mothers and monthly nurses.

Then the *helpers in the nursery* have a daily control of the safety, health, temper, and morals of young children; and a conscientious, careful, affectionate woman, instructed in the care of health and remedies for sudden accidents, is a rare treasure. These arduous duties are now extensively given to the inexperienced and the ignorant. It is a mournful fact that more science and care are given by professional trainers to the offspring of horses, cows, sheep, and hogs, than to the larger portion of children of the American people. Thus comes the fact that the mortality of the human offspring greatly exceeds that of the lower animals.

The most difficult and important duties of a woman are those of an *educator* in the family and the school. In the nursery, children are taught the care of their bodies, the use of language, the nature and properties of the world around them, and many social and moral duties, all before books are used. Then it is a mother's duty to select the school-teacher, and so to supervise, that health and intellectual training shall be duly secured. To this add the duties of training and controlling the helpers in the nursery and kitchen, and to a housekeeper and mother the duties of an *educator* stand first on the roll of responsibilities.

But the most weighty of all human responsibilities that rest upon every housekeeper, whether mother or only mistress of servants, are those which are consequent on the distinctive teachings of Jesus Christ; for, as the general rule, it is the mistress who is the chief minister of religion in the family state.

And this is the age above all the past, when all the foundations of religious faith are being undermined, and all the most important principles of morals assailed. What is the conscientious woman to do, when the truth and authority of the Bible, the doctrine of immortality after death, and even the existence of a God, are attacked, not only in newspapers and books, but even in respectable pulpit ministries? Surely, if she is to be prepared by culture, argument, and reflection for any of her many responsibilities, it is for those she is to bear as the *religious educator of the family state.* This topic will be referred to more definitely in the chapters on the Training of Children and Care of Servants, and in a note at the close of this volume.

It is for want of facilities for the proper scientific training of women for these multiform duties that they are so generally not educated to be healthy, or economical, or industrious, or properly qualified to be happy wives, or to train children and servants, or to preserve health in families and schools, or to practice a wise economy in the various departments of the family state. It is for want of such scientific training that the most important duties of the family, being disgraced and undervalued, are forsaken by the cultivated and refined, and, passing to the unskilled and vulgar, secure neither honorable social position nor liberal rewards. The poorest teacher of music, drawing, or French has higher position and reward than those who perform the most scientific, sacred, and difficult duties of the family state.

The true remedy for this state of things is to provide as liberally for the scientific training of woman for her profession as men have provided for theirs. A wide-spread attempt is organizing for the establishment of institutions to cover this very ground of educating woman for the specific duties of her profession. But there are many thousands who are already beyond the reach of such instruction, and thousands of others who could never avail themselves of it; and certain it is, that a gathering together, in a compact volume like the present one, of many facts and ideas bearing upon these all-important topics, will be of great advantage to readers, especially in remote districts, far from the conveniences of cities.

CHAPTER II.

A HEALTHFUL AND ECONOMICAL HOUSE.

At the head of this chapter is a sketch of what may be properly called a *Christian* house; that is, a house contrived for the express purpose of enabling every member of a family to labor with the hands for the common good, and by modes at once healthful, economical, and tasteful.

In the following drawings are presented modes of economizing time, labor, and expense by the *close packing of conveniences.* By such methods, small and economical houses

Fig. 7.

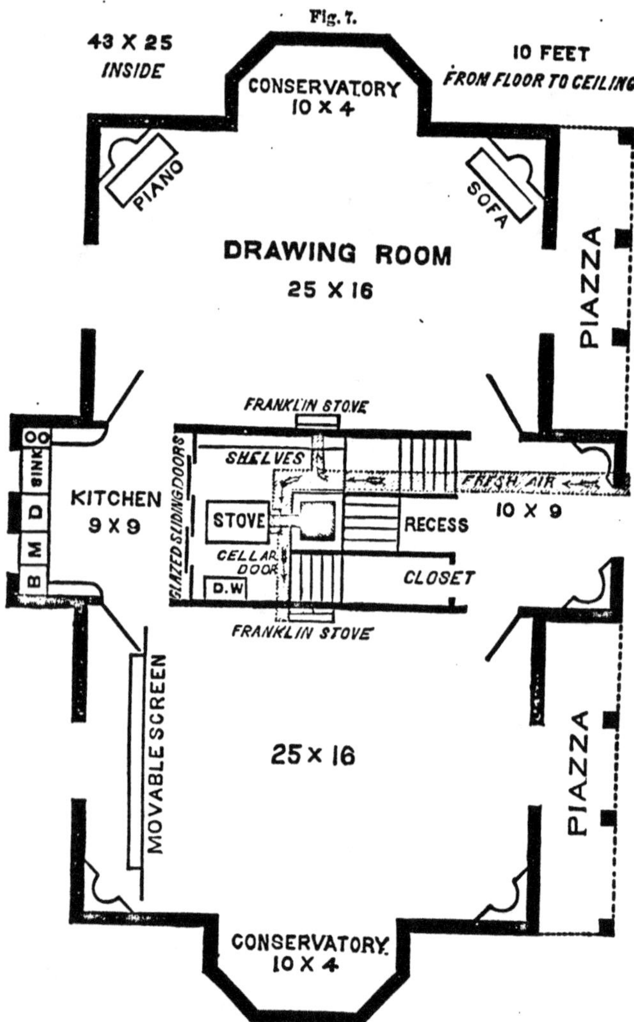

can be made to secure most of the comforts and many of the refinements of large and expensive ones. The cottage at the head of this chapter is projected on a plan which can

Fig. 8.

be adapted to a warm or cold climate with little change. By adding another story, it would serve a large family.

Fig. 7 shows the ground-plan of the first floor, the proportions being marked in the drawing. The piazzas each side of the front projection have sliding-windows to the floor, and can, by glazed sashes, be made greenhouses in winter. In a warm climate, piazzas can be made at the back side also.

The leading aim is to show how time, labor, and expense are saved, not only in the building, but in furniture and its arrangement. The conservatories are appendages not necessary to housekeeping, but useful in many ways.

The entry has arched recesses behind the front doors, (Fig. 8,) furnished with hooks for over-clothes in both—a box for overshoes in one, and a stand for umbrellas in the other. The roof of the recess is for statuettes, busts, or flowers. The stairs turn twice with broad steps, making a recess at the lower landing, where a table is set with a vase of flowers, (Fig. 9.) On one side of the recess is a closet, arched to correspond with the arch over the stairs. A bracket over the first broad stair,

Fig. 9.

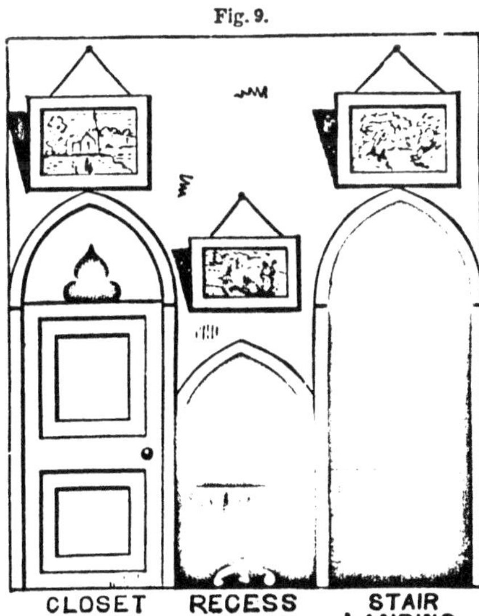

with flowers or statuettes, is visible from the entrance, and pictures can be hung as in the drawing.

The large room on the left can be made to serve the purpose of several rooms by means of a *movable screen.* By shifting this rolling screen from one part of the room to another, two apartments are always available, of any desired size within the limits of the large room. One side of the screen fronts what may be used for the parlor or sitting-room; the other side is arranged for bedroom conveniences. Of this, Fig. 10 shows the front side; covered first with strong

Fig. 10.

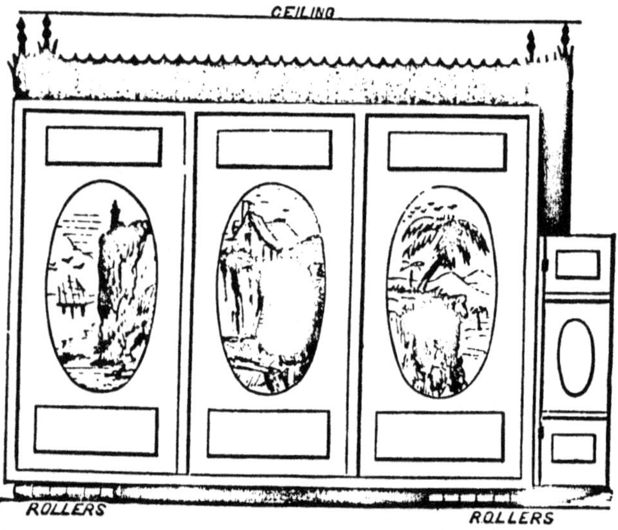

canvas, stretched and nailed on. Over this is pasted panel-paper, and the upper part is made to resemble an ornamental cornice by fresco-paper. Pictures can be hung in the panels, or be pasted on and varnished with white varnish. To prevent the absorption of the varnish, a wash of gum isinglass (fish-glue) must be applied twice.

Fig. 11 shows the back or inside of the movable screen, toward the part of the room used as the bedroom. On one side, and at the top and bottom, it has shelves with *shelf-*

Fig. 11.

boxes, which are cheaper and better than drawers, and much preferred by those using them. Handles are cut in the front and back side, as seen in Fig. 12. Half an inch space must be between the box and the shelf over it, and as much each side, so that it can be taken out and put in easily. The central part of the screen's interior is a wardrobe.

Fig. 12.

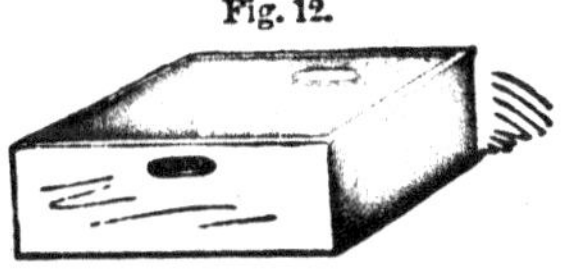

This screen must be so high as nearly to reach the ceiling, in order to prevent it from overturning. It is to fill the width of the room, except two feet on each side. A projecting cleat or strip, reaching nearly to the top of the screen, three inches wide, is to be screwed to the front sides, on which light frame doors are to be hung, covered with canvas and panel-paper like the front of the screen. The inside of these doors is furnished with hook for clothing, for which the projection makes room. The whole screen is to be eighteen inches deep at the top and two feet deep at the base, giving a solid foundation. It is moved on four wooden rollers, one foot long and four inches in diameter. The pivots of the rollers and the parts where there is friction must be rubbed with hard soap, and then a child can move the whole easily.

A curtain is to be hung across the whole interior of the screen by rings, on a strong wire. The curtain should be in three parts, with lead or large nails in the hems to keep it in place. The wood-work must be put together with screws, as the screen is too large to pass through a door.

Fig. 13.

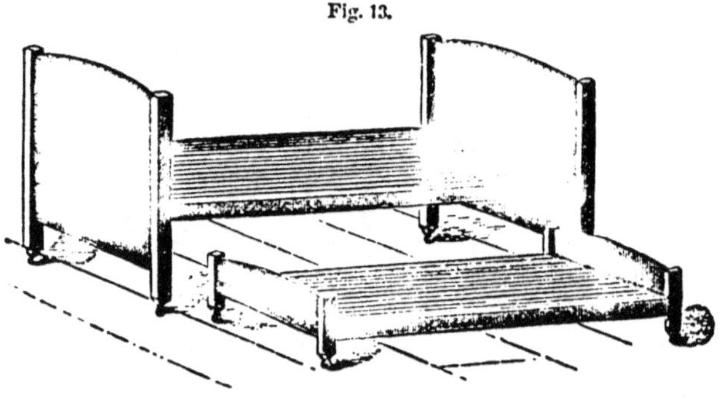

At the end of the room, behind the screen, are two couches, to be run one under the other, as in Fig. 13. The upper one is made with four posts, each three feet high and three inches square, set on casters two inches high. The frame is to be fourteen inches from the floor, seven feet long, two feet four inches wide, and three inches in thickness. At the head and at the foot is to be screwed a notched two-inch board, three inches wide, as in Fig. 14. The mortises are to be one inch wide and deep, and one inch apart, to receive slats made of ash, oak, or spruce, one inch square, placed lengthwise of the couch. The slats being small, and so near together, and running lengthwise, make a better spring frame than wire coils. If they warp, they can be turned. They must not be fastened at the ends, except

Fig. 14.

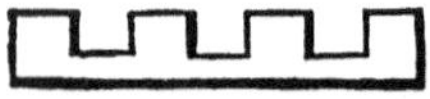

by insertion in the notches. Across the posts, and of equal height with them, are to be screwed head and foot boards.

The under couch is like the upper, except these dimensions: posts, nine inches high, including casters; frame, six feet two inches long, two feet four inches wide. The frame should be as near the floor as possible, resting on the casters.

The most healthful and comfortable mattress is made by a case, open in the centre and fastened together with buttons, as in Fig. 15; to be filled with oat straw, which is softer than wheat or rye. This can be adjusted to the figure, and often renewed.

Fig. 15.

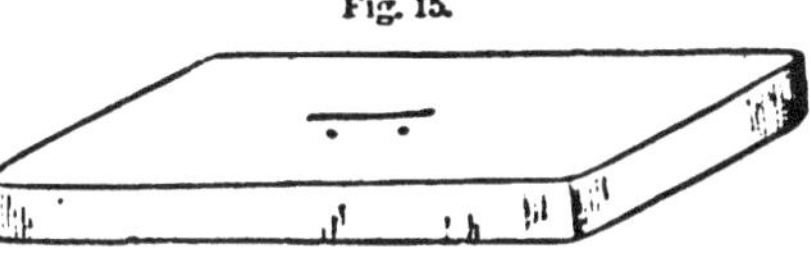

Fig. 16 represents the upper couch when covered, and the under couch put beneath it. The cover-lid should match the curtain of the screen; and the pillows, by day, should have a case of the same.

Fig. 16.

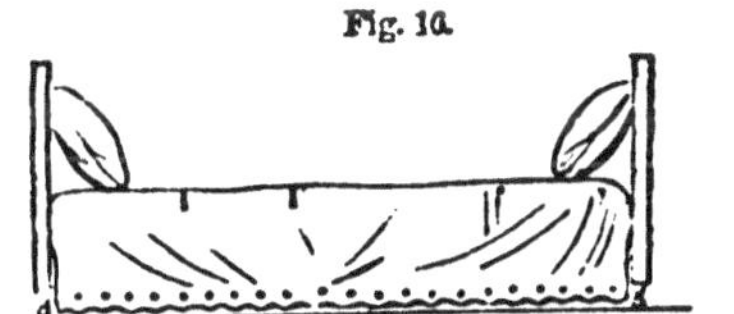

Fig. 17.

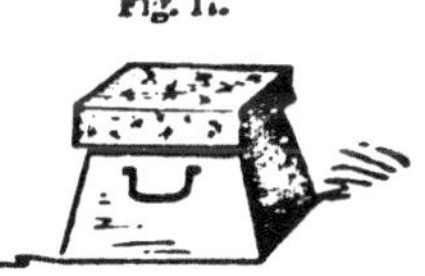

Fig. 17 is an ottoman, made as a box, with a lid on hinges. A cushion is fastened to this lid by strings at each corner, passing through holes in the box lid and tied inside. The cushion to be cut square, with side pieces; stuffed with hair, and stitched through like a mattress. Side handles are made by cords fastened inside with knots. The box must be two inches larger at the bottom than at the top, and the lid and cushion the same size as the bottom, to give it a tasteful shape. This ottoman is set on casters, and is a great convenience for holding articles, while serving also as a seat.

The expense of the screen, where lumber averages four dollars a hundred, and carpenter labor three dollars a day, would be about thirty dollars, and the two couches about six dollars. The material for covering might be cheap and yet pretty. A woman with these directions, and a son or husband who would use plane and saw, could thus secure much additional room, and also what amounts to two bureaus, two large trunks, one large wardrobe, and a wash-stand, for less than twenty dollars—the mere cost of materials. The screen and couches can be so arranged as to have one room serve first as a large and airy sleeping-room; then, in the morning, it may be used as sitting-room one side of the screen, and breakfast-room the other; and lastly, through the day it can be made a large parlor on the front side, and a sewing or retiring-room the other side. The needless spaces usually devoted to kitchen, entries, halls, back-stairs, pantries, store-rooms, and closets, by this method would be used in adding to the size of the large room, so variously used by day and by night.

Fig. 18 is an enlarged plan of the kitchen and stove-room. The chimney and stove-room are contrived to ventilate the whole house.

Between the two rooms glazed sliding-doors, passing each other, serve to shut out heat and smells from the kitchen. The sides of the stove-room must be lined with shelves; those on the side by the cellar stairs, to be one foot wide and eighteen inches apart; on the other side, shelves may be narrower, eight inches wide and nine inches apart. Boxes with lids, to receive stove utensils, must be placed near the stove.

On these shelves, and in the closet and boxes, can be placed every material used for cooking, all the table and cooking utensils, and all the articles used in house-work, and yet much spare room will be left. The cook's galley in a steamship has every article and utensil used in cooking for two hundred persons, in a space not larger than this stove-room, and so arranged that with one or two steps the cook can reach all he uses.

In contrast to this, in most large houses, the table furniture, the cooking materials and utensils, the sink, and the eating-room, are at such distances apart, that half the time and strength is employed in walking back and forth to collect and return the articles used.

Fig. 18.

FLOUR
COOK
DRAIN
SINK
PUMPS
SHELVS
SHELVS

KITCHEN
9 × 9
SHELVES
LOCKED CLOSET
SLIDING DOORS
D. W.
STOVE ROOM
SHELVES
SHELVES
9 × 7
STOVE
POT-BOX
FRANKLIN STOVE
FRANKLIN STOVE
CELLAR DOOR
POT BOX
HALL CLOSET
HALL RECESS
LANDING

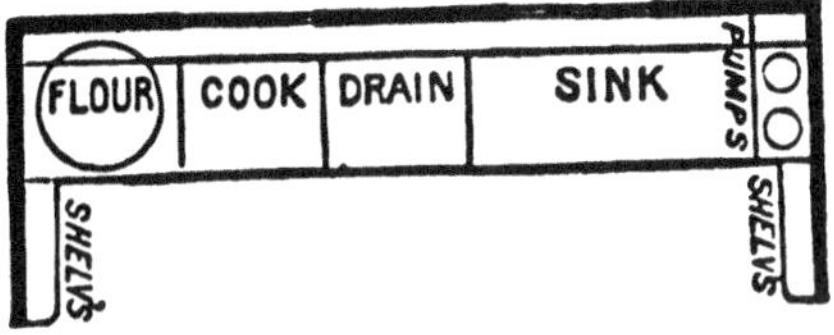

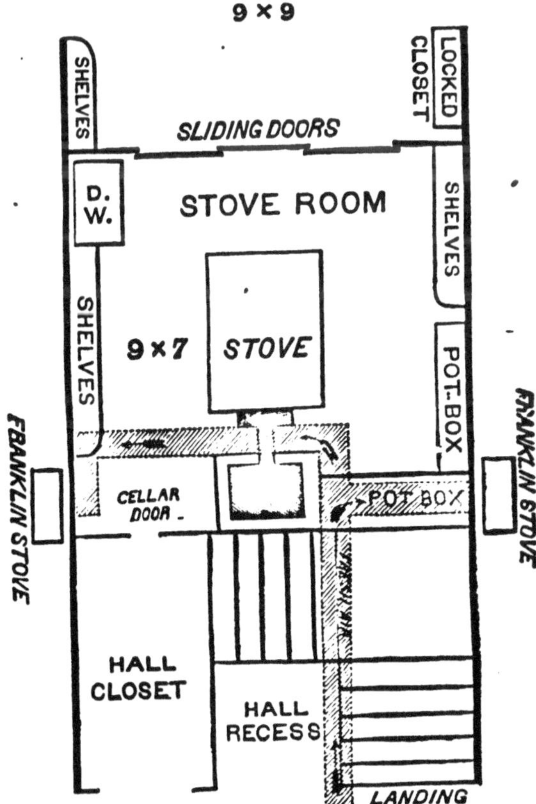

Fig. 19 is an enlarged plan of the sink and cooking-form. Two windows make a better circulation of air in warm weather, by having one open at top and the other at the bottom, while the light is better adjusted for working, in case of weak eyes.

Fig. 19.

The flour-barrel just fills the closet, which has a door for admission, and a lid to raise when used. Beside it is the form for cooking, with a molding-board laid on it; one side used for preparing vegetables and meat, and the other for molding bread. The sink has two pumps, for well and for rain-water—one having a forcing power to throw water into the reservoir in the garret, which supplies the water-closet and bath-room. On the other side of the sink is the dish-drainer, with a ledge on the edge next the sink, to hold the dishes, and grooves cut to let the water drain into the sink. It has hinges, so that it can either rest on the cook-form or be turned over and cover the sink. Under the sink are shelf-boxes placed on two shelves run into grooves, with other grooves above and below, so that one may move the shelves and increase or diminish the spaces between. The shelf-boxes can be used for scouring-materials, dish-towels, and dish-cloths; also to hold bowls for bits of butter, fats, etc. Under these two shelves is room for two pails, and a jar for soap-grease.

Under the cook-form are shelves and shelf-boxes for unbolted wheat, corn-meal, rye, etc. Beneath these, for white and brown sugar, are wooden can-pails, which are the best articles in which to keep these constant necessities. Beside them is the tin molasses-can with a tight, movable cover, and a cork in the spout. This is much better than a jug for molasses, and also for vinegar and oil, being easier to clean and to handle. Other articles and implements for cooking can be arranged on or under the shelves at the side and front. A small cooking-tray, holding pepper, salt, dredging-box, knife, and spoon, should stand close at hand by the stove, (Fig. 20.)

Fig. 20.

The articles used for setting tables are to be placed on the shelves at the front and side of the sink. Two tumbler-trays, made of pasteboard, covered with varnished fancy papers and divided by wires, (as shown in Fig. 21,) save many steps in setting and clearing table. Similar

Fig. 21.

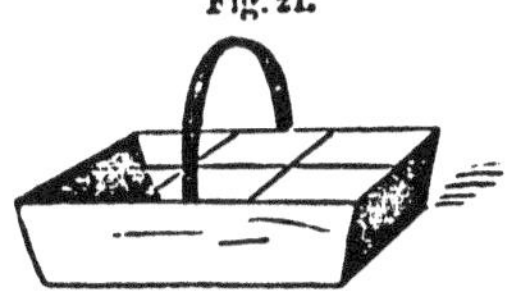

Fig. 22.

trays, (Fig. 22,) for knives and forks and spoons, serve the same purpose. The sink should be three feet long and three inches deep, its width matching the cook-form.

Fig. 23.

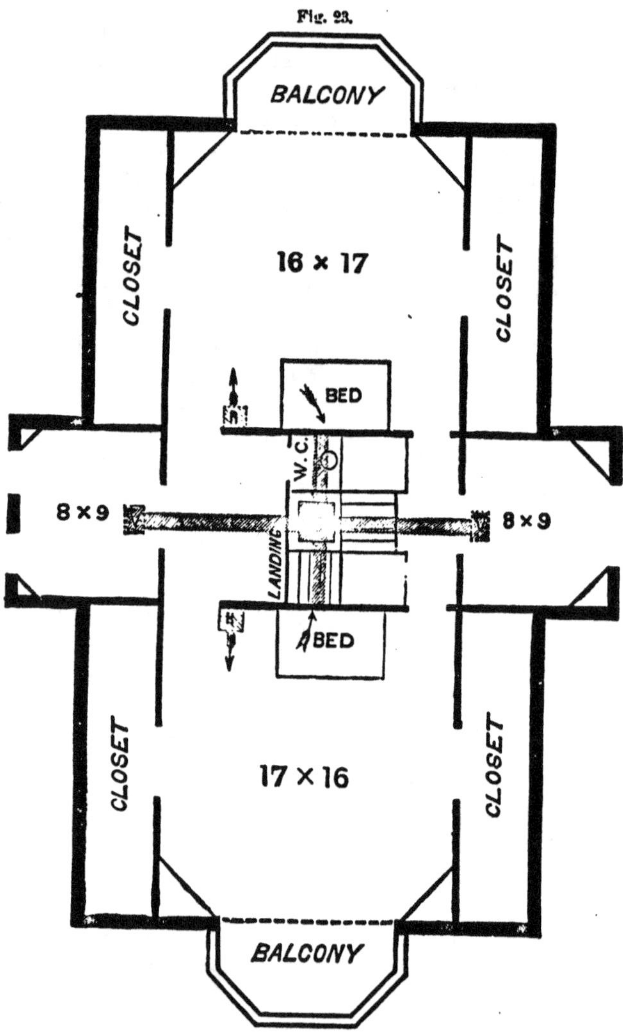

Fig. 23 is the second or attic story. The main objection to attic rooms is their warmth in summer, owing to the heated roof. This is prevented by so enlarging the closets

Fig. 24.

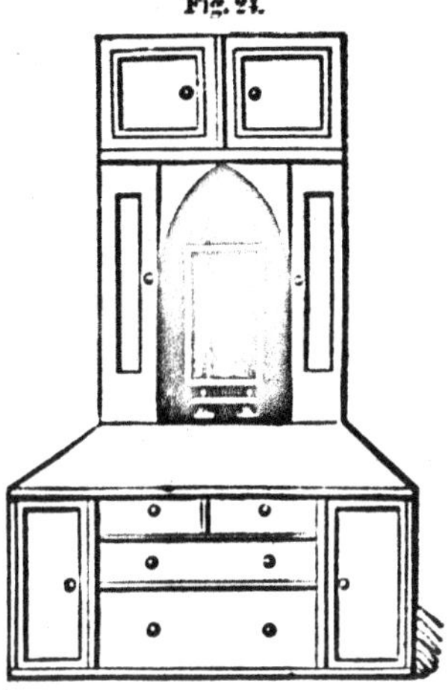

each side that their walls meet the ceiling under the garret floor, thus excluding all or most of the roof. In the bed-chambers, corner dressing-tables, as Fig. 24, instead of projecting bureaus, save much space for use, and give a handsome form and finish to the room. In the bath-room must be the opening to the garret, and a step-ladder to reach it. A reservoir in the garret, supplied by a forcing-pump in the cellar or at the sink, must be well supported by timbers, and the plumbing must be well done, or much annoyance will ensue.

The large chambers are to be lighted by large windows or glazed sliding-doors, opening upon the balcony. A roof can be put over the balcony and its sides inclosed by windows, and the chamber extend into it, and be thus much enlarged.

The water-closets must have the latest improvements for safe discharge, and there will be no trouble. They will cost no more than an outdoor building, and they relieve one from the most disagreeable house-labor.

Fig. 25.

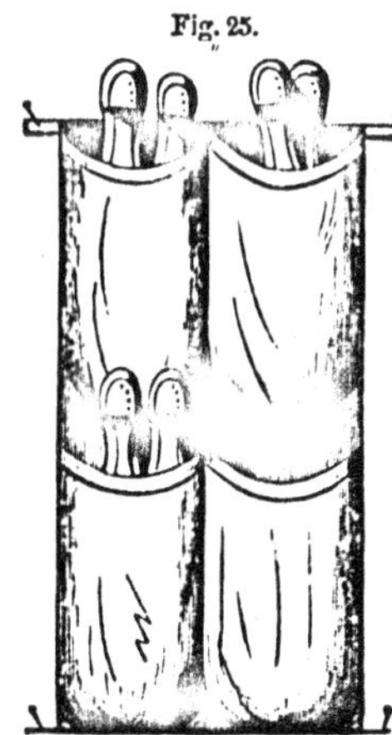

A great improvement, called *earth-closets*, will probably take the place of water-closets to some extent; though at present the water is the more convenient.

The method of ventilating all the chambers, and also the cellar, will be described in another place.

Fig. 25 represents a shoe-bag, that can be fastened to the side of a closet or closet-door.

Fig. 26 represents a piece-bag, and is a very great labor and space-saving invention. It is made of calico, and fastened to the side of a closet or a door, to hold all the bundles that are usually stowed in trunks and drawers. India-rubber or elastic tape drawn into hems to hold the contents

Fig. 26.

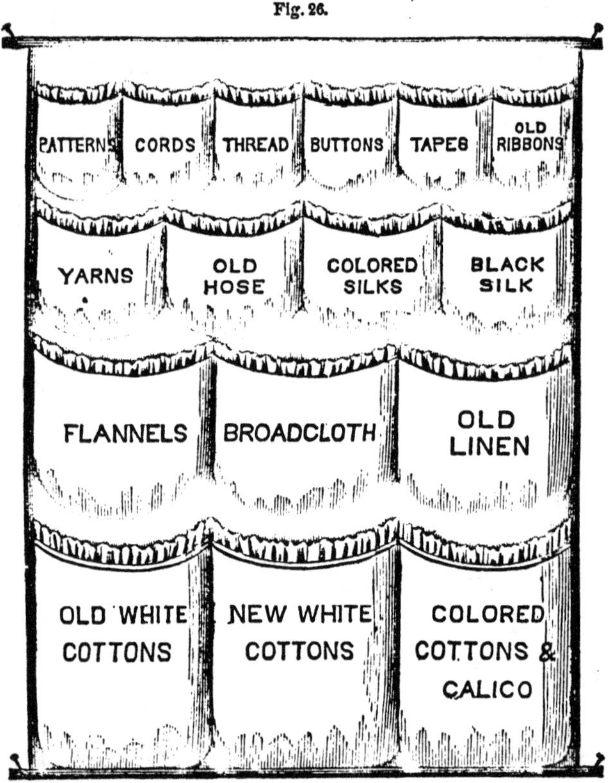

of the bag is better than tape-strings. Each bag should be labeled with the name of its contents, written with indelible ink on white tape sewed on to the bag. Such systematic arrangement saves much time and annoyance. Drawers or trunks to hold these articles can not be kept so easily in good order, and moreover, occupy spaces saved by this contrivance.

Fig. 27 is the basement. It has the floor and sides plastered, and is lighted with glazed doors. A form is raised close by the cellar stairs, for baskets, pails, and tubs. Here,

Fig. 27.

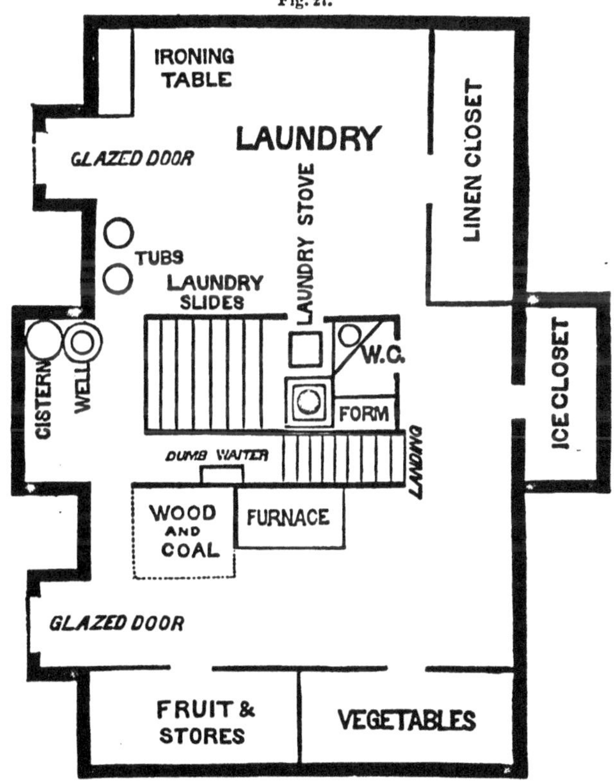

also, the refrigerator can be placed, or, what is better, an ice-closet can be made, as designated in the illustration. The floor of the basement must be an inclined plane toward a drain, and be plastered with water-lime. The wash-tubs have plugs in the bottom to let off water, and cocks and pipes over them bringing cold water from the reservoir in the garret and hot water from the laundry stove. This saves much heavy labor of emptying tubs and carrying water.

The laundry closet has a stove for heating irons, and also a kettle on top for heating water. Slides or clothes-frames are made to draw out to receive wet clothes, and then run into the closet to dry. This saves health as well as time and money, and the clothes are as white as when dried outdoors. The entrance to the kitchen is either through the basement or through the eating-room windows, made to slide.

The wood-work of the house, for doors, windows, etc., should be *oiled* chestnut, butternut, whitewood, and pine. This is cheaper, handsomer, and more easy to keep clean than painted wood.

In Fig. 7 are planned two conservatories, and few understand their value in the training of the young. They provide soil, in which children, through the winter months, can be starting seeds and plants for their gardens and raising valuable, tender plants. Every child should cultivate flowers and fruits to sell and to give away, and thus be taught to learn the value of money, and to practice both economy and benevolence.

According to the calculation of a house-carpenter, in a place where the *average* price of lumber is four dollars a hundred, and carpenter work three dollars a day, such a house can be built for sixteen hundred dollars. For those practicing the closest economy, two small families could occupy it, by dividing the kitchen, and yet have room enough. Or one large room and the chamber over it can be left till increase of family and means require enlargement.

A strong horse and carry-all, with a cow, garden, vineyard, and orchard, on a few acres, would secure all the substantial comforts found in great establishments, without the trouble of ill-qualified servants.

And if the parents and children were united in the daily labors of the house, garden, and fruit culture, such thrift, health, and happiness would be secured as is but rarely found among the rich.

Let us suppose a colony of cultivated and Christian people, having abundant wealth, who now are living as the wealthy usually do, emigrating to some of the beautiful Southern uplands, where are rocks, hills, valleys, and mountains as picturesque as those of New-England, where the thermometer but rarely reaches 90° in summer, and in winter as rarely sinks below freezing-point, so that outdoor labor goes on all the year, where the fertile soil is easily worked, where rich tropical fruits and flowers abound, where cotton and silk can be raised by children around their home, where the produce of vineyards and orchards finds steady markets by railroads ready-made; suppose such a colony, with a central church and school-room, library, hall for sports, and a common laundry, (taking the most trying part of domestic labor from each house)—suppose each family to train the children to labor with the hands as a healthful and honorable duty; suppose all this, which is perfectly practicable, would not the enjoyment of this life be increased, and also abundant treasures be laid up in heaven, by using the wealth thus economized in diffusing similar enjoyments and culture among the poor, ignorant, and neglected ones in desolated sections where many now are perishing for want of such Christian example and influences?

CHAPTER III.

ON HOME VENTILATION.

WHEN "the wise woman buildeth her house," the first consideration will be the health of the inmates. The first and most indispensable requisite for health is pure air, both by day and night.

If the parents of a family should daily withhold from their children a large portion of food needful to growth and health, and every night should administer to each a small dose of poison, it would be called murder of the most hideous character. But it is probable that more than one half of this nation are doing that very thing. The murderous operation is perpetrated daily and nightly, in our parlors, our bedrooms, our kitchens, our school-rooms; and even our churches are no asylum from the barbarity. Nor can we escape by our railroads, for even there the same dreadful work is going on.

The only palliating circumstance is the ignorance of those who commit these wholesale murders. As saith the Scripture, "The people do perish for lack of knowledge." And it is this lack of knowledge which it is woman's special business to supply.

The above statements will be illustrated by some account of the manner in which the body is supplied with healthful nutriment. There are two modes of nourishing the body, one is by food and the other by air. In the stomach the food is dissolved, and the nutritious portion is absorbed by the blood, and then is carried by blood-vessels tó the lungs, where it receives oxygen from the air we breathe. This oxygen is as necessary to the nourishment of the body as the food of the stomach. In a full-grown man weighing one hundred and fifty-four pounds, one hundred and eleven pounds consists of oxygen, obtained chiefly from the air we breathe. Thus the lungs feed the body with oxygen, as really as the stomach supplies the other food required.

The lungs occupy the upper portion of the body from the collar-bone to the lower ribs, and between their two lobes is placed the heart.

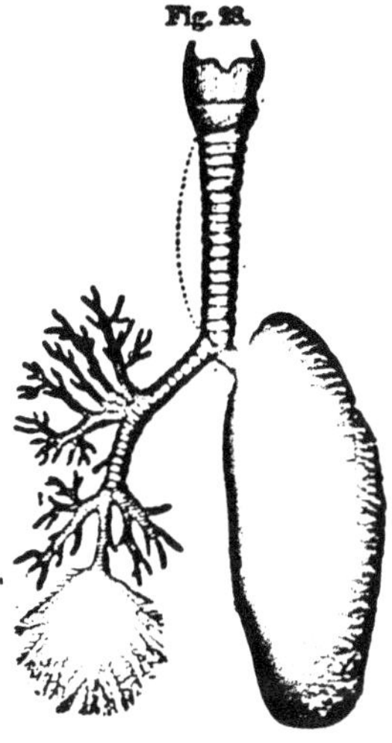
Fig. 28.

Fig. 28 shows the position of the lungs, though not the exact shape. On the right hand is the exterior of one of the lobes, and on the left hand are seen the branching tubes of the interior, through which the air we breathe passes to the exceedingly minute air-cells of which the lungs chiefly consist. Fig. 29 shows the outside of a cluster of these air-cells, and Fig. 30 is the inside view. The lining membrane of each air-cell is covered by a net-work of minute blood-vessels called *capillaries*, which, magnified several hundred times, appear in the microscope as at Fig. 31. Every air-cell has a blood-vessel that brings blood from the heart, which meanders through

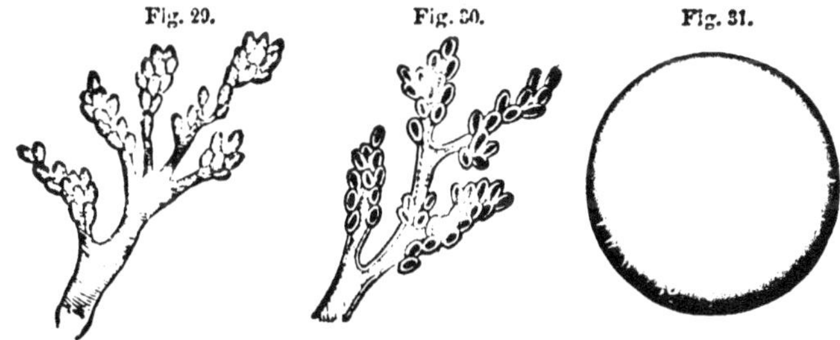
Fig. 29. Fig. 30. Fig. 31.

its capillaries till it reaches another blood-vessel that carries it back to the heart, as seen in Fig. 32. In this passage of the blood through these capillaries, the air in the air-cell imparts its oxygen to the blood, and receives in exchange carbonic acid and watery vapor which are expired at every breath into the atmosphere.

By calculating the number of air-cells in a small portion of the lungs, under a microscope, it is ascertained that there

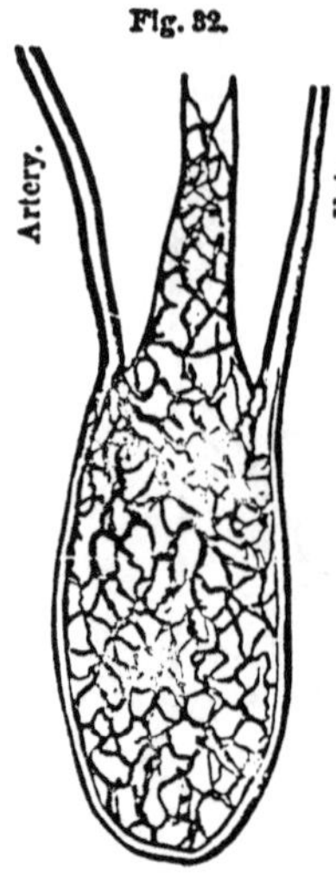

Fig. 32.

are no less than eighteen millions of these wonderful little purifiers and feeders of the body. By their ceaseless ministries, every grown person receives, each day, thirty-three hogsheads of air into the lungs to nourish and vitalize every part of the body, and also to carry off its impurities.

But the heart has a most important agency in this operation. Fig. 33 is a diagram of the heart, which is placed between the two lobes of the lungs. The right side of the heart receives the dark and impure blood, which is loaded with carbonic acid. It is brought from every point of the body by branching veins that unite in the upper and the lower *vena cava*, which discharge into the right side of the heart. This impure blood passes to the capillaries of the air-cells in the lungs, where it gives off carbonic acid, and, taking oxygen from the air, then returns to the left side of the heart, from whence it is sent out through the *aorta* and its myriad branching arteries to every part of the body.

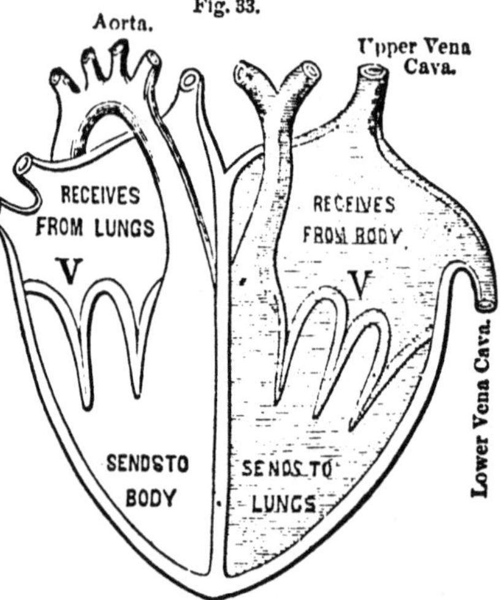

Fig. 33.

When the upper portion of the heart contracts, it forces both the pure blood from the lungs, and the impure blood from the body, through the valves marked V, V, into the lower part. When the lower portion contracts, it closes the valves and forces the impure blood into the lungs on one side, and also on the other side forces the purified blood through the aorta and arteries to all parts of the body.

As before stated, the lungs consist chiefly of air-cells, the walls of which are lined with minute blood-vessels; and we know that in every man these air-cells number *eighteen millions.*

Now every beat of the heart sends two ounces of blood into the minute, hair-like blood-vessels, called capillaries, that line these air-cells, where the air in the air-cells gives its oxygen to the blood, and in its place receives carbonic acid. This gas is then expired by the lungs into the surrounding atmosphere.

Thus, by this powerful little organ, the heart, no less than twenty-eight pounds of blood, in a common-sized man, is sent three times every hour through the lungs, giving out carbonic acid and watery vapor, and receiving the life-inspiring oxygen.

Whether all this blood shall convey the nourishing and invigorating oxygen to every part of the body, or return unrelieved of carbonic acid, depends entirely on the pureness of the atmosphere that is breathed.

Every time we think or feel, this mental action dissolves some particles of the brain and nerves, which pass into the blood to be thrown out of the body through the lungs and skin. In like manner, whenever we move any muscle, some of its particles decay and pass away. It is in the capillaries, which are all over the body, that this change takes place. The blood-vessels that convey the pure blood from the heart divide into myriads of little branches that terminate in capillary vessels like those lining the air-cells of the lungs. The blood meanders through these minute capillaries, depositing the oxygen taken from the lungs and the food of the stomach, and receiving in return the decayed matter, which is chiefly carbonic acid.

This carbonic acid is formed by the union of oxygen with *carbon* or *charcoal,* which forms a large portion of the food. Watery vapor is also formed in the capillaries by the union of oxygen with the hydrogen contained in the food and drink.

During this process in the capillaries, the bright red blood of the arteries changes to the purple blood of the veins, which is carried back to the heart, to be sent to be purified in the lungs as before described. A portion of the oxygen received in the lungs unites with the dissolved food sent from the stomach into the blood, and no food can nourish the body till it has received a proper supply of oxygen in the lungs. At every breath a half-pint of blood receives its needed oxygen in the lungs, and at the same time gives out an equal amount of carbonic acid and water.

Now this carbonic acid, if received into the lungs undiluted by sufficient air, is a fatal poison, causing certain death. When it is mixed with only a small portion of air, it is a slow poison, which imperceptibly undermines the constitution.

We now can understand how it is that all who live in houses where the breathing of inmates has deprived the air of oxygen, and loaded it with carbonic acid, may truly be said to be poisoned and starved; poisoned with carbonic acid, and starved for want of oxygen.

Whenever oxygen unites with carbon to form carbonic acid, or with hydrogen to form water, heat is generated. Thus it is that a kind of combustion is constantly going on in the capillaries all over the body. It is this burning of the decaying portions of the body that causes animal heat. It is a process similar to that which takes place when lamps and candles are burning. The oil and tallow, which are chiefly carbon and hydrogen, unite with the oxygen of the air and form carbonic acid and watery vapor, producing heat during the process. So in the capillaries all over the body, the carbon and hydrogen supplied to the blood by the food unite with the oxygen gained in the lungs, and cause the heat which is diffused all over the body.

The skin also performs an office similar to that of the lungs. In the skin of every adult there are no less than seven million minute perspirating tubes, each one-fourth of an inch long. If all these were united in one length, they would extend twenty-eight miles. These minute tubes are lined with capillary blood-vessels, which are constantly sending out not only carbonic acid, but other gases and particles of decayed matter. The skin and lungs together, in one day and night, throw out three-quarters of a pound of charcoal as carbonic acid, besides other gases and water.

While the bodies of men and animals are filling the air with the poisonous carbonic acid, and using up the life-giving oxygen, the trees and plants are performing an exactly contrary process; for they are absorbing carbonic acid and giving out oxygen. Thus, by a wonderful arrangement of the beneficent Creator, a constant equilibrium is preserved. What animals use is provided by vegetables, and what vegetables require is furnished by animals; and all goes on, day and night, without care or thought of man.

The human race in its infancy was placed in a mild and genial clime, where each separate family dwelt in tents, and breathed, both day and night, the pure air of heaven. And when they became scattered abroad to colder climes, the open fire-place secured a full supply of pure air. But civilization has increased economies and conveniences far ahead of the knowledge needed by the common people for their healthful use. Tight sleeping-rooms, and close, air-tight stoves, are now starving and poisoning more than one half of this nation. It seems impossible to make people know their danger. And the remedy for this is the light of knowledge and intelligence which it is woman's special mission to bestow, as she controls and regulates the ministries of a home.

The poisoning process is thus exhibited in Mrs. Stowe's "House and Home Papers," and can not be recalled too often:

"No other gift of God, so precious, so inspiring, is treated with such utter irreverence and contempt in the calculations of us mortals as this same air of heaven. A sermon on oxygen, if we had a preacher who understood the subject, might do more to repress sin than the most orthodox discourse to show when and how and why sin came. A minister gets up in a crowded lecture-room, where the mephitic air almost makes the candles burn blue, and bewails the deadness of the church—the church the while, drugged by the poisoned air, growing sleepier and sleepier, though they feel dreadfully wicked for being so.

"Little Jim, who, fresh from his afternoon's ramble in the fields, last evening said his prayers dutifully, and lay down to sleep in a most Christian frame, this morning sits up in bed with his hair bristling with crossness, strikes at his nurse, and declares he won't say his prayers—that he don't want to be good. The difference is, that the child, having slept in a close box of a room, his brain all night fed by poison, is in a mild state of moral insanity. Delicate women remark that it takes them till eleven or twelve o'clock to get up their strength in the morning. Query, Do they sleep with closed windows and doors, and with heavy bed-curtains?

"The houses built by our ancestors were better ventilated in certain respects than modern ones, with all their improvements. The great central chimney, with its open fire-places in the different rooms, created a constant current which carried off foul and vitiated air. In these days, how common is it to provide rooms with only a flue for a stove! This flue is kept shut in summer, and in winter opened only to admit a close stove, which burns away the vital portion of the air quite as fast as the occupants breathe it away. The sealing up of fire-places and introduction of air-tight stoves may, doubtless, be a saving of fuel; it saves, too, more than that; in thousands and thousands of cases it has saved people from all further human wants, and put an end forever to any needs short of the six feet of narrow earth which are man's only inalienable property. In other words, since the invention of air-tight stoves, thousands have died of slow poison.

"It is a terrible thing to reflect upon, that our northern winters last from November to May, six long months, in which many families confine themselves to one room, of which every window-crack has been carefully calked to make it air-tight, where an air-tight stove keeps the atmosphere at a temperature between eighty and ninety; and the inmates, sitting there with all their winter clothes on, become enervated both by the heat and by the poisoned air, for which there is no escape but the occasional opening of a door.

"It is no wonder that the first result of all this is such a delicacy of skin and lungs that about half the inmates are obliged to give up going into the open air during the six cold months, because they invariably catch cold if they do so. It is no wonder that the cold caught about the first of December has by the first of March become a fixed consumption, and that the opening of the spring, which ought to bring life and health, in so many cases brings death.

"We hear of the lean condition in which the poor bears emerge from their six months' wintering, during which they subsist on the fat which they have acquired the previous summer. Even so, in our long winters, multitudes of delicate people subsist on the daily waning strength which they acquired in the season when windows and doors were open, and fresh air was a constant luxury. No wonder we hear of spring fever and spring biliousness, and have thousands of nostrums for clearing the blood in the spring. All these things are the pantings and palpitations of a system run down under slow poison, unable to get a step farther.

"Better, far better, the old houses of the olden time, with their great roaring fires, and their bed-rooms where the snow came in and the wintry winds whistled. Then, to be sure, you froze your back while you burned your face, your water froze nightly in your pitcher, your breath congealed in ice-wreaths on the blankets, and you could write your name on the pretty snow-wreath that had sifted in through the window-cracks. But you woke full of life and vigor, you looked out into the whirling snow-storms without a shiver, and thought nothing of plunging through drifts as high as your head on your daily way to school. You jingled in sleighs, you snow-balled, you lived in snow like a snow-bird, and your blood coursed and tingled, in full tide of good, merry, real life, through your veins—none of the slow-creeping, black blood which clogs the brain and lies like a weight on the vital wheels!"

It is ascertained by experiments that breathing bad air tends so to reduce all the processes of the body, that less oxygen is demanded and less carbonic acid sent out. This, of course, lessens the vitality and weakens the constitution; and it accounts for the fact that a person of full health, accustomed to pure air, suffers from bad air far more than those who are accustomed to it. The body of strong and healthy persons demands more oxygen, and throws off more carbonic acid, and is distressed when the supply fails. But the one reduced by bad air feels little inconvenience, because all the functions of life are so slow that less oxygen is needed, and less carbonic acid thrown out. And the sensibilities being deadened, the evil is not felt. This provision of nature prolongs many lives, though it turns vigorous constitutions into feeble ones. Were it not for this change in the constitution, thousands in badly ventilated rooms and houses would come to a speedy death.

One of the results of unventilated rooms is *scrofula*. A distinguished French physician, M. Baudeloque, states that

"The repeated respiration of the same atmosphere is *the* cause of scrofula. If there be entirely pure air, there may be bad food, bad clothing, and want of personal cleanliness, but scrofulous disease will not exist. This disease *never* attacks persons who pass their lives in the open air, and *always* manifests itself when they abide in air which is unrenewed."

This writer illustrates this by the history of a French village where the inhabitants all slept in close, unventilated houses. Nearly all were seized with scrofula, and many families became wholly extinct, their last members dying "rotten with scrofula." A fire destroyed a large part of this village. Houses were then built to secure pure air, and scrofula disappeared from the part thus rebuilt.

We are informed by medical writers that defective ventilation is one great cause of diseased joints, as well as of diseases of the eyes, ears, and skin.

Foul air is the leading cause of tubercular and scrofulous consumption, so very common in our country. Dr. Guy, in his examination before public health commissioners in Great

Britain, says: "Deficient ventilation I believe to be more fatal than *all other causes* put together." He states that consumption is twice as common among tradesmen as among the gentry, owing to the bad ventilation of their stores and dwellings.

Says Dr. Dio Lewis, whose labors in the cause of health are well known:

"As a medical man I have visited thousands of sick-rooms, and have not found in *one in a hundred* of them a pure atmosphere. I have often returned from church doubting whether I had not committed a sin in exposing myself so long to its poisonous air. There are in our great cities churches costing fifty thousand dollars, in the construction of which not fifty cents were expended in providing means for ventilation. Ten thousand dollars for ornament, but not ten cents for pure air!

"Unventilated parlors, with gas-burners, (each consuming as much oxygen as several men,) made as tight as possible, and a party of ladies and gentlemen spending half the night in them! In 1861, I visited a legislative hall, the legislature being in session. I remained half an hour in the most impure air I ever breathed. Our school-houses are, some of them, so vile in this respect, that I would prefer to have my son remain in utter ignorance of books rather than to breathe, six hours every day, such a poisonous atmosphere. Theatres and concert-rooms are so foul that only reckless people continue to visit them. Twelve hours in a railway-car exhausts one, not by the journeying, but because of the devitalized air. While crossing the ocean in a Cunard steamer, I was amazed that men who knew enough to construct such ships did not know enough to furnish air to the passengers. The distress of sea-sickness is greatly intensified by the sickening air of the ship. Were carbonic acid *only black*, what a contrast there would be between our hotels in their elaborate ornament!

"Some time since I visited an establishment where one hundred and fifty girls, in a single room, were engaged in needle-work. Pale-faced, and with low vitality and feeble circulation, they were unconscious that they were breathing air that at once produced in me dizziness and a sense of suffocation. If I had remained a week with them, I should, by reduced vitality, have become unconscious of the vileness of the air!"

There is a prevailing prejudice against *night air* as unhealthful to be admitted into sleeping-rooms, which is owing wholly to sheer ignorance. In the night every body necessarily breathes night air and no other. When admitted from without into a sleeping-room, it is colder, and therefore heavier, than the air within, so it sinks to the bottom of the room and forces out an equal quantity of the impure air, warmed and vitiated by passing through the lungs of inmates. Thus the question is, Shall we shut up a chamber and breathe night air vitiated with carbonic acid or night air that is pure? The only real difficulty about night air is, that usually it is damper, and therefore colder and more likely to chill. This is easily remedied by sufficient bed-clothing.

One other very prevalent mistake is found even in books written by learned men. It is often thought that carbonic acid, being heavier than common air, sinks to the floor of sleeping-rooms, so that the low trundle-beds for children should not be used. This is all a mistake; for, as a fact, in close sleeping-rooms the purest air is below and the most impure above. It is true that carbonic acid is heavier than common air, when pure; but this it rarely is except in chemical experiments. It is the property of all gases, as well as of the two (oxygen and nitrogen) composing the atmosphere, that when brought together they always are entirely mixed, each being equally diffused. Thus the carbonic acid from the skin and lungs, being warmed in the body, rises, as does the common air, with which it mixes, toward the top of a room; so that usually there is more carbonic acid at the top than at the bottom of a room.* Both common air and carbonic acid expand and become lighter in the same proportions; that is, for every degree of added heat they expand at the rate of $\frac{1}{480}$ of their bulk.

* Professor Brewer, of the Yale Scientific School, says: "As a fact, often demonstrated by analysis, there is generally more carbonic acid near the ceiling than near the floor."

Here, let it be remembered, that in ill-ventilated rooms the carbonic acid is not the only cause of disease. Experiments seem to prove that other matter thrown out of the body, through the lungs and skin, is as truly excrement and in a state of decay as that ejected from the bowels, and as poisonous to the animal system. Carbonic acid has no odor; but we are warned by the disagreeable effluvia of close sleeping-rooms of the other poison thus thrown into the air from the skin and lungs. There is one provision of nature that is little understood, which saves the lives of thousands living in unventilated houses; and that is, the passage of pure air inward and impure air outward through the pores of bricks, wood, stone, and mortar. Were such dwellings changed to tin, which is not thus porous, in less than a week thousands and tens of thousands would be in danger of perishing by suffocation.

There are some recent scientific discoveries that relate to impure air which may properly be introduced here. It is shown by the microscope that *fermentation* is a process which generates extremely minute plants, that gradually increase till the whole mass is pervaded by this vegetation. The microscope also has revealed the fact that, in certain diseases, these microscopic plants are generated in the blood and other fluids of the body, in a mode similar to the ordinary process of fermentation.

And, what is very curious, each of these peculiar diseases generates diverse kinds of plants. Thus, in the typhoid fever, the microscope reveals in the fluids of the patient a plant that resembles in form some kinds of sea-weed. In chills and fever, the microscopic plant has another form, and in small-pox still another. A work has recently been published in Europe, in which representations of these various microscopic plants generated in the fluids of the diseased persons are exhibited, enlarged several hundred times by the microscope. All diseases that exhibit these microscopic plants are classed together, and are called *Zymotic*, from a Greek word signifying *to ferment.*

It is now regarded as probable that most of these diseases are generated by the microscopic plants which float in an impure or miasmatic atmosphere, and are taken into the blood by breathing.

Recent scientific investigations in Great Britain and other countries prove that the *power of resisting* these diseases depends upon the purity of the air which has been *habitually* inspired. The human body gradually accommodates itself to unhealthful circumstances, so that people can live a long time in bad air. But the "reserve power" of the body—that is, the power of resisting disease—is under such circumstances gradually destroyed, and then an epidemic easily sweeps away those thus enfeebled. The plague of London, that destroyed thousands every day, came immediately after a long period of damp, warm days, when there was no wind to carry off the miasma thus generated; while the people, by long breathing of bad air, were all prepared, from having sunk into a low vitality, to fall before the pestilence.

Multitudes of public documents show that the fatality of epidemics is always proportioned to the degree in which impure air has previously been respired. Sickness and death are therefore regulated by the degree in which air is kept pure, especially in case of diseases in which medical treatment is most uncertain, as in cholera and malignant fevers.

Investigations made by governmental authority, and by boards of health in this country and in Great Britain, prove that zymotic diseases ordinarily result from impure air generated by vegetable or animal decay, and that in almost all cases they can be prevented by keeping the air pure. The decayed animal matter sent off from the skin and lungs in a close, unventilated bedroom is one thing that generates these zymotic diseases. The decay of animal and vegetable matter in cellars, sinks, drains, and marshy districts is another cause; and the decayed vegetable matter thrown up by plowing up of decayed vegetable matter in the rich soil in new countries is another.

In the investigations made in certain parts of Great Britain, it appeared that in districts where the air is pure the deaths average eleven in one thousand each year; while in localities most exposed to impure miasma the mortality was forty-five in every thousand. At this rate, thirty-four persons in every thousand died from poisoned air, who would have preserved health and life by well-ventilated homes in a pure atmosphere. And, out of all who died, the proportion who owed their deaths to foul air was more than three-fourths. Similar facts have been obtained by boards of health in our own country.

Mr. Lewis Leeds gives statistics showing that in Philadelphia, by improved modes of ventilation and other sanitary methods, there was a saving of three thousand two hundred and thirty-seven lives in two years; and a saving of three-fourths of a million of dollars, which would pay the whole expense of the public schools. Philadelphia being previously an unusually cleanly and well-ventilated city, what would be the saving of life, health, and wealth were such a city as New York perfectly cleansed and ventilated?

CHAPTER IV.

ON WARMING A HOME.

THE laws that regulate the generation, diffusion, and preservation of heat as yet are a sealed mystery to thousands of young women who imagine they are completing a suitable education in courses of instruction from which most that is practical in future domestic life is wholly excluded. We therefore give a brief outline of some of the leading scientific principles which every housekeeper should understand and employ, in order to perform successfully one of her most important duties.

Concerning the essential nature of heat, and its intimate relations with the other great natural forces, light, electricity, etc., we shall not attempt to treat, but shall, for practical purposes, assume it to be a separate and independent force.

Heat or caloric, then, has certain powers or principles. Let us consider them:

First, we find *Conduction*, by which heat passes from one particle to another next to it; as when one end of a poker is warmed by placing the other end in the fire. The bodies which allow this power free course are called conductors, and those which do not are named non-conductors. Metals are good conductors; feathers, wool, and furs are poor conductors; and water, air, and gases are non-conductors.

Another principle of heat is *Convection*, by which water, air, and gases are warmed. This is, literally, the process of *conveying* heat from one portion of a fluid body to another by currents resulting from changes of temperature. It is secured by bringing one portion of a liquid or gas into contact with a heated surface, and thus it becomes lighter and expanded in volume. In consequence, the cooler and heavier particles above pressing downward, the lighter ones rise upward. Thus a constant motion of currents and interchange of particles is produced, until, as in a vessel of water, the whole body comes to an equal temperature. Air is heated in the same way. In case of a hot stove, the air that touches it is heated, becomes lighter, and rises, giving place to cooler and heavier particles, which, when heated, also ascend. It is owing to this process that the air of a room is warmest at the top and coolest at the bottom.

It is owing to this principle, also, that water and air can not be heated by fire from above. For the particles of these bodies, being non-conductors, do not impart heat to each other; and when the warmest are at the top, they can not take the place of cooler and heavier ones below.

Another principle of heat (which it shares with light) is *Radiation*, by which all things send out heat to surrounding cooler bodies. Some bodies will absorb radiated heat, others will reflect it, and others allow it to pass through them without either absorbing or reflecting. Thus, black and rough substances absorb heat, (or light,) colored and smooth articles reflect it, while air allows it to pass through without either absorbing or reflecting. It is owing to this that rough and black vessels boil water sooner than smooth and light-colored ones.

Another principle is *Reflection*, by which heat radiated to a surface is turned back from it when not absorbed or allowed to pass through; just as a ball rebounds from a wall; just as sound is thrown back from a hill, making echo; just as rays of light are reflected from a mirror.

There is no department of science, as applied to practical matters, which has so often baffled experimenters as the healthful mode of warming and ventilating houses. The British nation spent over a million on the House of Parliament for this end, and failed. Our own Government has spent half a million on the Capitol, with worse failure; and now it is proposed to spend a million more. The reason is, that the old open fire-place has been supplanted by less expensive modes of heating, destructive to health; and science has but just begun experiments to secure a remedy for the evil.

The open fire warms the person, the walls, the floors, and

the furniture by radiation, and these, together with the fire, warm the air by convection; for the air resting on the heated surfaces is warmed by convection, rises and gives place to cooler particles, causing a constant heating of its particles by movement. Thus, in a room with an open fire, the person is warmed in part by radiation from the fire and the surrounding walls and furniture, and in part by the warm air surrounding the body.

In regard to the warmth of air, the thermometer is not an exact index of its temperature. For all bodies are constantly radiating their heat to cooler adjacent surfaces until all come to the same temperature. This being so, the thermometer is radiating its heat to walls and surrounding objects, in addition to what is subtracted by the air that surrounds it, and thus the air is really several degrees warmer than the thermometer indicates. A room at 70° by the thermometer is usually filled with air five or more degrees warmer than this.

Now, the cold air is denser than warm, and therefore contains more oxygen. Consequently, the cooler the air inspired, the larger the supply of oxygen and of the vitality and vigor which it imparts. Thus, the great problem for economy of health is to warm the person as much as possible by radiated heat, and supply the lungs with cool air. For when we breathe air at from 16° to 20°, we take double the amount of oxygen that we do when we inhale it at 80° to 90°, and consequently can do a far greater amount of muscle and brain work.

Warming by an open fire is nearest to the natural mode of the Creator, who heats the earth and its furniture by the great central fire of heaven, and sends cool breezes for our lungs. But open fires involve great destruction of fuel and expenditure of money, and in consequence economic methods have been introduced, to the great destruction of health and life.

Whenever a family-room is heated by an open fire, it is duly ventilated, as the impure air is constantly passing off through the heated chimney, while, to supply the vacated space, the pure air presses in through the cracks of doors, windows, and floors. No such supply is gained for rooms warmed by stoves. And yet, from mistaken motives of economy, as well as from ignorance of the resulting evils, multitudes of householders are thus destroying health and shortening life, especially in regard to women and children who spend most of their time within doors. This is especially the case where air-tight stoves are used.

A common mode of warming is by heated air from a furnace. The chief objection to this is the loss of moisture and of all radiated heat, and the consequent necessity of breathing air which is debilitating, both from its heat and also from being usually deprived of the requisite moisture provided by the Creator in all outdoor air. Another objection is the fact that it is important to health to preserve an equal circulation of the blood, and the greatest impediment to this is a mode of heating which keeps the head in warmer air than the feet. This is especially deleterious in an age and country where active brains are constantly drawing blood from the extremities to the head. All furnace-heated rooms have coldest air at the feet, and warmest around the head.

What follows illustrates the principles on which several modes of ventilation are practiced.

It is the common property of both air and water to expand, become lighter and rise, just in proportion as they are heated; and therefore it is the invariable law that cool air sinks, thus replacing the warmer air below. Thus, whenever cool air enters a warm room, it sinks downward and takes the place of an equal amount of the warmer air, which is constantly tending upward and outward. This principle of all fluids is illustrated by the following experiment:

Take a glass jar about a foot high and three inches in diameter, and with a wire to aid in placing it aright, sink a small bit of lighted candle so as to stand in the centre at the bottom. (Fig. 34.) The candle will heat the air of the jar, which will rise a little on one side, while the colder air without will begin falling on the other side. These two currents will so conflict as finally to cease, and then the candle, having no supply of oxygen from fresh air, will begin to go out. Insert a bit of stiff paper so as to divide the

Fig. 34.

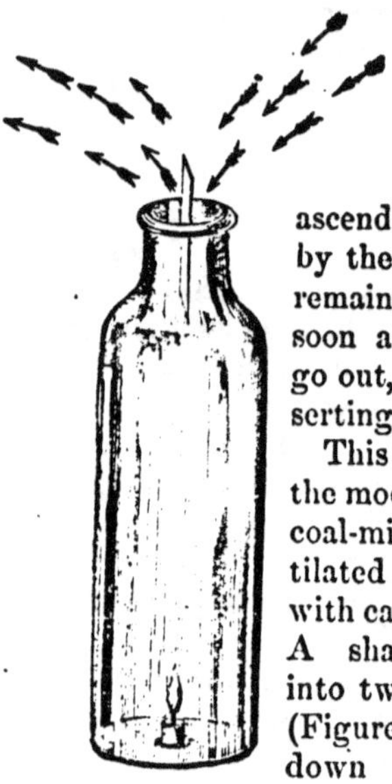

mouth of the jar, and instantly the cold and warm air are not in conflict as before, because a current is formed each side of the paper; the cold air descending on one side and the warm air ascending the other side, as indicated by the arrows. As long as the paper remains, the candle will burn, and as soon as it is removed, it will begin to go out, and can be restored by again inserting the paper.

Fig. 35.

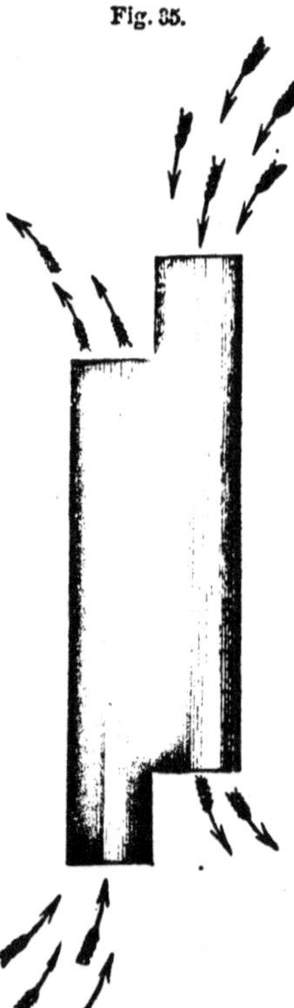

This illustrates the mode by which coal-mines are ventilated when filled with carbonic acid. A shaft divided into two passages, (Figure 35,) is let down into the mine, where the air is warmer than the outside air. Immediately the colder air outside presses down into the mine, through the passage which is highest, being admitted by the escape of an equal quantity of the warmer air, which rises through the lower passage of the shaft, this being the first available opening for it to rise through. A current is thus created, which continues as long as the inside air is warmer than that without the mine, and no longer. Sometimes a fire is kindled in the mine, in order to continue or increase the warmth, and consequent upward current of its air.

It is on this plan that many school-houses and manufactories have been ventilated. Its grand defect is, that it fails altogether when the air outside the house is at the same temperature as that within. This illustrates one of the cases where a "wise woman that buildeth her house" is greatly needed. For, owing to the ignorance of architects, house-builders, and men in general, they have been building school-houses, dwelling-houses, churches, and colleges, with the most absurd and senseless contrivances for ventilation, and all from not applying this principle of science. On this point, Professor Brewer, of the Scientific School of Yale College, writes thus:

"I have been in public buildings, (I have one in mind now, filled with dormitories,) which cost half a million, where they attempted to ventilate every room by a single flue, long and narrow, built into partition walls, and extending up into the capacious garret of the fifth story. Every room in the building had one such flue, with an opening into it at the floor and at the ceiling. It is needless to say that the whole concern was entirely useless. Had these flues been of proper proportions, and properly divided, the desired ventilation would have been secured." And this piece of ignorant folly was perpetrated in the midst of learned professors, teaching the laws of fluids and the laws of health!

In a cold climate and wintry weather, the grand impediment to ventilating rooms by opening doors or windows is the dangerous currents thus produced, which are so injurious to the delicate ones that for their sake it can not be done. Then, also, as a matter of economy, the poor can not afford to practice a method which carries off the heat generated by their stinted store of fuel. Even in a warm season and climate, there are frequent periods when the air without is damp and chilly, and yet at nearly the same temperature as that in the house. At such times even the opening of windows often has little effect in emptying a room of vitiated air.

The most successful mode of ventilating a house is by creating a current of warm air in a flue, into which an opening is made at both the top and the bottom of a room, to carry off the impure air, while a similar opening to admit outside air is made at the opposite side of the room. This is the mode employed in chemical laboratories for removing smells and injurious gases.

These statements give some idea of the evils to be remedied. But the most difficult point is *how* to secure the remedy; for often the attempt to secure pure air by one class of persons brings chills, colds, and disease on another class, from mere ignorance or mismanagement.

To illustrate this, it must be borne in mind that those who live in warm, close, and unventilated rooms are much more liable to take cold from exposure to draughts and cold air than those of vigorous vitality accustomed to breathe pure air.

Thus the strong and healthy husband, feeling the want of pure air in the night, and knowing its importance, keeps windows open, and makes such draughts that the wife, who lives all day in a close room and thus is low in vitality, can not bear the change, has colds, and sometimes perishes a victim to wrong modes of ventilation.

So, even in health-establishments, the patients will pass most of their days and nights in badly-ventilated rooms. But at times the physician, or some earnest patient, insists on a mode of ventilation that brings more evil than good to the delicate inmates.

The grand art of ventilating houses is by some method that will empty rooms of the vitiated air and bring in a supply of pure air *by small and imperceptible currents.*

But this important duty of a Christian woman is one that demands more science, care, and attention than almost any other; and yet, to prepare her for this duty has never been any part of female education. Young women are taught to draw mathematical diagrams and to solve astronomical problems; but few, if any, of them are taught to solve the problem of a house constructed to secure pure and moist air by day and night for all its inmates by safe methods.

We have seen the process through which the air is rendered unhealthful by close rooms and want of ventilation. Every person inspires air about twenty times each minute, using half a pint each time. At this rate, every pair of lungs vitiates one hogshead of air every hour. The membrane that lines the multitudinous air-cells of the lungs in which the capillaries are, should it be united in one sheet, would cover the floor of a room twelve feet square. Every breath brings a surface of air in contact with this extent of capillaries, by which the air inspired gives up most of its oxygen and receives carbonic acid in its stead. These facts furnish a guide for the proper ventilation of rooms. Just in proportion to the number of persons in a room or a house should be the amount of air brought in and carried out by arrangements for ventilation. But how rarely is this rule regarded in building houses or in the care of families by housekeepers!

As a guide to proportioning the air admitted and discharged to the number of persons, we have the following calculation: On an average, every adult vitiates about half a pint of air at each inspiration, and inspires twenty times a minute. This would amount to one hogshead of air vitiated every hour by every grown person. To keep the air pure, this amount should enter and be carried out every hour for each person. If, then, ten persons assemble in a dining-room, ten hogsheads of air should enter and ten be discharged each hour. By the same rule, a gathering of five hundred persons demands the entrance and discharge of five hundred hogsheads of air every hour, and a thousand persons require a thousand hogsheads of air every hour.

Therefore in calculating the size of registers and conductors, we must have reference to the number of persons who are to abide in a dwelling; while for rooms or halls intended for large gatherings a far greater allowance must be made.

The most successful arrangement for both warming and ventilation, is that employed by Lewis Leeds to ventilate the military hospitals, and also the treasury building at Washington. It is modeled strictly after the mode adopted by the Creator in warming and ventilating the earth, the home of his great earthly family. It aims to have a passage of pure air through every room, as the breezes pass over the hills, and to have a method of warming chiefly by radiation, as the earth is warmed by the sun. In addition to this, the air is to be provided with moisture, as it is supplied outdoors by exhalations from the earth and its trees and plants.

The mode of accomplishing this is by placing coils of steam, or hot-water pipes, under windows, which warm the parlor walls and furniture, partly by radiation, and partly by the air warmed on the heated surfaces of the coils. At the same time, by regulating registers, or by simply opening the lower part of the window, the pure air, guarded from immediate entrance into the room, is admitted directly upon the coils, so that it is partially warmed before it spreads through the room; and thus cold draughts are prevented. Then the vitiated air is drawn off through registers both at the top and bottom of the room, opening into a heated exhausting-flue, through which the constantly ascending current of warm air carries it off. These heated coils are often used for warming houses without any arrangement for carrying off the vitiated air, when, of course, their usefulness is gone.

The moisture may be supplied by a broad vessel placed on or close to the heated coils, giving a large surface for evaporation. When rooms are warmed chiefly by radiated heat, the air can be borne much cooler than in rooms warmed by hot-air furnaces, just as a person in the radiating sun can bear much cooler air than in the shade. A time will come when walls and floors will be contrived to radiate heat instead of absorbing it from the occupants of houses, as is generally the case at the present time, and then all can breathe pure and cool air.

We are now prepared to examine more in detail the modes of warming and ventilation employed in the dwellings planned for this work.

In doing this, it should be remembered that the aim is not to give plans of houses to suit the architectural taste or the domestic convenience of persons who intend to keep several servants, and care little whether they breathe pure or bad air, nor of persons who do not wish to educate their children to manual industry or to habits of close economy.

On the contrary, the aim is, first, to secure a house in which every room shall be perfectly ventilated both day and night, and that too without the watchful care and constant attention and intelligence needful in houses not provided with a proper and successful mode of ventilation.

The next aim is, to arrange the conveniences of domestic labor so as to save time, and also to render such work less repulsive than it is made by common methods, so that children can be trained to love house-work. And lastly, economy of expense in house-building is sought. These things should be borne in mind in examining the plans of this work.

In the dwelling-house, chap. ii., part ii., Fig. 7, a cast-iron pipe is made in sections, which are to be united, and the whole fastened at top and bottom in the centre of the warm-air flue by ears extending to the bricks, and fastened when the flue is in process of building. Projecting openings to receive the pipes of the furnace, the laundry stove, and two stoves in each story, should be provided in this cast-iron pipe, which must be closed when not in use. A large opening is to be made into the warm-air flue, and through this the kitchen stove-pipe is to pass, and be joined to the cast-iron chimney-pipe. Thus the smoke of the kitchen stove will warm the iron chimney-pipe, and this will warm the air of the flue, causing a current upward, and this current will draw the heat and smells of cooking out of the kitchen into the opening of the warm-air flue. Every room surrounding the chimney has an opening at the top and bottom into the warm-air flue for ventilation, as also have the bath-room and water-closets.

The pure air for rooms on the ground-floor is to be introduced by a wooden conductor one foot square, running under the floor from the front door to the stove-room, with cross branches to the two large rooms. The pure air passes through this, protected outside by wire netting, and delivered inside through registers in each room, as indicated in Fig. 7.

In case open Franklin stoves are used in the large rooms, the pure air from the conductor should enter behind them, and thus be partially warmed. The vitiated air is carried off at the bottom of the room through the open stoves, and also at the top by a register opening into a conductor to the exhausting warm-air shaft, which, it will be remembered, is the square chimney, containing the iron pipe which receives the kitchen stove-pipe. The stove-room receives pure air from the conductor, and sends off impure air and the smells of cooking by a register opening directly into the exhausting shaft; while its hot air and smoke, passing through the iron pipe, heat the air of the shaft, and produce the exhausting current.

The large chambers on the second floor (Fig. 18) have pure air conducted from the stove-room through registers that can be closed if the heat or smells of cooking are unpleasant. The air in the stove-room will always be moist from the water of the stove boiler.

The small chambers have pure air admitted from windows sunk at top half an inch; and the warm, vitiated air is conducted by a register in the ceiling which opens into a conductor to the exhausting warm-air shaft at the centre of the house, as shown in Fig. 23.

The basement or cellar is ventilated by an opening into the exhausting air-shaft, to remove impure air, and a small opening over each glazed door to admit pure air. The doors open out into a "well," or recess, excavated in the earth before the cellar, for the admission of light and air, neatly bricked up and whitewashed. The doors are to be made entirely of strong, thick glass sashes, and this will give light enough for laundry work—the tubs and ironing-table being placed closed to the glazed door. The floor must be plastered with water-lime, and the walls and ceiling be whitewashed, which will add reflected light to the room. There will thus be no need of other windows, and the house need not be raised above the ground. Several cottages have been built thus, so that the ground-floors and conservatories are nearly on the same level; and all agree that they are pleasanter than when raised higher.

When a window in any room is sunk at the top, it should have a narrow shelf in front inclined to the opening, so as to keep out the rain. In small chambers for one person, an inch opening is sufficient, and in larger rooms for two persons a two-inch opening is needed. The openings into the exhausting-air flue should vary from eight inches to twelve inches square, or more, according to the number of persons who are to sleep in the room.

The time when ventilation is most difficult is the medium weather in spring and fall, when the air, though damp, is similar in temperature outside and in. Then the warm-air flue is indispensable to proper ventilation. This is especially needed in a room used for school or church purposes.

Every room should have its air regulated not only as to its warmth and purity, but also as to its supply of moisture; and for this purpose will be found very convenient the instrument called the hygrodeik,* which shows at once the temperature and the moisture.

The preceding remarks illustrate the advantages of the cottage plan in respect to healthful ventilation. The economy of the mode of warming next demands attention. In the first place, it should be noted that the chimney being at the centre of the house, no heat is lost by its radiation through outside walls into open air, as is the case with all fire-places and grates that have their backs and flues joined to an outside wall.

In this plan all the radiated heat from the stove serves to warm the walls of adjacent rooms in cold weather; while in the warm season the non-conducting summer casings of the stove described in the next chapter send all the heat either into the exhausting warm-air shaft or into the central cast-iron pipe. In addition, the sliding doors of the stove-room (which should be only six feet high, meeting the partition coming from the ceiling), can be opened in cool days, and then the heat from the stove would temper the rooms each side of the kitchen. In hot weather they could be kept closed, except when the stove is used, and then opened only for a short time. The Franklin stoves in the large room would give the radiating warmth and cheerful blaze of an

* It is manufactured by N. M. Lowe, Boston, and sold by him and J. Queen & Co., Philadelphia.

open fire, while radiating heat also from all their surfaces. In cold weather the air of the larger chambers could be tempered by registers admitting warm air from the stove-room, which would always be sufficiently moistened by evaporation from the stationary boiler. The conservatories in winter, protected from frost by double sashes, would contribute agreeable moisture to the larger rooms. In case the size of a family required more rooms, another story could be ventilated and warmed by the same mode, with little additional expense.

We will next notice the economy of time, labor, and expense secured by this cottage plan. The laundry work being done in the basement, all the cooking, dish-washing, etc., can be done in the kitchen and stove-room on the ground-floor. But in case a larger kitchen is needed, the lounges can be put in the front part of the large room, and the movable screen placed so as to give a work-room adjacent to the kitchen, and the front side of the same be used for the eating-room. Where the movable screen is used, the floor should be oiled wood. A square piece of carpet can be put in the centre of the front part of the room, to keep the feet warm when sitting around the table, and small rugs can be placed before the lounges or other sitting-places, for the same purpose.

Most cottages are so divided by entries, stairs, closets, etc., that there can be no large rooms. But in this plan, by the use of the movable screen, two fine large rooms can be secured whenever the family work is over, while the conveniences for work will very much lessen the time required.

In certain cases, where the closest economy is needful, two small families can occupy the cottage, by having a movable screen in both rooms, and using the kitchen in common, or divide it and have two smaller stoves. Each kitchen will then have a window, and as much room as is given to the kitchen in great steamers that provide for several hundred.

Whoever plans a house with a view to economy must arrange rooms around a central chimney, and avoid all projecting appendages. Dormer-windows are far more expensive than common ones, and are less pleasant. Every addition projecting from a main building greatly increases expense of building, and still more of warming and ventilating.

It should be introduced, as one school exercise in every female seminary, to plan houses with reference to economy of time, labor, and expense, and also with reference to good architectural taste; and the teacher should be qualified to point out faults and give the instruction needed to prevent such mistakes in practical life. Every girl should be trained to be "a wise woman" that "buildeth her house" aright.

There is but one mode of ventilation yet tried that will, at all seasons of the year and all hours of the day and night, secure pure air without dangerous draughts, and that is by an exhausting warm-air flue. This is always secured by an open fire-place, so long as its chimney is kept warm by any fire. And in many cases, a fire-place with a flue of a certain dimension and height will secure good ventilation, *except* when the air without and within is at the same temperature.

When no exhausting warm-air flue can be used, the opening of doors and windows is the only resort. Every sleeping-room *without a fire-place that draws smoke well* should have a window raised at the bottom or sunk at the top at least an inch, with an inclined shelf outside or in, to keep out rain, and then it is properly ventilated, provided the air outside is colder than the inside air—but not otherwise. Or a door should be kept opened into a hall with an open window. Let the bed-clothing be increased, so as to keep warm in bed, and protect the head also, and then the more air comes into a sleeping-room the better for health.

In reference to the warming of rooms and houses already built, there is no doubt that stoves are the most economical mode, as they radiate heat and also warm by convection. The grand objection to their use is the difficulty of securing proper ventilation. If a room is well warmed by a stove, and then several small openings made for the entrance of a good supply of outdoor air, and by a mode that will prevent dangerous draughts, all is right as to pure air. But in this case the feet are always on cold floors, surrounded by the coldest air, while the head is in air of much higher temperature.

The writer believes that ere long the common mode of warming by furnaces will be banished as most pernicious to health, and constant sources of discomfort and economic waste. The reasons for this demand reference to some of the principles of pneumatics.

It has been shown how the air is heated by *convection*, or changing contact. It is thus the atmosphere is warmed, not by the rays of the sun passing through it, but by contact with the earth and other objects which have been warmed by radiated heat from the sun. The lower stratum of air being thus warmed, becomes lighter, and ascends, giving place to the cooler and heavier air. This process continues, so that the warmest air is always nearest the earth, and grows cooler as height increases.

The air has a strong attraction for water, and always holds a certain quantity as an invisible vapor. The warmer the air the more water it demands, and will draw it from all objects it can reach. When air cools, it deposits its invisible moisture as dew. When the air has all the water it can hold, it is said to be *saturated;* and when it cools so as to begin to deposit moisture, it is called the *dew point.*

When air holds all the moisture it can sustain, its moisture is said to be at 100 per cent.; when it holds only one-half as much as its temperature demands, it is said to be at 50 per cent.; and when it holds three-fourths of what its temperature requires, it is at 75 per cent.; and when only one-fourth, it holds 25 per cent.

In summer, outdoor air rarely holds less than half its *volume* of water; that is, a quart of air usually holds as much as a pint of invisible vapor. In 1838, at Harvard and Yale, at 70° Fahrenheit, the air held 80 per cent. of moisture; at New Orleans it often holds 90 per cent.; at the North, in fogs, the air often holds all it can, or is saturated—that is, holding 100 per cent. Thus it appears that the hotter the air, the more water is demanded by it for invisible vapor, and this it takes from all around.

Professor Bremer, of Yale College, states that 40 per cent. of moisture is needed to make air healthful. Now furnaces receive cold air containing little invisible moisture, and by heating it a demand is created for much more. This is sucked up, as by a sponge, from walls and furniture, and especially from the lungs and capillaries of our bodies, thus causing dryness and sometimes inflammation of lips, nose, eyes, throat, and lungs. Experiments prove that while 40 per cent. of moisture is needed for health, furnace-heated air rarely has as much as 20 per cent., even when a few quarts of water are evaporated in the furnace chamber. Thus the inmates of the house breathe dryer air than is ever breathed in the hottest deserts of Sahara.

Thus, for want of proper instruction, most American housekeepers who use stoves and furnaces not only poison their families with carbonic acid and carbonic oxide, and starve them for want of oxygen, but also diminish health and comfort for want of a due supply of moisture in the air. And often when a remedy is sought, by evaporating water in the furnace, or on the stove, it is without knowing that the amount evaporated depends, not on the quantity of water in the vessel, but on the extent of evaporating surface exposed to the air. A quart of water in a wide shallow pan will give more moisture than two gallons with a small surface exposed to heat.

There is also no little wise economy in keeping a proper supply of moisture in the air. For it is found that the body radiates its heat less in moist than in dry air, so that a person feels as warm at a lower temperature when the air has a proper supply of moisture, as in a much higher temperature of dry air. Of course, less fuel is needed to warm a house when water is evaporated in stove and furnace-heated rooms. It is said by those who have experimented, that the saving in fuel is twenty per cent. when the air is duly supplied with moisture.

There are other difficulties connected with furnaces which should be considered.

The human body is constantly radiating its heat to walls, floors, and cooler bodies around. At the same time, a thermometer is affected in the same way, radiating its heat to cooler bodies around, so that it always marks a lower degree of heat than actually exists in the warm air around it. Owing to these facts, the injected air of a furnace is always warmer than is good for the lungs, and much warmer than is ever needed in rooms warmed by radiation from fires or heated surfaces. The cooler the air we inspire, the more oxygen is received, the faster the blood circulates, and the greater is the vigor imparted to brain, nerves, and muscles.

Every woman ought to know all the dangers connected with furnaces and how to remedy them. The following may aid in this duty:

When a furnace does not draw well, it often is owing to the stoppage by fine ashes or soot, and then the smoke-flues must be cleaned. The fewer and more simple the smoke-flues the less this trouble will occur. Sometimes the shaking of a furnace makes cracks in joints, and this causes outflow of gas and also diminishes the draught.

When iron is very hot, it burns the particles floating in the air, making an unpleasant smell and dryness. A large furnace, therefore, is better than a small one that must be kept very hot.

Water should be evaporated in large surfaces, and so as to deposit dew on windows.

Heated air passes off by the shortest courses, and it is often the case that the more distant rooms thus warmed have no ventilation and little renewal from the furnace air, and this is often shown by a fetid smell.

Furnaces where air is heated in the furnace-chamber by coils of steam or by hot water, though costing more at first, require much less fuel, and do not involve the evils of warming by hot iron.

The safest and pleasantest way of warming a dwelling is by steam-coils, provided there are fire-places or hot-air flues to carry off bad air. Without these, this is the most unhealthful mode of all, as there is no fresh air brought in, and what is heated is breathed over and over, till it is poisonous.

The want of care in regulating the dampers of the air-box often makes a house cold, however great the furnace fire. A strong wind requires the dampers nearly closed, especially when it is on the side where the air enters from without. Every furnace should be supplied, not by cellar air, but by air taken through a shaft from a height, and so more pure.

Remember that an open fire, or an opening into a hot-air flue, will ventilate properly in all seasons and all weathers. The opening should be at both the top and bottom of the room.

CHAPTER V.

ON STOVES AND CHIMNEYS.

The simplest mode of warming a house and cooking food is by radiated heat from fires; but this is the most wasteful method, as respects time, labor, and expense. The most convenient, economical, and labor-saving mode of employing heat is by *convection*, as applied in stoves and furnaces; but for want of proper care and scientific knowledge this method has proved very destructive to health. When warming and cooking were done by open fires, houses were well supplied with pure air, as is rarely the case in rooms heated by stoves; for such is the prevailing ignorance on this subject, that as long as stoves save labor and warm the air, the great majority of people, especially among the ignorant, will use them in ways that involve debilitated constitutions and frequent disease.

The most common modes of cooking, where open fires are relinquished, are by the range and the cooking-stove. The range is inferior to the stove in these respects: it is less economical, demanding much more fuel; it endangers the dress of the cook while standing near for various operations; it requires more stooping than the stove while cooking; it will not keep a fire all night, as do the best stoves; it will not burn wood and coal equally well; and lastly, if it warms the kitchen sufficiently in winter, it is too warm for summer. Some prefer it because the fumes of cooking can be carried off; but stoves properly arranged accomplish this equally well.

After extensive inquiry and many personal experiments, the author has found a cooking-stove constructed on true scientific principles, which unites convenience, comfort, and economy, in a remarkable manner; and this is the one referred to in the kitchen of the cottage described in Chapter IV. Of this stove drawings and descriptions will now be given, as the best mode of illustrating the practical applications of these principles to the art of cooking, and to show how much American women have suffered, and how much they have been imposed upon for want of proper knowledge in this branch of their profession. And every woman can understand what follows with much less effort than young girls at high-schools give to the first problems of Geometry —for which they will never have any practical use, while attention to this problem of home affairs will cultivate the in-

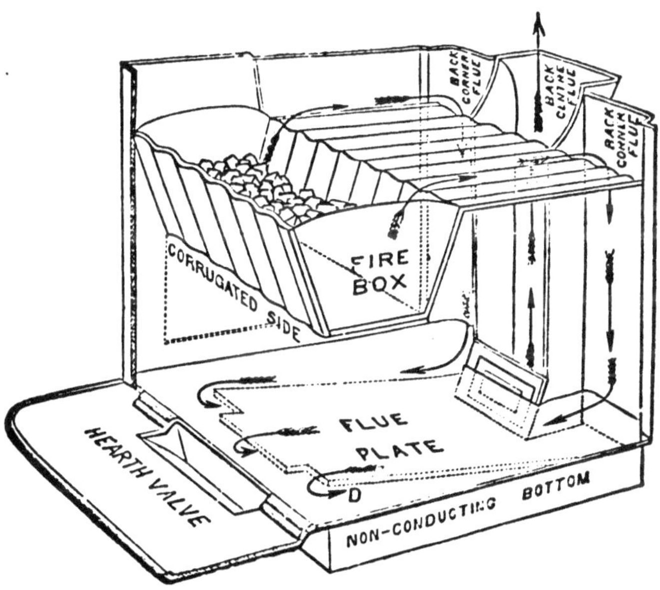

tellect quite as much as the abstract reasonings of Algebra and Geometry.

Fig. 36 represents a portion of the interior of this cooking-stove. First, notice the fire-box, which has corrugated (literally, wrinkled) sides, by which space is economized, so that as much heating surface is secured as if they were one-third larger; for the heat radiates from every part of the undulating surface, which is one-third greater in superficial extent than if it were plane. The shape of the fire-box also secures more heat by having oblique sides—which radiate more effectively into the oven beneath than if they were perpendicular, as illustrated by Figs. 37 and 38. It is also sunk into the oven, so as to radiate from three instead of from two sides. In most other stoves, the front of the fire-boxes with their grates are built so as to be the front of the stove itself, and radiate outward chiefly.

Fig. 37.

Model Stove.

Fig. 38.

Ordinary Stove.

The oven is the space under and around the back and front sides of the fire-box. The oven-bottom is not introduced in the diagram, but it is a horizontal plate between the fire-box and what is represented as the "flue-plate," which separates the oven from the bottom of the stove. The top of the oven is the horizontal corrugated plate passing from the rear edge of the fire-box to the back flues. These flues are three in number—the back centre-flue, which is closed to the heat and smoke coming over the oven from the fire-box by a damper, and the two back corner-flues. Down these two corner-flues passes the current of hot air and smoke, having first drawn across the corrugated oven-top. The arrows show its descent through these flues, from which it obliquely strikes and passes over the flue-plate, then under it, and then out through the centre back-flue, which is open at the bottom, up into the smoke-pipe.

The flue-plate is placed obliquely, to accumulate heat by forcing and compression; for the back space where the smoke enters from the corner-flues is largest, and decreases toward the front, so that the hot current is compressed in a narrow space, between the oven-bottom and the flue-plate at the place where the bent arrows are seen. Here again it enters a wider space, under the flue-plate, and proceeds to another narrow one, between the flue-plate and the bottom of the stove, and thus is compressed and retained longer than if not impeded by these various contrivances. The heat and smoke also strike the plate obliquely, and thus, by reflection from its surface, impart more heat than if the passage was a horizontal one.

The external radiation is regulated by the use of non-conducting plaster applied to the flue-plate and to the sides of the corner-flues, so that the heat is prevented from radiating in any direction except toward the oven. The doors, sides, and bottom of the stove are lined with tin casings, which hold a stratum of air which is a non-conductor. These casings are so arranged as to be removed whenever the weather becomes cold, so that the heat may then radiate into the kitchen. The outer edges of the oven are also similarly protected from loss of heat by tin casings and air-spaces, and the oven doors opening at the front of the stove are provided with the same economical savers of heat. High tin covers placed on the top prevent the heat from radiating from the top of the stove. These are exceedingly useful, as the space under them is well heated and arranged for baking, for heating irons, and many other incidental necessities. Cake and pies can be baked on the top, while the oven is used for bread or for meats. When all the casings and covers are on, almost all the heat is confined within the stove; and whenever heat for the room is wanted, opening the front oven doors turns it out into the kitchen.

Another contrivance is that of ventilating-holes in the front doors, through which fresh air is brought into the oven. This secures several purposes: it carries off the fumes of cooking meats, and prevents the mixing of flavors when different articles are cooked in the oven; it drives the heat that accumulates between the fire-box and front doors down around the oven, and equalizes its heat, so that articles need not be moved while baking; and lastly, as the air passes through the holes of the fire-box, it causes the burning of gases in the smoke, and thus increases heat. When wood or bituminous coal is used, perforated metal linings are put in the fire-box, and the result is the burning of smoke and gases that otherwise would pass into the chimney. This is a great discovery in the economy of fuel, which can be applied in many ways.

Heretofore most cooking-stoves have had dumping-grates,

which are inconvenient from the dust produced, are uneconomical in the use of fuel, and disadvantageous from too many or too loose joints. But recently this stove has been provided with a dumping-grate which also will sift ashes, and can be cleaned without dust and the other objectionable features of most dumping-grates.

Those who are taught to manage the stove properly keep the fire going all night, and equally well with wood or coal, thus saving the expense of kindling and the trouble of starting a new fire. When the fuel is of good quality, all that is needed in the morning is to draw the back-damper, shake the grate, and add more fuel.

Another remarkable feature of this stove is the extension-top, on which is placed a water reservoir, constantly heated by the smoke as it passes from the stove, through one or two uniting passages, to the smoke-pipe. Under this is placed a closet for warming and keeping hot the dishes, vegetables, meats, etc., while preparing for dinner. It is also very useful in drying fruit; and when large baking is required, a small appended pot for charcoal turns it into a fine large oven, that bakes as nicely as a brick oven.

Another useful appendage is a common tin oven, in which roasting can be done in front of the stove, the oven doors being removed for the purpose. The roast will be done as perfectly as by an open fire.

This stove is furnished with pipes for heating water, like the water-back of ranges, and these can be taken or left out at pleasure. So also the top covers, the baking stool and pot, and the summer-back, bottom, and side-casings can be used or omitted as preferred.

Fig. 39 exhibits the stove completed, with all its appendages, as they might be employed in cooking for a large family.

Its capacity, convenience, and economy as a stove may be estimated by the following fact: With proper management of dampers, one ordinary-sized coal-hod of anthracite coal will, for twenty-four hours, keep the stove running, keep seventeen gallons of water hot at all hours, bake pies and puddings in the warm closet, heat flat-irons under the back

Fig. 39.

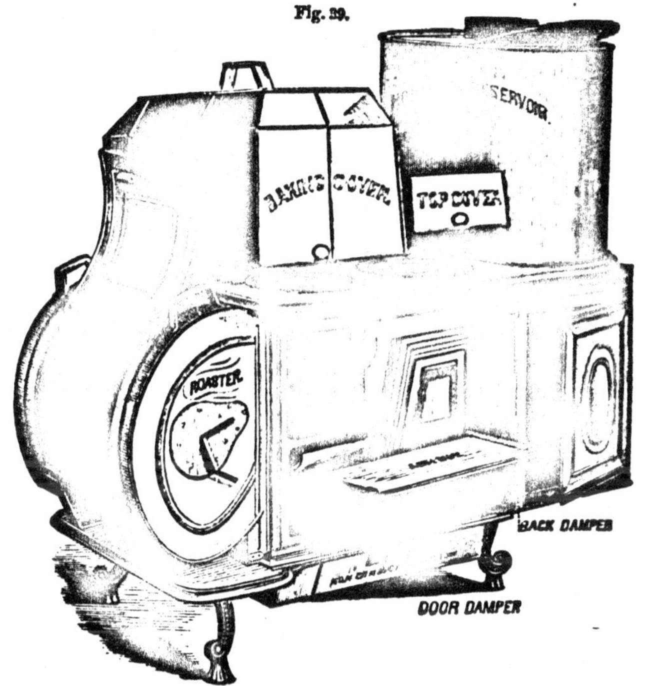

cover, boil tea-kettle and one pot under the front cover, bake bread in the oven, and cook a turkey in the tin roaster in front. The author has numerous friends who, after trying the best ranges, have dismissed them for this stove, and in two or three years cleared the whole expense by the saving of fuel.

The remarkable durability of this stove is another economic feature; for, in addition to its fine castings and nice-fitting workmanship, all the parts liable to burn out are so protected by linings, and other contrivances easily renewed, that the stove itself may pass from one generation to another, as do ordinary chimneys. The writer has visited in families where this stove had been in constant use for eighteen and twenty years, and was still as good as new. In most other families the stoves are broken, burned out, or thrown aside for improved patterns every four, five, or six years, and sometimes, to the knowledge of the writer, still oftener.

Another excellent point is that, although it is so complicated in its various contrivances as to demand intelligent management in order to secure all its advantages, it also can be used satisfactorily even when the mistress and maid are equally careless and ignorant of its distinctive merits. To such it offers all the advantages of ordinary good stoves, and is extensively used by those who take no pains to understand and apply its peculiar advantages.

But the writer has managed the stove herself in all the details of cooking, and is confident that any housekeeper of common sense who is instructed properly, and who also aims to have her kitchen affairs managed with strict economy, can easily train any servant who is willing to learn, so as to gain the full advantages offered. And even without any instructions at all except the printed directions sent with the stove, an intelligent woman can, by due attention, though not without, both manage it, and teach her children and servants to do likewise. And whenever this stove has failed to give the highest satisfaction, it has been either because the draught of the chimney was poor, or because the housekeeper was not apprised of its peculiarities, or because she did not give sufficient attention to the matter, or was not able or willing to superintend and direct its management.

The consequence has been that, in families where this stove has been understood and managed aright, it has saved nearly one-half of the fuel that would be used in ordinary stoves, constructed with the usual disregard of scientific and economic laws. And it is because we know this particular stove to be convenient, reliable, and economically efficient beyond ordinary experience, in the important housekeeping element of kitchen labor, that we devote to it so much space and pains to describe its advantageous points.*

* A letter to the author, inclosing twenty-five cents for expense of time and correspondence, will secure a circular with further account and directions for using this stove. Direct—Care of Dr. G. H. Taylor, New York city.

CHIMNEYS.

One of the most serious evils in domestic life is often found in chimneys that will not properly draw the smoke of a fire or stove. Although chimneys have been building for a thousand years, the artisans of the present day seem strangely ignorant of the true method of constructing them so as always to carry smoke upward instead of downward. It is rarely the case that a large house is built in which there is not some flue or chimney which "will not draw." One of the reasons why the stove described as excelling all others is sometimes cast aside for a poorer one is, that it requires a properly constructed chimney, and multitudes of women do not know how to secure it. The writer in early life shed many a bitter tear, drawn forth by smoke from an ill-constructed kitchen-chimney, and thousands all over the land can report the same experience.

The following are some of the causes and the remedies for this evil:

The most common cause of poor chimney draughts is too large an opening for the fire-place, either too wide or too high in front, or having too large a throat for the smoke. In a lower story, the fire-place should not be larger than thirty inches wide, twenty-five inches high, and fifteen deep. In the story above, it should be eighteen inches square and fifteen inches deep.

Another cause is too short a flue, and the remedy is to lengthen it. As a general rule, the longer the flue the stronger the draught; but in calculating the length of a flue, reference must be had to side-flues, if any open into it. Where this is the case, the length of the main flue is to be considered as extending only from the bottom to the point where the upper flue joins it, and where the lower flue will receive air from the upper side flue. If a smoky flue can not be increased in length, either by closing an upper flue or lengthening the chimney, the fire-place must be contracted so that all the air near the fire will be heated and thus pressed upward.

If a flue has more than one opening, in some cases it is

impossible to secure a good draught. Sometimes it will work well, and sometimes it will not. The only safe rule is to have a separate flue to each fire.

Another cause of poor draughts is too tight a room, so that the cold air from without can not enter to press the warm air up the chimney. The remedy is to admit a small current of air from without.

Another cause is two chimneys in one room, or in rooms opening together, in which the draught in one is much stronger than in the other. In this case the stronger draught will draw away from the weaker. The remedy is, for each room to have a proper supply of outside air; or, in a single room, to stop one of the chimneys.

Another cause is the too close vicinity of a hill or buildings higher than the top of the chimney, and the remedy for this is to raise the chimney.

Another cause is the descent into unused fire-places of smoke from other chimneys near. The remedy is to close the throat of the unused chimney.

Another cause is a door opening toward the fire-place on the same side of the room, so that its draught passes along the wall and makes a current that draws out the smoke. The remedy is to change the hanging of the door, so as to open another way.

Another cause is strong winds. The remedy is a turn-cap on top of the chimney.

Another cause is the roughness of the inside of a chimney, or projections which impede the passage of the smoke. Every chimney should be built of equal dimensions from bottom to top, with no projections into it, with as few bends as possible, and with the surface of the inside as smooth as possible.

Another cause of poor draughts is openings into the chimney of chambers for stove-pipes. The remedy is to close them, or insert stove-pipes that are in use.

Another cause is the falling out of brick in some part of the chimney so that outer air is admitted. The remedy is to close the opening.

The draught of a stove may be affected by most of these

causes. It also demands that the fire-place have a tight fire-board, or that the throat be carefully filled. For neglecting this, many a good stove has been thrown aside and a poor one taken in its place.

If all young women had committed to memory these causes of evil and their remedies, many a badly-built chimney might have been cured, and many smoke-drawn tears, sighs, ill tempers, and irritating words avoided.

But there are dangers in this direction which demand special attention. Where one flue has two stoves or fire-places, in rooms one above the other, in certain states of the atmosphere, the lower room being the warmer, the colder air and carbonic acid in the room above will pass down into the lower room through the opening for the stove or the fire-place.

This occurred not long since in a boarding-school, when the gas in a room above flowed into a lower one, and suffocated several to death. This room had no mode of ventilation, and several persons slept in it, and were thus stifled. Professor Brewer states a similar case in the family of a relative. An anthracite stove was used in the upper room; and on one still, close night, the gas from this stove descended through the flue and the opening into a room below, and stifled the sleepers.

CHAPTER VI.

ECONOMIC MODES OF BEAUTIFYING A HOME.

THE educating influence of works of natural beauty and of art can hardly be overestimated. Surrounded by such suggestions of the beautiful, and such reminders of history and art, children are constantly trained to correctness of taste and refinement of thought, and stimulated—sometimes to efforts at artistic imitation, always to the eager and intelligent inquiry about the scenes, the places, the incidents represented.

Just here, perhaps, we are met by some who impatiently exclaim, "But I have *no* money to spare for any thing of this sort. I am condemned to an absolute bareness, and beauty in my case is not to be thought of." It is for such that some economic modes of beautifying a home are here suggested.

Fig. 40.

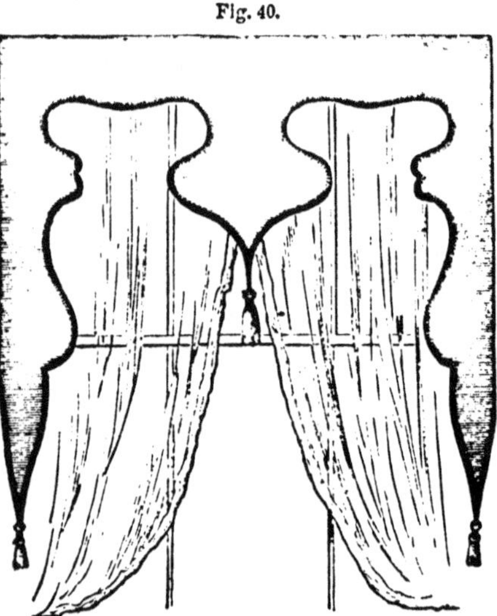

The cornices to your windows can be simply strips of wood covered with paper to match the bordering of your room, and the lambrequins, made of chintz like the lounge, could be trimmed with fringe or gimp of the same color. The patterns of these can be varied according to fancy, but simple designs are usually the prettiest. A tassel at

Fig. 41.

the lowest point greatly improves the appearance of the entire curtain.

The curtains can be made of plain white muslin, or some of the many styles that come for this purpose. If plain muslin is used, you can ornament them with hems an inch in width, in which insert a strip of gingham or chambray of the same color as your chintz. This will wash with the curtain without losing its color, or, should it fade, it can easily be drawn out and replaced.

The influence of white-muslin curtains in giving an air of grace and elegance to a room is astonishing. White curtains really create a room out of nothing. No matter how coarse the muslin, so it be white and hang in graceful folds there is a charm in it that supplies the want of multitude of other things.

The following is a sketch of a most attractive parlor, the owners being persons of taste and culture, and visited by the most wealthy and refined class, who are always delighted with its light, comfort, and beauty. In this parlor is the window, Fig. 40, page 192, with its lambrequins, and the window covered with flowers and greens, Fig. 41.

A straw matting, used six years, and still good.

Cheap drab-colored rugs, bordered with green, in front of the fire and under the centre-table. The cheap wall-paper is drab and green, with heavy green border for cornice. On one side is this window adorned with creepers, brackets with flower-pots, and hanging-baskets, as at Fig. 41, page 19 The other (see Fig. 40) window has lambrequins made of an old green worsted dress lined with coarse unbleached cotton trimmed with green gimp, and the tassels home-made from remnants of the old green dress. Cheap white lace with broad hems, in which strips of the green dress are drawn complete the window outfit.

On one side of the fire-place is a lounge made as illustrated by Fig. 16, page 139; and ottomans around are also made as illustrated in the same chapter. All are covered with drab cotton cloth, and trimmed with green.

Six chairs bought unpainted, and by the mistress of the house painted drab and green. Chromos and engravings i

Fig. 42.

cheap and tasteful frames, as illustrated in Figs. 42 and 43, adorn the walls, and German ivy and hanging-baskets of greens and flowers are in all tasteful arrangements. In cool weather a bright fire of dried walnut invites to a social gathering around its hospitable gleams, the fire-place being an open Franklin stove, so placed that its hearth is on a level with the floor, that there may be no cold feet. Such a stove unites economy with beauty and comfort. A prime charm of this room is its southern exposure, securing sunshine all the year, never shut out with shades or blinds except in the hottest days.

Fig. 43.

This lovely parlor was furnished with pictures and every other article for less than a hundred dollars, and was more beautiful and enjoyable than many of those which have demanded thousands for their outfit.

As a means of educating the ingenuity and the taste, you can make for yourselves pretty rustic frames in various modes. Take a very thin board, of the right size and shape, for the foundation or "mat;" saw out the inner oval or rectangular form to suit the picture. Nail on the edge a rustic frame made of branches of hard, seasoned wood, and garnish the corners with some pretty device; such, for instance, as a cluster of acorns; or, in place of the branches of trees, fasten on with glue small pine cones, with larger ones for corner ornaments. Or use the mosses of the wood or ocean shells for this purpose. It may be more convenient to get the mat or inner molding from a framer, or have it made by your carpenter, with a groove behind to hold a glass.

If you have in the house any broken-down arm-chair reposing in the oblivion of the garret, draw it out—drive a

Fig. 44.

nail here and there to hold it firm—stuff and pad, and stitch the padding through with a long upholsterer's needle, and cover it with the chintz like your other furniture and you create an easy-chair.

An ox-muzzle, flattened on one side and nailed to a board, as in Fig. 44, filled with spongy moss and feathery ferns, makes a lovely ornament; while suspended baskets holding cups or bowls of soil filled with drooping plants is another cheap ornament. A Ward case, which any ingenious boy can make of pine and common glass, is shown on the table at Fig. 41, page 193. It is a great source of enjoyment to children and invalids. The box at the bottom is to be lined with zinc, and have a hole for drainage covered with an inverted saucer, and there must be a door at one end. The soil must consist of broken charcoal at bottom, two inches deep, and over this some soil made of one-fourth fine sand, one-fourth meadow soil from under fresh turf, and two-fourths wood soil from under forest-trees. In this plant all sorts of ferns and swamp grasses, and make a border of money-plant or periwin-

Fig. 45.

kle. A bit of looking-glass, some shells, and bits of rock with a variety of mosses, flowers, and ferns that grow in the shade, can lend variety and beauty. When watering, set a pail under for it to drip intó. It needs only to keep this moss always damp, and to sprinkle these ferns occasionally with a whisk-broom, to have a most lovely ornament for your room or hall.

An old tin pan, painted green, with holes in the bottom, thus supplied with soil and ferns, makes a pretty parlor ornament. Or, take a salt-box or fig-box, and fill them with soil and plants, and use for hanging-baskets. The Ward case needs watering only once in two weeks, and most of these plants grow without sun in north windows. The fuchsias flourish also in the shade, as do striped spider-wort, smilax, saxifrage, and samentosa or Wandering Jew. German ivy growing in suspended bottles of water is a cheap ornament, and slips of nasturtions and verbenas will grow in north windows all winter. A sponge filled with flax-seed, hung by a cord and kept wet, is another cheap ornament, as is also a carrot scooped out, after the small part is cut out and hung up, till its tall, graceful shoots will mingle with flowers placed in it. A sweet-potato in a bowl of water, or suspended by a knitting-needle run through it and laid in a bowl half full of water, makes a verdant ornament. The flowers for a Ward case, in a room without sun, are, ground pine, prince's pine, trailing arbutus, partridge-berry, eyebrights, mosses. Fig. 45 is a stand for flowers, made of roots scraped and varnished.

Much of the beauty of furniture is secured by the tasteful combination of colors. There usually should be only two colors in addition to the white of the ceiling. Blue unites well with buff or corn color, or a yellow brown. Green combines well with drab, or white, or yellow. Scarlet or crimson unites well with gray or drab.

Those who cultivate parlor plants need these cautions: Too much water and want of fresh air make plants grow pale and spindling; so give fresh air every day. Wash leaves when covered with dust. Change soil once a year, or water with liquid manure. Pluck faded flowers, as much strength of a plant goes to make seed. Pick off fading green leaves. If flowers are wanted, use small pots. Do not shut out the sun, which human beings need as much as flowers. Use oil-cloth similar to the carpet, where flowers and sun abound. Shut out flies with wire netting in open windows, and also doors of the same. It costs much less than ill health and mournfully darkened rooms.

CHAPTER VII.

CARE OF HEALTH.

THERE is no point where a woman is more liable to suffer from a want of knowledge and experience than in reference to the health of a family committed to her care. Many a young lady who never had any charge of the sick; who never took any care of an infant; who never obtained information on these subjects from books, or from the experience of others; in short, with little or no preparation, has found herself the principal attendant in dangerous sickness, the chief nurse of a feeble infant, and the responsible guardian of the health of a whole family.

The care, the fear, the perplexity of a woman suddenly called to these unwonted duties, none can realize till they themselves feel it, or till they see some young and anxious novice first attempting to meet such responsibilities. To a woman of age and experience these duties often involve a measure of trial and difficulty at times deemed almost insupportable; how hard, then, must they press on the heart of the young and inexperienced!

There is no really efficacious mode of preparing a woman to take a rational care of the health of a family, except by communicating that knowledge in regard to the construction of the body and the laws of health which is the basis of the medical profession. Not that a woman should undertake the minute and extensive investigation requisite for a physician; but she should gain a general knowledge of first principles, as a guide to her judgment in emergencies when she can rely on no other aid.

With this end in view, in the preceding chapters some portions of the organs and functions of the human body have been presented, and others will now follow in connection with the practical duties which result from them.

On the general subject of health, one recent discovery of

science may here be introduced as having an important relation to every organ and function of the body, and as being one to which frequent reference will be made; and that is, the nature and operation of *cell-life.*

By the aid of the microscope, we can examine the minute construction of plants and animals, in which we discover contrivances and operations, if not so sublime, yet more wonderful and interesting, than the vast systems of worlds revealed by the telescope.

By this instrument it is now seen that the first formation, as well as future changes and actions, of all plants and animals are accomplished by means of small cells or bags containing various kinds of liquids. These cells are so minute that, of the smallest, some hundreds would not cover the dot of a printed *i* on this page. They are of diverse shapes and contents, and perform various different operations.

Fig. 46.

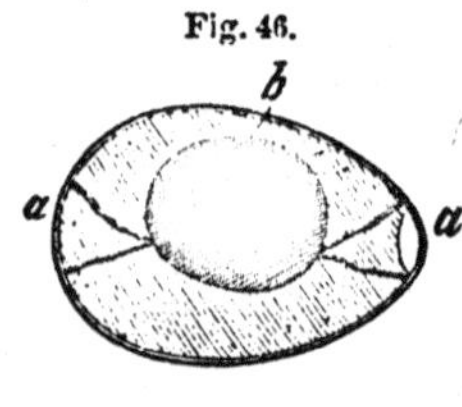

The first formation of every animal is accomplished by the agency of cells, and may be illustrated by the egg of any bird or fowl. The exterior consists of a hard shell for protection, and this is lined with a tough skin, to which is fastened the yelk, (which means the *yellow,*) by fibrous strings, as seen at *a*, *a*, in the diagram. In the yelk floats the germ-cell, *b*, which is the point where the formation of the future animal commences. The yelk, being lighter than the white, rises upward, and the germ being still lighter, rises in the yelk. This is to bring both nearer to the vitalizing warmth of the brooding mother.

New cells are gradually formed from the nourishing yelk around the germ, each being at first roundish in shape, and having a spot near the centre, called the nucleus. The reason why cells increase must remain a mystery until we can penetrate the secrets of vital force—probably forever. But the mode in which they multiply is as follows: The first change noticed in a cell, when warmed into vital activity, is the appearance of a second nucleus within it, while the cell gradually becomes oval in form, and then is drawn inward at the middle, like an hour-glass, till the two sides meet. The two portions then divide, and two cells appear, each containing its own germinal nucleus. These both divide again in the same manner, proceeding in the ratio of 2, 4, 8, 16, and so on, until most of the yelk becomes a mass of cells.

The central point of this mass, where the animal itself commences to appear, shows, first, a round-shaped figure, which soon assumes form like a pear, and then like a violin. Gradually the busy little cells arrange themselves to build up heart, lungs, brain, stomach, and limbs, for which the yelk and white furnish nutriment. There is a small bag of air fastened to one end inside of the shell; and when the animal is complete, this air is taken into its lungs, life begins, and out walks little chick, all its powers prepared, and ready to run, eat, and enjoy existence. Then, as soon as the animal uses its brain to think and feel, and its muscles to move, the cells which have been made up into these parts begin to decay, while new cells are formed from the blood to take their place. Thus with life commences the constant process of decay and renewal all over the body.

The liquid portion of the blood consists of material formed from food, air, and water. From this material the cells of the blood are formed: first, the white cells, which are incomplete in formation; and then the red cells, which are completed by the addition of the oxygen received from air in the lungs. Fig. 47 represents part of a magnified blood-vessel, *a*, *a*, in which the round cells are the white, and the oblong the red cells, floating in the blood. Surrounding the blood-vessels are the cells forming the adjacent membrane, *b b*, each having a nucleus in its centre.

Fig. 47.

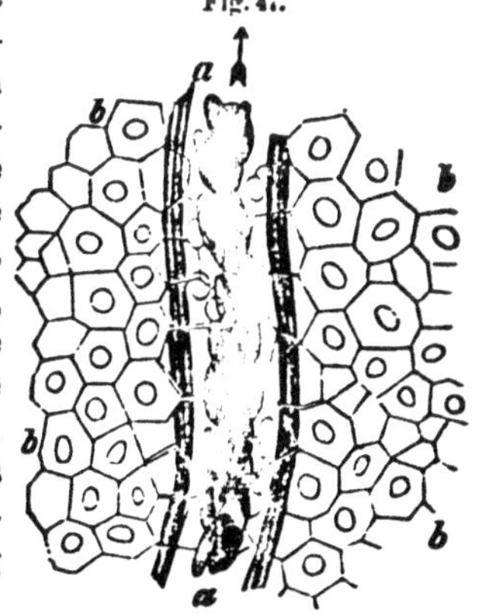

Cells have different powers of selecting and secreting diverse materials from the blood. Thus, some secrete bile to carry to the liver, others secrete saliva for the mouth, others take up the tears, and still others take material for the brain, muscles, and all other organs. Cells also have a converting power—of taking one kind of matter from the blood, and changing it to another kind. They are minute chemical laboratories all over the body, changing materials of one kind to another form in which they can be made useful.

Both animal and vegetable substances are formed of cells. But the vegetable cells take up and use unorganized, or simple, natural matter; whereas the animal cell only takes substances already organized into vegetable or animal life, and then changes one compound into another of different proportions and nature.

These curious facts in regard to cell-life have important relations to the general subject of the care of health, and also to the cure of disease, as will be noticed in following chapters.

THE NERVOUS SYSTEM.

There is another portion of the body which is so intimately connected with every other, that it is placed in this chapter as also having reference to every department in the general subject of the care of health.

The body has no power to move itself, but is a collection of instruments to be used by the mind in securing various kinds of knowledge and enjoyment. The organs through which the mind thus operates are the *brain* and *nerves.* The opposite drawing (Fig. 48) represents them.

The brain lies in the skull, and is divided into the large or upper brain, marked 1, and the small or lower brain, marked 2. From the brain runs the spinal marrow through the spine or backbone. From each side of the spine the large nerves run out into innumerable smaller branches to every portion of the body. The drawing shows only some of the larger branches. Those marked 3 run to the neck and organs of the chest; those marked 4 go to the arms; those below the arms, marked 3, go to the trunk; those marked 5 go to the legs; and the lowest of all go to the pelvic organs.

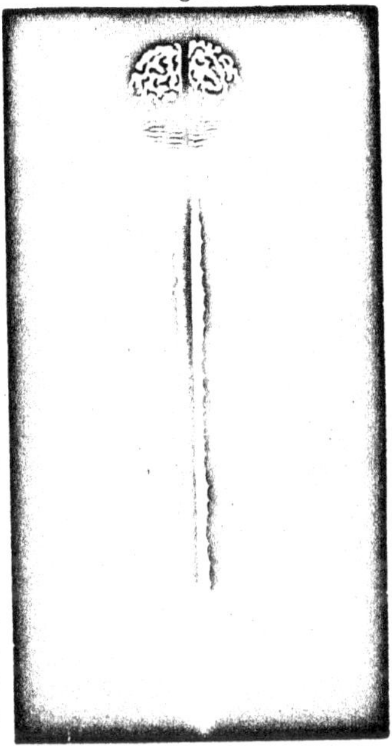

The brain and nerves consist of two kinds of nervous matter — the *gray*, which is supposed to be the portion that originates and controls a nervous fluid which imparts power of action; and the *white*, which seems to conduct this fluid to every part of the body.

Fig. 48.

The brain and nervous system are divided into distinct portions, each having different offices to perform, and each acting independently of the others; as, for example, one portion is employed by the mind in thinking, and in feeling pleasurable or painful mental emotions; another in moving the muscles; while the nerves that run to the nose, ears, eyes, tongue, hands, and surface generally, are employed in seeing, hearing, smelling, tasting, and feeling all physical sensations.

The *back* portion of the spinal marrow and the nerves that run from it are employed in *sensation*, or the *sense of feeling*. These nerves extend over the whole body, but are largely developed in the net-work of nerves in the skin. The *front* portion of the spinal marrow and its branches are employed in moving those muscles in all parts of the body which are controlled by the *will* or *choice* of the mind. These are called the *nerves of motion*.

The nerves of sensation and nerves of motion, although they start from different portions of the spine, are united in the same *sheath* or *cover*, till they terminate in the muscles. Thus, every muscle is moved by nerves of motion; while alongside of this nerve, in the same sheath, is a nerve of sensation. All the nerves of motion and sensation are connected with those portions of the brain used when we think, feel, and choose. By this arrangement the mind *knows* what is wanted in all parts of the body by means of the nerves of sensation, and then it *acts* by means of the nerves of motion.

For example, when we feel the cold air on the skin, the nerves of sensation report to the brain, and thus to the mind, that the body is growing cold. The mind thus knows that more clothing is needed, and *wills* to have the eyes look for it, and the hands and feet move to get it. This is done by the nerves of sight and of motion.

Next are the nerves of *involuntary motion*, which move all those parts of the head, face, and body that are used in breathing, and in other operations connected with it. By these we continue to breathe when asleep, and whether we will to do so or not. There are also some of the nerves of voluntary motion that are mixed with these, which enable the mind to stop respiration, or to regulate it to a certain extent. But the mind has no power to stop it for any great length of time.

There is another large and important system of nerves called the *sympathetic* or *ganglionic* system. It consists of small masses of gray and white nervous matter, that seem to be small brains with nerves running from them. These are called *ganglia*; and are arranged on each side of the spine, while small nerves from the spinal marrow run into them, thus uniting the sympathetic system with the nerves of the spine. These ganglia are also distributed around in various parts of the interior of the body, especially in the intestines, and all the different ganglia are connected with each other by nerves, thus making one system. It is the ganglionic system that carries on the circulation of the blood, the action of the capillaries, lymphatics, arteries, and veins, together with the work of secretion, absorption, and most of the internal working of the body, which goes forward without any knowledge or control of the mind.

Every portion of the body has nerves of sensation coming from the spine, and also branches of the sympathetic or ganglionic system. The object of this is to form a sympathetic communication between the several parts of the body, and also to enable the mind to receive, through the brain, some general knowledge of the state of the whole system. It is owing to this that, when one portion of the body is affected, other portions sympathize. For example, if one part of the body is diseased, the stomach may so sympathize as to lose all appetite until the disease is removed.

All the operations of the nervous system are performed by the influence of the nervous fluid, which is generated in the gray portions of the brain and ganglia. Whenever a nerve is cut off from its connection with these nervous centres, its power is gone, and the part to which it ministered becomes lifeless and incapable of motion.

The brain and nerves can be overworked, and can also suffer for want of exercise, just as the muscles do. It is necessary for the perfect health of the brain and nerves that the several portions be exercised sufficiently, and that no part be exhausted by overaction. For example, the nerves of sensation may be very much exercised, and the nerves of motion have but little exercise. In this case, one will be weakened by excess of work, and the other by the want of it.

It is found by experience that the proper exercise of the nerves of motion tends to reduce any extreme susceptibility of the nerves of sensation. On the contrary, the neglect of such exercise tends to produce an excessive sensibility in the nerves of sensation.

Whenever that part of the brain which is employed in thinking, feeling, and willing, is greatly exercised by hard study, or by excessive care or emotion, the blood tends to the brain to supply it with increased nourishment, just as it flows to the muscles when they are exercised. Over-exercise of this portion of the brain causes engorgement of the blood-vessels. This is sometimes indicated by pain, or by a sense of fullness in the head; but oftener the result is a debilitating drain on the nervous system, which depends for its supply on the healthful state of the brain.

The brain has, as it were, a fountain of supply for the nervous fluid, which flows to all the nerves, and stimulates them to action. Some brains have a larger, and some a smaller fountain; so that a degree of mental activity that would entirely exhaust one, would make only a small and healthful drain upon another.

The excessive use of certain portions of the brain tends to withdraw the nervous energy from other portions; so that when one part is debilitated by excess, another fails by neglect. For example, a person may so exhaust the brain-power in the excessive use of the nerves of motion by hard work, as to leave little for any other faculty. On the other hand, the nerves of feeling and thinking may be so used as to withdraw the nervous fluid from the nerves of motion, and thus debilitate the muscles.

Some animal propensities may be indulged to such excess as to produce a constant tendency of the blood to a certain portion of the brain and to the organs connected with it, and thus cause a constant and excessive excitement, which finally becomes a disease. Sometimes a paralysis of this portion of the brain results from such an entire exhaustion of the nervous fountain and of the overworked nerves.

Thus, also, the thinking portion of the brain may be so overworked as to drain the nervous fluid from other portions, which become debilitated by the loss. And in this way, also, the overworked portion may be diseased or paralyzed by the excess.

Sometimes the intellect and feelings may be confined to one subject so exclusively as to cause mental derangement on that subject when sane in all other respects. This is called a monomania.

The necessity for the *equal development* of all portions of the brain by an appropriate exercise of *all* the faculties of mind and body, and the influence of this upon happiness, is the most important portion of this subject, and will be more directly exhibited in another chapter.

The chief causes of debility of nerves, neuralgia, sciatica, and other diseases of the nerves, are exhaustion of the nervous fountain by excess of study, or of labor, or of mental excitement of *any* kind. All excess of feeling, or of intellectual or physical labor, decreases the nerve centres or fountains of nervous supply. Diseases also, and often medicines, have the same effect.

When the nerves are thus weakened their minute capillaries are not able to send forward the blood, and thus become swollen or congested, and then a change in the nerve substance follows.

The remedy for this is to withdraw the blood from the congested nerves, and this is secured by exercising the muscles, thus drawing the blood from nerves to muscles. When the patient is much debilitated this exercise should be done by an operator, as in the passive exercises of the movement cure; for in such cases the nerves and brain would be still more weakened by *voluntary* exercise of the patient. This shows the great mistake often made by attempts to remedy weak nerves and brain that need rest, by voluntary exercise of the muscles. It also shows the mischief often done in schools where to high intellectual excitement is added vigorous gymnastic exercises.

The chief benefit of the movement cure, especially as conducted by Dr. George Taylor, of New York City, consists in various apparatus invented by him, by which various parts of the body can be exercised while the brain and nerves of the patient are at rest. By these contrivances the congested blood of the capillaries is drawn from the diseased part and all the healthful functions restored, while the patient is at rest as to any voluntary exertion of brain and nerves. When the strength will permit, voluntary exercises adapted to each case are combined with the passive movement effected by an operator:

The following are the effects of the mechanical and involuntary movements by machinery or by an operator:

They produce increased motion of particles, and so increase of absorption and nutrition.

They increase contractile power in the capillaries, and thus remedy congestion.

They direct nervous energy to defective parts and remove obstructions.

They increase respiration, and thus increase the life-giving oxygen and animal heat, while they repress excess in other congested parts.

They increase nutrition, and also the secretion and discharge of morbid matter from diseased or weakened parts.

CHAPTER VIII.

DOMESTIC EXERCISE.

In a work which aims to influence women to train the young to honor domestic labor and to seek healthful exercise in home pursuits, there is special reason for explaining the construction of the muscles and their connection with the nerves, these being the chief organs of motion.

The muscles, as seen by the naked eye, consist of very fine fibres or strings, bound up in smooth, silky casings of thin membrane. But each of these visible fibres or strings the microscope shows to be made up of still finer strings, numbering from five to eight hundred in each fibre. And each of these microscopic fibres is a series or chain of elastic cells, which are so minute that one hundred thousand would scarcely cover a capital O on this page.

The peculiar property of the cells which compose the muscles is their elasticity, no other cells of the body having this property. At Fig. 49 is a diagram representing a microscopic muscular fibre, in which the cells are relaxed, as in

Fig. 49. a

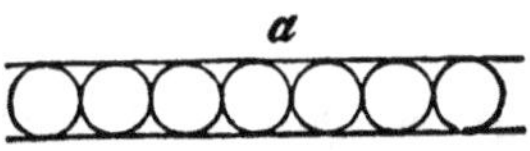

Fig. 50. b

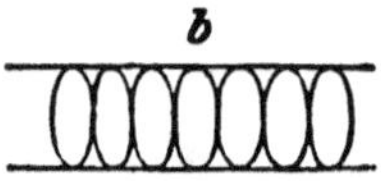

the natural state of rest. But when the muscle contracts, each of its numberless cells in all its small fibres becomes widened, making each fibre of the muscle shorter and thicker, as at Fig. 50. This explains the cause of the swelling out of muscles when they act.

Every motion in every part of the body has a special muscle to produce it, and many have other muscles to restore the part moved to its natural state. The muscles that move or bend any part are called *flexors*, and those that restore the natural position are called *extensors*.

Fig. 51 represents the muscles of the arm after the skin and flesh are removed. They are all in smooth, silky cases, laid over each other, and separated both by the smooth membranes that encase them and by layers of fat, so as to move easily without interfering with each other. They are fastened to the bones by strong tendons and cartilages; and around the wrist, in the drawing, is shown a band of cartilage to confine them in place. The muscle marked 8 is the extensor that straightens the fingers after they have been closed by a flexor on the other side of the arm. In like manner, each motion of the arm and fingers has one muscle to produce it and another to restore to the natural position.

Fig. 51.

The muscles are dependent on the brain and nerves for power to move. It has been shown that the gray matter of the brain and spinal marrow furnishes the stimulating power that moves the muscles, and causes sensations of touch on the skin, and the other sensations of the several senses. The white part of the brain and spinal marrow consists solely of conducting tubes to transmit this influence. Each of the minute fibrils of the muscles has a small conducting nerve connecting it with the brain or spinal marrow, and in this respect each muscular fibril is separate from every other.

When, therefore, the mind wills to move a flexor muscle of the arm, the gray matter sends out the stimulus through the nerves to the cells of each individual fibre of that muscle, and they contract. When this is done, the nerve of sensation reports it to the brain and mind. If the mind desires to return the arm to its former position, then follows the willing, and consequent stimulus sent through the nerves to the corresponding muscle; its cells contract, and the limb is restored.

When the motion is a compound one, involving the action of several muscles at the same time, a multitude of impressions are sent back and forth to and from the brain through the nerves. But the person acting thus is unconscious of all this delicate and wonderful mechanism. He wills the movement, and instantly the requisite nervous power is sent to the required cells and fibres, and they perform the motions required. Many of the muscles are moved by the sympathetic system, over which the mind has but little control.

Among the muscles and nerves so intimately connected run the minute capillaries of the blood, which furnish nourishment to all.

Fig. 52 represents an artery at *a*, which brings pure blood to a muscle from the heart. After meandering through the capillaries at *c*, to distribute oxygen and food from the stomach, the blood enters the vein, *b*, loaded with carbonic acid and water taken up in the capillaries, to be carried to the lungs or skin, and thrown out into the air.

Fig. 52.

The manner in which the exercise of the muscles quickens the circulation of the blood will now be explained. The veins abound in every part of every muscle, and the large veins have *valves* which prevent the blood from flowing backward. If the wrist is grasped tightly, the veins of the hand are immediately swollen. This is owing to the fact that the blood is prevented from flowing toward the heart by this pressure, and by the vein-valves from returning into the arteries; while the arteries themselves, being placed deeper down, are not so compressed, and continue to send the blood into the hand, and thus it accumulates. As soon as this pressure is removed, the blood springs onward from the restraint with accelerated motion. This same process takes place when any of the muscles are exercised. The contraction of any muscle presses some of the veins, so that the blood can not flow the natural way, while the valves in the veins prevent its flowing backward. Meantime the arteries continue to press the blood along until the veins become swollen. Then, as soon as the muscle ceases its contraction, the blood flows faster from the previous accumulation.

If, then, we use a number of muscles, and use them strongly and quickly, there are so many veins affected in this way as to quicken the whole circulation. The heart receives blood faster, and sends it to the lungs faster. Then the lungs work quicker, to furnish the oxygen required by the greater amount of blood. The blood returns with greater speed to the heart, and the heart sends it out with quicker action through the arteries to the capillaries. In the capillaries, too, the decayed matter is carried off faster, and then the stomach calls for more food to furnish new and pure blood. Thus it is that exercise gives new life and nourishment to every part of the body.

It is the universal law of the human frame that *exercise* is indispensable to the health of the several parts. Thus, if a blood-vessel be tied up, so as not to be used, it shrinks, and becomes a useless string; if a muscle be condemned to inaction, it shrinks in size and diminishes in power; and thus it is also with the bones. Inactivity produces softness, debility, and unfitness for the functions they are designed to perform.

Now, the nerves, like all other parts of the body, gain and lose strength according as they are exercised. If they have too much or too little exercise, they lose strength; if they are exercised to a proper degree, they gain strength. When the mind is continuously excited, by business, study, or the imagination, the nerves of emotion and sensation are kept in constant action, while the nerves of motion are unemployed. If this is continued for a long time, the nerves of sensation lose their strength from overaction, and the nerves of motion lose their power from inactivity. In consequence, there is a morbid excitability of the nervous, and a debility of the muscular system, which make all exertion irksome and wearisome.

The only mode of preserving the health of these systems is to keep up in them an equilibrium of action. For this purpose, occupations must be sought which exercise the muscles and interest the mind; and thus the equal action of both kinds of nerves is secured. This shows why exercise is so much more healthful and invigorating when the mind is interested than when it is not. As an illustration, let a person go shopping with a friend, and have nothing to do but look on. How soon do the continuous walking and standing weary! But, suppose one, thus wearied, hears of the arrival of a very dear friend: she can instantly walk off a mile or two to meet her, without the least feeling of fatigue. By this is shown the importance of furnishing, for young persons, exercise in which they will take an interest. Long and formal walks, merely for exercise, though they do some good, in securing fresh air and some exercise of the muscles, would be of triple benefit if changed to amusing sports, or to the cultivation of fruits and flowers, in which it is impossible to engage without acquiring a great interest.

It shows, also, why it is far better to trust to useful domestic exercise at home than to send a young person out to walk for the mere purpose of exercise. Young girls can seldom be made to realize the value of health, and the need of exercise to secure it, so as to feel much interest in walking abroad, when they have no other object. But if they are brought up to minister to the comfort and enjoyment of themselves and others by performing domestic duties, they will constantly be interested and cheered in their exercise by the feeling of usefulness and the consciousness of having performed their duty.

There are few young persons, it is hoped, who are brought up with such miserable habits of selfishness and indolence that they can not be made to feel happier by the consciousness of being usefully employed. And those who have never been accustomed to think or care for any one but themselves, and who seem to feel little pleasure in making themselves useful, by wise and proper influences can often be gradually awakened to the new pleasure of benevolent exertion to promote the comfort and enjoyment of others. And the more this sacred and elevating kind of enjoyment is tasted, the greater is the relish induced. Other enjoyments often cloy; but the heavenly pleasure secured by virtuous industry and benevolence, while it satisfies at the time, awakens fresh desires for the continuance of so ennobling a good.

It is an interesting illustration of the benevolence and wisdom of our Maker, that the appropriate duties of the family, uniting intellectual, social, and moral with both sedentary and active pursuits, are exactly fitted to employ every faculty in a healthful proportion. And it is a sad violation of the laws of health to so divide family employments that one class use muscle too much, and the other the brain to excess.

CHAPTER IX.

HEALTHFUL FOOD AND DRINKS.

THE person who decides what shall be the food and drink of a family, and the modes of its preparation, is the one who decides, to a greater or less extent, what shall be the health of that family. It is the opinion of most medical men that intemperance in eating is one of the most fruitful of all causes of disease and death. If this be so, the woman who wisely adapts the food and cooking of her family to the laws of health removes one of the greatest risks which threatens the lives of those under her care. But, unfortunately, there is no other duty that has been involved in more doubt and perplexity. Were one to believe all that is said and written on this subject, the conclusion probably would be, that there is not one solitary article of food on God's earth which it is healthful to eat. Happily, however, there are general principles on this subject which, if understood and applied, will prove a safe guide to any woman of common sense; and it is the object of the present chapter to set forth these principles.

All material things on earth, whether solid, liquid, or gaseous, can be resolved into sixty-two simple substances, only fourteen of which are in the human body; and these, in certain proportions, in all mankind.

Thus, in a man weighing 154 lbs. are found 111 lbs. oxygen gas and 14 lbs. hydrogen gas, which, united, form water; 21 lbs. carbon; 3 lbs. 8 oz. nitrogen gas; 1 lb. 12 oz. 190 grs. phosphorus; 2 lbs. calcium, the chief ingredient of bones; 2 oz. fluorine; 2 oz. 219 grs. sulphur; 2 oz. 47 grs. chlorine; 2 oz. 116 grs. sodium; 100 grs. iron; 290 grs. potassium; 12 grs. magnesium; and 2 grs. silicon.

These simple substances are constantly passing out of the body through the lungs, skin, and other excreting organs.

It is found that certain of these simple elements are used

for one part of the body and others for other parts, and this in certain regular proportions. Thus, carbon is the chief element of fat, and also supplies the fuel that combines with oxygen in the capillaries to produce animal heat. The nitrogen which we gain from our food and the air is the chief element of muscle; phosphorus is the chief element of brain and nerves; and calcium or lime is the hard portion of the bones. Iron is an important element of blood; and silicon supplies the hardest parts of the teeth, nails, and hair.

Water, which is composed of the two gases oxygen and hydrogen, is the largest portion of the body, forming its fluids; there is four times as much of carbon as there is of nitrogen in the body; while there is only two per cent. as much phosphorus as carbon. A man weighing one hundred and fifty-four pounds, who leads an active life, takes into his stomach daily from two to three pounds of solid food, and from five to six pounds of liquid. At the same time he takes into his lungs, daily, four or five thousand gallons of air. This amounts to three thousand pounds of nutriment received through stomach and lungs, and then expelled from the body, in one year; or about twenty times the man's own weight.

It is found that the simple elements will not nourish the body in their natural state, but only when organized, either as vegetable or animal food; and, to the dismay of the Grahamite or vegetarian school, it is now established by chemists that animal and vegetable food contain the same elements, and in nearly the same proportions.

Thus, in animal food, carbon predominates in fats, while in vegetable food it shows itself in sugar, starch, and vegetable oils. Nitrogen is found in animal food in the albumen, fibrine, and caseine; while in vegetables it is in gluten, albumen, and caseine.

It is also a curious fact that, in all articles of food, the elements that nourish diverse parts of the body are divided into separable portions, and also that the proportions correspond in a great degree to the wants of the body. For example, a kernel of wheat contains all the articles demanded for every part of the body. Fig. 53 represents, upon an enlarged scale, the position and proportions of the chief elements required. The white central part is the largest in quantity, and is chiefly carbon in the form of starch, which supplies fat and fuel for the capillaries. The shaded outer portion is chiefly nitrogen, which nourishes the muscles; and the dark spot at the bottom is principally phosphorus, which nourishes the brain and nerves. And these elements are in due proportion to the demands of the body. A portion of the outer covering of a wheat-kernel holds lime, silica, and iron, which are needed by the body, and which are found in no other part of the grain. The woody fibre is not digested, but serves, by its bulk and stimulating action, to facilitate digestion. It is, therefore, evident that bread made of unbolted flour is more healthful than that made of superfine flour. For the process of bolting removes all the woody fibre; the lime needed for the bones; the silica for hair, nails, and teeth; the iron for the blood; and most of the nitrogen and phosphorus needed for muscles, brain, and nerves.

Fig. 53.

Experiments on animals prove that fine flour alone, which is chiefly carbon, will not sustain life more than a month, while unbolted flour furnishes all that is needed for every part of the body. There are cases where persons can not use such coarse bread, on account of its irritating action on inflamed coats of the stomach. For such, a kind of wheaten grit is provided, containing all the kernel of the wheat, except the outside woody fibre.

From these statements it may be seen that one of the chief mistakes in providing food for families has been in changing the proportions of the elements nature has fitted for our food. Thus, fine wheat is deprived by bolting of some of the most important of its nourishing elements, leaving carbon chiefly, which, after supplying fuel for the capillaries, must, if in excess, be sent out of the body; thus needlessly taxing all the excreting organs. So milk, which contains all the elements needed by the body, has the cream taken out and used for butter, which again is chiefly carbon. Then, sugar and molasses, cakes and candies, are chiefly carbon, and supply but very little of other nourishing elements, while, to make them safe, much exercise in cold and pure air is necessary. And yet it is the children of the rich, housed in chambers and school-rooms most of their time, who are fed with these dangerous dainties, thus weakening their constitutions, and inducing fevers, colds, and many other diseases.

The proper digestion of food depends on the wants of the body, and on its power of appropriating the aliment supplied. The best of food can not be properly digested when it is not needed. All that the system requires will be used, and the rest will be thrown out by the several excreting organs, which thus are frequently overtaxed, and vital forces are wasted. Even food of poor quality may digest well if the demands of the system are urgent. The way to increase digestive power is to increase the demand for food by pure air and exercise of the muscles, quickening the blood, and arousing the whole system to a more rapid and vigorous rate of life.

We are now ready to consider intelligently the following general principles in regard to the proper selection of food:

Vegetable and animal food are equally healthful if apportioned to the given circumstances.

In cold weather, carbonaceous food, such as butter, fats, sugar, molasses, etc., can be used more safely than in warm weather. And they can be used more safely by those who exercise in the open air than by those of confined and sedentary habits.

Students who need food with little carbon, and women who live in the house, should always seek coarse bread, fruits, and lean meats, and avoid butter, oils, sugar, and molasses, and articles containing them.

Many students and women using little exercise in the open air grow thin and weak, because the vital powers are exhausted in throwing off excess of food, especially of the carbonaceous. The liver is especially taxed in such cases, being unable to remove all the excess of carbonaceous matter from the blood, and thus "biliousness" ensues, particularly on the approach of warm weather, when the air brings less oxygen than in cold.

It is found, by experiment, that the supply of gastric juice, furnished from the blood by the arteries of the stomach, is proportioned, not to the amount of food put into the stomach, but to the wants of the body; so that it is possible to put much more into the stomach than can be digested. To guide and regulate in this matter, the sensation called *hunger* is provided. In a healthy state of the body, as soon as the blood has lost its nutritive supplies, the craving of hunger is felt, and then, if the food is suitable, and is taken in the proper manner, this sensation ceases as soon as the stomach has received enough to supply the wants of the system. But our benevolent Creator, in this as in our other duties, has connected enjoyment with the operation needful to sustain our bodies. In addition to the allaying of hunger, the gratification of the palate is secured by the immense variety of food, some articles of which are far more agreeable than others.

This arrangement of Providence, designed for our happiness, has become, either through ignorance or want of self-control, the chief cause of the many diseases and sufferings which afflict those classes who have the means of seeking a variety to gratify the palate. If mankind had only one article of food, and only water to drink, though they would have less enjoyment in eating, they would never be tempted to put any more into the stomach than the calls of hunger require. But the customs of society, which present an incessant change, and a great variety of food, with those various condiments which stimulate appetite, lead almost every person very frequently to eat merely to gratify the palate, after the stomach has been abundantly supplied, so that hunger has ceased.

When too great a supply of food is put into the stomach, the gastric juice dissolves only that portion which the wants of the system demand. Most of the remainder is ejected in an unprepared state; the absorbents take portions of it into the system; and all the various functions of the body, which depend on the ministries of the blood, are thus gradually and imperceptibly injured. Very often, intemperance in eating produces immediate results, such as colic, headaches, pains of indigestion, and vertigo.

But the more general result is a gradual undermining of all parts of the human frame; thus imperceptibly shortening life, by so weakening the constitution that it is ready to yield, at every point, to any uncommon risk or exposure. Thousands and thousands are passing out of the world, from diseases occasioned by exposures which a healthy constitution could meet without any danger. It is owing to these considerations that it becomes the duty of every woman who has the responsibility of providing food for a family to avoid a variety of tempting dishes. It is a much safer guide to have only one kind of healthy food for each meal, rather than the too abundant variety which is often met at the tables of almost all classes in this country. When there is to be any variety of dishes, they ought not to be successive, but so arranged as to give the opportunity of selection. How often is it the case that persons, by the appearance of a favorite article, are tempted to eat merely to gratify the palate, when the stomach is already adequately supplied. All such intemperance wears on the constitution, and shortens life. It not unfrequently happens that excess in eating produces a morbid appetite, which must constantly be denied.

But the organization of the digestive organs demands not only that food should be taken in proper quantities, but that it be taken at proper times.

Fig. 54 shows one important feature of the digestive organs relating to this point. The part marked L M shows the muscles of the inner coat of the stomach, which run in one direction, and C M shows the muscles of the outer coat, running in another direction.

Fig. 54.

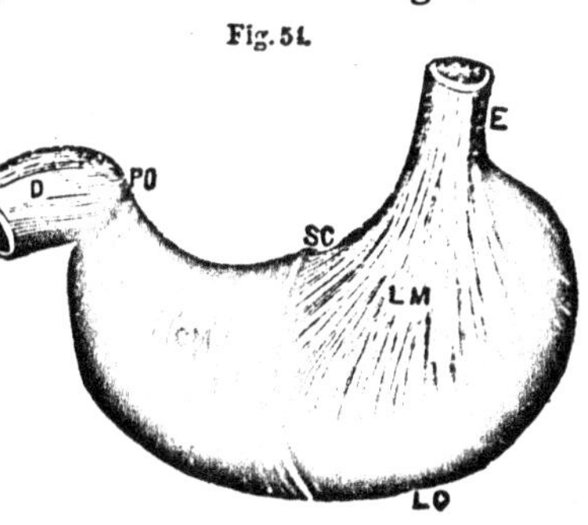

As soon as the food enters the stomach, the muscles are excited by the nerves, and the *peristaltic motion* commences: this is a powerful and constant exercise of the muscles of the stomach, which continues until the process of digestion is complete. During this time the blood is withdrawn from other parts of the system, to supply the demands of the stomach, which is laboring hard with all its muscles. When this motion ceases, and the digested food has gradually passed out, nature requires that the stomach should have a period of repose. And if another meal be eaten immediately after one is digested, the stomach is set to work again before it has had time to rest, and before a sufficient supply of gastric juice is provided.

The general rule, then, is, that three hours be given to the stomach for labor, and two for rest; and in obedience to this, five hours, at least, ought to elapse between every two regular meals. In cases where exercise produces a flow of perspiration, more food is needed to supply the loss; and strong laboring men may safely eat as often as they feel the want of food. So, young and healthy children, who gambol and exercise much, and whose bodies grow fast, may have a more frequent supply of food. But, as a general rule, meals should be five hours apart, and eating between meals avoided. There is nothing more unsafe and wearing to the constitution than a habit of eating at any time merely to gratify the palate. When a tempting article is presented, every person should exercise sufficient self-denial to wait till the proper time for eating arrives. Children, as well as grown persons, are often injured by eating between their regular meals, thus weakening the stomach by not affording it any time for rest.

As a general rule, the quantity of food actually needed by the body depends on the amount of muscular exercise taken. A laboring man in the open fields probably throws off from his skin and lungs a much larger amount than a person of sedentary pursuits. In consequence of this, he demands a greater amount of food and drink.

Those persons who keep their bodies in a state of health by sufficient exercise can always be guided by the calls of hunger. They can eat when they feel hungry, and stop when hunger ceases; and thus they will calculate exactly right. But the difficulty is, that a large part of the community, especially women, are so inactive in their habits that they seldom feel the calls of hunger. They habitually eat, merely to gratify the palate. This produces such a state of the system that they lose the guide which Nature has provided. They are not called to eat by hunger, nor admonished, by its cessation, when to stop. In consequence of this, such persons eat what pleases the palate, till they feel no more inclination for the article. It is probable that three-fourths of the women in the wealthier circles sit down to each meal without any feeling of hunger, and eat merely on account of the gratification thus afforded them. Such persons find their appetite to depend almost solely upon the kind of food on the table. This is not the case with those who take the exercise which Nature demands. They approach their meals in such a state that almost any kind of food is acceptable.

Persons who have a strong constitution, and take much exercise, may eat almost any thing with apparent impunity; but young children who are forming their constitutions, and persons who are delicate and who take but little exercise, are very dependent for health on a proper selection of food.

It is found that there are some kinds of food which afford nutriment to the blood, and do not produce any other effect on the system. There are other kinds which are not only nourishing, but *stimulating*, so that they quicken the functions of the organs on which they operate. The condiments used in cookery, such as pepper, mustard, and spices, are of this nature. There are certain states of the system when these stimulants may be beneficial; such cases can only be pointed out by medical men.

Persons in perfect health, and especially young children, never receive any benefit from such kind of food; and just in proportion as condiments operate to quicken the labors of the internal organs, they tend to wear down their powers. A person who thus keeps the body working under an unnatural excitement *lives faster* than Nature designed, and the constitution is worn out just so much the sooner. A woman, therefore, should provide dishes for her family which are free from these stimulating condiments.

In regard to articles which are the most easily digested, only general rules can be given. Tender meats are digested more readily than those which are tough, or than many kinds of vegetable food. The farinaceous articles, such as rice, flour, corn, potatoes, and the like, are the most nutritious, and most easily digested. The popular notion, that meat is more nourishing than bread, is a great mistake. Good bread contains more nourishment than butcher's meat. The meat is more *stimulating*, and for this reason is more readily digested.

A perfectly healthy stomach can digest almost any healthful food; but when the digestive powers are weak, every stomach has its peculiarities, and what is good for one is hurtful to another. In such cases, experiment alone can decide which are the most digestible articles of food. A person whose food troubles him must deduct one article after another, till he learns by experience which is the best for digestion. Much evil has been done by assuming that the powers of one stomach are to be made the rule in regulating every other.

The most unhealthful kinds of food are those which are made so by bad cooking; such as sour and heavy bread, cakes, pie-crust, and other dishes consisting of fat mixed and cooked with flour. Rancid butter and high-seasoned food are equally unwholesome. The fewer mixtures there are in cooking, the more healthful is the food likely to be.

There is one caution as to the *mode* of eating which seems peculiarly needful to Americans. It is indispensable to good digestion that food be well chewed and taken slowly. It needs to be thoroughly chewed and mixed with saliva, in order to prepare it for the action of the gastric juice, which, by the peristaltic motion, will be thus brought into contact with every one of the minute portions. It has been found that a solid lump of food requires much more time and labor of the stomach for digestion than divided substances.

It has also been found that as each bolus, or mouthful, enters the stomach, the latter closes, until the portion received has had some time to move around and combine with the gastric juice, and that the orifice of the stomach resists the entrance of any more till this is accomplished. But, if the eater persists in swallowing fast, the stomach yields; the food is then poured in more rapidly than the organ can perform its duty of preparative digestion, and evil results are sooner or later developed. This exhibits the folly of those hasty meals so common to travelers and to men of business, and shows why children should be taught to eat slowly.

After taking a full meal, it is very important to health that no great bodily or mental exertion be made till the labor of the stomach is over. Intense mental effort draws the blood to the head, and muscular exertions draw it to the muscles; and in consequence of this, the stomach loses the supply which it requires when performing its office. When the blood with its stimulating effects is thus withdrawn from the stomach, the adequate supply of gastric juice is not afforded, and indigestion is the result. The heaviness which follows a full meal is the indication which Nature gives of the need of quiet. When the meal is moderate, a sufficient quantity of gastric juice is exuded in an hour, or an hour and a half; after which, labor of body and mind may safely be resumed.

Extremes of heat or cold are injurious to the process of digestion. Taking hot food or drink habitually, tends to debilitate all the organs thus needlessly excited. In using cold substances, it is found that a certain degree of warmth in the stomach is indispensable to their digestion; so that when the gastric juice is cooled below this temperature it ceases to act. Indulging in large quantities of cold drinks, or eating ice-creams, after a meal, tends to reduce the temperature of the stomach, and thus to stop digestion. This shows the folly of those refreshments, in convivial meetings, where the guests are tempted to load the stomach with a variety such as would require the stomach of a stout farmer to digest; and then to wind up with ice-creams, thus lessening whatever ability might otherwise have existed to digest the heavy load. The fittest temperature for drinks, if taken when the food is in the digesting process, is blood-heat. Cool drinks, and even ice, can be safely taken at other times, if not in excessive quantity. When the thirst is excessive, or the body weakened by fatigue, or when in a state of perspiration, large quantities of cold drinks are injurious.

Fluids taken into the stomach are not subject to the slow process of digestion, but are immediately absorbed and carried into the blood. This is the reason why liquid nourishment, more speedily than solid food, restores from exhaustion. The minute vessels of the stomach absorb its fluids, which are carried into the blood, just as the minute extremities of the arteries open upon the inner surface of the stomach, and there exude the gastric juice from the blood.

Highly-concentrated food, having much nourishment in a small bulk, is not favorable to digestion, because it can not be properly acted on by the muscular contractions of the stomach, and is not so minutely divided as to enable the gastric juice to act properly. This is the reason why a certain *bulk* of food is needful to good digestion; and why those people who live on whale-oil and other highly nourishing food, in cold climates, mix vegetables and even sawdust with it, to make it more acceptable and digestible. So in civilized lands, fruits and vegetables are mixed with more highly concentrated nourishment. For this reason, also, soups, jellies, and arrow-root should have bread or crackers mixed with them. This affords another reason why coarse bread, of unbolted wheat, so often proves beneficial. Where, from inactive habits or other causes, the bowels become constipated and sluggish, this kind of food proves the appropriate remedy.

One fact on this subject is worthy of notice. In England, under the administration of William Pitt, for two years or more there was such a scarcity of wheat that, to make it hold out longer, Parliament passed a law that the army should have all their bread made of unbolted flour. The result was, that the health of the soldiers improved so much as to be a subject of surprise to themselves, the officers, and the physicians. These last came out publicly and declared that the soldiers never before were so robust and healthy; and that disease had nearly disappeared from the army. The civic physicians joined and pronounced it the healthiest bread; and for a time schools, families, and public institutions used it almost exclusively. Even the nobility, convinced by these facts, adopted it for their common diet, and the fashion continued a long time after the scarcity ceased, until more luxurious habits resumed their sway.

We thus see why children should not have cakes and candies allowed them between meals. Besides being largely carbonaceous, these are highly concentrated nourishments, and should be eaten with more bulky and less nourishing substances. The most indigestible of all kinds of food are fatty and oily substances, if heated. It is on this account that pie-crust and articles boiled and fried in fat or butter are deemed not so healthful as other food.

The following, then, may be put down as the causes of a debilitated constitution from the misuse of food: Eating *too much*, eating *too often*, eating *too fast*, eating food and condiments that are *too stimulating*, eating food that is *too warm* or *too cold*, eating food that is *highly concentrated*, without a proper admixture of less nourishing matter, and eating hot food that is *difficult of digestion.*

It is a point fully established by experience that the full development of the human body and the vigorous exercise of all its functions can be secured without the use of stimulating drinks. It is, therefore, perfectly safe to bring up children never to use them, no hazard being incurred by such a course.

It is also found by experience that there are two evils incurred by the use of stimulating drinks. The first is, their positive effect on the human system. Their peculiarity consists in so exciting the nervous system that all the functions of the body are accelerated, and the fluids are caused to move quicker than at their natural speed. This increased motion of the animal fluids always produces an agreeable effect on the mind. The intellect is invigorated, the imagination is excited, the spirits are enlivened; and these effects are so agreeable that all mankind, after having once experienced them, feel a great desire for their repetition.

But this temporary invigoration of the system is always followed by a diminution of the powers of the stimulated organs; so that, though in all cases this reaction may not be perceptible, it is invariably the result. It may be set down as the unchangeable rule of physiology, that stimulating drinks deduct from the powers of the constitution in exactly the proportion in which they operate to produce temporary invigoration.

The second evil is the temptation which always attends the use of stimulants. Their effect on the system is so agreeable, and the evils resulting are so imperceptible and distant, that there is a constant tendency to increase such excitement, both in frequency and power; and the more the system is thus reduced in strength, the more craving is the desire for that which imparts a temporary invigoration. This process of increasing debility and increasing craving for the stimulus that removes it, often goes to such an extreme that the passion is perfectly uncontrollable, and mind and body perish under this baleful habit.

In this country there are three forms in which the use of such stimulants is common; namely, *alcoholic drinks*, *opium mixtures*, and *tobacco*. These are all alike in the main peculiarity of imparting that extra stimulus to the system which tends to exhaust its powers.

Multitudes in this nation are in the habitual use of some one of these stimulants; and each person defends the indulgence by certain arguments:

First, that the desire for stimulants is a natural propensity implanted in man's nature, as is manifest from the universal tendency to such indulgences in every nation. From this it is inferred that it is an innocent desire, which ought to be gratified to some extent, and that the aim should be to keep it within the limits of temperance, instead of attempting to exterminate a natural propensity.

This is an argument which, if true, makes it equally proper for not only men, but women and children, to use opium, brandy, or tobacco as stimulating principles, provided they are used temperately. But if it be granted that perfect health and strength can be gained and secured without these stimulants, and that their peculiar effect is to diminish the power of the system in exactly the same proportion as they stimulate it, then there is no such thing as a temperate use, unless they are so diluted as to destroy any stimulating power; and in this form they are seldom desired.

The other argument for their use is, that they are among the good things provided by the Creator for our gratification; that, like all other blessings, they are exposed to abuse and excess; and that we should rather seek to regulate their use than to banish them entirely.

This argument is based on the assumption that they are, like healthful foods and drinks, necessary to life and health, and injurious only by excess. But this is not true; for whenever they are used in any such strength as to be a gratification, they operate to a greater or less extent as stimulants, and to just such extent they wear out the powers of the constitution; and it is abundantly proved that they are not, like food and drink, necessary to health. Such articles are designed for medicine, and not for common use. There can be no argument framed to defend the use of one of them which will not justify women and children in most dangerous indulgences.

There are some facts recently revealed by the microscope in regard to alcoholic drinks which every woman should understand and regard. It has been shown in a previous chapter that every act of mind, either by thought, feeling, or choice, causes the destruction of certain cells in the brain and nerves. It now is proved by microscopic science* that the kind of nutrition furnished to the brain by the blood to a certain extent decides future feelings, thoughts, and volitions. The cells of the brain not only abstract from the blood the healthful nutrition, but also are affected in shape, size, color, and action by unsuitable elements in the blood. This is especially the case when alcohol is taken into the stomach, from whence it is always carried to the brain. The consequence is, that it affects the nature and action of the brain-cells, until a habit is formed which is *automatic;* that is, the mind loses the power of controlling the brain in its development of thoughts, feelings, and choices as it would in the natural state, and is itself controlled by the brain.

* For these statements the writer is indebted to Maudsley, a recent writer on Microscopic Physiology.

In this condition a real disease of the brain is created, called *oino-mania*, and the only remedy is total abstinence, and that for a long period, from the alcoholic poison. And what makes the danger more fearful is, that the brain-cells never are so renewed but that this pernicious stimulus will bring back the disease in full force, so that a man once subject to it is never safe except by maintaining perpetual and total abstinence from every kind of alcoholic drink. Dr. Day, who for many years has had charge of an inebriate asylum, states that he witnessed the dissection of the brain of a man once an inebriate, but for many years in practice of total abstinence, and found its cells still in the weak and unnatural state produced by earlier indulgences.

There has unfortunately been a difference of opinion among medical men as to the use of alcohol. Liebig, the celebrated writer on animal chemistry, having found that both sugar and alcohol were heat-producing articles of food, framed a theory that alcohol is burned in the lungs, giving off carbonic acid and water, and thus serving to warm the body. But modern science has proved that it is in the capillaries that animal heat is generated, and it is believed that alcohol lessens instead of increasing the power of the body to bear the cold. Sir John Ross, in his Arctic voyage, proved by his own experience and that of his men that cold-water drinkers could bear cold longer and were stronger than any who used alcohol.

Carpenter, a standard writer on physiology, says the objection to a habitual use of even small quantities of alcoholic drinks is, that "they are universally admitted to possess a poisonous character," and "tend to produce a morbid condition of body;" while "the capacity for enduring extremes of heat and cold, or of mental or bodily labor, is diminished rather than increased by their habitual employment."

Professor J. Bigelow, of Harvard University, says: "Alcohol is highly stimulating, heating, and intoxicating, and its effects are so fascinating that when once experienced there is danger that the desire for them may be perpetuated."

Dr. Bell and Dr. Churchill, both high medical authorities,

especially in lung disease, for which whisky is often recommended, come to the conclusion that "the opinion that alcoholic liquors have influence in preventing the deposition of tubercle is destitute of any foundation; on the contrary, their use predisposes to tubercular deposition." And "where tubercle exists, alcohol has no effect in modifying the usual course, neither does it modify the morbid effects on the system."

Professor Youmans, of New York, says: "It has been demonstrated that alcoholic drinks prevent the natural changes in the blood, and obstruct the nutritive and reparative functions." He adds: "Chemical experiments have demonstrated that the action of alcohol on the digestive fluid is to destroy its active principle, the *pepsin*, thus confirming the observations of physiologists, that its use gives rise to serious disorders of the stomach, and malignant aberration of the whole economy." It is true that some scientific men teach that alcohol, tobacco, and opium are safe, and even useful, in certain quantities, though there is no way to know what is the safe and useful point. Usually it is men who habitually use some of these dangerous articles who hold this view.

We are now prepared to consider the great principles of science, common sense, and religion, which should guide every woman who has any kind of influence or responsibility on this subject.

It is allowed by all medical men that pure water is perfectly healthful, and supplies all the liquid needed by the body; and also that by proper means, which ordinarily are in the reach of all, water can be made sufficiently pure.

It is allowed by all that milk, and the juices of fruits, when taken into the stomach, furnish water that is always pure, and that our bread and vegetable food also supply it in large quantities. There are besides a great variety of agreeable and healthful beverages, made from the juices of fruit, containing no alcohol; and agreeable drinks, such as milk, cocoa, and chocolate, that contain no stimulating principles, and which are nourishing and healthful.

As one course, then, is perfectly safe, and another involves great danger, it is wrong and sinful to choose the path of danger. There is no peril in drinking pure water, milk, the juices of fruits, and infusions that are nourishing and harmless. But there is great danger to the young, and to the commonwealth, in patronizing the sale and use of alcoholic drinks. The religion of Christ, in its distinctive feature, involves generous self-denial for the good of others, especially for the weaker members of society. It is on this principle that St. Paul sets forth his own example: "If meat make my brother to offend, I will eat no flesh while the world standeth, lest I make my brother to offend." And again he teaches, "We, then, that are strong ought to bear the infirmities of the weak, and not to please ourselves."

This Christian principle also applies to the common drinks of the family, tea and coffee. It has been shown that the great end for which Jesus Christ came, and for which he instituted the family state, is the training of our whole race to virtue and happiness, with chief reference to an immortal existence. In this mission, of which woman is chief minister, the distinctive feature is self-sacrifice of the wiser and stronger members to save and to elevate the weaker ones. The children and the servants are these weaker members, who by ignorance and want of habits of self-control are in most danger. It is in this aspect that we are to consider the expediency of using tea and coffee in a family.

These drinks are a most extensive cause of much of the nervous debility and suffering endured by American women; and relinquishing them would save an immense amount of such suffering. Moreover, all housekeepers will allow that they can not regulate these drinks in their kitchens, where the ignorant use them to excess. There is little probability that the present generation will make so decided a change in their habits as to give up these beverages; but the subject is presented rather in reference to forming the habits of children.

It is a fact that tea and coffee are at first seldom or never agreeable to children. It is the mixture of milk, sugar, and water, that reconciles them to a taste which in this manner gradually becomes agreeable. Now, suppose that those who provide for a family conclude that it is not *their* duty to give up entirely the use of stimulating drinks, may not the case appear different in regard to teaching their children to love such drinks? Let the matter be regarded thus: The experiments of physiologists all prove that stimulants are not needful to health, and that, as the general rule, they tend to debilitate the constitution. Is it right, then, for a parent to tempt a child to drink what is not needful, when there is a probability that it will prove, to some extent, an undermining drain on the constitution? Some constitutions can bear much less excitement than others; and in every family of children there is usually one or more of delicate organization, and consequently peculiarly exposed to dangers from this source. It is this child who ordinarily becomes the victim to stimulating drinks. The tea and coffee which the parents and the healthier children can use without immediate injury gradually sap the energies of the feebler child, who proves either an early victim or a living martyr to all the sufferings that debilitated nerves inflict. Can it be right to lead children where all allow that there is some danger, and where in many cases disease and death are met, when another path is known to be perfectly safe?

The impression common in this country, that *warm drinks*, especially in winter, are more healthful than cold, is not warranted by any experience, nor by the laws of the physical system. At dinner cold drinks are universal, and no one deems them injurious. It is only at the other two meals that they are supposed to be hurtful.

"*Water* is a safe drink for all constitutions, provided it be resorted to in obedience to the dictates of natural thirst only, and not of habit. Unless the desire for it is felt, there is no occasion for its use during a meal.

"The primary effect of all distilled and fermented liquors is to *stimulate the nervous system and quicken the circulation.* In infancy and childhood the circulation is rapid and easily excited, and the nervous system is strongly acted upon even by the slightest external impressions. Hence, slight causes of irritation readily excite febrile and convulsive disorders. In youth, the natural tendency of the constitution is still to excitement, and consequently, as a general rule, the stimulus of fermented liquors is injurious."

These remarks by Dr. Combe show that parents, who find that stimulating drinks are not injurious to themselves, may mistake in inferring from this that they will not be injurious to their children.

He continues thus: "In mature age, when digestion is good, and the system in full vigor, if the mode of life be not too exhausting, the nervous functions and general circulation are in their best condition, and require no stimulus for their support. The bodily energy is then easily sustained by nutritious food and a regular regimen, and consequently artificial excitement only increases the wasting of the natural strength."

It may be asked, in this connection, why the stimulus of animal food is not to be regarded in the same light as that of stimulating drinks. In reply, a very essential difference may be pointed out. Animal food furnishes nutriment to the organs which it stimulates, but stimulating drinks excite the organs to quickened action without affording any nourishment.

It has been supposed by some that tea and coffee have at least a degree of nourishing power. But it is proved that it is the milk and sugar, and not the main portion of the drink, which imparts the nourishment. Tea has not one particle of nourishing properties; and what little exists in the coffee-berry is lost by roasting it in the usual mode. All that these articles do is simply *to stimulate without nourishing.*

Although there is little hope of banishing these drinks, there is still a chance that something may be gained in attempts to regulate their use by the rules of temperance. If, then, a housekeeper can not banish tea and coffee entirely, she may use her influence to prevent excess, both by her instructions, and by the power of control committed more or less to her hands.

It is important for every housekeeper to know that the health of a family very much depends on the *purity* of water used for cooking and drinking. There are three causes of impure and unhealthful water. One is, the existence in it of vegetable or animal matter, which can be remedied by filtering through sand and charcoal. Another cause is, the existence of mineral matter, especially in limestone countries, producing diseases of the bladder. This is remedied, in a measure, by boiling, which secures a deposit of the lime on the vessel used. The third cause is, the corroding of zinc and lead used in pipes and reservoirs, producing oxides that are slow poisons. The only remedy is prevention, by having supply-pipes made of iron, like gas-pipe, instead of zinc and lead; or the lately invented lead pipe lined with tin, which metal is not corrosive. The obstacle to this is, that the trade of the plumbers would be greatly diminished by the use of reliable pipes. When water must be used from supply-pipes of lead or zinc, it is well to let the water run some time before drinking it, and to use as little as possible, taking milk instead; and being further satisfied for inner necessities by the water supplied by fruits and vegetables. The water in these is always pure. But in using milk as a drink, it must be remembered that it is also rich food, and that less of other food must be taken when milk is thus used, or bilious troubles will result from excess of food.

The use of opium, especially by women, is usually caused at first by medical prescriptions containing it. All that has been stated as to the effect of alcohol in the brain is true of opium, while to break a habit thus induced is almost hopeless. Every woman who takes or who administers this drug is dealing as with poisoned arrows, whose wounds are without cure.

The use of tobacco in this country, and especially among young boys, is increasing at a fearful rate. On this subject we have the unanimous opinion of all medical men, the following being specimens.

A distinguished medical writer thus states the case: "Every physician knows that the agreeable sensations that tempt to the use of tobacco are caused by *nicotine*, which is a rank poison, as much so as prussic acid or arsenic. When smoked, the poison is absorbed by the blood of the mouth, and carried to the brain. When chewed, the nicotine passes to the blood through the mouth and stomach. In both cases, the whole nervous system is thrown into abnormal excitement to expel the poison, and it is this excitement that causes agreeable sensations. The excitement thus caused is invariably followed by a diminution of nervous power, in exact proportion to the preceding excitement to expel the evil from the system."

Few will dispute the general truth and effect of the above statement, so that the question is one to be settled on the same principle as applies to the use of alcoholic drinks. Is it, then, according to the generous principles of Christ's religion, for those who are strong and able to bear this poison, to tempt the young, the ignorant, and the weak to a practice not needful to any healthful enjoyment, and which leads multitudes to disease, and often to vice? For the use of tobacco tends always to lessen nerve-power, and probably every one out of five that indulges in its use awakens a morbid craving for increased stimulus, lessens the power of self-control, diminishes the strength of the constitution, and sets an example that influences the weak to the path of danger and of frequent ruin.

The great danger of this age is an increasing, intense worldliness, and disbelief in the foundation principle of the religion of Christ, that we are to reap through everlasting ages the consequences of habits formed in this life. In the light of his Word, they only who are truly wise "shall shine as the firmament, and they that turn many to righteousness, as the stars, forever and ever."

It is increased *faith* or *belief* in the teachings of Christ's religion, as to the influence of this life upon the *life to come*, which alone can save our country and the world from that inrushing tide of sensualism and worldliness now seeming to threaten the best hopes and prospects of our race.

And woman, as the chief educator of our race, and the prime minister of the family state, is bound, in the use of meats and drinks, to employ the powerful and distinctive motives of the religion of Christ in forming habits of temperance and benevolent self-sacrifice for the good of others.

CHAPTER X.

CLEANLINESS.

Both the health and comfort of a family depend, to a great extent, on cleanliness of the person and the family surroundings. True cleanliness of person involves the scientific treatment of the skin. This is the most complicated organ of the body, and one through which the health is affected more than through any other; and no persons can or will be so likely to take proper care of it as those by whom its construction and functions are understood.

Fig. 55 is a very highly magnified portion of the skin. The layer marked 1 is the outside, very thin skin, called the *cuticle* or *scarf skin*. This consists of transparent layers of minute cells, which are constantly decaying and being renewed, and the white scurf that passes from the skin to the clothing is a decayed portion of these cells. This part of the skin has neither nerves nor blood-vessels.

Fig. 55.

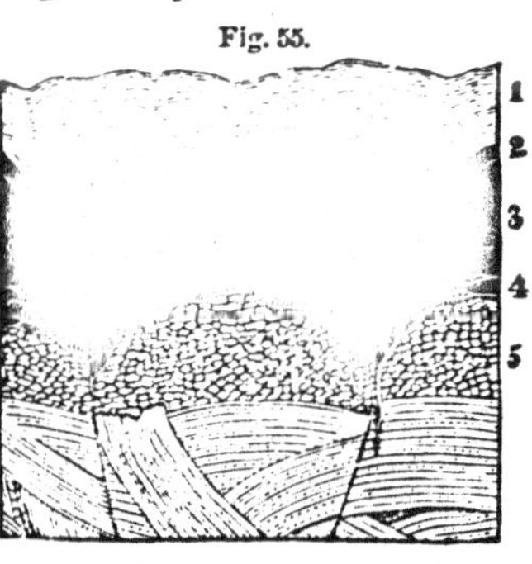

The dark layer, marked 2, 7, 8, is that portion of the true skin which gives the external color marking diverse races. In the portion of the dark layer marked 3, 4, is seen a network of nerves which run from two branches of the nervous trunks coming from the spinal marrow. These are nerves of sensation, by which the sense of touch or feeling is performed. Fig. 56 represents the blood-vessels, (intermingled with the nerves of the skin,) which divide into minute capillaries, that act like the capillaries of the lungs, taking oxygen from the air, and giving out carbonic acid. At *a* and *b* are seen the roots of two hairs, which abound in certain

Fig. 56.

parts of the skin, and are nourished by the blood of the capillaries.

At Fig. 57 is a magnified view of another set of vessels, called the *lymphatics* or *absorbents*. These are extremely minute vessels that interlace with the nerves and blood-vessels of the skin. Their office is to aid in collecting the useless, injurious, or decayed matter, and carry it to certain reservoirs, from which it passes into some of the large veins, to be thrown out through the lungs, bowels, kidneys, or skin. These *absorbent* or *lymphatic vessels* have mouths opening on the surface of the true skin, and, though covered by the cuticle, they can absorb both liquids and solids that are placed in close contact with the skin. In proof of this, one of the main trunks of the lymphatics in the hand can be cut off from all communication with other portions, and tied up; and if the hand is immersed in milk a given time, it will be found that the milk has been absorbed through the cuticle and fills the lymphatics. In this way long-continued blisters on the skin will introduce the blistering matter into the blood through the absorbents, and then the kidneys will take it up from the blood passing through them to carry it out of the body, and thus become irritated and inflamed by it.

Fig. 57.

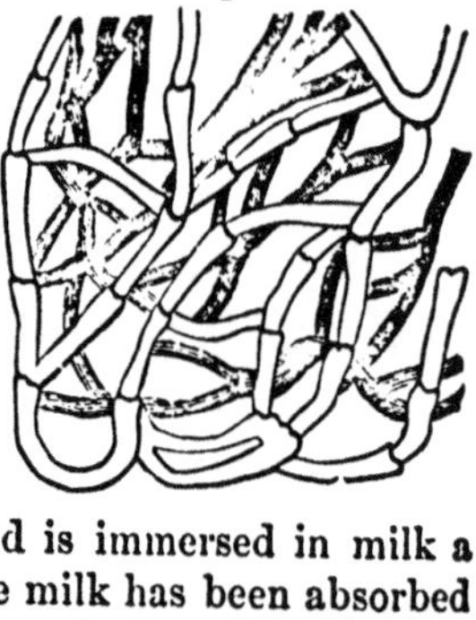

There are also oil-tubes, imbedded in the skin, that draw off oil from the blood. This issues on the surface, and spreads over the cuticle to keep it soft and moist.

But the most curious part of the skin is the system of innumerable minute perspiration-tubes. Fig. 58 is a drawing of one very greatly magnified. These tubes open on the

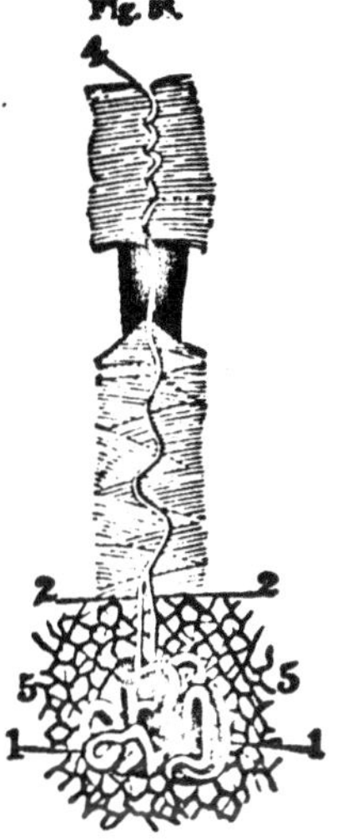

Fig. [illegible].

cuticle, and the openings are called pores of the skin. They descend into the true skin, and there form a coil, as is seen in the drawing. These tubes are hollow, like a pipe-stem, and their inner surface consists of wonderfully minute capillaries filled with the impure venous blood. And in these small tubes the same process is going on as takes place when the carbonic acid and water of the blood are exhaled from the lungs. The capillaries of these tubes through the whole skin of the body are thus constantly exhaling the noxious and decayed particles of the body, just as the lungs pour them out through the mouth and nose.

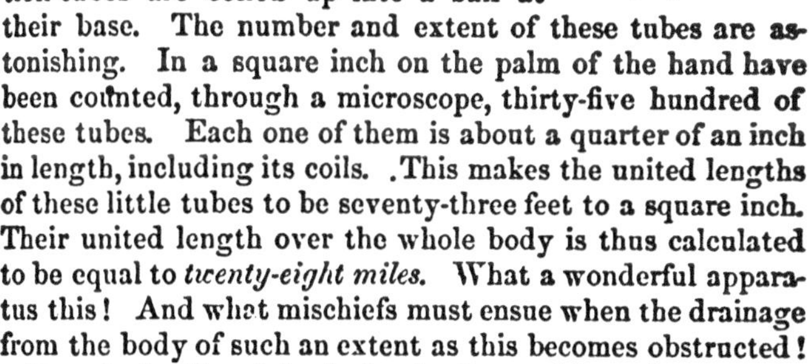

It has been shown that the perspiration-tubes are coiled up into a ball at their base. The number and extent of these tubes are astonishing. In a square inch on the palm of the hand have been counted, through a microscope, thirty-five hundred of these tubes. Each one of them is about a quarter of an inch in length, including its coils. This makes the united lengths of these little tubes to be seventy-three feet to a square inch. Their united length over the whole body is thus calculated to be equal to *twenty-eight miles.* What a wonderful apparatus this! And what mischiefs must ensue when the drainage from the body of such an extent as this becomes obstructed!

But the inside of the body also has a skin, as have all its organs. The interior of the head, the throat, the gullet, the lungs, the stomach, and all the intestines, are lined with a skin. This is called the *mucous membrane,* because it is constantly secreting from the blood a slimy substance called *mucus.* When it accumulates in the lungs, it is called *phlegm.* This inner skin also has nerves, blood-vessels, and lymphatics. The outer skin joins to the inner at the mouth, the nose, and other openings of the body, and there is a constant sympathy between the two skins, and thus between the inner organs and the surface of the body.

SECRETING ORGANS.

Those vessels of the body which draw off certain portions of the blood and change it into a new form, to be employed for service or to be thrown out of the body, are called *secreting organs.* The skin in this sense is a secreting organ, as its perspiration-tubes secrete or separate the bad portions of the blood, and send them off.

Of the internal secreting organs, the *liver* is the largest. Its chief office is to secrete from the blood all matter not properly supplied with oxygen. For this purpose, a set of veins carries the blood of all the lower intestines to the liver, where the imperfectly oxidized matter is drawn off in the form of *bile*, and accumulated in a reservoir called the *gall-bladder.* Thence it passes to the place where the smaller intestines receive the food from the stomach, and there it mixes with this food. Then it passes through the long intestines, and is thrown out of the body through the rectum. This shows how it is that want of pure and cool air and exercise causes excess of bile, from lack of oxygen. The liver also has arterial blood sent to nourish it, and corresponding veins to return this blood to the heart. So there are two sets of blood-vessels for the liver—one to secrete the bile, and the other to nourish the organ itself.

The kidneys secrete from the arteries that pass through them all excess of water in the blood, and certain injurious substances. These are carried through small tubes to the bladder, and thence thrown out of the body.

The *pancreas*, a whitish gland situated in the abdomen below the stomach, secretes from the arteries that pass through it the pancreatic juice, which unites with the bile from the liver, in preparing the food for nourishing the body.

There are certain little glands near the eyes that secrete the tears, and others near the mouth that secrete the saliva, or spittle.

These organs all have arteries sent to them to nourish them, and also veins to carry away the impure blood. At the same time, they secrete from the arterial blood the peculiar fluid which it is their office to supply.

All the food that passes through the lower intestines which is not drawn off by the lacteals or by some of these secreting organs, passes from the body through a passage called the rectum.

Learned men have made very curious experiments to ascertain how much the several organs throw out of the body. It is found that the skin throws off five out of eight pounds of the food and drink, or probably about three or four pounds a day. The lungs throw off one quarter as much as the skin, or about a pound a day. The remainder is carried off by the kidneys and lower intestines.

There is such a sympathy and connection between all the organs of the body, that when one of them is unable to work, the others perform the office of the feeble one. Thus, if the skin has its perspiration-tubes closed up by a chill, then all the poisonous matter that would have been thrown out through them must be emptied out either by the lungs, kidneys, or bowels.

When all these organs are strong and healthy, they can bear this increased labor without injury. But if the lungs are weak, the blood sent from the skin by the chill engorges the weak blood-vessels, and produces an inflammation of the lungs. Or it increases the discharge of a slimy mucous substance, that exudes from the skin of the lungs. This fills up the air-vessels, and would very soon end life, were it not for the spasms of the lungs, called *coughing*, which throw off this substance.

If, on the other hand, the bowels are weak, a chill of the skin sends the blood into all the blood-vessels of the intestines, and produces inflammation there, or else an excessive secretion of the mucous substance, which is called a *diarrhea.* Or if the kidneys are weak, there is an increased secretion and discharge from them, to an unhealthy and injurious extent.

This connection between the skin and internal organs is shown, not only by the internal effects of a chill on the skin, but by the sympathetic effect on the skin when these internal organs suffer. For example, there are some kinds of food that will irritate and influence the stomach or the bowels;

and this, by sympathy, will produce an immediate eruption on the skin. Some persons, on eating strawberries, will immediately be affected with a nettle-rash. Others can not eat certain shell-fish without being affected in this way. Many humors on the face are caused by a diseased state of the internal organs with which the skin sympathizes.

This short account of the construction of the skin, and of its intimate connection with the internal organs, shows the philosophy of those modes of medical treatment that are addressed to this portion of the body.

It is on this powerful agency that the steam-doctors rely, when, by moisture and heat, they stimulate all the innumerable perspiration-tubes and lymphatics to force out from the body a flood of unnaturally excited secretions; while it is "kill or cure," just as the chance may meet or oppose the demands of the case. It is the skin, also, that is the chief basis of medical treatment in the Water Cure, whose slow processes are as much safer as they are slower.

At the same time, it is the ill-treatment or neglect of the skin which, probably, is the cause of disease and decay to an incredible extent. The various particulars in which this may be seen will now be pointed out. In the management and care of this wonderful and complex part of the body many mistakes have been made.

The most common one is the misuse of the bath, especially since cold-water cures have come into use. This mode of medical treatment originated with an ignorant peasant, amidst a population where outdoor labor had strengthened nerves and muscles and imparted rugged powers to every part of the body. It was then introduced into England and America without due consideration or knowledge of the diseases, habits, or real condition of patients, especially of women. The consequence was a mode of treatment too severe and exhausting; and many practices were spread abroad not warranted by true medical science.

But, in spite of these mistakes and abuses, the treatment of the skin for disease by the use of cold water has become an accepted doctrine of the most learned medical practitioners. It is now held by all such that fevers can be detected in their distinctive features by the thermometer, and that all fevers can be reduced by cold baths and packing in the wet sheet, in the mode employed in all water cures.

It has been supposed that large bath-tubs for immersing the whole person are indispensable to the proper cleaning of the skin. This is not so. A wet towel, applied every morning to the skin, followed by friction in pure air, is all that is absolutely needed; although a full bath is a great luxury. Access of air to every part of the skin, when its perspiratory tubes are cleared and its blood-vessels are filled by friction, is the best ordinary bath.

Children should be washed all over, every night or morning, to remove impurities from the skin. But in this process careful regard should be paid to the peculiar constitution of a child. Very nervous children sometimes revolt from cold water, and like a tepid bath; others prefer a cold bath; and nature should be the guide. It must be remembered that the skin is the great organ of sensation, and in close connection with brain, spine, and nerve-centres: so that what a strong nervous system can bear with advantage is too powerful and exhausting for another. As age advances, or as disease debilitates the body, great care should be taken not to overtax the nervous system by sudden shocks, or to diminish its powers by withdrawing animal heat to excess. Persons lacking robustness should bathe or use friction in a warm room; and if very delicate, should expose only a portion of the body at once to cold air. But an evening or morning washing and friction of the skin will save from colds and many other evils.

Johnson, a celebrated writer on agricultural chemistry, tells of an experiment by friction on the skin of pigs, whose skins are like that of the human race. He treated six of these animals with a curry-comb seven weeks, and left three other pigs untouched. The result was a gain of thirty-three pounds more of weight, with the use of five bushels less of food for those curried, than for the neglected ones. This result was owing to the fact that all the functions of the body were more perfectly performed when, by friction, the skin was kept free from filth and the blood in it exposed to the air. The same will be true of the human skin. A calculation has been made on this fact, by which it is estimated that a man, by proper care of his skin, would save over thirty-one dollars in food yearly, which at 6 per cent. is the interest on over five hundred dollars. If men will give as much care to their own skin as they give to currying a horse, they will gain both health and wealth.

CHAPTER XI.

CLOTHING.

THERE is no duty of those persons having control of a family where principle and practice are more at variance than in regulating the dress of young girls, especially at the most important and critical period of life. It is a difficult duty for parents and teachers to contend with the power of fashion, which at this time of a young girl's life is frequently the ruling thought, and when to be out of the fashion, to be odd and not dress as all her companions do, is a mortification and grief that no argument or instructions can relieve. The mother is often so overborne that, in spite of her better wishes, the daughter adopts modes of dress alike ruinous to health and to beauty.

The greatest protection against such an emergency is to train a child to understand the construction of her own body, and to impress upon her, in early days, her obligations to the invisible Friend and Guardian of her life, the "Former of her body and the Father of her spirit," who has committed to her care so precious and beautiful a casket. And the more she can be made to realize the skill and beauty of construction shown in her earthly frame, the more will she feel the obligation to protect it from injury and abuse.

It is a singular fact that the war of fashion has attacked most fatally what seems to be the strongest foundation and defense of the body, the bones. For this reason, the construction and functions of this part of the body will now receive attention.

The bones are composed of two substances, one animal, and the other mineral. The animal part is a very fine network, called *cellular membrane.* In this are deposited the harder mineral substances, which are composed principally of carbonate and phosphate of lime. In very early life, the bones consist chiefly of the animal part, and are then soft and pliant. As the child advances in age, the bones grow harder, by the gradual deposition of the phosphate of lime, which is supplied by the food, and carried to the bones by the blood. In old age, the hardest material preponderates; making the bones more brittle than in earlier life.

The bones are covered with a thin skin or membrane, filled with small blood-vessels which convey nourishment to them.

Where the bones unite with others to form joints, they are covered with *cartilage*, which is a smooth, white, elastic substance. This enables the joints to move smoothly, while its elasticity prevents injuries from sudden jars.

The joints are bound together by strong, elastic bands called *ligaments*, which hold them firmly and prevent dislocation.

Between the ends of the bones that unite to form joints are small sacks or bags, that contain a soft lubricating fluid. This answers the same purpose for the joints as oil in making machinery work smoothly, while the supply is constant and always in exact proportion to the demand.

If you will examine the leg of some fowl, you can see the cartilage that covers the ends of the bones at the joints, and the strong white ligaments that bind the joints together.

The health of the bones depends on the proper nourishment and exercise of the body as much as that of any other part. When a child is feeble and unhealthy, or when it grows up without exercise, the bones do not become firm and hard as they are when the body is healthfully developed by exercise. The size as well as the strength of the bones, to a certain extent, also depend upon exercise and good health. So also they depend on the food, for fine flour is deprived of the materials that form bone, and growing children often have weak bones from having this for common food.

The chief supporter of the body is the spine, which consists of twenty-four small bones, interlocked or hooked into each other, while between them are elastic cushions of cartilage which aid in preserving the upright, natural position. Fig. 59 shows three of the spinal bones, hooked into each other, the dark spaces showing the disks or flat circular plates of cartilage between them.

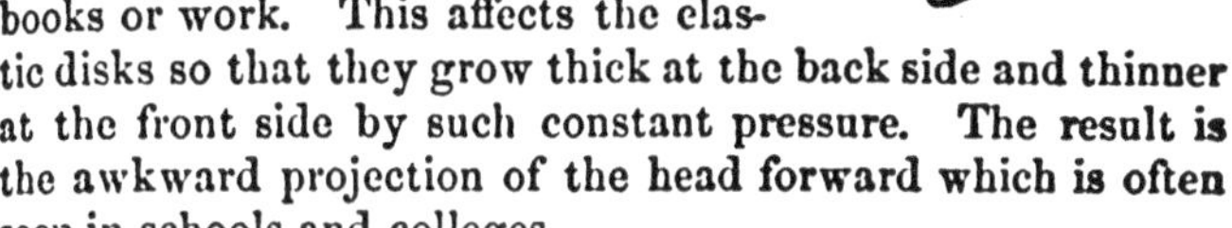
Fig. 59.

The spine is held in its proper position, partly by the ribs, partly by muscles, partly by aid of the elastic disks, and partly by the close packing of the intestines in front of it.

The upper part of the spine is often thrown out of its proper position by constant stooping of the head over books or work. This affects the elastic disks so that they grow thick at the back side and thinner at the front side by such constant pressure. The result is the awkward projection of the head forward which is often seen in schools and colleges.

Another distortion of the spine is produced by tight dress around the waist. The liver occupies the right side of the body and is a solid mass, while on the other side is the larger part of the stomach, which is often empty. The consequence of tight dress around the waist is a constant pressure of the spine toward the unsupported part where the stomach lies. Thus the elastic disks again are compressed, till they become thinner on one side than the other, and harden into that condition. This produces what is called the *lateral curvature of the spine*, making one shoulder higher than the other.

The evils consequent on modes of dress can never be remedied until the process of *breathing* is understood and its influence in preserving the position and healthful action of the pelvic organs in both sexes, but especially those of woman. And this has never been explained in any of our popular works on physiology.

In the diagram, Figs. 60, 61, D represents the diaphragm, which resembles an inverted bowl. Above it are the heart and lungs, marked H and L, and these are held up by blood-vessels and other supports above them. In this position of the diaphragm the air-vessels of the lungs are only partially filled with air, and there are two modes of increasing this

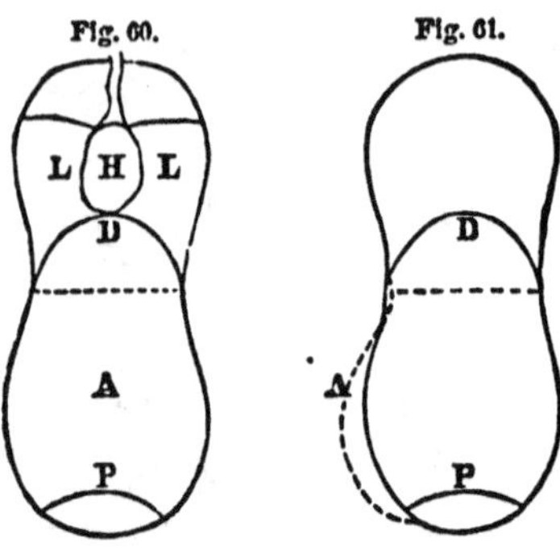

supply. One is by *chest* breathing, when the ribs are lifted upward and outward, making a vacuum in the air-vessels of the lungs. At the same time, the diaphragm is flattened by this expansion of the chest, as shown by the dotted lines. Then the air presses in through the nose and windpipe and fills the air-vessels, giving up its oxygen to the blood, and receiving carbonic acid and water, which are expired when the ribs and diaphragm return to their natural position.

The other mode of filling the lungs is by *abdominal* breathing, as illustrated by Fig. 61.

At D is a side view of the diaphragm in its natural position, and the dotted lines show its position when it is contracted and thus flattened. When the diaphragm contracts or flattens, a vacant space is left above it, and then the air rushes in to fill the vacuum, as it does when the ribs are raised. This flattening of the diaphragm presses all the viscera beneath it downward, and thus causes the abdomen to swell outward, as is represented by the dotted lines at A. Then, when the diaphragm returns to its natural state, a vacant space is made beneath it, and in consequence the viscera below rises to fill the vacuum, owing to the pressure of the atmosphere around the body; for it is said that "nature abhors a vacuum," by which is expressed a law of pneumatics in a popular adage. This law is, that when a vacuum is made in either air or water, the surrounding fluid presses from all sides, and from the bottom as strongly as from above. And thus, when a vacuum is made by the raising of the diaphragm, there is a pressure on all sides of the body, forcing the intestines upward to fill the vacuum thus made.

This enables us to explain that most curious and wonderful mode by which the upper viscera are prevented from sinking on to the lower, as secured chiefly by abdominal breathing.

The *pelvis* is the bony basin supporting the spine, to which the bones of the legs are fastened.

This basin holds the pelvic organs, consisting in one sex of the bladder and rectum, and in the other sex of the bladder, vagina, uterus, and rectum. These pelvic organs must enlarge by use, and so are placed in a spongy, yielding substance called *cellular membrane.* Now the liver, stomach, and all the intestines below the diaphragm, have *no support from above*, and so the question is, what sustains these organs, weighing from six to twelve pounds, so that they do not sink down on to the delicate pelvic organs below? The answer is, they are held up chiefly by *abdominal breathing*, as above explained. For at every rise of the diaphragm a vacuum is made above the abdominal viscera, lifting them upward, and this is done at every breath, and we breathe about twenty times each minute.

By this constant upward and downward movement of the abdominal viscera, the healthful and quickened circulation of the blood in all the myriad capillaries of both the abdominal and also the pelvic organs is promoted; for it has been shown on page 152 how alternate compression and relaxation of the veins promotes quickened circulation in all the veins and capillaries. Of course, any thing that impedes abdominal breathing interrupts this lifting operation, so that the upper intestines are left to gravitate on the pelvic organs. This stops the healthful flow of blood through the capillaries, and tends to produce congestion, inflammation, and cancerous accumulations in the pelvic organs.

All natural and healthful breathing unites both chest and abdominal breathing, as may be seen by watching a sleeping child. Clothing resting on the hips and abdomen, unsupported from the shoulders, is sure to impede abdominal breathing, and if heavy, to stop it entirely. In the present style of dress, when the clothing rests on hips and abdomen, and is unsupported by shoulder-straps, through most of the day this most healthful movement is interrupted, and thus the most efficient mode is taken of bringing on terrible suffering, both physical and mental.

Many a school-girl, whose waist was originally of a proper and healthful size, has gradually pressed the soft bones of youth until the lower ribs, that should rise and fall with every breath, become entirely unused, while heavy clothing or stiff corset-bones stop the abdominal breathing.

The pressure of the upper interior organs upon the lower ones by tight dress, is increased by the weight of clothing resting on the hips and abdomen. Corsets, as usually worn, have no support from the shoulders, and consequently all the weight of dress resting upon or above them presses upon the hips and abdomen, and this in such a way as to throw out of use, and thus weaken, the supporting muscles of the abdomen, and impede abdominal breathing.

Then the *stomach* begins to draw from above, instead of resting on the viscera beneath it. This in some cases causes dull and wandering pains, a sense of pulling at the centre of the chest, and a drawing downward at the pit of the stomach. Then, as the natural mode of support is really *gone*, there is what is often called "a feeling of *goneness*." This is sometimes relieved by food, which, so long as it remains in a solid form, helps to hold up the falling superstructure. This displacement of the stomach, liver, and spleen interrupts their healthful functions, and dyspepsia and biliary difficulties not unfrequently are the result.

As the stomach and its appendages fall downward, the breathing sometimes thus becomes quicker and shorter, on account of the elongated or debilitated condition of the assisting organs. Consumption not unfrequently results from this cause.

The *heart* also feels the evil. "Palpitations," "flutterings," "sinking feelings," all show that, in the language of Scripture, "the heart trembleth, and is moved out of its place."

Having the weight of all the unsupported organs above pressing them into unnatural and distorted positions, the passage of the food is interrupted, and inflammations, indurations, and constipation are the frequent result. Dreadful ulcers and cancers in the bowels may be traced in some instances to this cause.

Although these internal displacements are most common

among women, some foolish members of the other sex are adopting customs of dress, in girding the central portion of the body, that tend to similar results.

But this distortion brings upon woman peculiar distresses. The pressure of the whole superincumbent mass on the pelvic or lower organs induces sufferings proportioned in acuteness to the extreme delicacy and sensitiveness of the parts thus crushed. And the intimate connection of these organs with the brain and whole nervous system renders injuries thus inflicted the causes of the most extreme anguish, both of body and mind. This evil is becoming so common, not only among married women but among young girls, as to be a just cause for universal alarm.

How very common these sufferings are few but the medical profession can realize, because they are troubles that must be concealed. Many a woman is moving about in uncomplaining agony who, with any other trouble involving equal suffering, would be on her bed surrounded by sympathizing friends.

The terrible sufferings that are sometimes thus induced can never be conceived of, or at all appreciated from any use of language. Nothing that the public can be made to believe on this subject will ever equal the reality. Not only mature persons and mothers, but fair young girls sometimes, are shut up for months and years as helpless and suffering invalids from this cause. This may be found all over the land. And there frequently is a horrible extremity of suffering in certain forms of this evil, which no woman of feeble constitution dressing in present fashion can ever be certain may not be her doom. Not that in all cases this extremity is involved, but none can say who will escape it.

In regard to this, if one must choose for a friend or a child, on the one hand, the horrible torments inflicted by savage Indians or cruel inquisitors on their victims, or, on the other, the protracted agonies that result from such deformities and displacements, sometimes the former would be a merciful exchange. And yet this is the fate that is coming to meet the young as well as the mature in every direction.

And tender parents are unconsciously leading their lovely and hapless daughters to this awful doom.

There is no excitement of the imagination in what is here indicated. If the facts and details could be presented, they would send a groan of terror all over the land. For it is not one class, or one section, that is endangered. In every part of our country the evil is progressing.

And, as if these dreadful ills were not enough, there have been added methods of medical treatment at once useless, torturing to the mind, and involving great liability to immoralities.*

In hope of abating these evils, drawings are given (Fig. 62 and Fig. 63) of the front and back of a jacket that will pre-

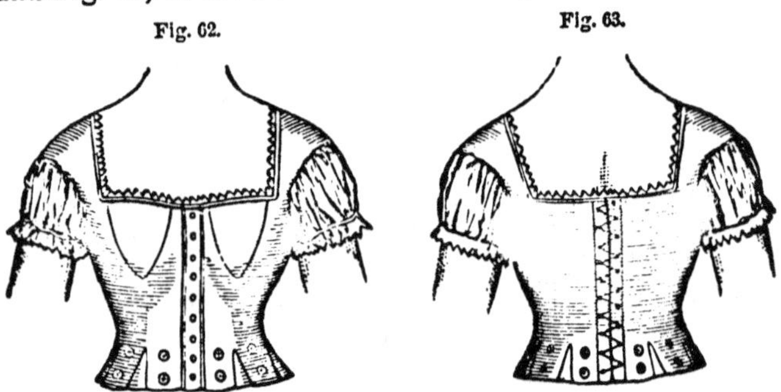

Fig. 62. Fig. 63.

serve the advantages of the corset without its evils. This jacket may at first be fitted to the figure with corsets underneath it, just like the waist of a dress. Then delicate whalebones can be used to stiffen the jacket, so that it will take the proper shape, when the corset may be dispensed with. The buttons below are to hold all articles of dress below the waist by button-holes. By this method the bust is supported as well as by corsets, while the shoulders support from above, as they should do, the weight of the dress below. No stiff bone should be allowed to press in front and the jacket should be so loose that a full breath can be inspired with ease while in a sitting position.

* Some extracts from medical writers in Note A will give the views of the most respected physicians all over the land on this point.

The proper way to dress a young girl is to have a cotton or flannel close-fitting jacket next the body, to which the drawers should be buttoned. Over this place the chemise; and over that, such a jacket as the one here drawn, to which should be buttoned the hoops and other skirts. Thus every article of dress will be supported by the shoulders. The sleeves of the jacket can be omitted, and in that case a strong lining, and also a tape binding, must surround the arm-hole, which should be loose.

It is hoped that increase of intelligence and moral power among mothers, and a combination among them to regulate fashions, may banish the pernicious practices that have prevailed. If a *school-girl dress* without corsets and without tight belts could be established as a fashion, it would be one step gained in the right direction. Then, if mothers could secure to their daughters daily domestic exercise in chambers, eating-rooms, and parlors in loose dresses, a still further advance would be secured.

A friend of the writer informs her that her daughter had her wedding outfit made up by a fashionable milliner in Paris, and every dress was beautifully fitted to the form, and yet was not compressing to any part. This was done too without the use of corsets, the stiffening being delicate and yielding whalebones.

Not only parents but all having the care of young girls, especially those at boarding-schools, have a fearful responsibility resting upon them in regard to this important duty.

In regard to the dressing of young children, much discretion is needed to adapt dress to circumstances and peculiar constitutions. The leading fact must be borne in mind, that the skin is made strong and healthful by exposure to light and pure air, while cold air, if not excessive, has a tonic influence. If the skin of infants is rubbed with the hand till red with blood, and then exposed naked to sun and air in a well-ventilated room, it will be favorable to health.

There is a constitutional difference in the skin of different children in regard to retaining the animal heat manufactured within, so that some need more clothing than others for comfort. Nature is a safe guide to a careful nurse and mother, and will indicate, by the looks and actions of a child, when more clothing is needful. As a general rule, it is safe for a healthful child to wear as little clothing as suffices to keep it from complaining of cold. Fifty years ago, it was not common for children to wear as much under-clothing as they now do. The writer well remembers how girls, though not of strong constitutions, used to play for hours in the snow-drifts without the protection of drawers, kept warm by exercise and occasional runs to an open fire. And multitudes of children grew to vigorous maturity through similar exposures to cold-air baths, and without the frequent colds and sicknesses so common among children of the present day, who are more carefully housed and warmly dressed. But care was taken that the feet should be kept dry and warmly clad, because, circulation being feebler in the extremities, this precaution was important.

It must also be considered that age brings with it decrease in vigor of circulation, and diminished generation of heat, so that more warmth of air and clothing is needed at an advanced period of life than is suitable for the young.

These are the general principles which must be applied with modification to each individual case. A child of delicate constitution must have more careful protection from cold air than is desirable for one more vigorous, while the leading general principle is retained that cold air is a healthful tonic for the skin whenever it does not produce an uncomfortable chilliness.

Sometimes it is asked, Why are women, especially young girls, so much more delicate and sickly than in former days? The true reply would be, it is because parents and teachers are doing every thing they can do to produce such mischiefs.

Sleeping in unventilated chambers; living in school-rooms and parlors heated to excess, and charged with poisonous gases; exposed to sudden variations of temperature from mismanagement; eating unhealthful food at irregular hours and to a dangerous excess; supplied with unhealthful confectionary to eat at any hour; indulging in exciting amusements, with late hours for sleep; the brain stimulated by a multitude of school duties and studies unrelieved by sufficient sleep or by muscular exercise; the dress contrived to impede vital functions, so as to force the upper organs on to the lower, generating the most cruel displacements and mental and bodily diseases; overheating the parts most injured by such treatment, and exposing the parts most important to keep warm; compressing feet and ankles so as to impede circulation, with high heels throwing all the muscles out of natural play, so as to increase all the dangerous tendencies to internal displacement; these are only one portion of the many contrivances adopted or allowed by parents and teachers to destroy the health of women and young girls.

CHAPTER XII.

EARLY RISING.

There is no practice which has been more extensively eulogized in all ages than early rising; and this universal impression is an indication that it is founded on true philosophy. For it is rarely the case that the common sense of mankind fastens on a practice as really beneficial, especially one that demands self-denial, without some substantial reason.

This practice, which may justly be called a domestic virtue, is one which has a peculiar claim to be styled American and democratic. The distinctive mark of aristocratic nations is a disregard of the great mass, and a disproportionate regard for the interests of certain privileged orders. All the customs and habits of such a nation are, to a greater or less extent, regulated by this principle. Now the mass of any nation must always consist of persons who labor at occupations which demand the light of day. But in aristocratic countries, especially in England, labor is regarded as the mark of the lower classes, and indolence is considered as one mark of a gentleman. This impression has gradually and imperceptibly, to a great extent, regulated their customs, so that, even in their hours of meals and repose, the higher orders aim at being different and distinct from those who, by laborious pursuits, are placed below them. From this circumstance, while the lower orders labor by day and sleep at night, the rich, the noble, and the honored sleep by day, and follow their pursuits and pleasures by night.

It will be found that the aristocracy of London breakfast near midday, dine after dark, visit and go to Parliament between ten and twelve at night, and retire to sleep toward morning. In consequence of this, the subordinate classes who aim at gentility gradually fall into the same practice. The influence of this custom extends across the ocean, and here, in this democratic land, we find many who measure their grade of gentility by the late hour at which they arrive at a party. And this aristocratic folly is growing upon us, so that throughout the nation the hours for visiting and retiring are constantly becoming later, while the hours for rising correspond in lateness.

The question, then, is one which appeals to American women as a matter of patriotism, and as having a bearing on those great principles of democracy which we conceive to be equally the principles of Christianity. Shall we form our customs on the assumption that labor is degrading and indolence genteel? Shall we assume, by our practice, that the interests of the great mass are to be sacrificed for the pleasures and honors of a privileged few? Shall we ape the customs of aristocratic lands, in those very practices which result from principles and institutions that we condemn? Shall we not rather take the place to which we are entitled, as the leaders, rather than the followers, in the customs of society, turn back the tide of aristocratic inroads, and carry through the whole, not only of civil and political but of social and domestic life, the true principles of democratic freedom and equality? The following considerations may serve to strengthen an affirmative decision:

The first relates to the health of a family. It is a universal law of physiology, that all living things flourish best in the light. Vegetables, in a dark cellar, grow pale and spindling. Children brought up in mines are always wan and stunted, while men become pale and cadaverous who live under ground. This indicates the folly of losing the genial influence which the light of day produces on all animated creation.

Sir James Wylie, of the Russian imperial service, states that in the soldiers' barracks three times as many were taken sick on the shaded side as on the sunny side; though both sides communicated, and discipline, diet, and treatment were the same. The eminent French surgeon, Dupuytren, cured a lady, whose complicated diseases baffled for years his own and all other medical skill, by taking her from a dark room to an abundance of daylight.

Florence Nightingale writes: "Second only to fresh air in importance for the sick is *light*. Not only daylight but direct sunlight is necessary to speedy recovery, except in a small number of cases. Instances, almost endless, could be given where, in dark wards, or wards with only northern exposure, or wards with borrowed light, even when properly ventilated, the sick could not be, by any means, made speedily to recover."

In the prevalence of cholera, it was invariably the case that deaths were more numerous in shaded streets, or in houses having only northern exposures, than in those having sunlight. Several physicians have stated to the writer that, in sunny exposures, women after childbirth gained strength much faster than those excluded from sunlight. In the writer's experience, great nervous debility has been always immediately lessened by sitting in the sun, and still more by lying on the earth and in open air, a blanket beneath, and head and eyes protected, under the direct rays of the sun.

Some facts in physiology and natural philosophy have a bearing on this subject. It seems to be settled that the red color of blood is owing to iron contained in the red blood-cells, while it is established as a fact that the sun's rays are metallic, having "vapor of iron" as one element. It is also true that want of light causes a diminution of the red and an increase of the imperfect white blood-cells, and that this sometimes results in a disease called *leucoemia*, while all who live in the dark have pale and waxy skins, and flabby, weak muscles. Thus it would seem that it is the sun that imparts the iron and color to the blood. These things being so, the customs of society that bring sleeping hours into daylight, and working and study hours into the night, are direct violations of the laws of health. The laws of health are the laws of God, and "sin is the trangression of law."

To this we must add the great neglect of economy as well as health in substituting unhealthful gas-light and poisonous, anthracite warmth, for the life-giving light and warmth of the sun. Millions and millions would be saved to this nation in fuel and light, as well as in health, by returning to the good old ways of our forefathers, to rise with the sun, and retire to rest "when the bell rings for nine o'clock."

The observations of medical men, whose inquiries have been directed to this point, have decided that from six to eight hours is the amount of sleep demanded by persons in health. Some constitutions require as much as eight, and others no more than six hours of repose. But eight hours is the maximum for all persons in ordinary health, with ordinary occupations. In cases of extra physical exertions, or the debility of disease, or a decayed constitution, more than this is required. Let eight hours, then, be regarded as the ordinary period required for sleep by an industrious people like the Americans.

It thus appears that the laws of our political condition, the laws of the natural world, and the constitution of our bodies, alike demand that we rise with the light of day to prosecute our employments, and that we retire in time for the requisite amount of sleep.

In regard to the effects of protracting the time spent in repose, many extensive and satisfactory investigations have been made. It has been shown that during sleep the body perspires most freely, while yet neither food nor exercise are ministering to its wants. Of course, if we continue our slumbers beyond the time required to restore the body to its usual vigor, there is an unperceived undermining of the constitution by this protracted and debilitating exhalation. This process, in a course of years, renders the body delicate and less able to withstand disease, and in the result shortens life. Sir John Sinclair, who has written a large work on the Causes of Longevity, states, as one result of his extensive investigations, that he has never yet heard or read of a single case of great longevity where the individual was not an early riser. He says that he has found cases in which the individual has violated some one of all the other laws of health, and yet lived to great age; but never a single instance in which any constitution has withstood that undermining consequent on protracting the hours of repose beyond the demands of the system.

Another reason for early rising is, that it is indispensable to a systematic and well-regulated family. At whatever hour the parents retire, children and domestics, wearied by play or labor, must retire early. Children usually awake with the dawn of light and commence their play, while domestics usually prefer the freshness of morning for their labors. If, then, the parents rise at a late hour, they either induce a habit of protracting sleep in their children and domestics, or else the family are up, and at their pursuits, while their supervisors are in bed.

Any woman who asserts that her children and domestics, in the first hours of day, when their spirits are freshest, will be as well regulated without her presence as with it, confesses that which surely is little for her credit. It is believed that any candid woman, whatever may be her excuse for late rising, will concede that if she could rise early it would be for the advantage of her family. A late breakfast puts back the work, through the whole day, for every member of a family; and if the parents thus occasion the loss of an hour or two to each individual, who, but for their delay in the morning, would be usefully employed, they alone are responsible for all this waste of time.

But the practice of early rising has a relation to the general interests of the social community, as well as to that of each distinct family. All that great portion of the community who are employed in business and labor find it needful to rise early; and all their hours of meals, and their appointments for business or pleasure, must be accommodated to these arrangements. Now, if a small portion of the community establish very different hours, it makes a kind of jostling in all the concerns and interests of society. The various appointments for the public, such as meetings, schools, and business hours, must be accommodated to the mass, and not to individuals. The few, then, who establish domestic habits at variance with the majority, are either constantly interrupted in their own arrangements, or else are interfering with the rights and interests of others. This is exemplified in the case of schools. In families where late rising is practiced, either hurry, irregularity, and neglect are engendered in the family, or else the interests of the school, and thus of the community, are sacrificed. In this and many other matters, it can be shown that the well-being of the bulk of the people is, to a greater or less extent, impaired by this self-indulgent practice. Let any teacher select the unpunctual scholars—a class who most seriously interfere with the interests of the school—and let men of business select those who cause them most waste of time and vexation, by unpunctuality; and it will be found that they are generally among the late risers, and rarely among those who rise early. Thus, late rising not only injures the person and family which indulge in it, but interferes with the rights and convenience of the community; while early rising imparts corresponding benefits of health, promptitude, vigor of action, economy of time, and general effectiveness, both to the individuals who practice it and to the families and community of which they are a part.

CHAPTER XIII.

DOMESTIC MANNERS.

Good manners are the expressions of benevolence in personal intercourse, by which we endeavor to promote the comfort and enjoyment of others, and to avoid all that gives needless uneasiness. It is the exterior exhibition of the divine precept, which requires us to do to others as we would that they should do to us. It is saying, by our deportment, to all around, that we consider their feelings, tastes, and conveniences, as equal in value to our own.

Good manners lead us to avoid all practices which offend the taste of others; all unnecessary violations of the conventional rules of propriety; all rude and disrespectful language and deportment; and all remarks which would tend to wound the feelings of others.

There is a serious defect in the manners of the American people, especially among the descendants of the Puritan settlers of New England, which can never be efficiently remedied, except in the domestic circle, and during early life. It is a deficiency in the free expression of kindly feelings and sympathetic emotions, and a want of courtesy in deportment. The causes which have led to this result may easily be traced.

The forefathers of this nation, to a wide extent, were men who were driven from their native land by laws and customs which they believed to be opposed both to civil and religious freedom. The sufferings they were called to endure, the subduing of those gentler feelings which bind us to country, kindred, and home; and the constant subordination of the passions to stern principle, induced characters of great firmness and self-control. They gave up the comforts and refinements of a civilized country, and came as pilgrims to a hard soil, a cold clime, and a heathen shore. They were continually forced to encounter danger, privation sickness, loneliness, and death; and all these their religion taught them to meet with calmness, fortitude, and submission. And thus it became the custom and habit of the whole mass to repress rather than to encourage the expression of feeling.

Persons who are called to constant and protracted suffering and privation are forced to subdue and conceal emotion; for the free expression of it would double their own suffering, and increase the sufferings of others. Those only who are free from care and anxiety, and whose minds are mainly occupied by cheerful emotions, are at full liberty to unveil their feelings.

It was under such stern and rigorous discipline that the first children in New-England were reared; and the manners and habits of parents are usually to a great extent transmitted to children. Thus it comes to pass that the descendants of the Puritans, now scattered over every part of the nation, are predisposed to conceal the gentler emotions, while their manners are calm, decided, and cold, rather than free and impulsive. Of course, there are very many exceptions to these predominating characteristics.

Other causes, to which we may attribute a general want of courtesy in manners, are certain incidental results of our domestic institutions. Our ancestors and their descendants have constantly been combating the aristocratic principle, which would exalt one class of men at the expense of another. They have had to contend with this principle, not only in civil but in social life. Almost every American, in his own person as well as in behalf of his class, has had to assume and defend the main principle of democracy—that every man's feelings and interests are equal in value to those of every other man. But, in doing this, there has been some want of clear discrimination. Because claims based on distinctions of mere birth, fortune, or position were found to be injurious, many have gone to the extreme of inferring that all distinctions involving subordinations are useless. Such would wrongfully regard children as equals to parents, pupils to teachers, domestics to their employers, and subjects to magistrates—and that, too, in all respects.

The fact that certain grades of superiority and subordination are needful, both for individual and public benefit, has not been clearly discerned; and there has been a gradual tendency to an extreme of the opposite view which has sensibly affected our manners. All the proprieties and courtesies which depend on the recognition of the relative duties of superior and subordinate have been warred upon; and thus we see, to an increasing extent, disrespectful treatment of parents, by children; of teachers, by pupils; of employers, by domestics; and of the aged, by the young. In all classes and circles there is a gradual decay in courtesy of address.

In cases, too, where kindness is rendered, it is often accompanied with a cold, unsympathizing manner, which greatly lessens its value; while kindness or politeness is received in a similar style of coolness, as if it were but the payment of a just due.

It is owing to these causes that the American people, especially the descendants of the Puritans, do not do themselves justice. For, while those who are near enough to learn their real character and feelings can discern the most generous impulses and the most kindly sympathies, they are often so veiled behind a composed and indifferent demeanor as to be almost entirely concealed from strangers.

These defects in our national manners it especially falls to the care of mothers, and all who have charge of the young, to rectify; and if they seriously undertake the matter, and wisely adapt means to ends, these defects will be remedied. With reference to this object, the following ideas are suggested:

The law of Christianity and of democracy, which teaches that all men are born equal in rights, and that their interests and feelings should be regarded as of equal value, seems to be adopted in aristocratic circles, with exclusive reference to the class in which the individual moves. The courtly gentleman addresses all of his own class with politeness and respect, and in all his actions seems to allow that the feelings and convenience of these others are to be regarded the same as his own. But his demeanor to those of inferior station is not based on the same rule.

Among those who make up aristocratic circles, such as are above them are deemed of superior, and such as are below of inferior, value. Thus, if a young, ignorant, and vicious coxcomb happens to have been born a lord, the aged, the virtuous, the learned, and the well-bred of another class must give his convenience the precedence, and must address him in terms of respect. So, sometimes, when a man of "noble birth" is thrown among the lower classes, he demeans himself in a style which, to persons of his own class, would be deemed the height of assumption and rudeness.

Now, the principles of democracy require that the same courtesy which we accord to our own circle shall be extended to every class and condition; and that distinctions of superiority and subordination shall depend, not on accidents of birth, fortune, or occupation, but solely on those mutual relations which the good of all classes equally require. The distinctions demanded in a democratic state are simply those which result from relations that are common to every class, and are for the benefit of all.

It is for the benefit of every class that children be subordinate to parents, pupils to teachers, the employed to their employers, and subjects to magistrates. In addition to this, it is for the general well-being that the comfort or convenience of the delicate and feeble should be preferred to that of the strong and healthy, who would suffer less by any deprivation; that precedence should be given to their elders by the young; and that reverence should be given to the hoary head.

The rules of good-breeding, in a democratic state, must be founded on these principles. It is indeed assumed that the value of the happiness of each individual is the same as that of every other; but as there must be occasions where there are advantages which all can not enjoy, there must be general rules for regulating a selection. Otherwise, there would be constant scrambling among those of equal claims, and brute force must be the final resort; in which case the strongest would have the best of every thing. The democratic rule, then, is, that superiors in age, station, or office, have precedence of subordinates; age and feebleness, of youth and strength; and the feebler sex, of more vigorous man.*

There is, also, a style of deportment and address which is appropriate to these different relations. It is suitable for a superior to secure compliance with his wishes from those subordinate to him by commands; but a subordinate must secure compliance with his wishes from a superior by request. (Although the kind and considerate manner to subordinates will always be found the most effective as well as the pleasantest, by those in superior station.) It is suitable for a parent, teacher, or employer, to admonish for neglect of duty; but not for an inferior to adopt such a course toward a superior. It is suitable for a superior to take precedence of a subordinate without any remark; but not for an inferior without previously asking leave, or offering an apology. It is proper for a superior to use language and manners of freedom and familiarity which would be improper from a subordinate to a superior.

The want of due regard to these proprieties occasions a great defect in American manners. It is very common to hear children talk to their parents in a style proper only between companions and equals; so, also, the young address their elders; those employed, their employers; and domestics, the members of the family and their visitors in a style which is inappropriate to their relative positions. But courteous address is required not merely toward superiors; every person desires to be thus treated, and therefore the law of benevolence demands such demeanor toward all whom we meet in the social intercourse of life. "Be ye courteous," is the direction of the apostle in reference to our treatment of *all.*

Good manners can be successfully cultivated only in early life and in the domestic circle. There is nothing which depends so much upon *habit* as the constantly recurring pro-

* The universal practice of this nation, in thus giving precedence to woman has been severely commented on by foreigners, and by some who would transfer all the business of the other sex to women, and then have them treated like men. But we hope this evidence of our superior civilization and Christianity may increase rather than diminish.

prieties of good-breeding; and if a child grows up without forming such habits, it is very rarely the case that they can be formed at a later period. The feeling that it is of little consequence how we behave at home if we conduct ourselves properly abroad, is a very fallacious one. Persons who are careless and ill-bred at home may imagine that they can assume good manners abroad; but they mistake. Fixed habits of tone, manner, language, and movements can not be suddenly altered; and those who are ill-bred at home, even when they try to hide their bad habits, are sure to violate many of the obvious rules of propriety, and yet be unconscious of it.

And there is nothing which would so effectually remove prejudice against our democratic institutions as the general cultivation of good-breeding in the domestic circle. Good manners are the exterior of benevolence, the minute and constant exhibitions of "peace and good-will;" and the nation, as well as the individual, which most excels in the external demonstration, as well as the internal principle, will be most respected and beloved.

It is only the training of the family state according to its true end and aim that is to secure to woman her true position and rights. When the family is instituted by marriage, it is man who is the head and chief magistrate by the force of his physical power and requirement of the chief responsibility; not less is he so according to the Christian law, by which, when differences arise, the husband has the deciding control, and the wife is to obey. "Where love is, there is no law;" but where love is not, the only dignified and peaceful course is for the wife, however much the man's superior, to "submit, as to God and not to man."

But this power of nature and of religion, given to man as the controlling head, involves to him especially the distinctive duty of the family state, *self-sacrificing love.* The husband is to "honor" the wife, to love her as himself, and thus to account her wishes and happiness as of equal value with his own. But more than this, he is to love her "as Christ loved the Church;" that is, he is to "suffer" for her, if need be, in order to support and elevate and ennoble her.

The father, then, is to set the example of self-sacrificing love and devotion; and the mother, of Christian obedience, when it is required. Every boy is to be trained for his future domestic position by labor and sacrifices for his mother and sisters. It is the brother who is to do the hardest and most disagreeable work, to face the storms, and perform the most laborious drudgeries. In the family circle, too, he is to give his mother and sister precedence in all the conveniences and comforts of home life.

It is only in those nations where the teachings and example of Christ have had most influence that man has ever assumed his obligations of self-sacrificing benevolence in the family. And even in Christian communities, the duty of wives to obey their husbands has been more strenuously urged, than the obligations of the husband to love his wife "as Christ loved the Church."

Here it is needful to notice that the distinctive duty of obedience to man does not rest on women who do not enter the relations of married life. A woman who inherits property, or who earns her own livelihood, can institute the family state, adopt orphan children, and employ suitable helpers in training them; and then to her will appertain the authority and rights that belong to man as the head of a family. And when every woman is trained to some self-supporting business, she will not be tempted to enter the family state as a subordinate, except by that love for which there is no need of law.

These general principles being stated, some details in regard to domestic manners will be enumerated.

In the first place, there should be required in the family a strict attention to the rules of precedence, and those modes of address appropriate to the various relations to be sustained. Children should always be required to offer their superiors in age or station the precedence in all comforts and conveniences, and always address them in a respectful tone and manner. The custom of adding, "Sir," or "Ma'am," to "Yes," or "No," is valuable, as a perpetual indication of a respectful recognition of superiority. It is now going out of fashion, even among the most well-bred people; probably from a want of consideration of its importance. Every remnant of courtesy of address in our customs should be carefully cherished by all who feel a value for the proprieties of good-breeding.

If parents allow their children to talk to them, and to the grown persons in the family, in the same style in which they address each other, it will be in vain to hope for the courtesy of manner and tone which good-breeding demands in the general intercourse of society. In a large family, where the elder children are grown up and the younger are small, it is important to require the latter to treat the elder in some sense as superiors. There are none so ready as young children to assume airs of equality; and if they are allowed to treat one class of superiors in age and character disrespectfully, they will soon use the privilege universally. This is the reason why the youngest children of a family are most apt to be pert, forward, and unmannerly.

Another point to be aimed at is, to require children always to acknowledge every act of kindness and attention, either by words or manner. If they are so trained as always to make grateful acknowledgments when receiving favors, one of the objectionable features in American manners will be avoided.

Again, children should be required to ask leave, whenever they wish to gratify curiosity, or use an article which belongs to another. And if cases occur when they can not comply with the rules of good-breeding—as, for instance, when they must step between a person and the fire, or take the chair of an older person—they should be taught either to ask leave or to offer an apology.

There is another point of good-breeding which can not, in all cases, be understood and applied by children in its widest extent. It is that which requires us to avoid all remarks which tend to embarrass, vex, mortify, or in any way wound the feelings of another. To notice personal defects; to allude to others' faults, or the faults of their friends; to speak disparagingly of the sect or party to which a person belongs; to be inattentive when addressed in conversation; to contradict flatly; to speak in contemptuous tones of opinions expressed by another; all these are violations of the rules of good-breeding, which children should be taught to regard. Under this head comes the practice of whispering and staring about when a teacher, or lecturer, or clergyman is addressing a class or audience. Such inattention is practically saying that what the person is uttering is not worth attending to; and persons of real good-breeding always avoid it. Loud talking and laughing in a large assembly, even when no exercises are going on; yawning and gaping in company; and not looking in the face a person who is addressing you, are deemed marks of ill-breeding.

Another branch of good manners relates to the duties of hospitality. Politeness requires us to welcome visitors with cordiality; to offer them the best accommodations; to address conversation to them; and to express, by tone and manner, kindness and respect. Offering the hand to all visitors at one's own house is a courteous and hospitable custom; and a cordial shake of the hand, when friends meet, would abate much of the coldness of manner ascribed to Americans.

Another point of good-breeding refers to the conventional rules of propriety and good taste. Of these, the first class relates to the avoidance of all disgusting or offensive personal habits: such as fingering the hair; obtrusively using a tooth-pick, or carrying one in the mouth after the needful use of it; cleaning the nails in presence of others; picking the nose; spitting on carpets; snuffing instead of using a handkerchief, or using the article in an offensive manner; lifting up the boots or shoes, as some men do, to tend them on the knee, or to finger them: all these tricks, either at home or in society, children should be taught to avoid.

Another topic, under this head, may be called *table manners*. To persons of good-breeding nothing is more annoying than violations of the conventional proprieties of the table. Reaching over another person's plate; standing up to reach distant articles, instead of asking to have them passed; using one's own knife and spoon for butter, salt, or sugar, when it is the custom of the family to provide separate utensils for the purpose; setting cups with the tea dripping from them on the table-cloth, instead of the mats or small plates furnished; using the table-cloth instead of the napkins; eating fast, and in a noisy manner; putting large pieces in the mouth; looking and eating as if very hungry, or as if anxious to get at certain dishes; sitting at too great a distance from the table, and dropping food; laying the knife and fork on the table-cloth, instead of on the edge of the plate; picking the teeth at the table: all these particulars children should be taught to avoid.

It is always desirable, too, to train children, when at table with grown persons, to be silent, except when addressed by others; or else their chattering will interrupt the conversation and comfort of their elders. They should always be required, too, to wait in silence till all the older persons are helped.

When children are alone with their parents, it is desirable to lead them to converse and to take this as an opportunity to form proper conversational habits. But it should be a fixed rule that, when strangers are present, the children are to listen in silence, and only reply when addressed. Unless this is secured, visitors will often be condemned to listen to puerile chattering, with small chance of the proper attention due to guests and superiors in age and station.

Children should be trained, in preparing themselves for the table or for appearance among the family, not only to put their hair, face, and hands in neat order, but also their nails, and to habitually attend to this latter whenever they wash their hands.

There are some very disagreeable tricks which many children practice even in families counted well-bred. Such, for example, are drumming with the fingers on some piece of furniture, or humming a tune while others are talking, or interrupting conversation by pertinacious questions, or whistling in the house instead of outdoors, or speaking several at once and in loud voices to gain attention. All these are violations of good-breeding, which children should be trained to avoid, lest they should not only annoy as children, but practice the same kind of ill manners when mature. In all assemblies for public debate, a chairman or moderator is appointed whose business it is to see that only one person speaks at a time, that no one interrupts a person when speaking, that no needless noises are made, and that all indecorums are avoided. Such an officer is sometimes greatly needed in family circles.

Children should be encouraged freely to use lungs and limbs outdoors, or in hours for sport in the house. But at other times, in the domestic circle, gentle tones and manners should be cultivated. The words *gentleman* and *gentlewoman* came originally from the fact that the uncultivated and ignorant classes used coarse and loud tones, and rough words and movements; while only the refined circles habitually used gentle tones and gentle manners. For the same reason, those born in the higher circles were called "of gentle blood." Thus it came that a coarse and loud voice, and rough, ungentle manners, are regarded as vulgar and plebeian.

All these things should be taught to children gradually, and with great patience and gentleness. Some parents, with whom good manners are a great object, are in danger of making their children perpetually uncomfortable, by suddenly surrounding them with so many rules that they must inevitably violate some one or other a great part of the time. It is much better to begin with a few rules, and be steady and persevering with these till a habit is formed, and then take a few more, thus making the process easy and gradual. Otherwise, the temper of children will be injured; or, hopeless of fulfilling so many requisitions, they will become reckless and indifferent to all.

If a few brief, well-considered, and sensible rules of good manners could be suspended in every school-room, and the children all required to commit them to memory, it probably would do more to remedy the defects of American manners, and to advance universal good-breeding, than any other mode that could be so easily adopted.

But, in reference to those who have enjoyed advantages for the cultivation of good manners, and who duly estimate its importance, one caution is necessary. Those who never have had such habits formed in youth are under disadvantages which no benevolence of temper can altogether remedy. They may often violate the tastes and feelings of others, not from a want of proper regard for them, but from ignorance of custom, or want of habit, or abstraction of mind, or from other causes which demand forbearance and sympathy, rather than displeasure. An ability to bear patiently with defects in manners, and to make candid and considerate allowance for a want of advantages, or for peculiarities in mental habits, is one mark of the benevolence of real good-breeding.

The advocates of monarchical and aristocratic institutions have always had great plausibility given to their views, by the seeming tendencies of our institutions to insubordination and bad manners. And it has been too indiscriminately conceded by the defenders of the latter that such are these tendencies, and that the offensive points in American manners are the necessary result of democratic principles.

But it is believed that both facts and reasoning are in opposition to this opinion. The following extract from the work of De Tocqueville, the great political philosopher of France, exhibits the opinion of an impartial observer, when comparing American manners with those of the English, who are confessedly the most aristocratic of all people.

He previously remarks on the tendency of aristocracy to make men more sympathizing with persons of their own peculiar class, and less so toward those of lower degree; and he then contrasts American manners with the English, claiming that the Americans are much the more affable, mild, and social. "In America, where the privileges of birth never existed, and where riches confer no peculiar rights on their possessors, men acquainted with each other are very ready to frequent the same places, and find neither peril nor disadvantage in the free interchange of their thoughts. If they meet by accident, they neither seek nor avoid intercourse; their manner is therefore natural, frank, and open." "If their demeanor is often cold and serious, it is never haughty nor constrained." But an "aristocratic pride is still extremely great among the English; and as the limits of aristocracy are still ill-defined, every body lives in constant dread lest advantage should be taken of his familiarity. Unable to judge at once of the social position of those he meets, an Englishman prudently avoids all contact with them. Men are afraid lest some slight service rendered should draw them into an unsuitable acquaintance; they dread civilities, and they avoid the obtrusive gratitude of a stranger as much as his hatred."

Thus, *facts* seem to show that when the most aristocratic nation in the world is compared, as to manners, with the most democratic, the judgment of strangers is in favor of the latter. And if good manners are the outward exhibition of the democratic principle of impartial benevolence and equal rights, surely the nation which adopts this rule, both in social and civil life, is the most likely to secure the desirable exterior. The aristocrat, by his principles, extends the exterior of impartial benevolence to his own class only; the democratic principle requires it to be extended *to all.*

There is reason, therefore, to hope and expect more refined and polished manners in America than in any other land; while all the developments of taste and refinement, such as poetry, music, painting, sculpture, and architecture, it may be expected, will come to as high a state of perfection here as in any other nation.

If this country increases in virtue and intelligence as it may, there is no end to the wealth which will pour in as the result of our resources of climate, soil, and navigation, and the skill, industry, energy, and enterprise of our countrymen. This wealth, if used as intelligence and virtue dictate, will furnish the means for a superior education to all classes, and every facility for the refinement of taste, intellect, and feeling.

Moreover, in this country, labor is ceasing to be the badge of a lower class; so that already it is disreputable for a man to be "a lazy gentleman." And this feeling must increase, till there is such an equalization of labor as will afford all the time needful for every class to improve the many advantages offered to them. Already, through the munificence of some of our citizens, there are literary and scientific advantages offered to all classes, rarely enjoyed elsewhere. In most of our large cities and towns the advantages of education now offered to the poorest classes, often without charge, surpass what, some years ago, most wealthy men could purchase for any price; and it is believed that a time will come when the poorest boy in America can secure advantages which will equal what the heir of the proudest peerage can now command.

The records of the courts of France and Germany, (as detailed by the Duchess of Orleans,) in and succeeding the brilliant reign of Louis the Fourteenth—a period which was deemed the acme of elegance and refinement—exhibit a grossness, a vulgarity, and a coarseness, not to be found among the very lowest of our respectable poor. And the biography of the English Beau Nash, who attempted to reform the manners of the gentry in the times of Queen Anne, exhibits violations of the rules of decency among the aristocracy which the commonest yeoman of this land would feel disgraced in perpetrating.

This shows that our lowest classes, at this period, are more refined than were the highest in aristocratic lands a hundred years ago; and another century may show the lowest classes in wealth, in this country, attaining as high a polish as adorns those who now are leaders of good manners in the courts of kings.

CHAPTER XIV.

THE PRESERVATION OF GOOD TEMPER IN THE HOUSEKEEPER.

There is nothing which has a more abiding influence on the happiness of a family than the preservation of equable and cheerful temper and tones in the housekeeper. A woman who is habitually gentle, sympathizing, forbearing, and cheerful, carries an atmosphere about her which imparts a soothing and sustaining influence, and renders it easier for all to do right, under her administration, than in any other situation.

The writer has known families where the mother's presence seemed the sunshine of the circle around her—imparting a cheering and vivifying power, scarcely realized till it was withdrawn. Every one, without thinking of it, or knowing why it was so, experienced a peaceful and invigorating influence as soon as he entered the sphere illumined by her smile and sustained by her cheering kindness and sympathy. On the contrary, many a good housekeeper, (good in every respect but this,) by wearing a countenance of anxiety and dissatisfaction, and by indulging in the frequent use of sharp and reprehensive tones, more than destroys all the comfort which otherwise would result from her system, neatness, and economy.

There is a secret, social sympathy which every mind, to a greater or less degree, experiences with the feelings of those around, as they are manifested by the countenance and voice. A sorrowful, a discontented, or an angry countenance produces a silent, sympathetic influence, imparting a sombre shade to the mind, while tones of anger or complaint still more effectually jar the spirits.

No person can maintain a quiet and cheerful frame of mind while tones of discontent and displeasure are sounding on the ear. We may gradually accustom ourselves to the evil till it is partially diminished; but it always is an evil which greatly interferes with the enjoyment of the family state. There are sometimes cases where the entrance of the mistress of a family seems to awaken a slight apprehension in every mind around, as if each felt in danger of a reproof, for something either perpetrated or neglected. A woman who should go around her house with a small stinging snapper, which she habitually applied to those whom she met, would be encountered with feelings very much like those which are experienced by the inmates of a family where the mistress often uses her countenance and voice to inflict similar penalties for duties neglected.

Yet there are many allowances to be made for housekeepers who sometimes imperceptibly and unconsciously fall into such habits. A woman who attempts to carry out any plans of system, order, and economy, and who has her feelings and habits conformed to certain rules, is constantly liable to have her plans crossed, and her taste violated, by the inexperience or inattention of those about her. And no housekeeper, whatever may be her habits, can escape the frequent recurrence of negligence or mistake which interferes with her plans.

It is probable that there is no class of persons in the world who have such incessant trials of temper, and temptations to be fretful, as American housekeepers; for a housekeeper's business is not, like that of the other sex, limited to a particular department, for which previous preparation is made. It consists of ten thousand little disconnected items, which can never be so systematically arranged that there is no daily jostling somewhere. And in the best-regulated families it is not unfrequently the case that some act of forgetfulness or carelessness from some member will disarrange the business of the whole day, so that every hour will bring renewed occasion for annoyance. And the more strongly a woman realizes the value of time, and the importance of system and order, the more will she be tempted to irritability and complaint.

The following considerations may aid in preparing a woman to meet such daily crosses with even a cheerful temper and tones.

In the first place, a woman who has charge of a large household should regard her duties as dignified, important, and difficult. The mind is so made as to be elevated and cheered by a sense of far-reaching influence and usefulness. A woman who feels that she is a cipher, and that it makes little difference how she performs her duties, has far less to sustain and invigorate her than one who truly estimates the importance of her station. A man who feels that the destinies of a nation are turning on the judgment and skill with which he plans and executes, has a pressure of motive and an elevation of feeling which are great safeguards against all that is low, trivial, and degrading.

So, an American mother and housekeeper who rightly estimates the long train of influence which will pass down to thousands whose destinies, from generation to generation, will be modified by those decisions of her will which regulate the temper, principles, and habits of her family, must be elevated above petty temptations which would otherwise assail her.

Again, a housekeeper should feel that she really has great difficulties to meet and overcome. A person who wrongly thinks there is little danger, can never maintain so faithful a guard as one who rightly estimates the temptations which beset her. Nor can one who thinks that they are trifling difficulties which she has to encounter, and trivial temptations to which she must yield, so much enjoy the just reward of conscious virtue and self-control as one who takes an opposite view of the subject.

A third method is, for a woman deliberately to calculate on having her best-arranged plans interfered with very often, and to be in such a state of preparation that the evil will not come unawares. So complicated are the pursuits, and so diverse the habits of the various members of a family, that it is almost impossible for every one to avoid interfering with the plans and taste of a housekeeper in some one point or another. It is, therefore, most wise for a woman to keep the loins of her mind ever girt, to meet such collisions with a cheerful and quiet spirit.

Another important rule is, to form all plans and arrangements in consistency with the means at command, and the character of those around. A woman who has a heedless husband, and young children, and incompetent domestics, ought not to make such plans as one may properly form who will not, in so many directions, meet embarrassment. She must aim at just as much as she can probably attain, and no more; and thus she will usually escape much temptation, and much of the irritation of disappointment.

The fifth, and a very important consideration, is, that system, economy, and neatness, are valuable only so far as they tend to promote the comfort and well-being of those affected. Some women seem to act under the impression that these advantages *must* be secured, at all events, even if the comfort of the family be the sacrifice. True, it is very important that children grow up in habits of system, neatness, and order; and it is very desirable that the mother give them every incentive, both by precept and example; but it is still more important that they grow up with amiable tempers, that they learn to meet the crosses of life with patience and cheerfulness; and nothing has a greater influence to secure this than a mother's example. Whenever, therefore, a woman can not accomplish her plans of neatness and order without injury to her own temper or to the temper of others, she ought to modify and reduce them until she can.

The sixth method relates to the government of the tones of voice. In many cases, when a woman's domestic arrangements are suddenly and seriously crossed, it is impossible not to feel some irritation. But it *is* always possible to refrain from angry tones. A woman can resolve that, whatever happens, she will not speak till she can do it in a calm and gentle manner. *Perfect silence* is a safe resort, when such control can not be attained as enables a person to speak calmly; and this determination, persevered in, will eventually be crowned with success.

Many persons seem to imagine that tones of anger are needful, in order to secure prompt obedience. But observation has convinced the writer that they are *never* necessary; that *in all cases* reproof administered in calm tones would be better. A case will be given in illustration.

A young girl had been repeatedly charged to avoid a certain arrangement in cooking. On one day, when company was invited to dine, the direction was forgotten, and the consequence was an accident which disarranged every thing, seriously injured the principal dish, and delayed dinner for an hour. The mistress of the family entered the kitchen just as it occurred, and at a glance saw the extent of the mischief. For a moment her eyes flashed and her cheeks glowed; but she held her peace. After a minute or so, she gave directions in a calm voice as to the best mode of retrieving the evil, and then left, without a word said to the offender.

After the company left, she sent for the girl, alone, and in a calm and kind manner pointed out the aggravations of the case, and described the trouble which had been caused to her husband, her visitors, and herself. She then portrayed the future evils which would result from such habits of neglect and inattention, and the modes of attempting to overcome them; and then offered a reward for the future, if, in a given time, she succeeded in improving in this respect. Not a tone of anger was uttered; and yet the severest scolding of a practiced Xantippe could not have secured such contrition, and determination to reform, as were gained by this method.

But similar negligence is often visited by a continuous stream of complaint and reproof, which, in most cases, is met either by sullen silence or impertinent retort, while anger prevents any contrition or any resolution of future amendment.

It is very certain that some ladies do carry forward a most efficient government, both of children and domestics, without employing tones of anger; and therefore they are not indispensable, nor on any account desirable.

Though some ladies of intelligence and refinement do fall unconsciously into such a practice, it is certainly very unlady-like, and in very bad taste, to *scold;* and the further a woman departs from all approach to it, the more perfectly she sustains her character as a lady.

Another method of securing equanimity amidst the trials

of domestic life is, to cultivate a habit of making allowances for the difficulties, ignorance, or temptations of those who violate rule or neglect duty. It is vain, and most unreasonable, to expect the consideration and care of a mature mind in childhood and youth; or that persons of such limited advantages as most domestics have enjoyed should practice proper self-control, and possess proper habits and principles.

Every parent and every employer needs daily to cultivate the spirit expressed in the divine prayer, "Forgive us our trespasses as we forgive those who trespass against us." The same allowances and forbearance which we supplicate from our Heavenly Father, and desire from our fellow-men in reference to our own deficiencies, we should constantly aim to extend to all who cross our feelings and interfere with our plans.

The last and most important mode of securing a placid and cheerful temper and tones is, by a constant belief in the influence of a superintending Providence. All persons are too much in the habit of regarding the more important events of life exclusively as under the control of Perfect Wisdom; but the fall of a sparrow, or the loss of a hair, they do not feel to be equally the result of his directing agency. In consequence of this, Christian persons who aim at perfect and cheerful submission to heavy afflictions, and who succeed to the edification of all about them, are sometimes sadly deficient under petty crosses. If a beloved child be laid in the grave, even if its death resulted from the carelessness of a domestic or of a physician, the eye is turned from the subordinate agent to the Supreme Guardian of all; and to him they bow, without murmur or complaint. But if a pudding be burned, or a room badly swept, or an errand forgotten, then vexation and complaint are allowed, just as if these events were not appointed by Perfect Wisdom as much as the sorer chastisement.

A woman, therefore, needs to cultivate the *habitual* feeling that all the events of her nursery and kitchen are brought about by the permission of our Heavenly Father; and that fretfulness or complaint in regard to these is, in fact, complaining at the appointments of God, and is really as sinful as unsubmissive murmurs amidst the sorer chastisements of his hand. And a woman who cultivates this habit of referring all the minor trials of life to the wise and benevolent agency of a heavenly Parent, and daily seeks his sympathy and aid to enable her to meet them with a quiet and cheerful spirit, will soon find it the perennial spring of abiding peace and content.

The power of religion to impart dignity and importance to the ordinary and seemingly petty details of domestic life greatly depends upon the degree of faith in the reality of a life to come, and of its eternal results. A woman who is training a family simply with reference to this life may find exalted motives as she looks forward to unborn generations, whose temporal prosperity and happiness are depending upon her fidelity and skill. But one who truly and firmly believes that this life is but the beginning of an eternal career to every immortal inmate of her home, and that the formation of tastes, habits, and character, under her care, will bring forth fruits of good or ill, not only through earthly generations, but through everlasting ages—such a woman secures a calm and exalted principle of action, and a source of peace which no earthly motives can impart.

CHAPTER XV.

HABITS OF SYSTEM AND ORDER.

ANY discussion of the equality of the sexes as to intellectual capacity seems frivolous and useless, both because it can never be decided, and because there would be no possible advantage in the decision. But one topic, which is often drawn into this discussion, is of far more consequence; and that is, the relative importance and difficulty of the duties a woman is called to perform.

It is generally assumed, and almost as generally conceded, that a housekeeper's business and cares are contracted and trivial; and that the proper discharge of her duties demands far less expansion of mind and vigor of intellect than the pursuits of the other sex. This idea has prevailed because women, as a mass, have never been educated with reference to their most important duties; while that portion of their employments which is of least value has been regarded as the chief, if not the sole, concern of a woman. The covering of the body, the convenience of residences, and the gratification of the appetite, have been too much regarded as the chief objects on which her intellectual powers are to be exercised.

But as society gradually shakes off the remnants of barbarism and the intellectual and moral interests of man rise, in estimation, above the merely sensual, a truer estimate is formed of woman's duties, and of the measure of intellect requisite for the proper discharge of them. Let any man of sense and discernment become the member of a large household, in which a well-educated and pious woman is endeavoring systematically to discharge her multiform duties; let him fully comprehend all her cares, difficulties, and perplexities; and it is probable he would coincide in the opinion that no statesman at the head of a nation's affairs had more frequent calls for wisdom, firmness, tact, discrimination, prudence, and versatility of talent, than such a woman.

She has a husband, to whose peculiar tastes and habits she must accommodate herself; she has children, whose health she must guard, whose physical constitutions she must study and develop, whose temper and habits she must regulate, whose principles she must form, whose pursuits she must guide. She has constantly changing domestics, with all varieties of temper and habits, whom she must govern, instruct, and direct; she is required to regulate the finances of the domestic state, and constantly to adapt expenditures to the means and to the relative claims of each department. She has the direction of the kitchen, where ignorance, forgetfulness, and awkwardness, are to be so regulated that the various operations shall each start at the right time, and all be in completeness at the same given hour. She has the claims of society to meet, visits to receive and return, and the duties of hospitality to sustain. She has the poor to relieve; benevolent societies to aid; the schools of her children to inquire and decide about; the care of the sick and the aged; the nursing of infancy; and the endless miscellany of odd items constantly recurring in a large family.

Surely it is a pernicious and mistaken idea that the duties which tax a woman's mind are petty, trivial, or unworthy of the highest grade of intellect and moral worth. Instead of allowing this feeling, every woman should imbibe, from early youth, the impression that she is in training for the discharge of the most important, the most difficult, and the most sacred and interesting duties that can possibly employ the highest intellect. She ought to feel that her station and responsibilities in the great drama of life are second to none, either as viewed by her Maker or in the estimation of all minds whose judgment is most worthy of respect.

She who is the mother and housekeeper in a large family is the sovereign of an empire, demanding more varied cares, and involving more difficult duties, than are really exacted of her who wears a crown and professedly regulates the interests of the greatest nation on earth.

There is no one thing more necessary to a housekeeper, in performing her varied duties, than *a habit of system and order;* and yet the peculiarly desultory nature of women's pursuits, and the embarrassments resulting from the state of domestic service in this country, render it very difficult to form such a habit. But it is sometimes the case that women who could and would carry forward a systematic plan of domestic economy do not attempt it, simply from a want of knowledge of the various modes of introducing it. It is with reference to such that various modes of securing system and order, which the writer has seen adopted, will be pointed out.

A wise economy is nowhere more conspicuous than in a systematic *apportionment of time* to different pursuits. There are duties of a religious, intellectual, social, and domestic nature, each having different relative claims on attention. Unless a person has some general plan of apportioning these claims, some will intrench on others, and some, it is probable, will be entirely excluded. Thus some find religious, social, and domestic duties so numerous, that no time is given to intellectual improvement. Others find either social, or benevolent, or religious interests excluded by the extent and variety of other engagements.

It is wise, therefore, for all persons to devise a systematic plan which they will at least keep in view and aim to accomplish, and by which a proper proportion of time shall be secured for all the duties of life.

In forming such a plan, every woman must accommodate herself to the peculiarities of her situation. If she has a large family and a small income, she must devote far more time to the simple duty of providing food and raiment than would be right were she in affluence, and with a small family. It is impossible, therefore, to draw out any general plan which all can adopt. But there are some *general principles*, which ought to be the guiding rules, when a woman arranges her domestic employments. These principles are to be based on Christianity, which teaches us to "seek first the kingdom of God," and to deem food, raiment, and the conveniences of life as of secondary account. Every woman, then, ought to start with the assumption that the moral and religious interests of her family are of more consequence than any worldly concern, and that, whatever else may be sacrificed, these shall be the leading object, in all her arrangements, in respect to time, money, and attention.

It is also one of the plainest requisitions of Christianity, that we devote some of our time and efforts to the comfort and improvement of others. There is no duty so constantly enforced, both in the Old and New Testament, as that of charity, in dispensing to those who are destitute of the blessings we enjoy. In selecting objects of charity, the same rule applies to others as to ourselves; their moral and religious interests are of the highest moment, and for them, as well as for ourselves, we are to "seek first the kingdom of God."

Another general principle is, that our intellectual and social interests are to be preferred to the mere gratification of taste or appetite. A portion of time, therefore, must be devoted to the cultivation of the intellect and the social affections.

Another is, that the mere gratification of appetite is to be placed last in our estimate; so that when a question arises as to which shall be sacrificed, some intellectual, moral, or social advantage, or some gratification of sense, we should invariably sacrifice the last.

As health is indispensable to the discharge of every duty, nothing which sacrifices that blessing is to be allowed in order to gain any other advantage or enjoyment. There are emergencies when it is right to risk health and life to save ourselves and others from greater evils; but these are exceptions, which do not militate against the general rule. Many persons imagine that if they violate the laws of health in order to attend to religious or domestic duties, they are guiltless before God. But such greatly mistake. We directly violate the law, "Thou shalt not kill," when we do what tends to risk or shorten our own life. The life and happiness of all his creatures are dear to our Creator; and he is as much displeased when we injure our own interests as when we injure those of others. The idea, therefore, that we are excusable if we harm no one but ourselves, is false and pernicious. These, then, are some general principles to guide a woman in systematizing her duties and pursuits.

The Creator of all things is a Being of perfect system and order; and, to aid us in our duty in this respect, he has divided our time by a regularly returning day of rest from worldly business. In following this example, the intervening six days may be subdivided to secure similar benefits. In doing this, a certain portion of time must be given to procure the means of livelihood, and for preparing food, raiment, and dwellings. To these objects some must devote more, and others less, attention. The remainder of time not necessarily thus employed might be divided somewhat in this manner: The leisure of two afternoons and evenings could be devoted to religious and benevolent objects, such as religious meetings, charitable associations, school visiting, and attention to the sick and poor. The leisure of two other days might be devoted to intellectual improvement and the pursuits of taste. The leisure of another day might be devoted to social enjoyments, in making or receiving visits; and that of another, to miscellaneous domestic pursuits, not included in the other particulars.

It is probable that few persons could carry out such an arrangement very strictly; but every one can make a systematic apportionment of time, and at least *aim* at accomplishing it; and they can also compare with such a general outline the time which they actually devote to these different objects, for the purpose of modifying any mistaken proportions.

Without attempting any such systematic employment of time, and carrying it out, so far as they can control circumstances, most women are rather driven along by the daily occurrences of life; so that, instead of being the intelligent regulators of their own time, they are the mere sport of circumstances. There is nothing which so distinctly marks the difference between weak and strong minds as the question whether they control circumstances or circumstances control them.

It is very much to be feared that the apportionment of time actually made by most women exactly inverts the order required by reason and Christianity. Thus the furnishing a needless variety of food, the conveniences of dwellings, and the adornments of dress, often take a larger portion of time than is given to any other object. Next after this comes intellectual improvement; and last of all, benevolence and religion.

It may be urged that it is indispensable for most persons to give more time to earn a livelihood, and to prepare food, raiment, and dwellings, than to any other object. But it may be asked, how much of the time devoted to these objects is employed in preparing varieties of food not necessary, but rather injurious, and how much is spent for those parts of dress and furniture not indispensable, and merely ornamental? Let a woman subtract from her domestic employments all the time given to pursuits which are of no use, except as they gratify a taste for ornament, or minister increased varieties to tempt the appetite, and she will find that much which she calls "domestic duty," and which prevents her attention to intellectual, benevolent, and religious objects, should be called by a very different name.

No woman has a right to give up attention to the higher interests of herself and others for the ornaments of person or the gratification of the palate. To a certain extent, these lower objects are lawful and desirable; but when they intrude on nobler interests, they become selfish and degrading. Every woman, then, when employing her hands in ornamenting her person, her children, or her house, ought to calculate whether she has devoted *as much* time to the really more important wants of herself and others. If she has not, she may know that she is doing wrong, and that her system or apportioning her time and pursuits should be altered.

Some persons endeavor to systematize their pursuits by apportioning them to particular hours of each day. For example, a certain period before breakfast is given to devotional duties; after breakfast, certain hours are devoted to exercise and domestic employments; other hours, to sewing, or reading, or visiting; and others, to benevolent duties. But in most cases it is more difficult to systematize the hours of each day than it is to secure some regular division of the week.

In regard to the minutiæ of family work, the writer has

known the following methods to be adopted. Monday, with some of the best housekeepers, is devoted to preparing for the labors of the week. Any extra cooking, the purchasing of articles to be used during the week, the assorting of clothes for the wash, and mending such as would otherwise be injured—these, and similar items, belong to this day. Tuesday is devoted to washing, and Wednesday to ironing. On Thursday, the ironing is finished off, the clothes are folded and put away, and all articles which need mending are put in the mending-basket and attended to. Friday is devoted to sweeping and house-cleaning. On Saturday, and especially the last Saturday of every month, every department is put in order; the casters and table furniture are regulated, the pantry and cellar inspected, the trunks, drawers, and closets arranged, and every thing about the house put in order for Sunday. By this regular recurrence of a particular time for inspecting every thing, nothing is forgotten till ruined by neglect.

Another mode of systematizing relates to providing proper supplies of conveniences, and proper places in which to keep them. Thus, some ladies keep a large closet, in which are placed the tubs, pails, dippers, soap-dishes, starch, bluing, clothes-lines, clothes-pins, and every other article used in washing; and in the same, or another place, is kept every convenience for ironing. In the sewing department, a trunk, with suitable partitions, is provided, in which are placed, each in its proper place, white thread of all sizes, colored thread, yarns for mending, colored and black sewing-silks and twist, tapes and bobbins of all sizes, white and colored welting-cords, silk braids and cords, needles of all sizes, papers of pins, remnants of linen and colored cambric, a supply of all kinds of buttons used in the family, black and white hooks and eyes, a yard-measure, and all the patterns used in cutting and fitting. These are done up in separate parcels, and labeled. In another trunk, or in a piece-bag, such as has been previously described, are kept all pieces used in mending, arranged in order. A trunk like the first mentioned will save many steps, and often much time and perplexity; while by purchasing articles thus by the quantity, they come much cheaper than if bought in little portions as they are wanted. Such a trunk should be kept locked, and a smaller supply for current use retained in a work-basket.

A full supply of all conveniences in the kitchen and cellar, and a place appointed for each article, very much facilitate domestic labor. For want of this, much vexation and loss of time is occasioned while seeking vessels in use, or in cleansing those employed by different persons for various purposes. It would be far better for a lady to give up some expensive article in the parlor, and apply the money thus saved for kitchen conveniences, than to have a stinted supply where the most labor is to be performed. If our countrywomen would devote more attention to comfort and convenience, and less to show, it would be a great improvement. Expensive mirrors and pier-tables in the parlor, and an unpainted, gloomy, ill-furnished kitchen, not unfrequently are found under the same roof.

Another important item in systematic economy is, the apportioning of *regular* employment to the various members of a family. If a housekeeper can secure the co-operation of *all* her family, she will find that "many hands make light work." There is no greater mistake than in bringing up children to feel that they must be taken care of and waited on by others, without any corresponding obligations on their part. The extent to which young children can be made useful in a family would seem surprising to those who have never seen a *systematic* and *regular* plan for utilizing their services. The writer has been in a family where a little girl of eight or nine years of age washed and dressed herself and young brother, and made their small beds, before breakfast; set and cleared all the tables for meals, with a little help from a grown person in moving tables and spreading cloths; while all the dusting of parlors and chambers was also neatly performed by her. A brother of ten years old brought in and piled all the wood used in the kitchen and parlor, brushed the boots and shoes, went on errands, and took all the care of the poultry. They were children whose parents could afford to hire servants to do this, but who chose to have their children grow up healthy and industrious, while proper instruction, system, and encouragement, made these services rather a pleasure than otherwise to the children.

Some parents pay their children for such services; but this is hazardous, as tending to make them feel that they are not bound to be helpful without pay, and also as tending to produce a hoarding, money-making spirit. But where children have no hoarding propensities, and need to acquire a sense of the value of property, it may be well to let them earn money for some extra services rather as a favor. When this is done, they should be taught to spend it for others as well as for themselves; and in this way a generous and liberal spirit will be cultivated.

There are some mothers who take pains to teach their boys most of the domestic arts which their sisters learn. The writer has seen boys mending their own garments, and aiding their mother or sisters in the kitchen, with great skill and adroitness; and at an early age they usually very much relish joining in such occupations. The sons of such mothers, in their college life, or in roaming about the world, or in nursing a sick wife or infant, find occasion to bless the forethought and kindness which prepared them for such emergencies. Few things are in worse taste than for a man needlessly to busy himself in women's work; and yet a man never appears in a more interesting attitude than when, by skill in such matters, he can save a mother or wife from care and suffering. The more a boy is taught to use his hands in every variety of domestic employment, the more his faculties, both of mind and body, are developed; for mechanical pursuits exercise the intellect as well as the hands. The early training of New-England boys, in which they turn their hand to almost every thing, is one great reason of the quick perceptions, versatility of mind, and mechanical skill, for which that portion of our countrymen is distinguished.

It is equally important that young girls should be taught to do some species of handicraft that generally is done by men, and especially with reference to the frequent emigration to new territories where well-trained mechanics are scarce. To hang wall-paper, repair locks, glaze windows, and mend various household articles, require a skill in the use of tools which every young girl should acquire. If she never has any occasion to apply this knowledge and skill by her own hands, she will often find it needful in directing and superintending incompetent workmen.

The writer has known one mode of systematizing the aid of the older children in a family, which, in some cases of very large families, it may be well to imitate. In the case referred to, when the oldest daughter was eight or nine years old, an infant sister was given to her as her special charge. She tended it, made and mended its clothes, taught it to read, and was its nurse and guardian through all its childhood. Another infant was given to the next daughter, and thus the children were all paired in this interesting relation. In addition to the relief thus afforded to the mother, the elder children were in this way qualified for their future domestic relations, and both older and younger bound to each other by peculiar ties of tenderness and gratitude.

In offering these examples of various modes of systematizing, one suggestion may be worthy of attention. It is not unfrequently the case that ladies who find themselves cumbered with oppressive cares, after reading remarks on the benefits of system, immediately commence the task of arranging their pursuits with great vigor and hope. They divide the day into regular periods, and give each hour its duty; they systematize their work, and endeavor to bring every thing into a regular routine. But in a short time they find themselves baffled, discouraged, and disheartened, and finally relapse into their former desultory ways, in a sort of resigned despair.

The difficulty in such cases is, that they attempt too much at a time. There is nothing which so much depends upon *habit* as a systematic mode of performing duty; and where no such habit has been formed, it is impossible for a novice to start at once into a universal mode of systematizing, which none but an adept could carry through. The only way for such persons is to begin with a little at a time. Let them select some three or four things, and resolutely at tempt to conquer at these points. In time, a habit will be formed of doing a few things at regular periods, and in a systematic way. Then it will be easy to add a few more; and thus, by a gradual process, the object can be secured, which would be vain to attempt by a more summary course.

Early rising is almost an indispensable condition to success in such an effort; but where a woman lacks either the health or the energy to secure a period for devotional duties before breakfast, let her select that hour of the day in which she will be least liable to interruption, and let her then seek strength and wisdom from the only true Source. At this time let her take a pen, and make a list of all the things which she considers as duties. Then let a calculation be made whether there be time enough, in the day or the week, for all these duties. If there be not, let the least important be stricken from the list, as not being duties, and therefore to be omitted. In doing this, let a woman remember that, though "what we shall eat, and what we shall drink, and wherewithal we shall be clothed," are matters requiring due attention, they are very apt to obtain a wrong relative importance, while intellectual, social, and moral interests receive too little regard.

In this country, eating, dressing, and household furniture and ornaments, take far too large a place in the estimate of relative importance; and it is probable that most women could modify their views and practice so as to come nearer to the Saviour's requirements. No woman has a right to put a stitch of ornament on any article of dress or furniture, or to provide one superfluity in food, until she is sure she can secure time for all her social, intellectual, benevolent, and religious duties. If a woman will take the trouble to make such a calculation as this, she will usually find that she has time enough to perform all her duties easily and well.

It is impossible for a conscientious woman to secure that peaceful mind and cheerful enjoyment of life which all should seek, who is constantly finding her duties jarring with each other, and much remaining undone which she feels that she ought to do. In consequence of this, there will be a sécret uneasiness which will throw a shade over the whole current of life, never to be removed till she so efficiently defines and regulates her duties that she can fulfill them all.

And here the writer would urge upon young ladies the importance of forming habits of system while unembarrassed with those multiplied cares which will make the task so much more difficult and hopeless. Every young lady can systematize her pursuits, to a certain extent. She can have a particular day for mending her wardrobe, and for arranging her trunks, closets, and drawers. She can keep her work-basket, her desk at school, and all her other conveniences, in their proper places and in regular order. She can have regular periods for reading, walking, visiting, study, and domestic pursuits. And by following this method in youth, she will form a taste for regularity and a habit of system which will prove a blessing to her through life.

CHAPTER XVI.

HEALTH OF MIND.

THERE is such an intimate connection between the body and mind, that the health of one can not be preserved without a proper care of the other. And it is from a neglect of this principle that some of the most exemplary and conscientious persons in the world suffer a thousand mental agonies from a diseased state of body, while others ruin the health of the body by neglecting the proper care of the mind.

When the mind is excited by earnest intellectual effort, or by strong passions, the blood rushes to the head and the brain is excited. Sir Astley Cooper records that, in examining the brain of a young man who had lost a portion of his skull, whenever "he was agitated by some opposition to his wishes," "the blood was sent with increased force to his brain," and the pulsations "became frequent and violent." The same effect was produced by any intellectual effort; and the flushed countenance which attends earnest study or strong emotions of interest of any kind, is an external indication of the suffused state of the brain from such causes.

In exhibiting the causes which injure the health of the mind, we shall find them to be partly physical, partly intellectual, and partly moral.

The first cause of mental disease and suffering is not unfrequently in the want of a proper supply of duly oxygenized blood. It has been shown that the blood, in passing through the lungs, is purified by the oxygen of the air combining with the superabundant hydrogen and carbon of the venous blood, thus forming carbonic acid and water, which are expired into the atmosphere. Every pair of lungs is constantly withdrawing from the surrounding atmosphere its healthful principle, and returning one which is injurious to human life.

When, by confinement and this process, the air is deprived of its appropriate supply of oxygen, the purification of the blood is interrupted, and it passes, without being properly prepared, into the brain, producing languor, restlessness, and inability to exercise the intellect and feelings. Whenever, therefore, persons sleep in a close apartment, or remain for a length of time in a crowded or ill-ventilated room, a most pernicious influence is exerted on the brain, and, through this, on the mind. A person who is often exposed to such influences can never enjoy that elasticity and vigor of mind which is one of the chief indications of its health. This is the reason why all rooms for religious meetings, and all school-rooms and sleeping apartments, should be so contrived as to secure a constant supply of fresh air from without. The minister who preaches in a crowded and ill-ventilated apartment loses much of his power to feel and to speak, while the audience are equally reduced in their capability of attending. The teacher who confines children in a close apartment diminishes their ability to study, or to attend to instructions. And the person who habitually sleeps in a close room impairs mental energy in a similar degree. It is not unfrequently the case that depression of spirits and stupor of intellect are occasioned solely by inattention to this subject.

Another cause of mental disease is the excessive exercise of the intellect or feelings. If the eye is taxed beyond its strength by protracted use, its blood-vessels become gorged, and the bloodshot appearance warns of the excess and the need of rest. The brain is affected in a similar manner by excessive use, though the suffering and inflamed organ can not make its appeal to the eye. But there are some indications which ought never to be misunderstood or disregarded. In cases of pupils at school or at college, a diseased state, from over-action, is often manifested by increased clearness of mind, and temporary ease and vigor of mental action. In one instance, known to the writer, a most exemplary and industrious pupil, anxious to improve every hour, and ignorant or unmindful of the laws of health, first manifested the diseased state of her brain and mind by demands for more studies, and a sudden and earnest activity in planning modes of improvement for herself and others. When warned of her danger, she protested that she never was better in her life; that she took regular exercise in the open air, went to bed in season, slept soundly, and felt perfectly well; that her mind was never before so bright and clear, and study never so easy and delightful. And at this time she was on the verge of derangement, from which she was saved only by an entire cessation of all intellectual efforts.

A similar case occurred, under the eye of the writer, from overexcited feelings. It was during a time of unusual religious interest in the community, and the mental disease was first manifested by the pupil bringing her hymn-book or Bible to the class-room, and making it her constant resort in every interval of school duty. It finally became impossible to convince her that it was her duty to attend to any thing else; her conscience became morbidly sensitive, her perceptions indistinct, her deductions unreasonable; and nothing but entire change of scene and exercise, and occupation of her mind by amusement, saved her. When the health of the brain was restored, she found that she could attend to the "one thing needful," not only without interruption of duty or injury to health, but rather so as to promote both. Clergymen and teachers need most carefully to notice and guard against the dangers here alluded to.

Any such attention to religion as prevents the performance of daily duties and needful relaxation is dangerous, and tends to produce such a state of the brain as makes it impossible to feel or judge correctly. And when any morbid and unreasonable pertinacity appears, much exercise and engagement in other interesting pursuits should be urged, as the only mode of securing the religious benefits aimed at. And whenever any mind is oppressed with care, anxiety, or sorrow, the amount of active exercise in the fresh air should be greatly increased, that the action of the muscles may withdraw the blood which, in such seasons, is constantly tending too much to the brain. At the same time, innocent and healthful amusement should be urged as a duty.

There has been a most appalling amount of suffering, derangement, disease, and death, occasioned by a want of attention to this subject, in teachers and parents. Uncommon precocity in children is usually the result of an unhealthy state of the brain; and in such cases medical men would now direct that the wonderful child should be deprived of all books and study, and turned to play out in the fresh air. Instead of this, parents frequently add fuel to the fever of the brain, by supplying constant mental stimulus, until the victim finds refuge in idiocy or an early grave. Where such fatal results do not occur, the brain in many cases is so weakened that the prodigy of infancy sinks below the medium of intellectual powers in after-life.

In our colleges, too, many of the most promising minds sink to an early grave, or drag out a miserable existence, from this same cause. And it is an evil as yet little alleviated by the increase of physiological knowledge. Every college and professional school, and every seminary for young ladies, needs a medical man or woman, not only to lecture on physiology and the laws of health, but empowered by official capacity to investigate the case of every pupil, and, by authority, to enforce such a course of study, exercise, and repose as the physical system requires. The writer has found by experience that in a large institution there is one class of pupils who need to be restrained by penalties from late hours and excessive study, as much as another class need stimulus to industry.

Under the head of excessive mental action must be placed the indulgence of the imagination in novel-reading and "castle-building." This kind of stimulus, unless counterbalanced by physical exercise, not only wastes time and energies, but undermines the vigor of the nervous system. The imagination was designed by our wise Creator as a charm and stimulus to animate to benevolent activity, and its perverted exercise seldom fails to bring a penalty.

Another cause of mental disease is the want of the appropriate exercise of the various faculties of the mind. On this point Dr. Combe remarks: "We have seen that, by disuse, muscles become emaciated, bone softens, blood-vessels are obliterated, and nerves lose their characteristic structure.

The brain is no exception to this general rule. The tone of it is also impaired by permanent inactivity, and it becomes less fit to manifest the mental powers with readiness and energy." It is "the withdrawal of the stimulus necessary for its healthy exercise which renders solitary confinement so severe a punishment, even to the most daring minds. It is a lower degree of the same cause which renders continuous seclusion from society so injurious to both mental and bodily health."

"Inactivity of intellect and of feeling is a very frequent predisposing cause of every form of nervous disease. For demonstrative evidence of this position, we have only to look at the numerous victims to be found among persons who have no call to exertion in gaining the means of subsistence, and no objects of interest on which to exercise their mental faculties, and who consequently sink into a state of mental sloth and nervous weakness." "If we look abroad upon society, we shall find innumerable examples of mental and nervous debility from this cause. When a person of some mental capacity is confined for a long time to an unvarying round of employment which affords neither scope nor stimulus for one half of the faculties, and, from want of education or society, has no external resources; the mental powers, for want of exercise, become blunted, and the perceptions slow and dull." "The intellect and feelings, not being provided with interests external to themselves, must either become inactive and weak, or work upon themselves and become diseased."

"The most frequent victims of this kind of predisposition are females of the middle and higher ranks, especially those of a nervous constitution and good natural abilities; but who, from an ill-directed education, possess nothing more solid than mere accomplishments, and have no materials for thought," and no "occupation to excite interest or demand attention." "The liability of such persons to melancholy, hysteria, hypochondriasis, and other varieties of mental distress, really depends on a state of irritability of the brain, induced by its imperfect exercise."

These remarks of a medical man illustrate the principles

before indicated—namely, that the demand of Christianity, that we live to save from eternal evils and promote the highest and eternal happiness of our race, has for its aim not only the general good, but the highest happiness of the individual in offering abundant exercise for all the noblest faculties.

A person possessed of wealth, who has nothing more noble to engage attention than seeking personal enjoyment, subjects the mental powers and moral feelings to a degree of inactivity utterly at war with health and mind. And the greater the capacities, the greater are the sufferings which result from this cause. Any one who has read the misanthropic wailings of Lord Byron has seen the necessary result of great and noble powers bereft of their appropriate exercise, and, in consequence, becoming sources of the keenest suffering.

It is this view of the subject which has often awakened feelings of sorrow and anxiety in the mind of the writer, while aiding in the development and education of superior feminine minds in the wealthier circles. Not because there are not noble objects for interest and effort abundant, and within reach of such minds, but because long-established custom has made it seem so quixotic to the majority, even of the professed followers of Christ, for a woman of wealth to practice any great self-denial, that few have independence of mind and Christian principle sufficient to overcome such an influence. The more a mind has its powers developed, the more does it aspire and pine after some object worthy of its energies and affections; and they are commonplace and phlegmatic characters who are most free from such deep-seated wants. Many a young woman, of fine genius and elevated sentiment, finds a charm in Lord Byron's writings, because they present a glowing picture of what, to a certain extent, must be felt by every well-developed mind which has no nobler object in life than the pursuit of self-gratification.

If young ladies of wealth could pursue their education under the full conviction that the increase of their powers and advantages increased their obligations to use all for the great and sublime end for which our Saviour toiled and suffered, and with some plan of benevolent enterprise in view, what new motives of interest would be added to their daily pursuits! And what blessed results would follow to our beloved country if all well-educated women carried out the principles of Christianity in the exercise of their developed powers!

The benevolent activities called forth in our late dreadful war illustrate the blessed influence on character and happiness in having a noble object for which to labor and suffer. In illustration of this may be mentioned the experience of one of the noble women who, in a sickly climate and fervid season, devoted herself to the ministries of a military hospital. Separated from an adored husband, deprived of wonted comforts and luxuries, and toiling in humble and unwonted labors, she yet recalls this as one of the happiest periods of her life. And it was not the mere exercise of benevolence and piety in ministering comfort and relieving suffering. It was, still more, the elevated enjoyment which only an enlarged and cultivated mind can attain, in the inspirations of grand and far-reaching results purchased by such sacrifice and suffering. It was in aiding to save her well-loved country from impending ruin, and to preserve to coming generations the blessings of true liberty, self-government, and the Christian life by which toils and suffering became triumphant joys.

Every Christian woman who "walks by faith and not by sight," who looks forward to the results of self-sacrificing labor for the ignorant and sinful as they will enlarge and expand through everlasting ages, may rise to the same elevated sphere of experience and happiness.

On the contrary, the more highly cultivated the mind devoted to mere selfish enjoyment, the more are the sources of true happiness closed, and the soul left to helpless emptiness and unrest.

The indications of a diseased mind, owing to the want of the proper exercise of its powers, are apathy, discontent, a restless longing for excitement, a craving for unattainable good, a diseased and morbid action of the imagination, dissatisfaction with the world, and factitious interest in trifles which the mind feels to be unworthy of its powers. Such minds sometimes seek alleviation in exciting amusements; others resort to the grosser enjoyments of sense. Oppressed with the extremes of languor, or over-excitement, or apathy, the body fails under the wearing process, and adds new causes of suffering to the mind. Such the compassionate Saviour calls to his service, in the appropriate terms, "Come unto me, all ye that labor and are heavy laden, and I will give you rest. Take my yoke upon you, and learn of me," "and ye shall find rest unto your souls."

CHAPTER XVII.

CARE OF THE AGED.

ONE of the most interesting and instructive illustrations of the design of our Creator, in the institution of the family state, is the preservation of the aged after their faculties decay and usefulness in ordinary modes seems to be ended. By most persons this period of infirmities and uselessness is anticipated with apprehension, especially in the case of those who have lived an active, useful life, giving largely of service to others, and dependent for most resources of enjoyment on their own energies.

To lose the resources of sight or hearing, to become feeble in body, so as to depend on the ministries of others, and finally to gradually decay in mental force and intelligence, to many seems far worse than death. Multitudes have prayed to be taken from this life when their usefulness is thus ended.

But a true view of the design of the family state, and of the ministry of the aged and helpless in carrying out this design, would greatly lessen such apprehensions, and might be made a source of pure and elevated enjoyment.

The Christian virtues of patience with the unreasonable, of self-denying labor for the weak, and of sympathy with the afflicted, are dependent, to a great degree, on cultivation and habit, and these can be gained only in circumstances demanding the daily exercise of these graces. In this aspect, continued life in the aged and infirm should be regarded as a blessing and privilege to a family, especially to the young, and the cultivation of the graces that are demanded by that relation should be made a definite and interesting part of their education. A few of the methods to be attempted for this end will be suggested.

In the first place, the object for which the aged are preserved in life, when in many cases they would rejoice to depart, should be definitely kept in recollection, and a sense of gratitude and obligation be cultivated. They should be looked up to and treated as ministers sustained by our Heavenly Father in a painful experience, expressly for the good of those around them. This appreciation of their ministry and usefulness will greatly lessen their trials, and impart consolation. If, in hours of weariness and infirmity, they wonder why they are kept in a useless and helpless state to burden others around, they should be assured that they are not useless; and this not only by word, but, better still, by the manifestation of those virtues which such opportunities alone can secure.

Another mode of cheering the aged is to engage them in the domestic games and sports which unite the old and the young in amusement. Many a weary hour may thus be enlivened for the benefit of all concerned. And here will often occur opportunities of self-denying benevolence in relinquishing personal pursuits and gratification thus to promote the enjoyment of the infirm and dependent. Reading aloud is often a great source of enjoyment to those who by age are deprived of reading for themselves. So the effort to gather news of the neighborhood and impart it, is another mode of relieving those deprived of social gatherings.

There is no period in life when those courtesies of good-breeding which recognize the relations of superior and inferior should be more carefully cherished than when there is need of showing them toward those of advancing age. To those who have controlled a household, and still more to those who in public life have been honored and admired, the decay of mental powers is peculiarly trying, and every effort should be made to lessen the trial by courteous attention to their opinions, and by avoiding all attempts to controvert them, or to make evident any weakness or fallacy in their conversation.

In regard to the decay of bodily or mental faculties, much more can be done to prevent or retard them than is generally supposed, and some methods for this end which have been gained by observation or experience will be presented.

As the exercise of all our faculties tends to increase their power, unless it be carried to excess, it is very important that the aged should be provided with useful employment suited to their strength and capacity. Nothing hastens decay so *fast* as to remove the *stimulus* of useful activity. It should become a study with those who have the care of the aged to interest them in some useful pursuit, and to convince them that they are in some measure actively contributing to the general welfare. In the country and in families where the larger part of the domestic labor is done without servants, it is very easy to keep up an interest in domestic industrial employments. The tending of a small garden in summer, the preparation of fuel and food, the mending of household utensils—these and many other occupations of the hands will keep alive activity and interest in a man; while for women there are still more varied resources. There is nothing that so soon hastens decay and lends acerbity to age as giving up all business and responsibility, and every mode possible should be devised to prevent this result.

As age advances, all the bodily functions move more slowly, and consequently the generation of animal heat, by the union of oxygen and carbon in the capillaries, is in smaller proportion than in the midday of life. For this reason some practices, safe for the vigorous, must be relinquished by the aged; and one of these is the use of the cold bath. It has often been the case that rheumatism has been caused by neglect of this caution. More than ordinary care should be taken to preserve animal heat in the aged, especially in the hands and the feet.

In many families will be found an aged brother, or sister, or other relative who has no home, and no claim to a refuge in the family circle but that of kindred. Sometimes they are poor and homeless, for want of a faculty for self-supporting business; and sometimes they have peculiarities of person or disposition which render their society undesirable. These are cases where the pitying tenderness of the Saviour should be remembered, and for his sake patient kindness and tender care be given, and he will graciously accept it as an offering of love and duty to himself. "Inasmuch as ye have done it to the least of these my brethren, ye have done it to me."

It is sometimes the case that even parents in old age have had occasion to say, with the forsaken King Lear, "How sharper than a serpent's tooth it is to have a thankless child!" It is right training in early life alone that will save from this.

In the opening of China and the probable influx of its people, there is one cause for congratulation to a nation that is failing in the virtue of reverence. The Chinese are distinguished above all other nations for their respect for the aged, and especially for their reverence for aged parents and conformity to their authority, even to the last. This virtue is cultivated to a degree that is remarkable, and has produced singular and favorable results on the national character, which it is hoped may be imparted to the land to which they are flocking in such multitudes. For with all their peculiarities of pagan philosophy and their Oriental eccentricities of custom and practical life, they are everywhere renowned for their uniform and elegant courtesy—a most commendable virtue, and one arising from habitual deference to the aged more than from any other source.

But every person, in approaching the trials and helplessness of age, needs to consider that the very performance of these duties toward one's self by all around may tend to induce a selfish and exacting spirit, or querulous complaints at forgetfulness or neglect. And constant service and petting may tempt to self-indulgent uselessness. Approaching age sometimes leads to the relinquishment of active life; and this tends to induce imbecility of body and mind, which, like all instruments, are kept bright by use. The course of wisdom is to redouble exertions in cultivating self-denying regard for the convenience and comfort of others, and perpetuating, as far as possible, useful labors.

One of the most lovely and beautiful features in a family circle is the aged father or mother sympathizing in the joys and sorrows of the young, and watching for occasions to please and serve all around.

CHAPTER XVIII.

THE CARE OF DOMESTIC ANIMALS.

ONE of the most interesting illustrations of the design of our benevolent Creator in establishing the family state is the nature of the domestic animals connected with it. At the very dawn of life, the infant watches with delight the graceful gambols of the kitten, and soon makes it a playmate. Meantime, its outcries when hurt appeal to kindly sympathy, and its sharp claws to fear; while the child's mother has a constant opportunity to inculcate kindness and care for weak and ignorant creatures. Then the dog becomes the outdoor playmate and guardian of early childhood, and he also guards himself by cries of pain, and protects himself by his teeth. At the same time, his faithful loving nature and caresses awaken corresponding tenderness and care; while the parent, again, has a daily opportunity to inculcate these virtues toward the helpless and dependent. As the child increases in knowledge and reason, the horse, cows, poultry, and other domestic animals come under his notice. These do not ordinarily express their hunger or other sufferings by cries of distress, but depend more on the developed reason and humanity of man. And here the parent is called upon to instruct a child in the nature and wants of each, that he may intelligently provide for their sustenance and for their protection from injury and disease.

To assist in this important duty of home life, which so often falls to the supervision of woman, the following information is prepared through the kindness of one of the editors of a prominent, widely known agricultural paper.

Domestic animals are very apt to catch the spirit and temper of their masters. A surly man will be very likely to have a cross dog and a biting horse. A passionate man will keep all his animals in moral fear of him, making them snappish, and liable to hurt those of whom they are not afraid.

It is, therefore, most important that all animals should be treated uniformly with kindness. They are all capable of returning affection, and will show it very pleasantly if we manifest affection for them. They also have intuitive perceptions of our emotions which we can not conceal. A sharp, ugly dog will rarely bite a person who has no fear of him. A horse knows, the moment a man mounts or takes the reins, whether he is afraid or not; and so it is with other animals.

If live stock can not be well fed, they ought not to be kept. One well-wintered horse is worth as much as two that drag through on straw, and by browsing the hedgerows. The same is true of oxen, and emphatically so of cows. The owner of a half-starved dog loses the use of him almost altogether; for at the very time—the night—when he is most needed as a guard, he must be off scouring the country for food.

Shelter in winter is most important for cows. They should have good tight stables or byres, well ventilated, and so warm that water in a pail will only freeze a little on the top the severest nights. Oxen should have the same stabling, though they bear cold better. Horses in stables will bear almost any degree of cold, if they have all they can eat. Sheep, except young lambs, are well enough sheltered in dry sheds, with one end open. Cattle, sheep, and dogs do not sweat as horses do, they "loll;" that is, water or slabber runs from their tongues; hence they are not liable to take cold as the horse is. Hogs bear cold pretty well; but they eat enough to convince any one that true economy lies in giving them warm styes in winter, for the colder they are the more they eat. Fowls will not lay in cold weather unless they have light and warm quarters.

Cleanliness is indispensable, if one would keep his animals healthy. In their wild state all our domestic animals are very clean, and, at the same time, very healthy. The hog is not naturally a dirty animal, but quite the reverse. He enjoys currying as much as a horse or cow, and would be as careful of his litter as a cat if he had a fair chance.

Horses ought to be groomed daily; cows and oxen as often as twice a week; dogs should be washed with soap-suds frequently. Stables should be cleaned out daily. Absorbents of liquid in stables should be removed as often as they become wet. Dry earth is one of the best absorbents, and is especially useful in the fowl-house. Hogs in pens should have straw for their rests or lairs, and it should be often renewed.

Parasitic Vermin.—These are lice, fleas, ticks, the scale insects, and other pests which afflict our live stock. There are many ways of destroying them; the best and safest is a free use of *carbolic acid soap.* The larger animals, as well as hogs, dogs, and sheep, may be washed in strong suds of this soap without fear, and the application repeated after a week. This generally destroys both the creatures and their eggs. Hen lice are best destroyed by greasing the fowls, and dusting them with flower of sulphur. Sitting hens must never be greased, but the sulphur may be dusted freely in their nests, and it is well to put it in all hens' nests.

Salt and Water.—All animals except poultry require salt, and all free supplies of fresh water.

Light.—Stables, or places where any kind of animals are confined, should have plenty of light. Windows are not more important in a house than in a barn. The *sun* should come in freely; and if it shines directly upon the stock, all the better. When beeves and sheep are fattening very rapidly, the exclusion of the light makes them more quiet, and fatten faster; but their state is an unnatural and hardly a healthy one.

Exercise in the open air is important for breeding animals. It is especially necessary for horses of all kinds. Cows need very little, and swine none, unless kept for breeding.

Breeding.—Always use thorough-bred males, and improvement is certain.

Horses.—The care which horses require varies with the circumstances in which the owner is placed, and the uses to which they are put. In general, if kept stabled, they should be fed with good upland hay, almost as much as they will eat; and if absent from the stable, and at work most of the day, they should have all they will eat of hay, together with four to eight quarts of oats or an equal weight of other grain or meal. Barley is good for horses, and so is dry corn. Corn-meal put upon cut hay, wet and well mixed, is good, steady feed, if not in too large quantities. Four quarts a day may be fed unmixed with other grain; but if the horse be hard worked and needs more, mix the meal with wheat bran, or linseed-oil-cake meal, or use corn and oats ground together; carrots are especially wholesome. A quart of linseed-oil-cake meal, daily, is an excellent occasional addition to a horse's feed, when carrots can not be had. It gives lustre to his coat, and brings the new coat of hair out in the spring. A stabled horse needs daily exercise, as much as to trot three miles. Where a horse is traveling, it is well to give him six quarts of oats in the morning, four at noon, and six at night.

Thorough grooming is indispensable to the health of horses. Especial care should be taken of the legs and fetlocks, that no dirt remain to cause that distressing disease, *grease* or *scratches*, which results from filthy fetlocks and standing in dirty stables. When a horse comes in from work on muddy roads with dirty legs, they should be immediately cleaned, the dirt brushed off, then rubbed with straw; then, if very dirty, washed clean and rubbed dry with a piece of sacking. A horse should never stand in a draught of cold air, if he can not turn and put his back to it. If sweaty or warm from work, he should be blanketed, if he is to stand a minute in the winter air. If put at once into the stable, he should be stripped and rubbed down with straw actively for five minutes or more, and then blanketed. The blanket must be removed in an hour, and the horse given water and feed, if it is the usual time. It will not hurt him to eat hay when hot, unless he be thoroughly exhausted, when all food should be withheld for a while.

It is very comforting to a tired horse, when he is too hot to drink, to sponge out his mouth with cool water. A horse should never drink when very hot, nor be turned into a yard to "cool off," even in summer, neither should he be turned out to pasture before he is quite cool.

Cows.—Gentle but firm treatment will make a cow easy to milk and to handle in every way. If stabled or yarded, cows should have access to water at all times, or have it frequently offered to them. Clover hay is probably the best steady food for milch cows. Cornstalks cut up, thoroughly soaked with water for half a day, and then sprinkled with corn or oil-cake meal, is perhaps unsurpassed as good winter food for milch cows. The amount of meal may vary. With plenty of oil-meal, there is little danger of feeding too much, as that is loosening to the bowels, and a safe, nutritious article. Corn-meal alone, in large quantities, is too heating. Roots should, if possible, form part of the diet of a milch cow, especially before and soon after calving; feed well before this period, yet not to make the cow very fat; but it is better to err in that way than to have her "come in" thin. Take the calf away from the mother as soon as it stands up, and the separation will worry neither dam nor young. This is always best, unless the calf is to be kept with the cow. The calf will soon learn to drink its food, if two fingers be held in its mouth. Let it have all the first drawn milk for three days as soon as milked; after this, skimmed milk warmed to blood heat. Soon a little fine scalded meal may be mixed with the milk; and it will, at three to five weeks old, nibble hay and grass. It is well, also, to keep a box containing some dry wheat-bran and fine corn-meal mixed in the calf-pen, so that calves may take as much as they like.

In milking, put the fingers around the teat close to the bag; then firmly close the forefingers of each hand alternately, immediately squeezing with the other fingers. The forefingers prevent the milk flowing back into the bag, while the others press it out. Sit with the left knee close to the right hind leg of the cow, the head pressed against her flank, the left hand always ready to ward off a blow from her feet, which the gentlest cow may give almost without knowing it, if her tender teats be cut by long nails, or if a wart be hurt, or her bag be tender. She must be stripped *dry* every time she is milked, or she will dry up; and if she gives much milk, it pays to milk three times a day, as nearly eight hours apart as possible. Never stop while milking till done, as this will cause the cow to stop giving milk.

To tether a cow, tie her by one hind leg, making the rope fast above the fetlock joint, and protecting the limb with a piece of an old boot-leg or similar thing. The knot must be one that will not slip; regular fetters of iron bound with leather are much better.

A cow should go unmilked two months before calving, and her milk should not be used by the family till four days after that time.

Swine.—The filthy state of hog-pens is allowed on account of the amount of manure they will make by working over all sorts of vegetable matter, spoiled hay, weeds, etc., etc. This is unhealthy for the family near and also for the animal. The hog is, naturally, a cleanly animal, and if given a chance he will keep himself very neat and clean. Breeding sows should have the range of a small pasture, and be regularly fed. They need fresh water constantly, and often suffer for lack of it when they have liquid swill which they do not like to drink. All hogs should have a warm, dry, well-littered pen to lie in, away from flies and disturbance of any kind. They are fond of charcoal, and it is worth while frequently to throw a few handfuls where they can get at it. It has a very beneficial effect on the appetite, regulates the tone of the stomach and digestive organs, and can not do any harm. Pigs ought always to be well fed and kept growing fast; and when being fattened, they should be penned always, the herd being sorted so that all may have an equal chance. It is well to feed soft corn in the ear; but hard corn should always be ground and cooked for pigs.

Sheep.—In the winter, sheep need deep, well-littered, dry sheds, dry yards, and hay, wheat, or oat straw, as much as they will eat. They should be kept gaining by grain regularly fed to them, and so distributed that each gets its share. Corn, either whole or ground, or oil-cake meal, or both, are used for fattening sheep. They will easily surfeit themselves on any grain except oil-meal, which is very safe feed for them, and usually economical. Strong sheep will often drive the weaker ones away, and so get more than their share of food and make themselves sick. This must be guarded against, and the flock sorted, keeping the weaker and stronger apart.

Sheep are very useful in clearing land of brush and certain weeds, which they gnaw down and kill. To accomplish this, the land must be overstocked, and it is best not to keep sheep on short pasturage more than a few weeks at a time; but if they are returned after a few days, it will serve as good a purpose as if they were to be kept on all the time. Sheep at pasture must be restrained by good fences, or they will be a great nuisance. Dog-proof hedge fences of Osage orange are to be highly recommended, wherever this plant will grow. Mutton sheep will generally pay better to raise than merinos, but they need more care.

Poultry.—Few objects of labor are more remunerative than poultry, raised on a moderate scale. *Turkeys*, when young, need great care; some animal food, dry, warm quarters, and must be kept out of the wet grass, and kept in when it rains. As soon as fledged they become very hardy, and, with free range, will almost take care of themselves. *Geese* need water and good grass pasture. *Ducks* do very well without water to swim in, if they have all they need to drink. They will lay a great many eggs if kept shut in a pen until say eight o'clock in the morning. If let out earlier, they wander away, and will hide their nests, and lay only about as many eggs as they can cover. It is best to set ducks' eggs under hens, and to keep young ducks shut up in a dry roomy pen for four weeks, at least. *Fowls* need light, warm, dry quarters in winter, plenty of feed, but not too much. They relish animal food, and ought to have some frequently to make them lay. Pork or beef scrap-cake can be bought for two to three cents a pound, and is very good for them. Any kind of grain is good for poultry. Nothing is better than wheat screenings. Early-hatched chickens must be kept in a warm, dry, sunny room, with plenty of gravel, and the hen should have no more than eight or nine chickens to brood; though in summer one hen will take good care of fifteen. Little chickens, turkeys, and ducks need frequent feeding, and must have their water changed often. It is well to grease the body of the hen and the heads of the chicks with lard, in order to prevent their becoming lousy.

Hens set about twenty days, and should be well fed and watered. Cold or damp weather is bad for young fowls, and when they have been chilled, pepper-corns are a good remedy, in addition to the warmth of an inclosed dry place.

The most absorbing part of the "Woman's question" of the present time is the remedy for the varied sufferings of women who are widows or unmarried, and without means of support. As yet, few are aware how many sources of lucrative enterprise and industry lie open to woman in the employments directly connected with the family state. A woman can invest capital in the dairy and qualify herself to superintend a dairy farm as well as a man. And if she has no capital of her own, if well trained for this business, she can find those who have capital ready to furnish—an investment that, well managed, will become profitable. And, too, the raising of poultry, of hogs, and of sheep are all within the reach of a woman with proper abilities and training for this business. So that, if a woman chooses, she can find employment both interesting and profitable in studying the care of domestic animals.

Bees.—But one of the most profitable as well as interesting kinds of business for a woman is the care of bees. In a recent agricultural report it is stated that one lady bought four hives for ten dollars, and in five years she was offered one thousand five hundred dollars for her stock, and refused it as not enough. In addition to this increase of her capital, in one of these five years she sold twenty-two hives and four hundred and twenty pounds of honey. It is also stated that in five years one man, from six colonies of bees to start with, cleared eight thousand pounds of honey and one hundred and fifty-four colonies of bees.

It is hoped a time is at hand when every woman will be trained to some employment by which she can secure to herself an independent home and means to support a family, in case she does not marry, or is left a widow, with herself and a family to maintain.

CHAPTER XIX.

CARE OF THE SICK.

It is interesting to notice in the histories of our Lord the prominent place given to the care of the sick. When he first sent out the apostles, it was to heal the sick as well as to preach. Again, when he sent out the seventy, their first command was to "heal the sick," and next to say, "the kingdom of God has come nigh unto you." The body was to be healed first, in order to attend to the kingdom of God, even when it was "brought nigh."

Jesus Christ spent more time and labor in the cure of men's bodies than in preaching, even if we subtract those labors with his earthly father by which family homes were provided. When he ascended to the heavens, his last recorded words to his followers, as given by Mark, were, that his disciples should "lay hands on the sick," that they might recover. Still more directly is the duty of care for the sick exhibited in the solemn allegorical description of the last day. It was those who visited the sick that were the blessed; it was those who did not visit the sick who were told to "depart." Thus are we abundantly taught that one of the most sacred duties of the Christian family is the training of its inmates to care and kind attention to the sick.

Every woman who has the care of young children, or of a large family, is frequently called upon to advise what shall be done for some one who is indisposed, and often in circumstances where she must trust solely to her own judgment. In such cases, some err by neglecting to do any thing at all till the patient is quite sick; but a still greater number err from excessive and injurious dosing.

The two great causes of the ordinary slight attacks of illness in a family are, sudden chills, which close the pores of the skin, and thus affect the throat, lungs, or bowels; and the excessive or improper use of food. In most cases of illness from the first cause, bathing the feet, retiring to a warm bed, and some hot aperient drink to induce perspiration, are suitable remedies.

In case of illness from improper food, or excess in eating, *fasting* for one or two meals, to give the system time and chance to relieve itself, is the safest remedy. Sometimes a gentle cathartic of castor-oil may be needful; but it is best first to try fasting. A safe relief from injurious articles in the stomach is an emetic of warm water; but to be effective, several tumblerfuls must be given in quick succession, and till the stomach can receive no more.

The following extract from a discourse of Dr. Burne, before the London Medical Society, contains important information: "In civilized life, the causes which are most generally and continually operating in the production of diseases are, affections of the mind, improper diet, and retention of the intestinal excretions. The undue retention of excrementitious matter allows of the absorption of its more liquid parts, which is a cause of great impurity to the blood, and the excretions, thus rendered hard and knotty, act more or less as extraneous substances, and, by their irritation, produce a determination of blood to the intestines and to the neighboring viscera, which ultimately ends in inflammation. It also has a great effect on the whole system; causes a determination of blood to the head, which oppresses the brain and dejects the mind; deranges the functions of the stomach; causes flatulency; and produces a general state of discomfort."

Dr. Combe remarks on this subject: "In the natural and healthy state, under a proper system of diet, and with sufficient exercise, the bowels are relieved regularly once every day." *Habit* "is powerful in modifying the result, and in sustaining healthy action when once fairly established. Hence the obvious advantage of observing as much regularity in relieving the system, as in taking our meals." It is often the case that soliciting nature at a regular period once a day, will remedy constipation without medicine, and induce a regular and healthy state of the bowels. "When however, as most frequently happens, the constipation arises from the absence of all assistance from the abdominal and respiratory muscles, the first step to be taken is, again to solicit their aid; first, by removing all impediments to free respiration, such as stays, waistbands, and belts; secondly, by resorting to such active exercise as shall call the muscles into full and regular action;* and lastly, by proportioning the quantity of food to the wants of the system, and the condition of the digestive organs.

"If we employ these means systematically and perseveringly, we shall rarely fail in at last restoring the healthy action of the bowels, with little aid from medicine. But if we neglect these modes, we may go on for years, adding pill to pill, and dose to dose, without ever attaining the end at which we aim.

"There is no point in which a woman needs more knowledge and discretion than in administering remedies for what seem slight attacks, which are not supposed to require the attention of a physician. It is little realized that purgative drugs are unnatural modes of stimulating the internal organs, tending to exhaust them of their secretions, and to debilitate and disturb the animal economy. For this reason, they should be used as little as possible; and fasting, and perspiration, and the other methods pointed out, should always be first resorted to."

When medicine must be given, it should be borne in mind that there are various classes of purgatives, which produce very diverse effects. Some, like salts, operate to thin the

* The most effective mode of exercising the abdominal and respiratory muscles, in order to remedy constipation, is by a continuous alternate contraction of the muscles of the abdomen and diaphragm. By contracting the muscles of the abdomen, the intestines are pressed inward and upward, and then the muscles of the diaphragm above contract and press them downward and outward. Thus the blood is drawn to the torpid parts to stimulate to the healthful action, while the agitation moves their contents downward. An invalid can thus exercise the abdominal muscles in bed. The proper time is just after a meal. This exercise, continued ten minutes a day, including short intervals of rest, and persevered in for a week or two, will cure most ordinary cases of constipation, provided proper food is taken. Coarse bread and fruit are needed for this purpose in most cases.

blood, and reduce the system; others are stimulating; and others have a peculiar operation on certain organs. Of course, great discrimination and knowledge are needed, in order to select the kind which is suitable to the particular disease, or to the particular constitution of the invalid. This shows the folly of using the many kinds of pills, and other quack medicines, where no knowledge can be had of their composition. Pills which are good for one kind of disease might operate as poison in another state of the system.

It is very common in cases of colds, which affect the lungs or throat, to continue to try one dose after another for relief. It will be well to bear in mind at such times, that all which goes into the stomach must be first absorbed into the blood before it can reach the diseased part; and that there is some danger of injuring the stomach, or other parts of the system, by such a variety of doses, many of which, it is probable, will be directly contradictory in their nature, and thus neutralize any supposed benefit they might separately impart.

When a cold affects the head and eyes, and also impedes breathing through the nose, great relief is gained by a wet napkin spread over the upper part of the face, covering the nose except an opening for breath. This is to be covered by folds of flannel fastened over the napkin with a handkerchief. So also a wet towel over the throat and whole chest, covered with folds of flannel, often relieves oppressed lungs.

Ordinarily, a cold can be arrested on its first symptoms by coverings in bed and a bottle of hot water, securing free perspiration. Often, at its first appearance, it can be stopped by a spoonful or two of hot whisky, or any alcoholic liquor, in hot water, taken on going to bed. Warm covering to induce perspiration will assist the process. These simple remedies are safest. Perspiration should always be followed by a towel-bath of cool water in a warm room or by a fire.

It is very unwise to tempt the appetite of a person who is indisposed. The cessation of appetite is the warning of nature that the system is in such a state that food can not be easily digested. When food is to be given to one who has no desire for it, beef-tea is the best in most cases.

The following suggestions may be found useful in regard to nursing the sick: As nothing contributes more to the restoration of health than pure air, it should be a primary object to keep a sick-room well ventilated. At least twice in the twenty-four hours, the patient should be well covered, and fresh air freely admitted from out-of-doors. After this, if need be, the room should be restored to a proper temperature by the aid of an open fire. Bedding and clothing should also be well aired, and frequently changed, as the exhalations from the body, in sickness, are peculiarly deleterious. Frequent ablutions of the whole body, if possible, are very useful; and for these warm water may be employed, when cold water is disagreeable.

A sick-room should always be kept very neat and in perfect order; and all haste, noise, and bustle should be avoided. In order to secure neatness, order, and quiet, in case of long illness, the following arrangements should be made: Keep a large box for fuel, which will need to be filled only twice in twenty-four hours. Provide also and keep in the room or an adjacent closet, a small tea-kettle, a saucepan, a pail of water for drinks and ablutions, a pitcher, a covered porringer, two pint bowls, two tumblers, two cups and saucers, two wine-glasses, two large and two small spoons; also a dish in which to wash these articles; a good supply of towels, and a broom. Keep a slop-bucket near by to receive the wash of the room. Procuring all these articles at once will save much noise and confusion.

Whenever medicine or food is given, spread a clean towel over the person or bed-clothing, and get a clean handkerchief, as nothing is more annoying to a weak stomach than the stickiness and soiling produced by medicine and food.

Keep the fire-place neat, and always wash all articles and put them in order as soon as they are out of use. A sick person has nothing to do but look about the room; and when every thing is neat and in order, a feeling of comfort is induced, while disorder, filth, and neglect are constant objects of annoyance which, if not complained of, are yet felt.

One very important particular in the case of those who are delicate in constitution, as well as in the case of the sick, is the preservation of warmth, especially in the hands and the feet. The *equal* circulation of the blood is an important element for good health, and this is impossible when the extremities are habitually or frequently cold. It is owing to this fact that the coldness caused by wetting the feet is so injurious. In cases where disease or a weak constitution causes a feeble or imperfect circulation, great pains should be taken to dress the feet and hands warmly, especially around the wrists and ankles, where the blood-vessels are nearest to the surface and thus most exposed to cold. Warm elastic wristlets and anklets would save many a feeble person from increasing decay or disease.

When the circulation is feeble from debility or disease, the union of carbon and oxygen in the capillaries is slower than in health, and therefore care should be taken to preserve the heat thus generated by warm clothing and protection from cold draughts. In nervous debility it is peculiarly important to preserve the animal heat, for its excessive loss especially affects weak nerves. Many an invalid is carelessly and habitually suffering cold feet, who would recover health by proper care to preserve animal heat, especially in the extremities. Hot fomentations in most cases will be as good as a blister, less painful, and safer.

Always prepare food for the sick in the neatest and most careful manner. It is in sickness that the senses of smell and taste are most susceptible of annoyance; and often, little mistakes or negligences in preparing food will take away all appetite.

Food for the sick should be cooked on coals, that no smoke may have access to it; and great care must be taken to prevent, by stirring, any adherence to the bottom of the cooking vessel, as this always gives a disagreeable taste.

Keeping clean handkerchiefs and towels at hand, cooling the pillows, sponging the hands with water, (with care to dry them thoroughly,) swabbing the mouth with a clean linen rag on the end of a stick, are modes of increasing the comfort of the sick. Always throw a shawl over a sick person when raised up.

Be careful to understand a physician's directions, and *to*

obey them implicitly. If it be supposed that any other person knows better about the case than the physician, dismiss the physician, and employ that person in his stead.

It is always best to consult the physician as to where medicines shall be purchased, and to show the articles to him before using them, as great impositions are practiced in selling old, useless, and adulterated drugs. Always put labels on phials of medicine, and keep them out of the reach of children.

Be careful to label all powders, and particularly all *white powders*, as many poisonous medicines in this form are easily mistaken for others which are harmless.

In nursing the sick, always speak gently and cheeringly; and, while you express sympathy for their pain and trials, stimulate them to bear all with fortitude, and with resignation to the Heavenly Father, who "doth not willingly afflict," and "who causeth all things to work together for good to them that love him." Offer to read the Bible or other devotional books, whenever it is suitable, and will not be deemed obtrusive.

Every woman should be trained for the office of nurse to the sick, and some who have special traits that fit them for it should make it their daily professional business. The indispensable qualities in a good nurse are common sense, conscientiousness, and sympathetic benevolence.

Persons may be conscientious and benevolent, and possess good judgment in many respects, and yet be miserable nurses of the sick for want of training and right knowledge.

"*Knowledge*, the assurance that one knows what to do, always gives *presence of mind*—and presence of mind is important not only in a sick-room but in every home. Who has not known consternation in a family when some one has fainted, or been burned, or cut, while none were present who knew how to stop the flowing blood, or revive the fainting, or apply the saving application to the burn? And yet knowledge and efficiency in such cases would save many a life, and be a most fitting and desirable accomplishment in every woman."

"We are slow to learn the mighty influence of common

agencies, and the greatness of little things, in their bearing upon life and health. The woman who believes it takes no strength to bear a little noise or some disagreeable announcements, and loses patience with the weak, nervous invalid who is agonized with creaking doors or shoes, or loud, shrill voices, or rustling papers, or sharp, fidgety motions, or the whispering so common in sick-rooms and often so acutely distressing to the sufferer, will soon correct such misapprehensions by herself experiencing a nervous fever."

Here the writer would put in a plea for the increasing multitudes of nervous sufferers not confined to a sick-room, and yet exposed to all the varied sources of pain incident to an exhausted nervous system, which often cause more intolerable and also more wearing pain than other kinds of suffering.

"An exceeding acuteness of the senses is the result of many forms of nervous disease. A heavy breath, an unwashed hand, a noise that would not have been noticed in health, a crooked table-cover or bed-spread, may disturb or oppress; and more than one invalid has spoken in my hearing of the sickening effect produced by the nurse tasting her food, or blowing in her drinks to make them cool. One woman, and a sensible woman too, told me her nurse had turned a large cushion upon her bureau with the back part in front. She determined not to be disturbed nor to speak of such a trifle, but after struggling *three hours* in vain to banish the annoyance, she was forced to ask to have the cushion placed right."

In this place should be mentioned the suffering caused to persons of reduced nervous power not only by the smoke of tobacco, but by the fetid effluvium of it from the breath and clothing of persons who smoke. Many such are sickened in society and in car-traveling, and to a degree little imagined by those who gain a dangerous pleasure at the frequent expense of the feeble and suffering.

"It is often exceedingly important to the very weak, who can take but very little nutriment, to have that little whenever they want it. I have known invalids sustain great injury and suffering; when exhausted for want of food, they have had to wait and wait, feeling as if every minute was an hour, while some well-fed nurse delayed its coming. Said a lady, 'It makes me hungry now to think of the meals she brought me upon that little waiter when I was sick—such brown thin toast, such good broiled beef, such fragrant tea, and every thing looking so exquisitely nice! If at any time I did not think of any thing I wanted, nor ask for food, she did not annoy me with questions, but brought some little delicacy at the proper time, and when it came I could take it.'

"If there is one purpose of a personal kind for which it is especially desirable to lay up means, it is for being well nursed in sickness; yet in the present state of society this is absolutely impossible, even to the wealthy, because of the scarcity of competent nurses. Families worn down with the long and extreme illness of a member require relief from one whose feelings will be less taxed, and who can better endure the labor.

"But, alas! how often is it impossible, for love or money, to obtain one capable of taking the burden from the exhausted sister or mother or daughter, and how often in consequence they have died prematurely or struggled through weary years with a broken constitution. Appeal to those who have made the trial, and you will find that very seldom have they been able to have those who by nature or by training were competent for their duties. Ignorant, unscrupulous, inattentive—how often they disturb and injure the patient! A physician told me that one of his patients had died because the nurse, contrary to orders, had at a critical period washed her with cold water. One is known who, by stealth, quieted a fretful child with laudanum, and of others who exhausted the sick by incessant talking. One lady said that when, to escape this distressing garrulity, she closed her eyes, the nurse exclaimed, aloud, 'Why, she is going to sleep while I am talking to her.'

"A few only of the sensible, quiet, and loving women, whose presence everywhere is a blessing, have qualified themselves and followed nursing as a business. Heaven bless that few! What a sense of relief pervades a family when such an one has been procured; and what a treasure seemed found!

"There is very commonly an extreme susceptibility in the sick to the *moral atmosphere* about them. They feel the healthful influence of the presence of a true-hearted attendant and repose in it, though they may not be able to define the cause; while dissimulation, falsehood, recklessness, coarseness, jar terribly and injuriously on their heightened sensibilities. 'Are the Sisters of Charity really better nurses than most other women?' asked an intelligent lady who had seen much of our military hospitals. 'Yes, they are,' was the reply. 'Why should it be so?' 'I think it is because with them it is a work of self-abnegation, and of duty to God; and they are so quiet and self-forgetful in its exercise that they do it better, while many other women show such self-consciousness and are so fussy!"

Is there any reason why every Protestant woman should not be trained for this self-denying office as *a duty owed to God?*

We can not better close this chapter than by one more quotation from an intelligent and attractive writer: "The good nurse is an artist. Oh the pillowy, soothing softness of her touch, the neatness of her simple, unrustling dress, the music of her assured yet gentle voice and tread, the sense of security and rest inspired by her kind and hopeful face, the promptness and attention to every want, the repose that like an atmosphere encircles her, the evidence of heavenly goodness and love that she diffuses!" Is not such an art as this worth much to attain?

In training children to the Christian life, one very important opportunity occurs whenever sickness appears in the family or neighborhood. The repression of disturbing noises, the speaking in tones of gentleness and sympathy, the small offices of service or nursing in which children can aid, should be inculcated as ministering to the Lord and Elder Brother of man, who has said, "Inasmuch as ye have done it unto one of the least of these my brethren, ye have done it to me."

One of the blessed opportunities for such ministries is given to children in the cultivation of flowers. The entrance into a sick-room of a smiling, healthful child, bringing an offering of flowers raised by its own labor, is like an angel of comfort and love, "and alike it blesseth him who gives and him who takes."

A time is coming when the visitation of the sick, as a part of the Christian life, will hold a higher consideration than is now generally accorded, especially in the cases of uninteresting sufferers who have nothing to attract kind attentions, except that they are suffering children of our Father in heaven, and "one of the least" of the brethren of Jesus Christ.

CHAPTER XX.

FIRES AND LIGHTS.

A SHALLOW fire-place saves wood, and gives out more heat than a deeper one. A false back of brick may be put up in a deep fire-place. Hooks for holding up the shovel and tongs, a hearth-brush and bellows, and brass knobs to hang them on, should be furnished to every fire-place. An iron bar across the andirons aids in keeping the fire safe and in good order. Steel furniture is neater, handsomer, and more easily kept in order than that made of brass.

Use green wood for logs, and mix green and dry wood for the fire; and then the wood-pile will last much longer. Walnut, maple, hickory, and oak wood are best; chestnut or hemlock is bad, because it snaps. Do not buy a load in which there are many crooked sticks. Learn how to measure and calculate the solid contents of a load, so as not to be cheated. A cord of wood should be equivalent to a pile eight feet long, four feet wide and four feet high; that is, it contains (8+4+4=128) one hundred and twenty-eight cubic or solid feet. A city "load" is usually one third of a cord. Have all your wood split and piled under cover for winter. Have the green-wood logs in one pile, dry-wood in another, oven-wood in another, kindlings and chips in another, and a supply of charcoal to use for broiling and ironing in another place. Have a brick bin for ashes, and never allow them to be put in wood. When quitting fires at night, never leave a burning stick across the andirons, nor on its end, without quenching it. See that no fire adheres to the broom or brush; remove all articles from the fire, and have two pails filled with water in the kitchen where they will not freeze.

STOVES AND GRATES.

Rooms heated by stoves should always have some opening for the admission of fresh air, or they will be injurious to health. The dryness of the air which they occasion should be remedied by placing a vessel filled with water on the stove, otherwise the lungs or eyes will be injured. A large number of plants in a room prevents this dryness of the air. Where stove-pipes pass through fire-boards, the hole in the wood should be much larger than the pipe, so that there may be no danger of the wood taking fire. The unsightly opening thus occasioned should be covered with tin. When pipes are carried through floors or partitions, they should always pass either through earthen crocks, or what are known as tin stove-pipe thimbles, which may be found in any stove store or tinsmith's. Lengthening a pipe will increase its draught.

For those who use *anthracite coal*, that which is broken or screened is best for grates, and the nut-coal for small stoves. Three tons are sufficient in the Middle States, and four tons in the Northern, to keep one fire through the winter. That which is bright, hard, and clean, is best; and that which is soft, porous, and covered with damp dust, is poor. It will be well to provide two barrels of charcoal for kindling to every ton of anthracite coal. Grates for *bituminous coal* should have a flue nearly as deep as the grate; and the bars should be round and not close together. The better draught there is, the less coal-dust is made. Every grate should be furnished with a poker, shovel, tongs, blower, coal-scuttle, and holder for the blower. The latter may be made of woolen, covered with old silk, and hung near the fire.

Coal-stoves should be carefully put up, as cracks in the pipe, especially in sleeping-rooms, are dangerous.

LIGHTS.

Professor Phin, of the *Manufacturer and Builder*, has kindly given us some late information on this important topic, which will be found valuable.

In choosing the source of our light, the great points to be considered are, first, the influence on the eyes; and secondly, economy. It is poor economy to use a bad light. Modern houses in cities, and even in large villages, are furnished with gas; where gas is not used, sperm-oil, kerosene or coal-oil, and candles are employed. Gas is the cheapest, (or ought to be;) and if properly used, is as good as any. Good sperm-oil burned in an Argand lamp—that is, a lamp with a circular wick, like the astral lamp and others—is perhaps the best; but it is expensive and attended with many inconveniences. Good kerosene-oil gives a light which leaves little to be desired. Candles are used only on rare occasions, though many families prefer to manufacture into candles the waste grease that accumulates in the household. The economy of any source of light will depend so much upon local circumstances that no absolute directions can be given.

The effect produced by light on the eyes depends upon the following points: First, *Steadiness.* Nothing is more injurious to the eyes than a flickering, unsteady flame. Hence, all flames used for light-giving purposes ought to be surrounded with glass chimneys or small shades. No naked flame can ever be steady. Second, *Color.* This depends greatly upon the temperature of the flame. A hot flame gives a bright, white light; a flame which has not a high temperature gives a dull, yellow light, which is very injurious to the eyes. In the naked gas-jet a large portion of the flame burns at a low temperature, and the same is the case with the flame of the kerosene lamp when the height of the chimney is not properly proportioned to the amount of oil consumed; a high wick needs a high chimney. In the case of a well-trimmed Argand oil-lamp, or an Argand burner for gas, the flame is in general most intensely hot, and the light is of a clear white character.

The third point which demands attention is the *amount of heat* transmitted from the flame to the eyes. It often happens that people, in order to economize light, bring the lamp quite close to the face. This is a very bad habit. The heat is more injurious than the light. Better burn a larger flame, and keep it at a greater distance.

It is also well that various-sized lamps should be provided to serve the varying necessities of the household in regard to quantity of light. One of the very best forms of lamp is that known as the "student's reading-lamp," which is, in the burner, an Argand. Provide small lamps with handles for carrying about, and broad-bottomed lamps for the kitchen, as these are not easily upset. Hand and kitchen lamps are best made of metal, unless they are to be used by very careful persons.

Sperm-oil, lard, tallow, etc., have been superseded to such an extent by kerosene that it is scarcely worth while to give any special directions in regard to them. In the choice of kerosene, attention should be paid to two points: its *safety*, and its *light-giving qualities.* Kerosene is not a simple fluid, like water; but is a mixture of several liquids, all of which boil at different temperatures. Good kerosene-oil should be purified from all that portion which boils or evaporates at a low temperature; for it is the production of this vapor, and its mixture with atmospheric air, that gives rise to those terrible explosions which sometimes occur when a light is brought near a can of poor oil. To test the oil in this respect, pour a little into an iron spoon, and heat it over a lamp until it is moderately warm to the touch. If the oil produces vapor which can be set on fire by means of a flame held a short distance above the surface of the liquid, it is bad. Good oil poured into a tea-cup or on the floor does not easily take fire when a light is brought in contact with it. Poor oil will instantly ignite under the same circumstances, and hence the breaking of a lamp filled with poor oil is always attended by great peril of a conflagration. Not only the safety but also the light-giving qualities of kerosene are greatly enhanced by the removal of these volatile and dangerous oils. Hence, while good kerosene should be clear in color, and free from all matters which can gum up the wick and thus interfere with free circulation and combustion, it should also be perfectly safe. It ought to be kept in a cool, dark place, and carefully excluded from the air.

The care of lamps requires so much attention and discretion, that many ladies choose to do this work themselves, rather than trust it with domestics. To do it properly, provide the following things: an old waiter to hold all the articles used; a lamp-filler, with a spout, small at the end, and turned up to prevent oil from dripping; proper wicks, and a basket or box to hold them; a lamp-trimmer made for the purpose, or a pair of *sharp* scissors; a small soap-cup and soap; some washing soda in a broad-mouthed bottle; and several soft cloths to wash the articles and towels to wipe them. If every thing, after being used, is cleansed from oil and then kept neatly, it will not be so unpleasant a task as it usually is to take care of lamps.

The inside of lamps and oil-cans should be cleansed with soda dissolved in water. Be careful to drain them well, and not to let any gilding or bronze be injured by the soda coming in contact with it. Put one table-spoonful of soda to one quart of water. Take the lamp to pieces and clean it as often as necessary. Wipe the chimney at least once a day, and wash it whenever mere wiping fails to cleanse it. Some persons, owing to the dirty state of their chimneys, lose half the light which is produced. Keep dry fingers in trimming lamps. Renew the wicks before they get too short. They should never be allowed to burn shorter than an inch and a half.

In regard to *shades*, which are always well to use on lamps or gas, those made of glass or porcelain are now so cheap that we can recommend them as the best without any reservation. Plain shades, making the light soft and even, do not injure the eyes. Lamps should be lighted with a strip of folded or rolled paper, of which a quantity should be kept on the mantel-piece. Weak eyes should always be especially shaded from the lights. Small screens, made for the purpose, should be kept at hand. A person with weak eyes can use them safely much longer when they are protected from the glare of the light. Fill the entry-lamp every day, and cleanse and fill night-lanterns twice a week, if used often. A good night-lamp is made with a small one-wicked lamp and a roll of tin to set over it. Have some holes made in the bottom of this cover, and it can then be used to heat articles. Very cheap floating tapers can be bought to burn in a tea-cup of oil through the night.

TO MAKE CANDLES.

The nicest candles are those run in molds. For this purpose, melt together one quarter of a pound of white wax, one quarter of an ounce of camphor, two ounces of alum, and ten ounces of suet or mutton-tallow. Soak the wicks in lime-water and saltpetre, and when dry, fix them in the molds and pour in the melted tallow. Let them remain one night to cool; then warm them a little to loosen them, draw them out, and when they are hard, put them in a box in a dry and cool place.

To make dipped candles, cut the wicks of the right length, double them over rods, and twist them. They should first be dipped in lime-water or vinegar, and dried. Melt the tallow in a large kettle, filling it to the top with hot water, when the tallow is melted. Put in wax and powdered alum, to harden them. Keep the tallow hot over a portable furnace, and fill the kettle with hot water as fast as the tallow is used up. Lay two long strips of narrow board on which to hang the rods; and set flat pans under, on the floor, to catch the grease. Take several rods at once, and wet the wicks in the tallow; straighten and smooth them when cool. Then dip them as fast as they cool, until they become of the proper size. Plunge them obliquely and not perpendicularly; and when the bottoms are too large, hold them in the hot grease till a part melts off. Let them remain one night to cool; then cut off the bottoms, and keep them in a dry, cool place. Cheap lights are made by dipping rushes in tallow, the rushes being first stripped of nearly the whole of the hard outer covering, and the pith alone being retained with just enough of the tough bark to keep it stiff.

CHAPTER XXI.

ON THE CARE OF ROOMS.

In selecting the furniture of parlors, some reference should be had to correspondence of shades and colors. Curtains should be darker than the walls; and, if the walls and carpets be light, the chairs should be dark, and *vicè versa.* Pictures always look best on light walls.

In selecting carpets for rooms much used, it is poor economy to buy cheap ones. *Ingrain* carpets, of close texture, and the *three-ply* carpets, are best for common use. *Brussels* carpets do not wear so long as the three-ply ones, because they can not be turned. *Wilton* carpets wear badly, and *Venetians* are good only for halls and stairs.

In selecting colors, avoid those in which there are any black threads; as they are usually rotten. The most tasteful carpets are those which are made of various shades of the same color, or of all shades of only two colors; such as brown and yellow, or blue and buff, or salmon and green, or all shades of green, or of brown. All very dark shades should be brown or green, but not black.

In laying down carpets, it is a bad practice to put straw under them, as this makes them wear out in spots. Straw matting, laid under carpets, makes them last much longer, as it is smooth and even, and the dust sifts through it. In buying carpets, always get a few yards over, to allow for waste in matching figures.

In cutting carpets, make them three or four incher shorter than the room, to allow for stretching. Begin to cut *in the middle* of a figure, and it will usually match better. Many carpets match in two different ways, and care must be taken to get the right one. Sew a carpet on the wrong side, with double waxed thread, and with the *ball-stitch.* This is done by taking a stitch on the breadth next you, pointing the needle toward you; and then taking a stitch on the other breadth, pointing the needle from you. Draw the thread tightly, but not so as to pucker. In fitting a breadth to the hearth, cut slits in the right place, and turn the piece under. Bind *the whole* of the carpet with carpet-binding, nail it with tacks, having bits of leather under the heads. To stretch the carpet, use a carpet-fork, which is a long stick, ending with notched tin, like saw-teeth. This is put in the edge of the carpet, and pushed by one person, while the nail is driven by another. Cover blocks or bricks with carpeting like that of the room, and put them behind tables, doors, sofas, etc., to preserve the walls from injury by knocking, or by the dusting-cloth.

Cheap footstools, made of a square plank, covered with tow-cloth, stuffed, and then covered with carpeting, with worsted handles, look very well. Sweep carpets as seldom as possible, as it wears them out. To shake them often is good economy. In cleaning carpets, use damp tea leaves, or wet Indian meal, throwing it about, and rubbing it over with the broom. The latter is very good for cleansing carpets made dingy by coal-dust. In brushing carpets in ordinary use, it will be found very convenient to use a large flat dust-pan, with a perpendicular handle a yard high, put on so that the pan will stand alone. This can be carried about and used without stooping, brushing dust into it with a common or small whisk broom. The pan must be very large, or it will be upset.

When carpets are taken up, they should be hung on a line, or laid on long grass, and whipped, first on one side, and then on the other, with pliant whips. If laid aside, they should be sewed up tight in linen, having snuff or tobacco put along all the crevices where moths could enter. Shaking pepper, from a pepper-box, round the edge of the floor, under a carpet, prevents the access of moths.

Carpets can be best washed on the floor, thus: First shake them; and then, after cleaning the floor, stretch and nail them upon it. Then scrub them in cold soap-suds, having half a tea-cupful of ox-gall to a bucket of water. Then wash off the suds with a cloth in fair water. Set open the doors and windows for two days or more. Imperial Brussels, Venetian, ingrain, and three-ply carpets can be washed thus; but Wilton and other plush carpets can not. Before washing them, take out grease with a paste made of potter's clay, ox-gall, and water.

Straw matting is the best for chambers and summer parlors. The checked, of two colors, is not so good to wear. The best is the cheapest in the end. When washed, it should be done with salt water, wiping it dry; but frequent washing injures it. Bind matting with cotton binding. Sew breadths together like carpeting. In joining the ends of pieces, ravel out a part, and tie the threads together, turning under a little of each piece, and then, laying the ends close, nail them down, with nails having kid under their heads.

In hanging pictures, put them so that the lower part shall be opposite the eye. Cleanse the glass of pictures with whiting, as water endangers the pictures. Gilt frames can be much better preserved by putting on a coat of copal varnish, which, with proper brushes, can be bought of carriage or cabinet makers. When dry, it can be washed with fair water. Wash the brush in spirits of turpentine.

Curtains, ottomans, and sofas covered with worsted, can be cleansed by wheat bran rubbed on with flannel. Dust Venetian blinds with feather brushes. Buy light-colored ones, as the green are going of fashion. Strips of linen or cotton, on rollers and pulleys, are much in use, to shut out the sun from curtains and carpets. Paper curtains, pasted on old cotton, are good for chambers. Put them on rollers having cords nailed to them, so that when the curtain falls the cord will be wound up. Then, by pulling the cord, the curtain will be rolled up.

House-cleaning should be done in dry, warm weather. Several friends of the writer maintain that cleaning paint, and windows, and floors in *hard, cold* water, without any soap, using a flannel wash-cloth, is much better than using warm suds. It is worth trying. In cleaning in the common way, sponges are best for windows, and clean water only should be used. They should be first wiped with linen, and then with old silk. The outside of windows should be washed with a long brush made for the purpose; and they should be rinsed, by throwing upon them water containing a little saltpetre.

When inviting company, mention in the note the day of the month and week, and the hour for coming. Provide a place for ladies to dress their hair, with a glass, pins, and combs. A pitcher of cold water and a tumbler should be added. When the company is small, it is becoming a common method for the table to be set at one end of the room, the lady of the house to pour out tea, and the gentlemen of the party to wait on the ladies and themselves. When tea is sent round, always send a tea-pot of hot water to weaken it, and a slop-bowl, or else many persons will drink their tea much stronger than they wish.

Let it ever be remembered that the burning of lights and the breath of guests are constantly exhausting the air of its healthful principle; therefore avoid crowding many guests into one room. Do not tempt the palate by a great variety of unhealthful dainties. Have a warm room for departing guests, that they may not become chilled before they go out.

A parlor should be furnished with candle and fire screens, for those who have weak eyes; and if, at table, a person sits with the back near the fire, a screen should be hung on the back of the chair, as it is very injurious to the whole system to have the back heated.

Pretty baskets, for flowers or fruits, on centre-tables, can be made thus: Knit, with coarse needles, all the various shades of green and brown, into a square piece. Press it with a hot iron, and then ravel it out. Buy a pretty-shaped wicker-basket, or make one of stiff millinet, or thin pasteboard, cut the worsted into bunches, and sew them on, to resemble moss. Then line the basket, and set a cup or dish of water in it, to hold flowers, or use it for a fruit-basket. Handsome fire-boards are made by nailing black foundation-muslin to a frame the size of the fire-place, and then cutting out flowers from wall-paper and pasting them on the muslin, according to the fancy.

Mahogany furniture should be made in the spring, and stand some months before it is used, or it will shrink and warp. Varnished furniture should be rubbed only with silk, except occasionally, when a little sweet-oil should be rubbed over, and wiped off carefully. For unvarnished furniture, use beeswax, a little softened with sweet-oil; rub it in with a hard brush, and polish with woolen and silk rags. Some persons rub in linseed-oil; others mix beeswax with a little spirits of turpentine and rosin, making it so that it can be put on with a sponge, and wiped off with a soft rag. Others keep in a bottle the following mixture: two ounces of spirits of turpentine, four table-spoonfuls of sweet-oil, and one quart of milk. This is applied with a sponge, and wiped off with a linen rag.

Hearths and jambs, of brick, look best painted over with black-lead, mixed with soft soap. Wash the bricks which are nearest the fire with redding and milk, using a painter's brush. A sheet of zinc, covering the whole hearth, is cheap, saves work, and looks very well. A tinman can fit it properly.

Stone hearths should be rubbed with a paste of powdered stone, (to be procured of the stone-cutters,) and then brushed with a stiff brush. Kitchen-hearths, of stone, are improved by rubbing in lamp-oil.

Stains can be removed from marble by oxalic acid and water, or oil of vitriol and water, left on fifteen minutes, and then rubbed dry. Gray marble is improved by linseed-oil. Grease can be taken from marble by ox-gall and potter's clay wet with soap-suds, (a gill of each). It is better to add, also, a gill of spirits of turpentine. It improves the looks of marble to cover it with this mixture, leaving it two days, and then rubbing it off.

Unless a parlor is in constant use, it is best to sweep it only once a week, and at other times use a whisk-broom and dust-pan. When a parlor with handsome furniture is to be swept, cover the sofas, centre-table, piano, books, and mantel-piece, with old cottons, kept for the purpose. Remove the rugs, and shake them, and clean the jambs, hearth, and fire-furniture. Then sweep the room, moving every article. Dust the furniture with a dust-brush and a piece of old silk. A painter's brush should be kept to remove dust from ledges and crevices. The dust-cloths should be often shaken and washed, or else they will soil the walls and furniture when they are used. Dust ornaments, and fine books, with feather brushes, kept for the purpose.

ON THE CARE OF BREAKFAST AND DINING ROOMS.

An eating-room should have in it a large closet, with drawers and shelves, in which should be kept all the articles used at meals. This, if possible, should communicate with the kitchen by a sliding window, or by a door, and have in it a window, and also a small sink, made of marble or lined with zinc, which will be a great convenience for washing nice articles. If there be a dumb-waiter, it is best to have it connected with such a closet. It may be so contrived, that, when it is down, it shall form part of the closet floor.

A table-rug, or crumb-cloth, is useful to save carpets from injury. Bocking, or baize, is best. Always spread the same side up, or the carpet will be soiled by the rug. Table-mats are needful, to prevent injury to the table from the warm dishes. Tea-cup-mats, or small plates, are useful to save the table-cloths from dripping tea or coffee. Butter-knives for the butter-plate, and salt-spoons for salt dishes, are designed to prevent those disgusting marks which are made when persons use their own knives to take salt or butter. A sugar-spoon should be kept in or by the sugar-dish, for the same purpose. Table-napkins, of diaper, are often laid by each person's plate, for use during the meal, to save the table-cloth and pocket-handkerchief. To preserve the same napkin for the same person, each member of the family has a given number, and the napkins are numbered to correspond, or else are slipped into ivory rings, which are numbered. A stranger has a clean one at each meal. Table-cloths should be well starched, and ironed on the right side, and always, when taken off, folded in the ironed creases. *Doilies* are colored napkins, which, when fruit is offered, should always be furnished, to prevent a person from staining a nice handkerchief, or permitting the fruit-juice to dry on the fingers.

Casters and salt-stands should be put in order, every

morning, when washing the breakfast things. Always, if possible, provide *fine* and *dry* table-salt, as many persons are much disgusted with that which is dark, damp, and coarse. Be careful to keep salad-oil closely corked, or it will grow rancid. Never leave the salt-spoons in the salt, nor the mustard-spoon in the mustard, as they are thereby injured. Wipe them immediately after the meal.

For table-furniture, French china is deemed the nicest, but it is liable to the objection of having plates so made that salt, butter, and similar articles, will not lodge on the edge, but slip into the centre. Select knives and forks which have weights in the handles, so that, when laid down, they will not touch the table. Those with riveted handles last longer than any others. Horn handles (except buck-horn) are very poor. The best are cheapest in the end. Knives should be sharpened once a month, unless they are kept sharp by the mode of scouring.

ON SETTING TABLES.

Neat housekeepers observe the manner in which a table is set more than any thing else; and, to a person of good taste, few things are more annoying than to see the table placed askew; the table-cloth soiled, rumpled, and put on awry; the plates, knives, and dishes thrown about without any order; the pitchers soiled on the outside, and sometimes within; the tumblers dim; the caster out of order; the butter pitched on the plate, without any symmetry; the salt coarse, damp, and dark; the bread cut in a mixture of junks and slices; the dishes of food set on at random, and without mats; the knives dark or rusty, and their handles greasy; the tea-furniture all out of order, and every thing in similar style. And yet, many of these negligences will be met with at the tables of persons who call themselves well bred, and who have wealth enough to make much outside show. One reason for this is, the great difficulty of finding domestics who will attend to these things in a proper manner, and who, after they have been repeatedly instructed, will not neglect nor forget what has been said to them. The writer has known cases where much has been gained by placing the following rules in plain sight, in the place where the articles for setting tables are kept.

RULES FOR SETTING A TABLE.

1. Lay the rug square with the room, and also smooth and even; then set the table also square with the room, and see that the *legs* are in the right position to support the leaves.

2. Lay the table-cloth square with the table, *right side up*, smooth and even.

3. Put on the tea-tray (for breakfast or tea) square with the table; set the cups and saucers at the front side of the tea-tray, and the sugar, slop-bowls, and cream-cup at the back side. Lay the sugar-spoon or tongs on the sugar-bowl.

4. Lay the plates around the table at equal intervals, and the knives and forks at regular distances, each in the same particular manner, with a cup-mat or cup-plate to each, and a napkin at the right side of each person.

5. If meat be used, set the caster and salt-cellars in the centre of the table; then lay mats for the dishes, and place the carving-knife and fork and steel by the master of the house. Set the butter on two plates, one on either side, with a butter-knife by each.

6. Set the tea or coffee-pot on a mat, at the right hand of the tea-tray, (if there be not room upon it.) Then place the chairs around the table, and call the family.

FOR DINNER.

1. Place the rug, table, table-cloth, plates, knives and forks, and napkins, as before directed, with a tumbler by each plate. In cold weather, set the plates where they will be warmed.

2. Put the caster in the centre, and the salt-stands at two oblique corners, of the table, the latter between two large spoons crossed. If more spoons be needed, lay them on each side of the caster, crossed. Set the pitcher on a mat, either at a side-table, or, when there is no waiter, on the dining-table. Water looks best in glass decanters.

3. Set the bread on the table, when there is no waiter. Some take a fork and lay a piece on the napkin or tumbler

by each plate. Others keep it in a tray, covered with a white napkin to keep off flies. Bread for dinner is often cut in small junks, and not in slices.

4. Set the principal dish before the master of the house, and the other dishes in a regular manner. Put the carving-knife, fork, and steel by the principal dish, and also a knife-rest, if one be used.

5. Put a small knife and fork by the pickles, and also by any other dishes which need them. Then place the chairs.

ON WAITING AT TABLE.

A domestic who waits on the table should be required to keep the hair and hands in neat order, and have on a clean apron. A small tea-tray should be used to carry cups and plates. The waiter should announce the meal (when ready) to the mistress of the family, then stand by the eating-room door till all are in, then close the door, and step to the left side of the lady of the house. When all are seated, the waiter should remove the covers, taking care first to invert them, so as not to drop the steam on the table-cloth or guests. In presenting articles, go to the left side of the person. In pouring water, never entirely fill the tumbler. The waiter should notice when bread or water is wanting, and hand it without being called. When plates are changed, be careful not to drop knives or forks. Brush off crumbs, with a crumb-brush, into a small waiter.

When there is no domestic waiter, a light table should be set at the left side of the mistress of the house, on which the bread, water, and other articles not in immediate use can be placed.

ON CARVING AND HELPING AT TABLE.

It is considered an accomplishment for a lady to know how to carve well at her own table. It is not proper to stand in carving. The carving-knife should be sharp and thin. To carve fowls (which should always be laid with the breast uppermost,) place the fork in the breast, and take off the wings and legs without turning the fowl; then cut out the merry-thought, cut slices from the breast, take out the collar bone, cut off the side pieces, and then cut the carcass in two. Divide the joints in the leg of a turkey.

In helping the guests, when no choice is expressed, give a piece of both the white and dark meat, with some of the stuffing. Inquire whether the guest will be helped to each kind of vegetable, and put the gravy on the plate, and not on any article of food.

In carving a sirloin, cut thin slices from the side next to you, (it must be put on the dish with the tenderloin underneath;) then turn it, and cut from the tenderloin. Help the guest to both kinds.

In carving a leg of mutton or a ham, begin by cutting across the middle to the bone. Cut a tongue across, and not lengthwise, and help from the middle part.

Carve a fore-quarter of lamb by separating the shoulder from the ribs, and then dividing the ribs. To carve a loin of veal, begin at the smaller end and separate the ribs. Help each one to a piece of the kidney and its fat. Carve pork and mutton in the same way.

To carve a fillet of veal, begin at the top, and help to the stuffing with each slice. In a breast of veal, separate the breast and brisket, and then cut them up, asking which part is preferred. In carving a pig, it is customary to divide it, and take off the head, before it comes to the table; as, to many persons, the head is very revolting. Cut off the limbs, and divide the ribs. In carving venison, make a deep incision down to the bone, to let out the juices; then turn the broad end of the haunch toward you, cutting deep, in thin slices. For a saddle of venison, cut from the tail toward the other end, on each side, in thin slices. Warm plates are very necessary with venison and mutton, and in winter are desirable for all meats.

ON THE CARE OF CHAMBERS AND BEDROOMS.

Every mistress of a family should see not only that all sleeping-rooms in her house *can be* well ventilated at night, but that they actually are so. Where there is no open fireplace to admit the pure air from the exterior, a door should be left open into an entry, or room where fresh air is admitted; or else a small opening should be made in the top and bottom of a window, taking care not to allow a draught of air to cross the bed. The debility of childhood, the lassitude of domestics, and the ill health of families, are often caused by neglecting to provide a supply of pure air. Straw matting is best for a chamber carpet, and strips of woolen carpeting may be laid by the side of the bed. Where chambers have no closets, a *wardrobe* is indispensable. A low square box, set on casters, with a cushion on the top, and a drawer on one side to put shoes in, is a great convenience in dressing the feet. An old Champagne basket, fitted up with a cushion on the lid, and a valance fastened to it to cover the sides, can be used for the same purpose.

Another convenience, for a room where sewing is done in summer, is a fancy jar, set in one corner, to receive clippings, and any other rubbish. It can be covered with prints or paintings, and varnished, and then looks very prettily.

The trunks in a chamber can be improved in looks and comfort by making cushions of the same size and shape, stuffed with hay and covered with chintz, with a frill reaching nearly to the floor.

Every bed-chamber should have a wash-stand, bowl, pitcher, and tumbler, with a wash-bucket under the stand, to receive slops. A light screen, made like a clothes-frame, and covered with paper or chintz, should be furnished for bedrooms occupied by two persons, so that ablutions can be performed in privacy. It can be ornamented, so as to look well anywhere. A little frame, or towel-horse, by the wash-stand, on which to dry towels, is a convenience. A wash-stand should be furnished with a sponge or wash-cloth, and a small towel, for wiping the basin after using it. This should be hung on the wash-stand or towel-horse, for constant use. A soap-dish, and a dish for tooth-brushes, are neat and convenient, and each person should be furnished with two towels; one for the feet, and one for other purposes.

It is in good taste to have the curtains, bed-quilt, valance, and window-curtains of similar materials. In making feather-beds, side-pieces should be put in, like those of mattresses, and the bed should be well filled, so that a person will not be buried in a hollow, which is not healthful, save in extremely cold weather. Feather-beds should never be used except in cold weather. At other times, a thin mattress of hair, cotton and moss, or straw, should be put over them. A simple strip of broad straw matting, spread over a feather-bed, answers the same purpose. Nothing is more debilitating than, in warm weather, to sleep with a feather-bed pressing round the greater part of the body. Pillows stuffed with papers an inch square are good for summer, especially for young children, whose heads should be kept cool. The cheapest and best covering of a bed, for winter, is a *cotton comforter*, made to contain three or four pounds of cotton, laid in bats or sheets, between covers tacked together at regular intervals. They should be three yards square, and less cotton should be put at the sides that are tucked in. It is better to have two thin comforters to each bed, than one thick one; as then the covering can be regulated according to the weather.

Few domestics will make a bed properly without much attention from the mistress of the family. The following directions should be given to those who do this work:

Open the windows, and lay off the bed-covering, on two chairs, at the foot of the bed. After the bed is well aired, shake the feathers, from each corner to the middle; then take up the middle, and shake it well, and turn the bed over. Then push the feathers in place, making the head higher than the foot, and the sides even, and as high as the middle part. Then put on the bolster and the under sheet, so that the wrong side of the sheet shall go next the bed, and the *marking* come at the head, tucking in all around. Then put on the pillows, even, so that the open ends shall come to the sides of the bed, and then spread on the upper sheet, so that the wrong side shall be next the blankets and the marked end at the head. This arrangement of sheets is to prevent the part where the feet lie from being reversed, so as to come to the face, and also to prevent the parts soiled by the body from coming to the bed-tick and blankets. Then put on the other covering, except the outer one, tucking in all around, and then turn over the upper sheet, at the head, so as to show a part of the pillows. When the pillow-cases are clean and smooth, they look best outside of the cover, but not otherwise. Then draw the hand along the side of the pillows, to make an even indentation, and then smooth and shape the whole outside. A nice housekeeper always notices the manner in which a bed is made; and in some parts of the country it is rare to see this work properly performed.

The writer would here urge every mistress of a family who keeps more than one domestic to provide them with single beds, that they may not be obliged to sleep with all the changing domestics, who come and go so often. Where the room is too small for two beds, a narrow truckle-bed under another will answer. Domestics should be furnished with washing conveniences in their chambers, and be encouraged to keep their persons and rooms neat and in order.

ON PACKING AND STORING ARTICLES.

Fold a gentleman's coat thus: Lay it on a table or bed, the inside downward, and unroll the collar. Double each sleeve once, making the crease at the elbow, and laying them so as to make the fewest wrinkles, and parallel with the skirts. Turn the fronts over the back and sleeves, and then turn up the skirts, making all as smooth as possible.

Fold a shirt thus: One that has a bosom-piece inserted, lay on a bed, bosom downward. Fold each sleeve twice, and lay it parallel with the sides of the shirt. Turn the two sides, with the sleeves, over the middle part, and then turn up the bottom, with two folds. This makes the collar and bosom lie, unpressed, on the outside.

Fold a frock thus: Lay its front downward, so as to make the first creases in folding come in the side breadths. To do this, find the middle of the side breadths by first putting the middle of the front and back breadths together. Next, fold over the side creases so as just to meet the slit behind. Then fold the skirt again, so as to make the backs lie together within and the fronts without. Then arrange the waist and sleeves, and fold the skirt around them.

In packing trunks for traveling, put all heavy articles at

the bottom, covered with paper, which should not be printed, as the ink rubs off. Put coats and pantaloons into linen cases, made for the purpose, and furnished with strings. Fill all crevices with small articles; as, if a trunk is not full, nor tightly packed, its contents will be shaken about and get injured. Under-clothing packs closer by being rolled tightly, instead of being folded.

Bonnet-boxes, made of light wood, with a lock and key, are better than the paper bandboxes so annoying to travelers. Carpet-bags are very useful, to carry the articles to be used on a journey. The best ones have sides inserted, iron rims, and a lock and key. A large silk traveling-bag, with a double linen lining, in which are stitched receptacles for tooth-brush, combs, and other small articles, is a very convenient article for use when traveling.

A bonnet-cover, made of some thin material, like a large hood with a cape, is useful to draw over the bonnet and neck, to keep off dust, sun, and sparks from a steam-engine. Green veils are very apt to stain bonnets when damp.

In packing household furniture for moving, have each box numbered, and then have a book, in which, as each box is packed, note down the number of the box, and the order in which its contents are packed, as this will save much labor and perplexity when unpacking. In packing china and glass, wrap each article separately in paper, and put soft hay or straw at bottom and all around each. Put the heaviest articles at the bottom, and on the top of the box write, "This side up."

ON THE CARE OF THE KITCHEN, CELLAR, AND STORE-ROOM.

If parents wish their daughters to grow up with good domestic habits, they should have, as one means of securing this result, a neat and cheerful kitchen. A kitchen should always, if possible, be entirely above-ground, and well lighted. It should have a large sink, with a drain running under-ground, so that all the premises may be kept sweet and clean. If flowers and shrubs be cultivated around the doors and windows, and the yard near them be kept well turfed, it will add very much to their agreeable appearance. The walls should often be cleaned and whitewashed, to promote a neat look and pure air. The floor of a kitchen should be painted, or, which is better, covered with an oil-cloth. To procure a kitchen oil-cloth as cheaply as possible, buy cheap tow cloth, and fit it to the size and shape of the kitchen. Then have it stretched, and nailed to the south side of the barn, and with a brush cover it with a coat of thin rye paste. When this is dry, put on a coat of yellow paint, and let it dry for a fortnight. It is safest to first try the paint, and see if it dries well, as some paint never will dry. Then put on a second coat, and, at the end of another fortnight, a third coat. Then let it hang two months, and it will last, uninjured, for many years. The longer the paint is left to dry, the better. If varnished, it will last much longer.

A sink should be scalded out every day, and occasionally with hot ley. On nails, over the sink, should be hung three good dish-cloths, hemmed, and furnished with loops—one for dishes not greasy, one for greasy dishes, and one for washing pots and kettles. These should be put in the wash every week. The lady who insists upon this will not be annoyed by having her dishes washed with dark, musty, and greasy rags, as is too frequently the case.

Under the sink should be kept a slop-pail; and, on a shelf by it, a soap-dish and two water-pails. A large boiler, of warm soft water, should always be kept over the fire, well covered, and a hearth-broom and bellows be hung near the fire. A clock is a very important article in the kitchen, in order to secure regularity at meals.

ON WASHING DISHES.

No item of domestic labor is so frequently done in a negligent manner by domestics as this. A full supply of conveniences will do much toward a remedy of this evil. A swab, made of strips of linen, tied to a stick, is useful to wash nice dishes, especially small, deep articles. Two or three towels, and three dish-cloths, should be used. Two large tin tubs, painted on the outside, should be provided; one for washing, and one for rinsing; also, a large old waiter, on which to drain the dishes. A soap-dish, with hard soap, and a fork, with which to use it, a slop-pail, and two pails for water, should also be furnished. Then, if there be danger of neglect, the following rules for washing dishes, legibly written, may be hung up by the sink, and it will aid in promoting the desired care and neatness.

RULES FOR WASHING DISHES.

1. Scrape the dishes, putting away any food which may remain on them, and which it may be proper to save for future use. Put grease into the grease-pot, and whatever else may be on the plates, into the slop-pail. Save tea-leaves, for sweeping. Set all the dishes, when scraped, in regular piles; the smallest at the top.

2. Put the nicest articles in the wash-dish, and wash them in hot suds, with the swab or nicest dish-cloth. Wipe all metal articles as soon as they are washed. Put all the rest into the rinsing-dish, which should be filled with hot water. When they are taken out, lay them to drain on the waiter. Then rinse the dish-cloth and hang it up, wipe the articles washed, and put them in their places.

3. Pour in more hot water, wash the greasy dishes with the dish-cloth made for them; rinse them, and set them to drain. Wipe them, and set them away. Wash the knives and forks, *being careful that the handles are never put in water;* wipe them, and then lay them in a knife-dish to be scoured.

4. Take a fresh supply of clean suds, in which wash the milk-pans, buckets, and tins. Then rinse and hang up this dish-cloth, and take the other; with which wash the roaster, gridiron, pots, and kettles. Then wash and rinse the dish-cloth, and hang it up. Empty the slop-bucket and scald it. Dry metal tea-pots and tins before the fire. Then put the fire-place in order, and sweep and dust the kitchen.

Some persons keep a deep and narrow vessel, in which to wash knives with a swab, so that a careless domestic *can not* lay them in the water while washing them. This article can be carried into the eating-room, to receive the knives and forks when they are taken from the table.

KITCHEN FURNITURE.

Crockery.—Brown earthen pans are said to be best for milk and for cooking. Tin pans are lighter, and more convenient, but are too cold for many purposes. Tall earthen jars with covers are good to hold butter, salt, lard, etc. Acids should never be put into the red earthenware, as there is a poisonous ingredient in the glazing which the acid takes off. Stone ware is better and stronger, and safer every way than any other kind.

Iron Ware.—Many kitchens are very imperfectly supplied with the requisite conveniences for cooking. When a person has sufficient means, the following articles are all desirable: A nest of iron pots, of different sizes, (they should be slowly heated when new;) a long iron fork, to take out articles from boiling water; an iron hook with a handle, to lift pots from the crane; a large and small gridiron, with grooved bars, and a trench to catch the grease; a Dutch oven, called also a bake-pan: two skillets, of different sizes, and a spider, or flat skillet, for frying; a griddle, a waffle-iron, tin and iron bake and bread pans; two ladles, of different sizes; a skimmer; iron skewers; a toasting-iron; two tea-kettles, one small and one large one; two brass kettles, of different sizes, for soap-boiling, etc. Iron kettles lined with porcelain are better for preserves. The German are the best. Too hot a fire will crack them, but with care in this respect they will last for many years.

Portable charcoal furnaces, of iron or clay, are very useful in summer, in washing, ironing, and stewing, or making preserves. If used in the house, a strong draught must be made, to prevent the deleterious effects of the charcoal. A box and mill, for spice, pepper, and coffee, are needful to those who use these articles. Strong knives and forks, a sharp carving-knife, an iron cleaver and board, a fine saw, steelyards, chopping-tray and knife, an apple-parer, steel for sharpening knives, sugar-nippers, a dozen iron spoons, also a large iron one with a long handle, six or eight flat-irons, one of them very small, two iron-stands, a ruffle-iron, a crimping-iron, are also desirable.

Tin Ware.—Bread-pans· large and small patty-pans; cake-pans, with a centre tube to insure their baking well; pie-dishes, (of block-tin;) a covered butter-kettle; covered kettles to hold berries; two saucepans; a large oil-can, (with a cock;) a lamp-filler; a lantern; broad-bottomed candlesticks for the kitchen; a candle-box; a funnel; a reflector for baking warm cakes; an oven or tin-kitchen; an apple-corer; an apple-roaster: an egg-boiler; two sugar-scoops, and flour and meal scoop; a set of mugs; three dippers; a pint, quart, and gallon measure; a set of scales and weights; three or four pails, painted on the outside; a slop-bucket with a tight cover, painted on the outside; a milk-strainer; a gravy-strainer; a colander; a dredging-box; a pepper-box; a large and small grater; a cheese-box; also a large box for cake, and a still larger one for bread, with tight covers. Bread, cake, and cheese, shut up in this way, will not grow dry as in the open air.

Wooden Ware.—A nest of tubs; a set of pails and bowls; a large and small sieve; a beetle for mashing potatoes; a spade or stick for stirring butter and sugar; a bread-board, for molding bread and making pie-crust; a coffee-stick; a clothes-stick; a mush-stick; a meat-beetle, to pound tough meat; an egg-beater; a ladle, for working butter; a bread-trough, (for a large family;) flour-buckets, with lids, to hold sifted flour and Indian meal; salt-boxes; sugar-boxes; starch and indigo boxes; spice-boxes; a bosom-board; a skirt-board; a large ironing-board; two or three clothes-frames; and six dozen clothes-pins.

Basket Ware.—Baskets of all sizes, for eggs, fruit, marketing, clothes, etc.; also chip-baskets. When often used, they should be washed in hot suds.

Other Articles.—Every kitchen needs a box containing balls of brown thread and twine, a large and small darning-needle, rolls of waste paper and old linen and cotton, and a supply of common holders. There should also be another box, containing a hammer, carpet-tacks, and nails of all sizes, a carpet-claw, screws and a screw-driver, pincers, gimlets of several sizes, a bed-screw, a small saw, two chisels, (one to use for button-holes in broadcloth,) two awls, and two files.

In a drawer or cupboard should be placed cotton table-cloths for kitchen use; nice crash towels for tumblers, marked T T; coarser towels for dishes marked T; six large roller-towels; a dozen hand-towels, marked H T; and a dozen hemmed dish-cloths with loops. Also two thick linen pudding or dumpling cloths, a jelly-bag made of white flannel, to strain jelly, a starch-strainer, and a bag for boiling clothes.

In a closet should be kept, arranged in order, the following articles: the dust-pan, dust-brush, and dusting-cloths, old flannel and cotton for scouring and rubbing, large sponges for washing windows and looking-glasses, a long brush for cobwebs, and another for washing the outside of windows, whisk-brooms, common brooms, a coat-broom or brush, a whitewash-brush, a stove-brush, shoe-brushes and blacking, articles for cleaning tin and silver, leather for cleaning metals, bottles containing stain-mixtures and other articles used in cleansing.

CARE OF THE CELLAR.

A cellar should often be whitewashed, to keep it sweet. It should have a drain to keep it perfectly dry, as standing water in a cellar is a sure cause of disease in a family. It is very dangerous to leave decayed vegetables in a cellar. Many a fever has been caused by the poisonous miasm thus generated. The following articles are desirable in a cellar: a safe, or movable closet, with sides of wire or perforated tin, in which cold meats, cream, and other articles should be kept; (if ants be troublesome, set the legs in tin cups of water;) a refrigerator, or a large wooden box, on feet, with a lining of tin or zinc, and a space between the tin and wood filled with powdered charcoal, having at the bottom a place for ice, a drain to carry off the water, and also movable shelves and partitions. In this articles are kept cool. It should be cleaned once a week. Filtering-jars, to purify water, should also be kept in the cellar. Fish and cabbages in a cellar are apt to scent a house, and give a bad taste to other articles.

STORE-ROOM.

Every house needs a store-room, in which to keep tea, coffee, sugar, rice, candles, etc. It should be furnished with jars having labels, a large spoon, a fork, sugar and flour scoops, a towel, and a dish-cloth.

CHAPTER XXII.

THE CARE OF YARDS AND GARDENS.

FIRST, let us say a few words on the *Preparation of Soil.* If the garden soil be clayey and adhesive, put on a covering of sand, three inches thick, and the same depth of well-rotted manure. Spade it in as deep as possible, and mix it well. If the soil be sandy and loose, spade in clay and ashes. Ashes are good for all kinds of soil, as they loosen those which are close, hold moisture in those which are sandy, and destroy insects. The best kind of soil is that which will hold water the longest without becoming hard when dry.

To prepare Soil for Pot-plants, take one fourth part of common soil, one fourth part of well-decayed manure, and one half of vegetable mold, from the woods or from a chip-yard. Break up the manure fine, and sift it through a lime-screen, (or coarse wire sieve.) These materials must be thoroughly mixed. When the common soil which is used is adhesive, and indeed in most other cases, it is necessary to add sand, the proportion of which must depend on the nature of the soil.

To prepare a Hot-Bed, dig a pit six feet long, five feet wide, and thirty inches deep. Make a frame of the same size, with the back two feet high, the front fifteen inches, and the sides sloped from the back to the front. Make two sashes, each three feet by five, with the panes of glass lapping like shingles instead of having cross-bars. Set the frame over the pit, which should then be filled with fresh horse-dung which has not lain long nor been sodden by water. Tread it down hard; then put into the frame light and very rich soil, six or eight inches deep, and cover it with the sashes for two or three days. Then stir the soil, and sow the seeds in shallow drills, placing sticks by them, to mark the different kinds. Keep the frame covered with the glass whenever it is cold enough to chill the plants; but at all other times admit fresh air, which is indispensable to their health. When the sun is quite warm, raise the glasses enough to admit air, and cover them with matting or blankets, or else the sun may kill the young plants. Water the bed at evening with water which has stood all day, or, if it be fresh drawn, add a little warm water. If there be too much heat in the bed, so as to scorch or wither the plants, lift the sashes, water freely, shade by day; make deep holes with stakes, and fill them up when the heat is reduced. In very cold nights, cover the sashes and frame with straw-mats.

For Planting Flower Seeds.—Break up the soil till it is very soft, and free from lumps. Rub that nearest the surface between the hands, to make it fine. Make a circular drill a foot in diameter. Seeds are to be planted either deeper or nearer the surface, according to their size. For seeds as large as sweet peas, the drill should be half an inch deep. The smallest seeds must be planted very near the surface, and a very little fine earth be sifted over them. After covering them with soil, beat them down with a trowel, so as to make the earth as compact as it is after a heavy shower. Set up a stick in the middle of the circle, with the name of the plant heavily written upon it with a dark lead-pencil. This remains more permanent if white-lead be first rubbed over the surface. Never plant when the soil is very wet. In very dry times, water the seeds at night. Never use very cold water. When the seeds are small, many should be planted together, that they may assist each other in breaking the soil. When the plants are an inch high, thin them out, leaving only one or two, if the plant be a large one like the balsam; five or six, when it is of a medium size; and eighteen or twenty of the smaller size. Transplanting, unless the plant be lifted with a ball of earth, retards the growth about a fortnight. It is best to plant at two differerent times, lest the first planting should fail, owing to wet or cold weather.

To plant Garden Seeds, make the beds from one to three yards wide; lay across them a board a foot wide, and with a stick make a furrow on each side of it, one inch deep. Scatter the seeds in this furrow, and cover them. Then lay the board over them, and step on it, to press down the earth. When the plants are an inch high, thin them out, leaving spaces proportioned to their sizes. Seeds of similar species, such as melons and squashes, should not be planted very near to each other, as this causes them to degenerate. The same kinds of vegetables should not be planted in the same place for two years in succession. The longer the rows are, the easier is the after-culture.

Transplanting should be done at evening, or, which is better, just before a shower. Take a round stick sharpened at the point, and make openings to receive the plants. Set them a very little deeper than they were before, and press the soil firmly round them. Then water them, and cover them for three or four days, taking care that sufficient air be admitted. If the plant can be removed without disturbing the soil around the root, it will not be at all retarded by transplanting. Never remove leaves and branches, unless a part of the roots be lost.

To Re-pot House Plants, renew the soil every year, soon after the time of blossoming. Prepare soil as previously directed. Loosen the earth from the pot by passing a knife around the sides. Turn the plant upside down, and remove the pot. Then remove all the matted fibres at the bottom, and all the earth, except that which adheres to the roots. From woody plants, like roses, shake off all the earth. Take the new pot, and put a piece of broken earthenware over the hole at the bottom, and then, holding the plant in the proper position, shake in the earth around it. Then pour in water to settle the earth, and heap on fresh soil till the pot is even full. Small pots are considered better than large ones, as the roots are not so likely to rot from excess of moisture.

In the Laying out of Yards and Gardens, there is room for much judgment and taste. In planting trees in a yard, they should be arranged in groups, and never planted in straight lines, nor sprinkled about as solitary trees. The object of this arrangement is to imitate Nature, and secure some spots of dense shade and some of clear turf. In yards which are covered with turf, beds can be cut out of it, and raised for flowers. A trench should be made around, to prevent the grass from running on them. These beds can be made in the shape of crescents, ovals, or other fanciful forms.

In laying out beds in gardens and yards, a very pretty bordering can be made by planting them with common flax-seed, in a line about three inches from the edge. This can be trimmed with shears, when it grows too high.

For transplanting Trees, the autumn is the best time. Take as much of the root as possible, especially the little fibres, which should never become dry. If kept long before they are set out, put wet moss around them and water them. Dig holes larger than the extent of the roots; let one person hold the tree in its former position, and another place the roots carefully as they were before, cutting off any broken or wounded root. *Be careful not to let the tree be more than an inch deeper than it was before.* Let the soil be soft and well manured; shake the tree as the soil is shaken in, that it may mix well among the small fibres. Do not tread the earth down, while filling the hole; but, when it is full, raise a slight mound of say four inches deep around the stem to hold water, and fill it. Never cut off leaves nor branches, unless some of the roots are lost. Tie the trees to a stake, and they will be more likely to live. Water them often.

The Care of House Plants is a matter of daily attention, and well repays all labor expended upon it. The soil of house plants should be renewed every year, as previously directed. In winter, they should be kept as dry as they can be without wilting. Many house plants are injured by giving them too much water, when they have little light and fresh air. This makes them grow spindling. The more fresh air, warmth, and light they have, the more water is needed. They ought not to be kept very warm in winter, nor exposed to great changes of atmosphere. Forty degrees is a proper temperature for plants in winter, when they have little sun and air. When plants have become spindling, cut off their heads entirely, and cover the pot in the earth, where it has the morning sun only. A new and flourishing head will spring out. Few house plants can bear the sun at noon. When insects infest plants, set them in a closet or under a barrel, and burn tobacco under them. The smoke kills any insect enveloped in it. When plants are frozen, cold water and a gradual restoration of warmth are the best remedies. Never use very cold water for plants at any season.

THE PROPAGATION OF PLANTS.

This is an occupation requiring much attention and constant care. Bulbous roots are propagated by offsets; some growing on the top, others around the sides. Many plants are propagated by cutting off twigs, and setting them in earth, so that two or three eyes are covered. To do this, select a side shoot, ten inches long, two inches of it being of the preceding year's growth, and the rest the growth of the season when it is set. Do this when the sap is running, and put a piece of crockery at the bottom of the shoot when it is buried. One eye, at least, must be under the soil. Water it, and shade it in hot weather.

Plants are also propagated by layers. To do this, take a shoot which comes up near the root, bend it down so as to bring several eyes under the soil, leaving the top aboveground. If the shoot be cut half through, in a slanting direction, at one of these eyes, before burying it, the result is more certain. Roses, honeysuckles, and many other shrubs are readily propagated thus. They will generally take root by being simply buried; but cutting them as here directed is the best method. Layers are more certain than cuttings.

Budding and Grafting, for all woody plants, are favorite methods of propagation. In all such plants there is an outer and inner bark, the latter containing the sap vessels, in which the nourishment of the tree ascends. The success of grafting or inoculating consists in so placing the bud or graft that the sap vessels of the inner bark shall exactly join those of the plant into which they are grafted, so that the sap may pass from one into the other.

The following are directions for *budding*, which may be performed at any time from July to September:

Select a smooth place on the stock into which you are to insert the bud. Make a horizontal cut across the rind through to the firm wood; and from the middle of this, make a slit downward perpendicularly, an inch or more long, through to the wood. Raise the bark of the stock on each side of the perpendicular cut, for the admission of the bud, as is shown in the annexed cut, (Figure 64). Then take a shoot of this year's growth, and slice from it a bud, taking an inch below and an inch above it, and some portion of the wood under it. Then carefully slip off the woody part under the bud. Examine whether the eye or germ of the bud be perfect. If a little hole appear in that part, the bud has lost its root, and another must be selected. Insert the bud, so that *a*, of the bud, shall pass to a, of the stock; then *b*, of the bud, must be cut off, to match the cut b, in the stock, and fitted exactly to it, as it is this alone which insures success. Bind the parts with fresh bass or woolen yarn, beginning a little below the bottom of the perpendicular slit, and winding it closely around every part, except just over the eye of the bud, until you arrive above the horizontal cut. Do not bind it too tightly, but just sufficient to exclude air, sun, and wet. This is to be removed after the bud is firmly fixed and begins to grow.

Fig. 64.

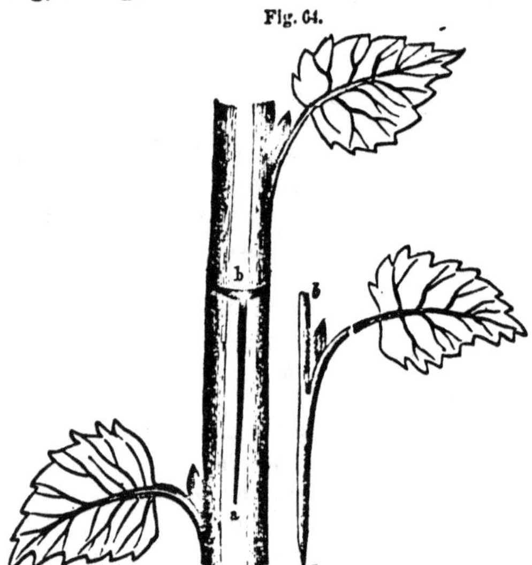

Seed-fruit can be budded into any other seed fruit, and

stone-fruit into any other stone-fruit; but stone and seed fruits can not be thus mingled.

Rose-bushes can have a variety of kinds budded into the same stock. Hardy roots are the best stocks. The branch above the bud must be cut off the next March or April after the bud is put in. Apples and pears are more easily propagated by ingrafting than by budding.

Ingrafting is a similar process to budding, with this advantage, that it can be performed on large trees; whereas budding can be applied only on small ones. The two common kinds of ingrafting are whip-grafting and split-grafting. The first kind is for young trees, and the other for large ones.

Fig. 65.

The time for ingrafting is from May to October. The cuttings must be taken from horizontal shoots, between Christmas and March, and kept in a damp cellar. In performing the operation, cut off in a sloping direction (as seen in Fig. 65) the tree or limb to be grafted. Then cut off in a corresponding slant the slip to be grafted on. Then put them together, so that the inner bark of each shall match exactly on one side, and tie them firmly together with yellow yarn. It is not essential that both be of equal size; if the bark of each meet together exactly on *one* side, it answers the purpose. But the two must not differ much in size. The slope should be an inch and a half, or more, in length. After they are tied together, the place should be covered with a salve or composition of bees-wax and rosin. A mixture of clay and cow-dung will answer the same purpose. This last must be tied on with a cloth. Grafting is more convenient than budding, as grafts can be sent from a great distance; whereas buds must be taken in July or August, from a shoot of the present year's growth, and can not be sent to any great distance.

The next cut (Fig. 66) exhibits the mode called stock-grafting; *a* being the limb of a large tree, which is sawed off and split, and is to be held open by a small wedge till the grafts are put in. A graft inserted in the limb is shown at *b*, and at *c* is one not inserted, but designed to be put in at *d*, as two grafts can be put into a large stock. In inserting the graft, be careful to make the edge of the inner bark of the graft meet exactly the edge of the inner bark of the stock; for on this success depends. After the grafts are put in, the wedge must be withdrawn, and the whole of the stock be covered with the thick salve or composition before mentioned, reaching from where the grafts are inserted to the bottom of the slit. Be careful not to knock or move the grafts after they are put in.

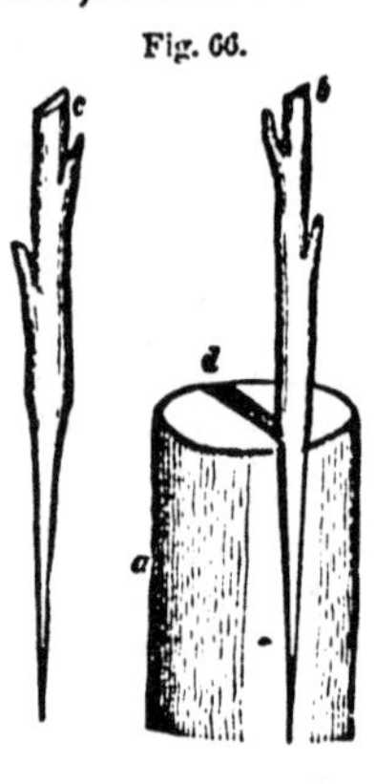

Fig. 66.

Pruning is an operation of constant exercise, for keeping plants and trees in good condition. The following rules are from a distinguished horticulturist: Prune off all dead wood, and all the little twigs on the main limbs. Retrench branches, so as to give light and ventilation to the interior of the tree. Cut out the straight and perpendicular shoots which give little or no fruit; while those which are most nearly horizontal, and somewhat curving, give fruit abundantly and of good quality, and should be sustained. Superfluous and ill-placed buds may be rubbed off at any time; and no buds pushing out after midsummer should be spared. In choosing between shoots to be retained, preserve the lowest placed, and on lateral shoots those which are nearest the origin. When branches cross each other so as to rub, remove one or the other. Remove all suckers from the roots of trees or shrubs. Prune after the sap is in full circulation, (except in the case of grapes,) as the wounds then heal best. Some think it best to prune before the sap begins to run. Pruning-shears, and a pruning-pole, with a chisel at the end, can be procured of those who deal in agricultural utensils.

Thinning is also an important but very delicate operation. As it is the office of the leaves to absorb nourishment from the atmosphere, they should never be removed, except to mature the wood or fruit. In doing this, remove such leaves as shade the fruit, as soon as it is ready to ripen. To do it earlier impairs the growth. Do it gradually at two different times. Thinning the fruit is important, as tending to increase its size and flavor, and also to promote the longevity of the tree. If the fruit be thickly set, take off one half at the time of setting. Revise in June, and then in July, taking off all that may be spared. One *very large* apple to every square foot is a rule that may be a sort of guide in other cases. According to this, two hundred large apples would be allowed to a tree whose extent is fifteen feet by twelve. If any person think this thinning excessive, let him try two similar trees, and thin one as directed and leave the other unthinned. It will be found that the thinned tree will produce an equal weight, and fruit of much finer flavor.

THE CULTIVATION OF FRUIT.

By a little attention to this matter, a lady with the help of her children can obtain a rich abundance of all kinds of fruit. The writer has resided in families where little boys of eight, ten, and twelve years old amused themselves, under the direction of their mother, in planting walnuts, chestnuts, and hazelnuts, for future time; as well as in planting and inoculating young fruit-trees of all descriptions. A mother who will take pains to inspire a love for such pursuits in her children, and who will aid and superintend them, will save them from many temptations, and at a trifling expense secure to them and herself a rich reward in the choicest fruits. The information given in this work on this subject may be relied on as sanctioned by the most experienced nurserymen.

The soil for a nursery should be rich, well dug, dressed with well-decayed manure, free from weeds, and protected from cold winds. Fruit-seeds should be planted in the autumn, an inch and a half or two inches deep, in ridges four or five feet apart, pressing the earth firmly over the seeds. While growing, they should be thinned out, leaving the best ones a foot and a half apart. The soil should be kept loose, soft, and free from weeds. They should be inoculated or ingrafted when of the size of a pipe-stem; and in a year after this may be transplanted to their permanent stand.

Peach-trees sometimes bear in two years from budding, and in four years from planting if well kept.

In a year after transplanting, take pains to train the head aright. Straight upright branches produce *gourmands*, or twigs bearing only leaves. The side branches, which are angular or curved, yield the most fruit. For this reason, the limbs should be trained in curves, and perpendicular twigs should be cut off if there be need of pruning. The last of June is the time for this. Grass should never be allowed to grow within four feet of a large tree, and the soil should be kept loose to admit air to the roots. Trees in orchards should be twenty-five feet apart. The soil *under* the top soil has much to do with the health of the trees. If it be what is called *hard-pan*, the trees will deteriorate. Trees need to be manured and to have the soil kept open and free from weeds.

Filberts can be raised in any part of this country.

Figs can be raised in the Middle, Western, and Southern States. For this purpose, in the autumn loosen the roots on one side, and bend the tree down to the earth on the other; then cover it with a mound of straw, earth, and boards, and early in the spring raise it up and cover the roots.

Currants grow well in any but a wet soil. They are propagated by cuttings. The old wood should be thinned in the fall and manure be put on. They can be trained into small trees.

Gooseberries are propagated by layers and cuttings. They are best when kept from suckers and trained like trees. One-third of the old wood should be removed every autumn.

Raspberries do best when shaded during a part of the day. They are propagated by layers, slips, and suckers. There is one kind which bears monthly; but the varieties of this and all other fruits are now so numerous that we can easily find those which are adapted to the special circumstances of the case.

Strawberries require a light soil and vegetable manure. They should be transplanted in April or September, and be set eight inches apart, in rows nine inches asunder, and in beds which are two feet wide, with narrow alleys between them. A part of these plants are *non-bearers*. These have large flowers with showy stamens and high black anthers. The *bearers* have short stamens, a great number of pistils, and the flowers are every way less showy. In blossom-time, pull out all the non-bearers. Some think it best to leave one non-bearer to every twelve bearers, and others pull them all out. Many beds never produce any fruit, because all the plants in them are non-bearers. Weeds should be kept from the vines. When the vines are matted with young plants, the best way is to dig over the beds in cross lines, so as to leave some of the plants standing in little squares, while the rest are turned under the soil. This should be done over a second time in the same year.

To raise Grapes, manure the soil, and keep it soft and free from weeds. A gravelly or sandy soil and a south exposure are best. Transplant the vines in the early spring, or better in the fall. Prune them the first year, so as to have only two main branches, taking off all other shoots as fast as they come. In November, cut off all of these two branches except four eyes. The second year, in the spring, loosen the earth around the roots, and allow only two branches to grow, and every month take off all side shoots. When they are very strong, preserve only a part, and cut off the rest in the fall. In November, cut off all the two main stems except eight eyes. After the second year, no more pruning is needed, except to reduce the side shoots, for the purpose of increasing the fruit. All the pruning of grapes (except nipping side shoots) must be done when the sap is not running, or they will bleed to death. Train them on poles, or lattices, to expose them to the air and sun. Cover tender vines in the autumn. Grapes are propagated by cuttings, layers, and seeds. For cuttings, select in the autumn well-ripened wood of the former year, and take five joints for each. Bury them till April; then soak them for some hours, and set them out *aslant*, so that all the eyes but one shall be covered.

Apples, grapes, and such like fruit can be preserved in their natural state by packing them when dry and solid in dry sand or sawdust, putting alternate layers of fruit and cotton, sawdust or sand. Some sawdust gives a bad flavor to the fruit.

Modes of preserving Fruit-Trees.—Heaps of ashes or tanner's bark around peach-trees prevent the attack of the worm. The *yellows* is a disease of peach-trees, which is spread by the pollen of the blossom. When a tree begins to turn yellow, take it away with all its roots, before it blossoms again, or it will infect other trees. Planting tansy around the roots of fruit-trees is a sure protection against worms, as it prevents the moth from depositing her egg. Equal quantities of salt and saltpetre, put around the trunk of a peach-tree, half a pound to a tree, improve the size and flavor of the fruit. Apply this about the first of April; and if any trees have worms already in them, put on half the quantity in addition in June. To young trees just set out, apply one ounce in April, and another in June, close to the stem. Sandy soil is best for peaches.

Apple-trees are preserved from insects by a wash of strong lye to the body and limbs, which, if old, should be first scraped. Caterpillars should be removed by cutting down their nests in a damp day. Boring a hole in a tree infested with worms, and filling it with sulphur, will often drive them off immediately.

The *fire-blight* or *brûlure* in pear-trees can be stopped by cutting off all the blighted branches. It is supposed by some to be owing to an excess of sap, which is remedied by diminishing the roots.

The *curculio*, which destroys plums and other stone-fruit, can be checked only by gathering up all the fruit that falls, (which contains their eggs,) and destroying it. The *canker-worm* can be checked by applying a bandage around the body of the tree, and every evening smearing it with fresh tar.

CHAPTER XXIII.

SEWING, CUTTING, AND FITTING.

THE customs of the American people are more conformed to those principles of the Christian family state which demand protecting care for the weaker members, than those of any other nation. Nowhere is this fact more apparent than in the division of labor to the boys and girls of one family. The outdoor work, all that is most disagreeable, and the heaviest labor, is taken by the boys, while the indoor family-work is reserved for the girls. Of this indoor labor a part is sedentary, such as sewing, and a part is light labor, such as dish-washing, cooking, sweeping, dusting, and general care of the house. The laundry gives the hardest woman's work; but this is not daily, nor so severe as the outdoor employments of men, while it can be so divided among several women, or be so regulated in various ways, as never to involve excessive labor. Young women wash and iron, as a daily business, six and eight hours a day, and yet continue healthful and cheerful. Such is the distinctive construction of woman's form, that labor with the muscles of the arms and trunk, such as is demanded in washing and ironing, is peculiarly favorable to the perfect development and support of the most delicate and most important portion of her body.

But while the general arrangements of family labor have been conformed to the true Christian principle, there have been certain extremes in our customs which it is important to remedy. This is often exhibited in houses when the members of a family assemble in an evening, and the girls all have some useful employment of the hands, while the boys look on and do nothing.

Again, at other times, we see broken locks, windows unglazed, and furniture needing repair, all making necessary a kind of work women could easily perform, and yet left neglected because the men do not find time or are unskilled for the performance. In a country like ours, the emergencies of the family state often demand the exchange of the ordinary labor of men and women. Frequently, in newer settlements, no servants can be found, while the wife and mother is confined by sickness. In such emergencies, skill in performing woman's work is a great blessing to a man and his family. So the soldiers, sailors, engineers, and all roving men need the skill of the needle that preserves clothing from waste. In our late war, millions would have been saved had all the soldiers been taught to sew in their boyhood.

In this view of the case, industrial schools, to teach both boys and girls all the economic skill of the family state, are of great importance, and a department for this purpose should be connected with every school, especially the public schools, where most of the children will earn their own livelihood and be exposed to many chances of a roving life.

Attempts have been made to introduce sewing into public schools, and usually with little or no success, from many combining difficulties. One of them arises from the increased number of classes for this purpose; which would be relieved by having boys taught to sew in the same class with girls. Another difficulty has been the providing of materials for sewing and the previous cutting and fitting needed, which the parents refuse to supply. A method which meets these and other difficulties, and which has been successfully tried in industrial schools in England, will now be described.

Let a fund be provided by school officers, or by contribution, to provide needles, thread, scissors, and thimbles of various sizes, and place them in the care of the teacher. Let two half-days of the week be devoted to this and other industrial employments, giving, as a reward for success in careful, neat, and quick accomplishment of the duties, the time left beyond that used in the task as holiday hours.

Let the first lesson be the use of scissors, in cutting straight slips of newspaper, thus training the eye and fingers to expert measurement and motion. Whoever excels in the performance of the allotted task in less than the allotted time is to be rewarded with the time, thus gained, for play.

Next, let the class cut broad strips of paper, and practice doubling them in a *hem*, first narrow and then broad. This also cultivates the eyes and trains the fingers.

Then give a lesson to teach the use of the thimble, using a needle without thread, and paper slips to set the needle through.

Let the class now have pieces of cheap and thin unbleached cotton, and cut off from it strips two inches wide, being directed to *cut by a thread.* At first a thread may be drawn to guide the eye. Then, these strips are to be cut into pieces five or six inches long, *turned down and pinched* to prepare for oversewing, and then put together and *basted* with a needle and thread, the teacher setting the example.

This last operation is intended to prepare two strips to be sewed together by *oversewing.* In this operation *colored* thread should be used in order to make the stitches show more distinctly. Meantime, the pupil is trained to make the stitches *equal in depth*, and also at *equal distances.*

The teacher is to be provided with a blank book for each pupil, and on the first page is to be inscribed, *Oversewing.* Beneath this word is to be fastened a specimen of the stitch, as soon as the pupil has attained the degree of excellence and accuracy required.

The next lesson is *Hemming.* To prepare for this, let the scholars first cut, out of newspaper, pieces three inches square, and fold a hem on each side till it is even and smooth.

Then the unbleached cotton is to be given to be cut and prepared in the same way. Finally, the hemming-stitch is to be taught, and the child be required to practice till the stitches are *equal* in size and *regular* in both *slant* and *distances.* When this is well executed, the specimen is to be fastened to another page of the child's book, under the word *Hemming.* In the same way, the various stitches used for running up seams, for felling, darning, whipping, buttonholing, stitching, and gathering, should be taught on small pieces of white or unbleached cotton, using colored thread.

The books in which are fastened the finished specimens of sewing should be preserved by the teacher and exhibited at the school examinations, as an encouragement to excellence. In England, the ladies of wealth and rank take pains to establish and superintend, among the poor, industrial schools in which are taught other domestic work as well as sewing; and, as the consequence, their servants and dependents are well trained for the duties of their station. It is hoped that American ladies will make similar efforts for the children of the poorer classes, and employ all their influence to promote industrial training in our common schools; and also, to see that instruction in these important matters be given to their own daughters, who may become mistresses and directors of future homes, or who, in the constantly changing fortunes of our land, may need to perform as well as to guide the doing of these homely duties.

It is a mistake to suppose that sewing-machines lessen the importance of hand-sewing. All the mending for a family, and much of the altering of clothing and house furniture, must be done only by the hand. In all poor families that own no machine, and in all cases where persons travel, the whole sewing needed must be done by hand.

It is especially for the benefit of the poor who can not have machines, that all the children of our common schools should be taught not only to sew, but to mend and to cut and fit common garments. Hard-working mothers can not teach this art, and the school-teacher is the proper person to do it. Nor should this be added to the ordinary severe and wearing labor of a teacher, but other less important branches should give place to this. It is the constant complaint of all who are seeking to help the destitute, that women are not trained properly to do any kind of domestic work, and there is no way in which philanthropy can be more wisely exerted than in urging the establishment of industrial schools.

It is the hope of the writer that a day is coming when *all* women will be made truly independent, by being trained in early life to employments by which they can secure a home and income for themselves, if they do not marry or if they become widows. This is what is done for daughters in European countries, and should be done in our own.

Institutions for training women to employments suitable for their sex should be established and *endowed*, the same as agricultural and other professional schools for men. When this is done, there will be a *liberal profession* for women of culture and refinement, securing to widows and unmarried women such advantages as have hitherto been enjoyed only by the more favored sex.

CHAPTER XXIV.

ACCIDENTS AND ANTIDOTES.

CHILDREN should be taught the following modes of saving life, health, and limbs in cases of sudden emergency, before a medical adviser can be summoned.

In case of a common cut, bind the lips of the wound together with a rag, and put on nothing else. If it is large, lay narrow strips of sticking-plaster obliquely across the wound. In some cases it is needful to draw a needle and thread through the lips of the wound, and tie the two sides together.

If an artery be cut, it must be tied as quickly as possible, or the person will soon bleed to death. The blood from an artery is a brighter red than that from the veins, and spirts out in jets at each beat of the heart. Take hold of the end of the artery and tie it or hold it tight till a surgeon comes. In this case, and in all cases of bad wounds that bleed much, tie a tight bandage near and above the wound, inserting a stick into the bandage and twisting as tight as can be borne, to stop the immediate effusion of blood.

Bathe bad bruises in hot water. Arnica-water hastens a cure, but is injurious and weakening to the parts when used too long and too freely.

A sprain is relieved from the first pains by hot fomentations, or the application of very hot bandages, but entire rest is the chief permanent remedy. The more the limb is used, especially at first, the longer the time required for the small broken fibres to knit together. The sprained leg should be kept in a horizontal position. When a leg is broken, tie it to the other leg, to keep it still till a surgeon comes. Tie a broken arm to a piece of thin wood, to keep it still till set.

In the case of bad burns that take off the skin, creosote-water is the best remedy. If this is not at hand, wood-soot (not coal,) pounded, sifted, and mixed with lard, is nearly as good, as such soot contains creosote. When a dressing is put on, do not remove it till a skin is formed under it. If nothing else is at hand for a bad burn, sprinkle flour over the place where the skin is off, and then let it remain, protected by a bandage. The chief aim is to keep the part without skin from the air.

In case of drowning, the aim should be to clear the throat, mouth, and nostrils, and then produce the natural action of the lungs in breathing as soon as possible, at the same time removing wet clothes and applying warmth and friction to the skin, especially the hands and feet, to start the circulation. The best mode of cleansing the throat and mouth of choking water is to lay the person on the face, and raise the head a little, clearing the mouth and nostrils with the finger, and then apply hartshorn or camphor to the nose. This is safer and surer than a common mode of lifting the body by the feet, or rolling on a barrel to empty out the water.

To start the action of the lungs, first lay the person on the face and press the back along the spine to expel all air from the lungs. Then turn the body nearly, but not quite over on to the back, thus opening the chest so that the air will rush in if the mouth is kept open. Then turn the body to the face again and expel the air, and then again nearly over on to the back; and so continue for a long time. Friction, dry and warm clothing, and warm applications, should be used in connection with this process. This is a much better mode than using bellows, which sometimes will close the opening to the windpipe. The above is the mode recommended by Dr. Marshall Hall, and is approved by the best medical authorities.

Certain articles are often kept in the house for cooking or medical purposes, and sometimes by mistake are taken in quantities that are poisonous.

Soda, *Saleratus*, *Potash*, or any other alkali, can be rendered harmless in the stomach by vinegar, tomato-juice, or any other acid. If sulphuric or oxalic acid are taken, pounded chalk in water is the best antidote. If those are not at hand, strong soap-suds have been found effective. Large quantities of tepid water should be drank after these antidotes are taken, so as to produce vomiting.

Lime or *baryta* and its compounds demand a solution of glauber salts or of sulphuric acid.

Iodine or *Iodide of Potassium* demands large draughts of wheat flour or starch in water, and then vinegar and water. The stomach should then be emptied by vomiting with as much tepid water as the stomach can hold.

Prussic Acid, a violent poison, is sometimes taken by children in eating the pits of stone-fruits or bitter almonds which contain it. The antidote is to empty the stomach by an emetic, and give water of ammonia or chloric water. Affusions of cold water all over the body, followed by warm hand friction, is often a remedy alone, but the above should be added if at command. *Antimony* and its compounds demand drinks of oak bark, or gall-nuts, or very strong green tea.

Arsenic demands oil or melted fat, with magnesia or lime water in large quantities, till vomiting occurs.

Corrosive Sublimate, (often used to kill vermin,) and any other form of mercury, requires milk or whites of eggs in large quantities. The whites of twelve eggs in two quarts of water, given in the largest possible draughts every three minutes till free vomiting occurs, is a good remedy. Flour and water will answer, though not so surely as the above. Warm water will help, if nothing else is in reach. The same remedy answers when any form of copper, or tin, or zinc poison is taken, and also for creosote.

Lead and its compounds require a dilution of Epsom or Glauber salts, or some strong acid drink, as lemon or tomatoes.

Nitrate of Silver demands salt water drank till vomiting occurs.

Phosphorus (sometimes taken by children from matches) needs magnesia and copious drinks of gum Arabic, or gum-water of any sort.

Alcohol, in dangerous quantities, demands vomiting with warm water.

When one is violently sick from excessive use of *tobacco*, vomiting is a relief, if it arise spontaneously. After that, or in case it does not occur, the juice of a lemon and perfect rest, in a horizonal position on the back, will relieve the nausea and faintness, generally soothing the foolish and overwrought patient into a sleep.

Opium demands a quick emetic. The best is a heaping table-spoonful of powdered mustard, in a tumblerful of warm water; or powdered alum in half-ounce doses and strong coffee alternately in warm water. Give acid drinks after vomiting. If vomiting is not elicited thus, a stomach-pump is demanded. Dash cold water on the head, apply friction, and use all means to keep the person awake and in motion.

Strychnia demands also quick emetics.

The stomach should be emptied always after taking any of these antidotes, by a warm-water emetic.

In case of bleeding at the lungs, or stomach, or throat, give a tea-spoonful of dry salt, and repeat it often. For bleeding at the nose, put ice or pour cold water on the back of the neck, keeping the head elevated.

If a person be struck with lightning, throw pailfuls of cold water on the head and body, and apply mustard poultices on the stomach, with friction of the whole body and inflation of the lungs, as in the case of drowning. The same mode is to be used when persons are stupefied by fumes of coal or bad air.

In thunder-storms, shut the doors and windows. The safest part of a room is its centre; and when there is a feather-bed in the apartment, that will be found the most secure resting-place.

A lightning-rod, if it be well pointed, and run deep into the earth, is a certain protection to a circle around it whose diameter equals the height of the rod above the highest chimney. But it protects *no farther* than this extent.

In case of fire, wrap about you a blanket, a shawl, a piece of carpet, or any other woolen cloth, to serve as protection. Never read in bed, lest you fall asleep, and the bed be set on fire. If your clothes get on fire, never run, but lie down, and roll about till you can reach a bed or carpet to wrap yourself in, and thus put out the fire. Keep young children in woolen dresses, to save them from the risk of fire.

16*

CHAPTER XXV.

ON THE RIGHT USE OF TIME AND PROPERTY.

It is probable that there is no one direction in which conscientious persons suffer so much doubt and perplexity as on the right apportionment of time and property. Clear views of duty on this subject can be gained only by reference to certain facts and principles of mind in connection with certain facts revealed by Jesus Christ.

It is a fact that whenever men notice any method which will *best* secure any end aimed at, they call it *right*. And so the word *right*, as men ordinarily use the term, signifies the method or rule for securing an end designed.

It is also a fact that all rational minds are so made as intuitively to feel or perceive that the end for which all things are made is, *not* to produce enjoyment or happiness of any sort or degree, but to produce the *best* good for all concerned both as to quality and amount.

In proof of this, we find that when any plan or action is proposed, and it is shown that on one alternative the *best* good of both the individual and society is secured, all rational minds decide that it is wise and right, and that the opposite alternative is foolish and wrong. There are endless diversities of opinion as to what *is* for the best good of individuals and society; but all agree that whatever is for the *best* good of all concerned is *right*. We therefore assume that it is an intuitive principle or belief in all rational minds, that *happiness-making on the best and largest scale is the end or purpose for which all things are made.*

We also find ourselves placed in a system of physical, intellectual, and social laws, by obedience to which happiness is gained, and that by disobedience to them happiness is destroyed. At the same time, the controlling principle of every mind is to gain happiness and escape pain or loss of happiness. This being so, we may assume that to gain the end for which we are made, or, in other words, *to act right*, we must obey these laws.

Again, we find every rational mind so made that it may be controlled by some leading desire of ruling purpose to which all other desires and purposes are subordinate, and that it is the nature of this ruling purpose which constitutes *moral character*. By moral character is meant that which results from our own choice instead of that which consists in qualities and propensities created by God. This ruling purpose that controls the mind sometimes, by a figure of speech is called the *heart*, which literally is the organ that controls the body.

Again, we find that in all ages and nations there are some men whose ruling purpose and chief desire is to do right, and that these persons are called the righteous or the virtuous men.

Again, we find that all decisions as to what is best and right are regulated by the *dangers* involved. If one course, with equal advantages, is free from danger, and the opposite involves danger, all men decide the former to be the right one. Thus, all questions of duty as to any course of action are regulated by the dangers which threaten ourselves or society. As an illustration of this fact, when the life of our nation was imperiled, privations, risks, and even death, were sometimes a duty, when in times of peace and prosperity such sacrifices would not be right but highly sinful.

The general principle thus illustrated is, that the standard of right and wrong in all practical affairs is regulated by the amount of danger to be met in alternate courses, one of which must be chosen. And thus it appears that every question of rectitude and duty is modified by circumstances; so that what would be a sin in one case would be a solemn duty in another.

Again, we find that the character of a righteous man is dependent on experience and instruction. For a child is born in utter ignorance of God's laws, and of his obligation to obey them; and it is only by the slow and gradual process of experience and training that he gains this knowledge. Still more is he dependent on educators for motives to excite to obedience. The great want of humanity is right instruction as to the laws by which the best good of all is secured, and powerful motives to induce obedience to these laws.

We are now prepared to notice the connection of these principles and facts with the facts revealed by Jesus Christ. The great and central fact thus made known is, that this life is only the beginning of an eternal existence, involving liability to dreadful dangers after death, and that, in estimating what is right and wise in character and conduct, we are to take into account these dangers, as regulating all questions of duty to ourselves and to our fellow-men. Of the nature of these dangers, we are informed that those who become righteous in this life will secure perpetuity of that character, and thus perfect and endless happiness; but that some will so fail that they never will attain this character, either in this life or the life to come, and so will forever reap the consequences of perpetuate and voluntary selfishness and sin. Still more momentous is the fact, that the number who are to be saved depends upon the self-denying labors of Christ's followers, and that so dreadful are the hazards of the life to come, that all consideration of earthly enjoyment should be made subordinate to the great end of escape for ourselves and for our fellow-men, whom we are to love and care for as we do for ourselves.

These facts and principles enable us clearly to comprehend the great law of rectitude and happiness given by God through Moses, and then more clearly explained and illustrated by Jesus Christ. All men are conscious of that *instinctive love* which we share in common with the brutes. This consists in pleasurable emotions in view of certain persons or things which afford us pleasure, attended by a desire to please those who cause such enjoyment to ourselves, or to those we love. Thus the mother, whether human or brute, feels instinctive love to her offspring; and thus all men feel this instinctive love to those who confer pleasure on themselves.

But Jesus Christ expressly discriminates, and explains that the great law of love (which, he says, it is the chief end of "the law and the prophets" to inculcate) is the *voluntary love* which consists in choosing to do right—that is, to make happiness on the best and largest scale. For the law is, "Thou shalt love the Lord thy God with all thy heart, and thy neighbor *as thyself.*" Now self-love consists not in pleasurable emotions in our own agreeable qualities, but in an instinctive, an all-controlling desire to make self happy.

This is the principle of mind which gives its true meaning to the great law of love, which in this aspect reads thus:

Thou shalt choose, for the chief end or controlling purpose, to make happiness on the greatest scale by obeying God's laws, and as the way to make him and all his creatures happy in the highest degree. And for this end you are to regard and treat the happiness of all in your reach as equal in value to your own.

This exposition of the great law of love is verified repeatedly in the New Testament: "This is the love of God, that ye keep his commandments."

"He that hath my commandments and keepeth them, he it is that loveth me."

"If a man love me, he will keep my words;"—"he that loveth me not, keepeth not my sayings."

"That the world may know that I love the Father, as the Father gave me commandment, even so I do."

We now are prepared to appreciate the new and most wonderful revelation ever made to the human race, and one which the wisest heathen philosophers never even conjectured.

Jesus Christ first revealed to mankind that our Creator is a loving Father to the whole human race; and that such is the eternal nature of things, that our highest possible happiness and escape from endless evil can be accomplished only by self-denying sacrifice and suffering, to save ourselves and others; and that our heavenly Father himself so loves us as to encounter such suffering to save us. For whatever views men form as to the divinity of Jesus Christ, or how his sufferings avail to save from danger in the life to come, all will concede that he teaches that God is represented as having made such a painful sacrifice as a father suffers in seeing a dear and lovely and only son subjected to long years of humiliation, of painful toils, and to a disgraceful and torturing death. And whatever opinions men form as to the nature and duration of future retributions, it is clear that Jesus Christ teaches that so great are our dangers, that every consideration of earthly enjoyment should be subordinate, and that our first interest and aim should be to secure escape to ourselves and our fellow-men.

And here we should notice that most comforting doctrine revealed by Jesus Christ, and that is, that our eternal welfare does not depend on our judging correctly as to what *is* for the best good of all concerned, both for this life and the life to come. On the contrary, we are assured that it is having our *heart*, or *chief desire*, set to do right by obeying all God's laws as fast as we learn what they are. "Sin is the transgression of law," and all men have sinned, and will continue to sin, sometimes from ignorance, sometimes from the force of temptation swaying from the prevailing desire and controlling purpose. And so the righteous men of olden times, though they committed heinous sins, were "men after God's own heart," because their "heart" was set to obey him in all things. And thus their failures were pardoned, and their eternal safety secured.

The same comforting assurance lessens the anxieties of those whose chief aim and desire is to obey Jesus Christ under the new obligations imposed by him. For the "*faith*" which saves our fellow-men both before and after Christ, is not the mere intellectual conviction; for the "devils thus believe and tremble." It is rather that faith which includes intellectual belief in his teachings, and the voluntary conformity of purpose and action to that belief.

So the "*repentance*" required is not mere sorrow for wrong-doing, but it consists in such sorrow as includes "ceasing to do evil, and learning to do well."

We now have the general principle which should regulate all expenditures both of time and property. And whenever any number of persons consistently and practically adopt this principle, they will become "a peculiar people."

The principle is this: The use of property and the use of time must be so regulated as to accomplish *all in our power*, *to save as many as possible* from ignorance of God's laws, and from disobedience to them. It must, in many cases, be difficult to decide as to the most successful way by which our time and property will avail to this end. But that this should be the first and chief object in all our plans, must be conceded by all who accept Jesus Christ as the only authorized teacher of truth and duty. He is the only man who has died and returned from the invisible world to tell us of our prospects there, and his authority is established by the highest evidence of which we can conceive. He is the only being authorized by God fully to explain his laws, both as to our highest happiness while on earth and our future eternal welfare. "There is no other name (or person) given under Heaven" to do this but Jesus Christ.

Having thus gained the main general principle, we may notice some rules to guide us as to the right apportionment of time and property. In employing our time, we are to make suitable allowance for sleep, for preparing and taking food, for securing the means of a livelihood, for intellectual improvement, for exercise and amusement, for social enjoyments, and for benevolent and religious duties. And it is the *right apportionment* of time to these various duties which constitutes its true economy.

In deciding respecting the rectitude of our pursuits, we are bound to aim at *the most* practical good as the ultimate object. With every duty of this life our benevolent Creator has connected some species of enjoyment, to draw us to perform it. Thus the palate is gratified by performing the duty of nourishing our bodies; the principle of curiosity is gratified in pursuing useful knowledge; the desire of approbation is gratified when we perform general social duties; and every other duty has an alluring enjoyment connected with it. But the great mistake of mankind has consisted in seeking the pleasures connected with these duties as the sole aim, without reference to the main end that should be held in view, and to which the enjoyment should be made subservient. Thus, men gratify the palate without reference to the question whether the body is properly nourished; and follow after knowledge without inquiring whether it ministers to good or evil; and seek amusements without reference to the great end to which they should minister.

In gratifying the implanted desires of our nature, we are bound so to restrain ourselves, by reason and conscience, as always to seek the main objects of existence—the *highest* good of ourselves and others; and never to sacrifice this for the mere gratification of our desires. We are to gratify appetite just so far as is consistent with health and usefulness, and the desire for knowledge just so far as will enable us to do most good by our influence and efforts, and no further. We are to seek social intercourse to that extent which will best promote domestic enjoyment and kindly feelings among neighbors and friends; and we are to pursue exercise and amusement only so far as will best sustain the vigor of body and mind.

The laws of the Supreme Ruler, when he became the civil as well as the religious Head of the Jewish theocracy, furnish an example which it would be well for all attentively to consider when forming plans for the apportionment of time and property. To properly estimate this example, it must be borne in mind that the main object of God was to set an example of the *temporal* rewards that follow obedience to the laws of the Creator, and at the same time to prepare religious teachers to extend the more enlarged views and duties resulting from the dangers of the future life revealed by Jesus Christ.

Before Christ came, the Jews were not required to go forth to other nations as teachers of religion, nor were the Jewish nation led to obedience by motives of a life to come. To them God was revealed both as a Father and a civil ruler, and obedience to laws relating solely to this life was all that was required. So low were they in the scale of civilization and mental development, that a system which confined them to one spot as an agricultural people, and prevented their growing very rich or having extensive commerce with other nations, was indispensable to prevent their relapsing into the low idolatries and vices of the nations around them, while temporal rewards and penalties were more effective than those of a life to come. Such faith in God, his laws, and those temporal rewards and penalties as secured habitual obedience, were all that was required.

The proportion of time and property which every Jew was required to devote to intellectual, benevolent, and religious purposes, was as follows:

In regard to property, they were required to give one-tenth of all their yearly income to support the Levites, the priests, and the religious service. Next, they were required to give the first-fruits of all their corn, wine, oil, and fruits, and the first-born of all their cattle, for the Lord's treasury, to be employed for the priests, the widow, the fatherless, and the stranger. The first-born, also, of their children, were the Lord's, and were to be redeemed by a specified sum paid into the sacred treasury. Besides this, they were required to bring a free-will offering to God every time they went up to the three great yearly festivals. In addition to this, regular yearly sacrifices of cattle and fowls were required of each family, and occasional sacrifices for certain sins or ceremonial impurities. In reaping their fields, they were required to leave the corners unreaped for the poor; not to glean their fields, olive-yards, or vineyards; and if a sheaf was left by mistake, they were not to return for it but leave it for the poor.

One-twelfth of the people were set apart, having no landed property, to be priests and teachers; and the other tribes were required to support them liberally.

In regard to the time taken from secular pursuits for the support of education and religion, an equally liberal amount was demanded. In the first place, one-seventh part of their time was taken for the weekly Sabbath, when no kind of work was to be done. Then the whole nation were required to meet at the appointed place three times a year, which, including their journeys and stay there, occupied about eight weeks, or another seventh part of their time. Then the Sabbatical year, when no agricultural labor was to be done, took another seventh of their time from their regular pursuits, as they were an agricultural people. This was the amount of time and property demanded by God, simply to sustain education, religion, and morality within the bounds of one nation.

It was promised to this nation, and fulfilled by constant miraculous interpositions, that in this life obedience to God's laws should secure health, peace, prosperity, and long life; while for disobedience was threatened war, pestilence, famine, and all temporal evils. These promises were constantly verified; and in the day of Solomon, when this nation was most obedient, the whole world was moved with wonder at its wealth and prosperity. But up to this time, no attempt was made by God to enlarge the obligations and motives by revelations as to the future life.

But "when the fullness of time had come," and the race of man was prepared to receive higher responsibilities, Jesus Christ came and "brought life and immortality to light" with a clearness never before revealed, and new and heavy responsibilities consequent on the dangers of the life to come. At the same time was revealed the fatherhood of God, not to the Jews alone, but to the whole human race, and the consequent brotherhood of man; and these revelations in many respects changed the whole standard of duty and obligation.

Christ came as "God manifest in the flesh," to set an example of self-sacrificing love, in rescuing the whole family of man from the dangers of the unseen world, and also to teach and train his disciples through all time to follow his example. And those who conform the most consistently to his teachings and example will aim at a standard of labor and self-denial far beyond that demanded of the Jews.

It is not always that men understand the economy of Providence in that unequal distribution of property which, even under the most perfect form of government, will always exist. Many, looking at the present state of things, imagine that the rich, if they acted in strict conformity to the law of benevolence, would share all their property with their suffering fellow-men. But such do not take into account the inspired declaration that "a man's life consisteth not in the abundance of the things which he possesseth;" or, in other words, life is made valuable not by great possessions, but by such a *character* as prepares a man to enjoy what he holds. God perceives that human character can be most improved by that kind of discipline which exists when there is something valuable to be gained by industrious efforts. This stimulus to industry could never exist in a community where all are just alike, as it does in a state of society where every man sees possessed by others enjoyments which he desires, and may secure by effort and industry. So, in a community where all are alike as to property, there would be no chance to gain that noblest of all attainments, a habit of self-denying benevolence which toils for the good of others, and takes from one's own store to increase the enjoyments of another.

Instead, then, of the stagnation, both of industry and of benevolence, which would follow the universal and equable distribution of property, some men, by superior advantages of birth, or intellect, or patronage, come into possession of a great amount of capital. With these means they are enabled, by study, reading, and travel, to secure expansion of mind, and just views of the relative advantages of moral, intellectual, and physical enjoyments. At the same time, Christianity imposes obligations corresponding with the increase of advantages and means. The rich are not at liberty to spend their treasures chiefly for themselves. Their wealth is given by God, to be employed for the best good of mankind; and their intellectual advantages are designed, primarily, to enable them to judge correctly in employing their means most wisely for the general good.

Now suppose a man of wealth inherits ten thousand acres of real estate; it is not his duty to divide it among his poor neighbors and tenants. If he took this course, it is probable that most of them would spend all in thriftless waste and indolence, or in mere physical enjoyments. Instead, then, of thus putting his capital out of his hands, he is bound to retain and so to employ it as to raise his family and his neighbors to such a state of virtue and intelligence that they can secure far more, by their own efforts and industry, than he, by dividing his capital, could bestow upon them.

In this view of the subject, it is manifest that the unequal distribution of property is no evil. The great difficulty is, that so large a portion of those who hold much capital, instead of using their various advantages for the greatest good of those around them, employ them chiefly for selfish indulgences—thus inflicting as much mischief on themselves as results to others from their culpable neglect. A great portion of the rich seem to be acting on the principle that the more God bestows on them the less are they under obligation to practice any self-denial in fulfilling his benevolent plan of raising our race to intelligence and virtue, and thus to eternal happiness after death.

But there are cheering examples of the contrary spirit and prejudice, some of which will be here recorded, to influence and encourage others.

A lady of great wealth, high position, and elegant culture, in one of our large cities, hired and furnished a house adjacent to her own, and, securing the aid of another benevolent and cultivated woman, took twelve orphan girls of different ages, and educated them under their joint care. Not only time and money were given, but love and labor, just as if these were their own children; and as fast as one was provided for, another was taken.

In another city, a young lady, with property of her own, hired a house, and made it a home for homeless and unprotected women, who paid board when they could earn it, and found a refuge when out of employment.

In another city, the wife of one of its richest merchants took two young girls from the certain road to ruin among the vicious poor. She boarded them with a respectable farmer, and sent them to school; and every week went out, not only to supervise them, but to aid in training them to habits of neatness, industry, and obedience, just as if they were her own children.

Next she hired a large house near the most degraded part of the city, furnished it neatly, and with all suitable conveniences to work, and then rented to those among the most degraded whom she could bring to conform to a few simple rules of decency, industry, and benevolence — one of these rules being that they should pay her the rent every Saturday night. To this motley gathering she became chief counselor and friend, quieted their brawls, taught them to aid each other in trouble or sickness, and strove to introduce among them that law of patient love and kindness illustrated by her own example. The young girls in this tenement she assembled every Saturday at her own house, taught them to sing, heard them recite their Sunday-school lessons, to be sure these were properly learned; taught them to make and mend their own clothing, trimmed their bonnets, and took charge of their Sunday dress, that it might always be in order.

Of course, such benevolence drew a stream of ignorance and misery to her door; and so successful was her labor that she hired a second house, and managed it on the same plan. One hot day in August a friend found her combing the head of a poor, ungainly, foreign girl. She had persuaded a friend to take her from compassion, and she was returned because her head was in such a state. Finding no one else to do it, the lady herself bravely met the difficulty, and persevered in this daily ministry till the evil was remedied, and the poor girl thus secured a comfortable home and wages.

A young lady of wealth and position, with great musical culture and taste, found among the poor two young girls with fine voices and great musical talent. Gaining her parents' consent, the young lady took one of them home, trained her in music, and saw that her school education was secured; so that, when expensive masters and instruments were needed, the girl herself earned the money required, as a governess in a family of wealthy friends. Then she aided the sister; and, as the result, one of them is married happily to a man of great wealth, and the other is receiving a large income as a popular musical artist.

Another young girl, educated as a fine musician by her wealthy parents, at the age of sixteen was afflicted with weak eyes and a heart complaint. She strove to solace herself by benevolent ministries. By teaching music to children of wealthy friends, she earned the means to relieve and instruct, the suffering, ignorant, and poor.

These examples may suffice to show that, even among the most wealthy, abundant modes of self-denying benevolence may be found where there is a heart to seek them.

There is no direction in which a true Christian economy of time and money is more conspicuous than in the style of living adopted in the family state.

Those who build stately mansions, and lay out extensive grounds, and multiply the elegancies of life, to be enjoyed by themselves and a select few, "have their reward" in the enjoyments that end in this life. But those who, with equal means, adopt a style that enables them largely to devote time and wealth to the eternal welfare of their fellow-men, are laying up never-failing treasures in heaven, in the everlasting virtue, gratitude, and happiness of those they have thus saved and blessed.

By taking Christ as the example, by communion with him, and by daily striving to imitate his character and conduct, we may form such a temper of mind that "doing good" on that highest scale revealed by our Lord will become the chief and highest source of enjoyment. And this heavenly principle will grow stronger and stronger, until self-denial loses the more painful part of its character; and then, to save men from sin, and guide them to eternal happiness, will be so delightful and absorbing a pursuit, that all exertions regarded as the means to this end will be like the joyous efforts of men when they strive for a prize or a crown with the full hope of success.

In this view of the subject, efforts and self-denial for the good of others are to be regarded not merely as duties enjoined for the benefit of others, but as the moral training indispensable to the formation of that character on which depends our own happiness. This view exhibits the full meaning of the Saviour's declaration, "How hardly shall they that have riches enter into the kingdom of God!" He had before taught that the kingdom of heaven consisted not in such enjoyments as the worldly seek, but in the temper of self-denying benevolence like his own; and as the rich have far greater temptations to indolent self-indulgence, they are far less likely to acquire this temper than those who, by limited means, are inured to some degree of self-denial.

But on this point one important distinction needs to be

made; and that is, between the self-denial which has no other aim than mere self-mortification, and that which is exercised to secure greater good to ourselves and others. The first is the foundation of monasticism, penances, and all other forms of asceticism; the latter only is that which Christianity requires.

A second consideration, which may give definiteness to this subject, is, that aiming at a perfect character for ourselves and for others involves not the extermination of any principles of our nature, but rather the regulating of them, according to the rules of reason and religion; so that the lower propensities shall always be kept subordinate to nobler principles. Thus we are not to aim at destroying our appetites, or at needlessly denying them, but rather so to regulate them that they shall best secure the objects for which they were implanted. We are not to annihilate the love of praise and admiration, but so to control it that the favor of God shall be regarded more than the estimation of men. We are not to extirpate the principle of curiosity, which leads us to acquire knowledge, but so to direct it that all our acquisitions shall be useful, and not frivolous or injurious. And thus with all the principles of the mind. God has implanted no desires in our constitution which are evil and pernicious. On the contrary, all our constitutional propensities, either of mind or body, he designed we should gratify, whenever no evils would thence result either to ourselves or others. Such passions as envy, selfish ambition, contemptuous pride, revenge, and hatred, are to be exterminated; for they are either excesses or excrescences, not created by God, but rather the result of our own neglect to form habits of benevolence and self-control.

A third consideration is that, though the means for sustaining life and health are to be regarded as necessaries, without which no other duties can be performed, yet a very large portion of the time spent by most persons in easy circumstances for food, raiment, and dwellings, is for mere *superfluities;* which are right when they do not involve the sacrifice of higher interests, and wrong when they do. Life and health can be sustained in the humblest dwellings, with the plainest dress and the simplest food; and after taking from our means what is necessary for life and health, the remainder is to be so divided that the larger portion shall be given to supply the moral and intellectual wants of ourselves and others.

There are many so dependent on parents or husbands, as to suffer perplexity as to their own duty on this account. In reference to these difficulties, the first remark is, that we are never under obligations to do what is entirely out of our power; so that those persons who can not regulate their expenses or their charities are under no sort of obligation to do so. The second remark is, that, when a rule of duty is discovered, if we can not fully attain to it, we are bound to *aim* at it, and to fulfill it just so far as we can. We have no right to throw it aside because we shall find some difficult cases when we come to apply it. The third remark is, that no person can tell how much can be done till a faithful trial has been made. If a woman has never kept any accounts, nor attempted to regulate her expenditures by the right rule, nor used her influence with those that control her plans, to secure this object, she has no right to say how much she can or can not do till after a fair trial has been made.

Is it objected, How can we decide between superfluities and necessities? It is replied, that we are not required to judge exactly in all cases. Our duty is to use the means in our power to assist us in forming a correct judgment; to seek the Divine aid in freeing our minds from indolence and selfishness; and then to judge as well as we can in our endeavors rightly to apportion and regulate our expenses. Many persons seem to feel that they are bound to do better than they know how. But God is not so hard a master; and after we have used all proper means to learn the right way, if we then follow it according to our ability, we do wrong to feel misgivings, or to blame ourselves, if results come out differently from what seems desirable.

The results of our actions alone can never prove us deserving of blame. For men are often so placed that, owing to lack of intellect or means, it is impossible for them to decide correctly. To use all the means of knowledge within our reach, to seek Divine guidance by prayer, and then to judge with a candid and conscientious spirit, is all that God requires; and when we have done this, and the event seems to come out so as to seem unfortunate, we should never wish that we had decided otherwise; for this would be the same as wishing that we had not followed the dictates of judgment and conscience. As this is a world designed for discipline and trial, what seem untoward events are never to be construed as indications of the obliquity of our past decisions.

In making an examination on this subject, it is sometimes the case that a woman will count among the *necessaries* of life all the various modes of adorning the person or house practiced in the circle in which she moves; and after enumerating the many *duties* which demand attention, counting these as a part, she will come to the conclusion that she has no time, and but little money, to devote to personal improvement or to benevolent enterprises. This surely is not in agreement with the requirements of the Saviour, who calls on us to seek for others as well as ourselves, *first of all*, "the kingdom of God and his righteousness."

In order to act in accordance with the rule here presented, it is true that many would be obliged to give up the idea of conforming to the notions and customs of those with whom they associate, and compelled to adopt the maxim, "Be not conformed to this world." In many cases it would involve an entire change in the style of living. And the writer has the happiness of knowing more cases than one where persons who have come to similar views on this subject have given up large and expensive establishments, that they might keep a pure conscience, and regulate their charities more according to the requirements of Christianity.

In deciding what particular objects shall receive our benefactions, there are also general principles to guide us. The first is that presented by our Saviour, when, after urging the great law of benevolence, he was asked, "And who is my neighbor?" His reply, in the parable of "the Good Samaritan," teaches us that any human being whose wants are brought to our knowledge is our neighbor. The wounded man in that parable was not only a stranger, but he belonged to a foreign nation, peculiarly hated; and he had no claim, except that his wants were brought to the knowledge of the wayfaring man. From this we learn that the destitute of all nations become our neighbors as soon as their wants are brought to our knowledge.

Another general principle is this: that those who are most in need must be relieved in preference to those who are less destitute. On this principle it is that we think the followers of Christ should give more to supply those who are suffering for want of the bread of eternal life, than for those who are deprived of physical enjoyments. And another reason for this preference is the fact that many who give in charity have made such imperfect advances in civilization and Christianity, that the intellectual and moral wants of our race make but a feeble impression on the mind. Relate a pitiful tale of a family reduced to live for weeks on potatoes only, and many a mind would awake to deep sympathy, and stretch forth the hand of charity. But describe cases where the immortal mind is pining in stupidity and ignorance, or racked with the fever of baleful passions, and how small the number so elevated in sentiment and so enlarged in their views as to appreciate and sympathize in these far greater misfortunes! The intellectual and moral wants of our fellow-men, therefore, should claim the first place in Christian attention, both because they are most important, and because they are most neglected; while it should not be forgotten, in giving personal attention to the wants of the poor, that the relief of immediate physical distress is often the easiest way of touching the moral sensibilities of the destitute.

Another consideration to be borne in mind is, that in this country there is much less real need of charity in supplying physical necessities than is generally supposed by those who have not learned the more excellent way. This land is so abundant in supplies, and labor is in such demand, that every healthy person can earn a comfortable support; and if all the poor were instantly made virtuous, it is probable that there would be few physical wants which could not readily be supplied by the immediate friends of each sufferer. The sick, the aged, and the orphan would be the only objects of charity. In this view of the case, the primary effort in relieving the poor should be to furnish them the means of earning their own support, and to supply them with those moral influences which are most effectual in securing virtue and industry.

Another point to be attended to is the importance of maintaining a system of *associated* charities. There is no point in which the economy of charity has more improved, than in the present mode of combining many small contributions for sustaining enlarged and systematic plans of charity. If all the half-dollars which are now contributed to aid in organized systems of charity were returned to the donors, to be applied by the agency and discretion of each, thousands and thousands of the treasures now employed to promote the moral and intellectual wants of mankind would become entirely useless. In a democracy like ours, where few are very rich and the majority are in comfortable circumstances, this collecting and dispensing of drops and rills is the mode by which, in imitation of nature, the dews and showers are to distill on parched and desert lands. And every person, while earning a pittance to unite with many more, may be cheered with the consciousness of sustaining a grand system of operations which must have the most decided influence in raising all mankind to that perfect state of society which Christianity is designed to accomplish.

Another consideration relates to the indiscriminate bestowal of charity. Persons who have taken pains to inform themselves, and who devote their whole time to dispensing charities, unite in declaring that this is one of the most fruitful sources of indolence, vice, and poverty. From several of these the writer has learned that, by their own personal investigations, they have ascertained that there are large establishments of idle and wicked persons in most of our cities, who associate together to support themselves by every species of imposition. They hire large houses, and live in constant rioting on the means thus obtained. Among them are women who have or who hire the use of infant children;

others, who are blind, or maimed, or deformed, or who can adroitly feign such infirmities; and by these means of exciting pity, and by artful tales of woe, they collect alms, both in city and country, to spend in all manner of gross and guilty indulgences. Meantime many persons, finding themselves often duped by impostors, refuse to give at all; and thus many benefactions are withdrawn, which a wise economy in charity would have secured. For this and other reasons, it is wise and merciful to adopt the general rule, never to give alms till we have had some opportunity of knowing how they will be spent. There are exceptions to this, as to every general rule, which a person of discretion can determine. But the practice so common among benevolent persons of giving at least a trifle to all who ask, lest perchance they may turn away some who are really sufferers, is one which causes more sin and misery than it cures.

The writer has never known any system for dispensing charity more successful than the one by which a town or city is divided into districts, and each district is committed to the care of two ladies, whose duty it is to call on each family and leave a book for a child, or do some other deed of neighborly kindness, and make that the occasion for entering into conversation and learning the situation of all residents in the district. By this method the ignorant, the vicious, and the poor are discovered, and their physical, intellectual, and moral wants are investigated. In some places where the writer has known this mode pursued, each person retained the same district year after year; so that every poor family in the place was under the watch and care of some intelligent and benevolent lady, who used all her influence to secure a proper education for the children, to furnish them with suitable reading, to encourage habits of industry and economy, and to secure regular attendance on public religious instruction. Thus the rich and the poor were brought in contact in a way advantageous to both parties; and if such a system could be universally adopted, more would be done for the prevention of poverty and vice than all the wealth of the nation could avail for their relief. But this plan can not be successfully carried out in this manner, unless there is a large proportion of intelligent, benevolent, and self-denying persons who unite in a systematic plan.

But there is one species of "charity" which needs especial consideration. It is that spirit of kindly love which induces us to refrain from judging of the means and the relative charities of other persons. There have been such indistinct notions, and so many different standards of duty on this subject, that it is rare for two persons to think exactly alike in regard to the rule of duty. Each person is bound to inquire and judge for himself as to his own duty or deficiencies; but as both the resources and the amount of the actual charities of others are beyond our ken, it is as indecorous as it is uncharitable to sit in judgment on their decisions.

CHAPTER XXVI.

THE CARE OF INFANTS.

The topic of this chapter may well be prefaced by an extract from Herbert Spencer on the treatment of offspring. He first supposes that some future philosophic speculator, examining the course of education of the present period, should find nothing relating to the training of children, and that his natural inference would be that our schools were all for monastic orders, who have no charge of infancy and childhood. He then remarks, "Is it not an astonishing fact that, though on the treatment of offspring depend their lives or deaths and their moral welfare or ruin, yet that so little instruction on the treatment of offspring is ever given to those who will hereafter be parents? Is it not monstrous that the fate of a new generation should be left to the chances of unreasoning custom, or impulse, or fancy, joined with the suggestions of ignorant nurses and the prejudiced counsel of grandmothers?

"If a merchant should commence business without any knowledge of arithmetic or book-keeping, we should exclaim at his folly, and look for disastrous consequences. Or if, without studying anatomy, a man set up as a surgeon, we should wonder at his audacity, and pity his patients. But that parents should commence the difficult work of rearing children without giving earnest attention to the principles, physical, moral, or intellectual, which ought to guide them, excites neither surprise at the actors nor pity for the victims.

"To tens of thousands that are killed add hundreds of thousands that survive with feeble constitutions, and millions not so strong as they should be; and you will have some idea of the curse inflicted on their offspring by parents ignorant of the laws of life. Do but consider for a moment that the regimen to which children are subject is hourly telling upon them to their life-long injury or benefit, and that there are twenty ways of going wrong to one way of going right, and you will get some idea of the enormous mischief that is almost everywhere inflicted by the thoughtless, hap-hazard system in common use.

"When sons and daughters grow up sickly and feeble, parents commonly regard the event as a visitation of Providence. They assume that these evils come without cause, or that the cause is supernatural. Nothing of the kind. In some cases causes are inherited, but in most cases foolish management is the cause. Very generally parents themselves are responsible for this pain, this debility, this depression, this misery. They have undertaken to control the lives of their offspring, and with cruel carelessness have neglected to learn those vital processes which they are daily affecting by their commands and prohibitions. In utter ignorance of the simplest physiological laws, they have been, year by year, undermining the constitutions of their children, and so have inflicted disease and premature death, not only on them but also on their descendants.

"Equally great are the ignorance and consequent injury, when we turn from the physical to the moral training. Consider the young, untaught mother and her nursery legislation. A short time ago she was at school, where her memory was crammed with words and names and dates, and her reflective faculties scarcely in the slightest degree exercised —where not one idea was given her respecting the methods of dealing with the opening mind of childhood, and where her discipline did not in the least fit her for thinking out methods of her own. The intervening years have been spent in practicing music, fancy-work, novel-reading, and party-going, no thought having been given to the grave responsibilities of maternity, and scarcely any of that solid intellectual culture obtained which would fit her for such responsibilities; and now see her with an unfolding human character committed to her charge, see her profoundly ignorant of the phenomena with which she has to deal, undertaking to do that which can be done but imperfectly even with the aid of the profoundest knowledge!"

In view of such considerations, every young lady ought to learn how to take proper care of an infant; for, even if she is never to become the responsible guardian of a nursery, she will often be in situations where she can render benevolent aid to others in this most fatiguing and anxious duty.

The writer has known instances in which young ladies, who had been trained by their mothers properly to perform this duty, were in some cases the means of saving the lives of infants, and in others, of relieving sick mothers from intolerable care and anguish by their benevolent aid.

On this point Dr. Combe remarks: "All women are not destined, in the course of nature, to become mothers; but how very small is the number of those who are unconnected, by family ties, friendship, or sympathy, with the children of others! How very few are there who, at some time or other of their lives, would not find their usefulness and happiness increased, by the possession of a kind of knowledge intimately allied to their best feelings and affections! And how important is it to the mother herself, that her efforts should be seconded by intelligent instead of ignorant assistants!"

In order to be prepared for such benevolent ministries, every young lady should improve the opportunity, whenever it is afforded her, for learning how to wash, dress, and tend a young infant; and whenever she meets with such a work as Dr. Combe's, on the management of infants, she ought to read it, and *remember* its contents.

The directions that follow have been taken from standard medical writers, or have been examined and approved by the highest class of physicians, and also by judicious and experienced mothers.

Says Dr. Combe: "Nearly one half of the deaths occurring during the first two years of existence are ascribable to mismanagement, and to errors in diet. At birth, the stomach is feeble, and as yet unaccustomed to food; its cravings are consequently easily satisfied, and frequently renewed." "At that early age, there ought to be no fixed time for giving nourishment. The stomach can not be thus satisfied." "The active call of the infant is a sign, which needs never be mistaken."

"But care must be taken to determine between the crying of pain or uneasiness, and the call for food; and the practice of giving an infant food to stop its cries is often the means of increasing its sufferings. After a child has satisfied its hunger, from two to four hours, according to the age, should intervene before another supply is given.

"At birth, the stomach and bowels, never having been used, contain a quantity of mucous secretion, which requires to be removed. To effect this, Nature has rendered the first portions of the mother's milk purposely watery and laxative. Nurses, however, distrusting Nature, often hasten to administer some active purgative; and the consequence often is, irritation in the stomach and bowels, not easily subdued." It is only where the child is deprived of its mother's milk, as the first food, that some gentle laxative should be given.

"It is a common mistake to suppose that because a woman is nursing, she ought to live very fully, and to add an allowance of wine, porter, or other fermented liquor, to her usual diet. The only result of this plan is, to cause an unnatural fullness in the system, which places the nurse on the brink of disease, and retards rather than increases the food of the infant. More will be gained by the observance of the ordinary laws of health than by any foolish deviation, founded on ignorance."

There is no point on which medical men so emphatically lift the voice of warning as in reference to administering medicines to infants. It is so difficult to discover what is the matter with an infant, its frame is so delicate and so susceptible, and slight causes have such a powerful influence, that it requires the utmost skill and judgment to ascertain what would be proper medicines, and the proper quantity to be given.

Says Dr. Combe: "That there are cases in which active means must be promptly used to save the child, is perfectly true. But it is not less certain that these are cases of which no mother or nurse ought to attempt the treatment. As a general rule, where the child is well managed, medicine of any kind is very rarely required; and if disease were more generally regarded in its true light, not as something thrust into the system, which requires to be expelled by force, but as an aberration from a natural mode of action, produced by some external cause, we should be in less haste to attack it by medicine, and more watchful in its prevention. Accordingly, where a constant demand for medicine exists in a nursery, the mother may rest assured that there is something essentially wrong in the treatment of her children.

"Much havoc is made among infants by the abuse of medicines, which procure momentary relief but end by producing incurable disease; and it has often excited my astonishment to see how recklessly remedies of this kind are had recourse to, on the most trifling occasions, by mothers and nurses, who would be horrified if they knew the nature of the power they are wielding, and the extent of injury they are inflicting."

Instead, then, of depending on medicine for the preservation of the health and life of an infant, the following precautions and preventives should be adopted:

"Take particular care of the *food* of an infant. If it is nourished by the mother, her own diet should be simple, nourishing, and temperate. If the child be brought up 'by hand,' the milk of a new milch-cow, mixed with one-third water, and sweetened a little with *white* sugar, should be the only food given, until the teeth come. This is more suitable than any preparations of flour or arrowroot, the nourishment of which is too highly concentrated. Never give a child *bread*, *cake*, or *meat*, before the teeth appear. If the food appear to distress the child after eating, first ascertain if the milk be really from a new milch-cow, as it may otherwise be too old. Learn, also, whether the cow lives on proper food. Cows that are fed on *still-slops*, as is often the case in cities, furnish milk which is very unhealthful."

Be sure and keep a good supply of pure and fresh air in the nursery. On this point Dr. Bell remarks, respecting rooms constructed without fire-places and without doors or windows to let in pure air from without, "The sufferings of children of feeble constitutions are increased beyond measure by such lodgings as these. An action, brought by the commonwealth, ought to lie against those persons who build houses for sale or rent, in which rooms are so constructed as not to allow of free ventilation; and a writ of lunacy taken out against those who, with the common-sense experience which all have on this head, should spend any portion of their time, still more, should sleep, in rooms thus nearly air-tight."

After it is a month or two old, take an infant out to walk, or ride, in a little wagon, every fair and warm day; but be very careful that its feet, and every part of its body, are kept warm; and be sure that its eyes are well protected from the light. Weak eyes, and sometimes blindness, are caused by neglecting this precaution. Keep the head of an infant cool, never allowing too warm bonnets, nor permitting it to sink into soft pillows when asleep. Keeping an infant's head too warm very much increases nervous irritability, and this is the reason why medical men forbid the use of caps for infants. But the head of an infant should, especially while sleeping, be protected from draughts of air, and from getting cold.

Be very careful of the skin of an infant, as nothing tends so effectually to prevent disease. For this end, it should be washed all over every morning, and then gentle friction should be applied with the hand, to the back, stomach, bowels, and limbs. The head should be thoroughly washed every day, and then brushed with a soft hair-brush, or combed with a fine comb. If, by neglect, dirt accumulates under the hair, apply with the finger the yelk of an egg, and then the fine comb will remove it all without any trouble.

Dress the infant so that it will be always warm, but not so as to cause perspiration. Be sure and keep its feet *always* warm; and for this often warm them at a fire, and use long dresses. Keep the neck and arms covered. For this purpose, wrappers, open in front, made high in the neck, with long sleeves, to put on over the frock, are now very fashionable.

It is better for both mother and child, that it should not sleep on the mother's arm at night, unless the weather be extremely cold. This practice keeps the child too warm, and leads it to seek food too frequently. A child should ordinarily take nourishment but once or twice in the night. A crib beside the mother, with plenty of warm and light covering, is best for the child; but the mother must be sure that it is always kept warm.

Never cover a child's head so that it will inhale the air of its own lungs. In very warm weather, especially in cities, great pains should be taken to find fresh and cool air by rides and sailing. Walks in a public square in the cool of the morning, and frequent excursions in ferry or steamboats, would often save a long bill for medical attendance. In hot nights, the windows should be kept open, and the infant laid on a mattress, or on folded blankets. A bit of straw matting, laid over a feather-bed and covered with the under sheet, makes a very cool bed for an infant.

Cool bathing, in hot weather, is very useful; but the water should be very little cooler than the skin of the child. When the constitution is delicate, the water should be slightly warmed. Simply sponging the body freely in a tub, answers the same purpose as a regular bath. In very warm weather this should be done two or three times a day, always waiting two or three hours after food has been given.

"When the stomach is peculiarly irritable, (from teething,) it is of paramount necessity to withhold all the nostrums which have been so falsely lauded as 'sovereign cures for *cholera infantum*.' The true restoratives for a child threatened with disease are cool air, cool bathing, and cool drinks of simple water, in addition to *proper* food, at stated intervals."

In many cases, change of air from sea to mountain, or the reverse, has an immediate healthful influence and is superior to every other treatment. Do not take the advice of mothers who tell of this, that, and the other thing, which have proved excellent remedies in their experience. Children have different constitutions, and there are multitudes of different causes for their sickness; and what might cure one child, might kill another which *appeared* to have the same complaint. A mother should go on the general rule of giving an infant very little medicine, and then only by the direction of a discreet and experienced physician. And there are cases when, according to the views of the most distinguished and competent practitioners, physicians themselves are much too free in using medicines, instead of adopting preventive measures.

Do not allow a child to form such habits that it will not be quiet unless tended and amused. A healthy child should be accustomed to lie or sit in its cradle much of the time; but it should occasionally be taken up and tossed, or carried about for exercise and amusement. An infant should be encouraged to *creep*, as an exercise very strengthening and useful. If the mother fears the soiling of its nice dresses, she can keep a long slip or apron which will entirely cover the dress, and can be removed when the child is taken in the arms. A child should not be allowed, when quite young, to bear its weight on its feet very long at a time, as this tends to weaken and distort the limbs.

Many mothers, with a little painstaking, succeed in putting their infants into their cradle while awake, at regular hours for sleep; and induce regularity in other habits, which saves much trouble. During this training process a child may cry, at first, a great deal; but, for a healthy child, this use of the lungs does no harm, and tends rather to strengthen than to injure them, unless it becomes exceedingly violent. A child who is trained to lie or sit and amuse itself, is happier than one who is carried and tended a great deal, and thus rendered restless and uneasy when not so indulged.

The most critical period in the life of an infant is that of dentition or teething, especially at the early stages. An adult has thirty-two teeth, but young children have only twenty, which gradually loosen and are followed by the permanent teeth. When the child has ten teeth on each jaw, all that are added are the permanent set, which should be carefully perserved; this caution is needful, as sometimes decay in the first double teeth of the second set are supposed to be of the transient set, and are so neglected, or are removed instead of being preserved by plugging. When the first teeth rise so as to press against the gums, there is always more or less inflammation, causing nervous fretfulness, and the impulse to put every thing into the mouth. Usually there is disturbed sleep, a slight fever, and greater flow of saliva; this is often relieved by letting the child have ice to bite, tied in a rag.

Sometimes the disorder of the mouth extends to the whole system. In difficult teething, one symptom is the jerking back of the head when taking the breath, as if in pain, owing to the extreme soreness of the gums. This is, in extreme cases, attended with increased saliva and a gummy secretion in the corners of the eyes, itching of the nose, redness of cheeks, rash, convulsive twitching of lips and the muscles generally, fever, constipation, and sometimes by a diarrhea, which last is favorable if slight; difficulty of breathing, dilation of the pupils of the eyes, restless motion and moaning; and finally, if not relieved, convulsions and death. The most effective relief is gained by lancing the gums. Every woman, and especially every mother, should know the time and order in which the infant teeth come, and, when any of the above symptoms appear, should examine the mouth, and if a gum is swollen and inflamed, should either have a physician lance it, or if this can not be done, should perform the operation herself. A sharp pen-knife and steady hand, making an incision to touch the rising tooth, will cause no more pain than a simple scratch of the gum, and usually will give speedy relief.

The temporary teeth should not be removed until the new ones appear, as it injures the jaw and coming teeth; but as soon as a new tooth is seen pressing upward, the temporary tooth should be removed, or the new tooth will come out of its proper place. If there is not room where the new tooth appears, the next temporary tooth must be taken out. Great mischief has been done by removing the first teeth before the second appear, thus making a contraction of the jaw.

Most trouble with the teeth of young children comes from neglect to use the brush to remove the tartar that accumulates near the gum, causing disease and decay. This disease is sometimes called *scurvy*, and is shown by an accumulation around the teeth and by inflamed gums that bleed easily. Removal of the tartar by a dentist and cleaning the teeth after every meal with a brush will usually cure this evil, which causes loosening of the teeth and a bad breath.

Much injury is often done to teeth by using improper tooth-powder. The tooth-brush should be used after every meal, and floss silk pressed between the teeth to remove food lodged there. This method will usually save the teeth from decay till old age, and there is no need of tooth-powder.

When an infant seems ill during the period of dentition, the following directions from an experienced physician may be of service. It is now an accepted principle of the medical world that fevers are to be reduced by cold applications; but an infant demands careful and judicious treatment in this direction; some have extremely sensitive nerves, and cold is painful. For such, tepid sponging should be used near a fire, and the coldness increased gradually. The sensations of the child should be the guide. Usually, but not always, children that are healthy will learn by degrees to prefer cold water, and then it may safely be used.

When an infant becomes feverish, wrapping its body in a towel wrung out in tepid or cold water, and then keeping it warm in a woolen blanket, is a very safe and soothing remedy.

In case of constipation, this preparation of food is useful:

One table-spoonful of unbolted flour wet with cold water. Add one pint of hot water, and boil twenty minutes. Add, when taken up, one pint of milk. If the stomach seems delicate and irritable, strain out the bran, but in most cases retain it.

Where the mother's milk fails, and good cow's milk can not be insured, there are preparations of oat-meal and barley-meal that are next best. These may be used when the mother's milk is injured by ill health. A trial must be made to see which is best. Make a thin gruel, and add half a tea-spoonful of condensed milk, or four great spoonfuls of milk to a coffee-cup of the gruel for a young infant, and a full one for an older child.

In case of diarrhea, walk with the child in arms a great deal in the open air, and give it rice-water to drink.

The warmth and vital influences of the nurse are very important, and make this mode of exercise both more soothing and more efficacious, especially in the open air, the infant being warmly clad.

In case of feverishness from teething or from any other cause, wrap the infant in a towel wrung out in tepid water, and then wrap it in a woolen blanket. The water may be cooler according as the child is older and stronger. The evaporation of the water draws off the heat, while the moisture soothes the nerves, and usually the child will fall into a quiet sleep. As soon as it becomes restless, change the wet towel and proceed as before.

The leading physicians of Europe and of this country, in all cases of fevers, use cool water to reduce them, by this and other modes of application. This method is more soothing than any other, and is as effective for adults as for infants.

Some of the most distinguished physicians of New York who have examined this chapter give their full approval of the advice given. If there is still distrust as to this mode of using water to reduce fevers, it will be advantageous to read an address on the use of cold applications in fevers, delivered by Dr. William Neftel, before the New York Academy of Medicine, published in the *New York Medical Record* for November, 1868; this can be obtained by inclosing twenty cents to the editor, with the post-office address of the applicant.

CHAPTER XXVII.

THE MANAGEMENT OF YOUNG CHILDREN.

In regard to the physical education of children, Dr. Clark, Physician in Ordinary to the Queen of England, expresses views on one point in which most physicians would coincide. He says: "There is no greater error in the management of children than that of giving them animal diet very early. By persevering in the use of an over-stimulating diet, the digestive organs become irritated, and the various secretions immediately connected with digestion, and necessary to it, are diminished, especially the *biliary secretion*. Children so fed become very liable to attacks of fever and inflammation, affecting particularly the mucous membranes; and measles and other diseases incident to childhood are generally severe in their attacks."

The result of the treatment of the inmates of the Orphan Asylum at Albany is one which all who have the care of young children should deeply ponder. During the first six years of the existence of this institution, its average number of children was eighty. For the first three years, their diet was meat once a day, bread of fine flour, rice, Indian puddings, vegetables, fruit, and milk. Considerable attention was given to clothing, fresh air, and exercise; and they were bathed once in three weeks. During these three years, from four to six children, and sometimes more, were continually on the sick-list; one or two assistant nurses were necessary; a physician was called two or three times a week; and during this time there were between thirty and forty deaths. At the end of this period, the management was changed in these respects: daily ablutions of the whole body were practiced; bread of unbolted flour was substituted for that of fine wheat; and all animal food was banished. More attention, also, was paid to clothing, bedding, fresh air, and exercise.

The result was, that the nursery was vacated; the nurse and physician were no longer needed; and for two years not a single case of sickness or death occurred. The third year, also, there were no deaths, except those of two idiots and one other child, all of whom were new inmates, who had not been subjected to this treatment. The teachers of the children also testified there was a manifest increase of intellectual vigor and activity, while there was much less irritability of temper.

Let parents, nurses, and teachers reflect on the above statement, and bear in mind that stupidity of intellect, and irritability of temper, as well as ill health, are often caused by the mismanagement of the nursery in regard to the physical training of children.

There is probably no practice more deleterious than that of allowing children to eat at short intervals through the day. As the stomach is thus kept constantly at work, with no time for repose, its functions are deranged, and a weak or disordered stomach is the frequent result. Children should be required to keep cakes, nuts, and other good things, which should be sparingly given, till just before a meal, and then they will form a part of their regular supply. This is better than to wait till after their hunger is satisfied by food, when they will eat the niceties merely to gratify the palate, and thus overload the stomach and interrupt digestion.

In regard to the intellectual training of young children, some modification in the common practice is necessary, with reference to their physical well-being. More care is needful in providing *well-ventilated* school-rooms, and in securing more time for sports in the open air during school hours. It is very important to most mothers that their young children should be removed from their care during certain school hours; and it is very useful for quite young children to be subjected to the discipline of a school, and to intercourse with other children of their own age. And, with a suitable teacher, it is no matter how early children are sent to school, provided their health is not endangered by impure air, too much confinement, and too great mental stimulus, which is the chief danger of the present age.

In regard to the formation of the moral character, it has been too much the case that the discipline of the nursery has consisted of disconnected efforts to make children either do, or refrain from doing, certain particular acts. Do this, and be rewarded; do that, and be punished; is the ordinary routine of family government.

But children can be very early taught that their happiness, both now and hereafter, depends on the formation of *habits* of submission, self-denial, and benevolence. And all the discipline of the nursery can be conducted by parents, not only with this general aim in their own minds, but also with the same object daily set before the minds of the children. Whenever their wishes are crossed, or their wills subdued, they can be taught that all this is done, not merely to please the parent, or to secure some good to themselves or to others; but as a part of that merciful training which is designed to form such a character, and such habits, that they can hereafter find their chief happiness in giving up their will to God, and in living to do good to others, instead of living merely to please themselves.

It can be pointed out to them, that they must always submit their will to the will of God, or else be continually miserable. It can be shown how, in the nursery, and in the school, and through all future days, a child must practice the giving up of his will and wishes, when they interfere with the rights and comfort of others; and how important it is early to learn to do this, so that it will, by habit, become easy and agreeable. It can be shown how children who are indulged in all their wishes, and who are never accustomed to any self-denial, always find it hard to refrain from what injures themselves and others. It can be shown, also, how important it is for every person to form such habits of benevolence toward others that self-denial in doing good will become easy.

Parents have learned, by experience, that children can be constrained by authority and penalties to exercise self-denial, for *their own* good, till a habit is formed which makes the duty comparatively easy. For example, well-trained children can be accustomed to deny themselves tempting articles of food which are injurious, until the practice ceases to be painful and difficult; whereas an indulged child would be thrown into fits of anger or discontent when its wishes were crossed by restraints of this kind.

But it has not been so readily discerned that the same method is needful in order to form a habit of self-denial in doing good to others. It has been supposed that while children must be forced, by *authority*, to be self-denying and prudent in regard to their own happiness, it may properly be left to their own discretion whether they will practice any self-denial in doing good to others. But the more difficult a duty is, the greater is the need of parental authority in forming a habit which will make that duty easy.

In order to secure this, some parents turn their earliest efforts to this object. They require the young child always to offer to others a part of every thing which it receives; always to comply with all reasonable requests of others for service; and often to practice little acts of self-denial, in order to secure some enjoyment for others. If one child receives a present of some nicety, he is required to share it with all his brothers and sisters. If one asks his brother to help him in some study or sport, and is met with a denial, the parent requires the unwilling child to act benevolently, and give up some of his time to increase his brother's enjoyment. Of course, in such an effort as this discretion must be used as to the frequency and extent of the exercise of authority, to induce a habit of benevolence. But where parents deliberately aim at such an object, and wisely conduct their instructions and discipline to secure it, very much will be accomplished.

In regard to forming habits of obedience, there have been two extremes, both of which need to be shunned. One is, a stern and unsympathizing maintenance of parental authority, demanding perfect and constant obedience, without any attempt to convince a child of the propriety and benevolence of the requisitions, and without any manifestation of sympathy and tenderness for the pain and difficulties which are to be met. Under such discipline, children grow up to fear their parents, rather than to love and trust them; while some of the most valuable principles of character are chilled, or forever blasted.

In shunning this danger, other parents pass to the opposite extreme. They put themselves too much on the footing of equals with their children, as if little were due to superiority of relation, age, and experience. Nothing is exacted, without the implied concession that the child is to be a judge of the propriety of the requisition; and reason and persuasion are employed, where simple command and obedience would be far better. This system produces a most pernicious influence. Children soon perceive the position thus allowed them, and take every advantage of it. They soon learn to dispute parental requirements, acquire habits of forwardness and conceit, assume disrespectful manners and address, maintain their views with pertinacity, and yield to authority with ill-humor and resentment, as if their rights were infringed upon.

The medium course is for the parent to take the attitude of a superior in age, knowledge, and relation, who has a perfect *right* to control every action of the child, and that, too, without giving any reason for the requisitions. "Obey *because your parent commands*," is always a proper and sufficient reason: though not always the best to give.

But care should be taken to convince the child that the parent is conducting a course of discipline designed to make him happy; and in forming habits of implicit obedience, self-denial, and benevolence, the child should have the reasons for most requisitions kindly stated; never, however, on the demand of it from the child, as a right, but as an act of kindness from the parent.

It is impossible to govern children properly, especially those of strong and sensitive feelings, without a constant effort to appreciate the value which they attach to their enjoyments and pursuits. A lady of great strength of mind and sensibility once told the writer that one of the most acute periods of suffering in her whole life was occasioned by the burning up of some milkweed-silk by her mother. The child had found, for the first time, some of this shining and beautiful substance; was filled with delight at her discovery; was arranging it in parcels; planning its future use, and her pleasure in showing it to her companions—when her mother, finding it strewed over the carpet, hastily swept it into the fire, and that, too, with so indifferent an air, that the child fled away, almost distracted with grief and disappointment. The mother little realized the pain she had inflicted, but the child felt the unkindness so severely that for several days her mother was an object almost of aversion. While, therefore, the parent needs to carry on a steady course, which will oblige the child always to give up its will, whenever its own good or the greater claims of others require it, this should be constantly connected with the expression of a tender sympathy for the trials and disappointments thus inflicted.

Those, again, who will join with children and help them in their sports, will learn by this mode to understand the feelings and interests of childhood; while, at the same time, they secure a degree of confidence and affection which can not be gained so easily in any other way. And it is to be regretted that parents so often relinquish this most powerful mode of influence to domestics and playmates, who often use it in the most pernicious manner. In joining in such sports, older persons should never yield entirely the attitude of superiors, or allow disrespectful manners or address. And respectful deportment is never more cheerfully accorded, than in seasons when young hearts are pleased and made grateful by having their tastes and enjoyments so efficiently promoted.

Next to the want of all government, the two most fruitful sources of evil to children are, *unsteadiness* in government and *over-government*. Most of the cases in which the children of sensible and conscientious parents turn out badly, result from one or the other of these causes. In cases of unsteady government, either one parent is very strict, severe, and unbending, and the other excessively indulgent, or else the parents are sometimes very strict and decided, and at other times allow disobedience to go unpunished. In such cases, children, never knowing exactly when they can escape with impunity, are constantly tempted to make the trial.

The bad effects of this can be better appreciated by reference to one important principle of the mind. It is found to be universally true that, when any object of desire is put entirely beyond the reach of hope or expectation, the mind very soon ceases to long for it, and turns to other objects of pursuit. But so long as the mind is hoping for some good, and making efforts to obtain it, any opposition excites irritable feelings. Let the object be put entirely beyond all hope, and this irritation soon ceases.

In consequence of this principle, those children who are under the care of persons of steady and decided government know that, whenever a thing is forbidden or denied, it is out of the reach of hope; the desire, therefore, soon ceases, and they turn to other objects. But the children of undecided, or of over-indulgent parents, never enjoy this preserving aid. When a thing is denied, they never know but either coaxing may win it, or disobedience secure it without any penalty, and so they are kept in that state of hope and anxiety which produces irritation and tempts to insubordination. The children of very indulgent parents, and of those who are undecided and unsteady in government, are very apt to become fretful, irritable, and fractious.

Another class of persons, in shunning this evil, go to the other extreme, and are very strict and pertinacious in regard to every requisition. With them, fault-finding and penalties abound, until the children are either hardened into indifference of feeling and obtuseness of conscience, or else become excessively irritable or misanthropic.

It demands great wisdom, patience, and self-control, to escape these two extremes. In aiming at this, there are parents who have found the following maxims of very great value:

First: Avoid, as much as possible, the multiplication of rules and absolute commands. Instead of this, take the attitude of advisers. "My child, this is improper, I wish you would remember not to do it." This mode of address answers for all the little acts of heedlessness, awkwardness, or ill-manners so frequently occurring with children. There are cases when direct and distinct commands are needful, and in such cases a penalty for disobedience should be as steady and sure as the laws of nature. A barrel in the nursery, with a seat in it for the child, serves for a gentle and yet very effective solitary imprisonment, and is a most salutary penalty. Where such steadiness and certainty of penalty attend disobedience, children no more think of disobeying than they do of putting their fingers into a burning candle.

The next maxim is, Govern by rewards more than by penalties. Such faults as willful disobedience, lying, dishonesty, and indecent or profane language, should be punished with severe penalties, after a child has been fully instructed in the evil of such practices. But all the constantly recurring faults of the nursery, such as ill-humor, quarreling, carelessness, and ill-manners, may, in a great many cases, be regulated by gentle and kind remonstrances, and by the offer of some reward for persevering efforts to form a good habit. It is very injurious and degrading to any mind to be kept under the constant fear of penalties. *Love* and *hope* are the principles that should be mainly relied on in forming the habits of childhood.

Another maxim, and perhaps the most difficult, is, Do not govern by the aid of severe and angry tones. A single example will be given to illustrate this maxim. A child is disposed to talk and amuse itself at table. The mother requests it to be silent, except when needing to ask for food, or when spoken to by its older friends. It constantly forgets. The mother, instead of rebuking in an impatient tone, says, "My child, you must remember not to talk. I will remind you of it four times more, and after that, whenever you forget, you must leave the table and wait till we are done." If the mother is steady in her government, it is not probable that she will have to apply this slight penalty more than once or twice. This method is far more effectual than the use of sharp and severe tones, to secure attention and recollection, and often answers the purpose as well as offering some reward.

The writer has been in some families where the most efficient and steady government has been sustained without the use of a cross or angry tone; and in others, where a far less efficient discipline was kept up, by frequent severe rebukes and angry remonstrances. In the first case, the children followed the example set them, and seldom used severe tones to each other; in the latter, the method employed by the parents was imitated by the children, and cross words and angry tones resounded from morning till night in every portion of the household.

Another important maxim is, Try to keep children in a happy state of mind. Every one knows, by experience, that it is easier to do right and submit to rule when cheerful and happy, than when irritated. This is peculiarly true of children; and a wise mother, when she finds her child fretful and impatient, and thus constantly doing wrong, will often remedy the whole difficulty by telling some amusing story, or by getting the child engaged in some amusing sport. This strongly shows the importance of learning to govern children without the employment of angry tones, which always produce irritation.

Children of active, heedless temperament, or those who are odd, awkward, or unsuitable in their remarks and deportment, are often essentially injured by a want of patience and self-control in those who govern them. Such children often possess a morbid sensibility which they strive to conceal, or a desire of love and approbation, which preys like a famine on the soul. And yet they become objects of ridicule and rebuke to almost every member of the family, until their sensibilities are tortured into obtuseness or misanthropy. Such children, above all others, need tenderness and sympathy. A thousand instances of mistake or forgetfulness should be passed over in silence, while opportunities for commendation and encouragement should be diligently sought.

In regard to the formation of habits of self-denial in childhood, it is astonishing to see how parents who are very sensible often seem to regard this matter. Instead of inuring their children to this duty in early life, so that by habit it may be made easy in after-days, they seem to be studiously seeking to cut them off from every chance to secure such a preparation. Every wish of the child is studiously gratified; and, where a necessity exists of crossing its wishes, some compensating pleasure is offered in return. Such parents often maintain that nothing shall be put on their table which their children may not join them in eating. But where, so easily and surely as at the daily meal, can that habit of self-denial be formed which is so needful in governing the appetites, and which children must acquire, or be ruined? The food which is proper for grown persons is often unsuitable for children; and this is a sufficient reason for accustoming them to see others partake of delicacies which they must not share. Requiring children to wait till others are helped, and to refrain from conversation at table, except when addressed by their elders, is another mode of forming habits of self-denial and self-control. Requiring them to help others first, and to offer the best to others, has a similar influence.

In forming the moral habits of children, it is wise to take into account the peculiar temptations to which they are to be exposed. The people of this nation are eminently a trafficking people; and the present standard of honesty, as to trade and debts, is very low, and every year seems sinking still lower. It is, therefore, pre-eminently important that children should be trained to strict *honesty*, both in word and deed. It is not merely teaching children to avoid absolute lying, which is needed: *all kinds of deceit* should be guarded against, and all kinds of little dishonest practices be strenuously opposed. A child should be brought up with the determined principle never to *run in debt*, but to be content to live in a humbler way, in order to secure that true independence which should be the noblest distinction of an American citizen.

Quite as important in family and school training is enforcing the *law that protects character*, which is more precious than gold, while the most cruel sufferings result from want of honor and care in this respect. Especially is the enforcement of this law important at this period, when there are such constant and destructive examples of its violation both by the press and by general practice.

This law of benevolence and rectitude is this: every person who has established a fair character in any direction should have it upheld by *all*, as a protection against unproved rumors that impeach this character. Such rumors should *always* be met with the question, Is it *proved* by *proper* evidence? If it is not, then it is a slander, and whoever aids to circulate it should be treated as an abettor of slander.

To illustrate this, take a not uncommon case: A lady, who for thirty years held the highest character for purity, propriety, and good principles, was accused by a man of high position of following him with repeated solicitations for marriage. He offered no proof but his assertion, which was nullified by her denial. In this case, the man should have been treated as a slanderer, and those who aided in circulating his story as abettors of slander.

Every woman is especially interested in sustaining this law, for it is a dreadful mortification and disgrace to a delicate and refined woman to have certain questions even connected with her name. Not less so is it to a clergyman of keen sensibilities. And it is an insult to ask a person thus abused to furnish denials and defense. *Established character* should protect both the person thus maligned and also their nearest friends from hearing, much less from noticing, such mean and disgraceful assaults.

There is no more important duty devolving upon an educator than the cultivation of habits of modesty and propriety in young children. All indecorous words or deportment should be carefully restrained, and delicacy and reserve studiously cherished. It is a common notion, that it is important to secure these virtues to one sex more than to the other; and, by a strange inconsistency, the sex most exposed to danger is the one selected as least needing care. Yet a wise mother will be especially careful that her sons are trained to modesty and purity of mind.

The rule which should guide on this subject is this: Whenever health, life, or duty demand it, all connected with such topics and duties should be spoken of and done without embarrassment or restraint; but in no other circumstances. Thus in the Bible, instruction on the dangers and duties connected with our bodily organization are set forth in plain and simple language, to be read in public worship and in private by all. So, in medical, surgical, and nursing duties, the same freedom is demanded, and disapproval or opposition are deemed false modesty and foolish fastidiousness. But where there are no such demands for health and safety, then conversation, poetry, pictures, jokes, and coarse allusions are vulgar, indecent, and sinful.

Few mothers are sufficiently aware of the dreadful penalties which often result from indulged impurity of thought. If children, in *future* life, can be preserved from licentious associates, it is supposed that their safety is secured. But the records of our insane retreats, and the pages of medical writers, teach that even in solitude, and without being aware of the sin or the danger, children may inflict evils on themselves which not unfrequently terminate in disease, delirium, and death.

There is no necessity for explanations on this point any further than this, that certain parts of the body are not to be touched except for purposes of cleanliness, and that the most dreadful suffering comes from disobeying these commands. So in regard to practices and sins of which a young child will sometimes inquire, the wise parent will say, that this is what children can not understand, and about which they must not talk or ask questions. And they should be told that it is always a bad sign when children talk on matters which parents call vulgar and indecent, and that the company of such children should be avoided. Disclosing details of wrong-doing to young and curious children, often leads to the very evils feared. But parents and teachers, in this age of danger, should be well informed and watchful; for it is not unfrequently the case that servants and school-mates will teach young children practices which exhaust the nervous system, and bring on paralysis, mania, and death.

But there are social dangers during and after childhood which demand from mothers and teachers such instructions as are rarely given; and yet, for the want of it, the most dreadful vices and sufferings ensue.

The evils and dangers here indicated can never be understood or appreciated till mothers and teachers gain that knowledge of the construction of the body, and the dangers connected with duties of the family state, which is now confined almost entirely to the medical profession, while physicians, by false customs and false modesty on the part of women, are constrained to a reticence which is dangerous and often fatal. The difficulty can be wisely met, not by public lectures or by pulpit ministries. It is in the privacy of the nursery and the school-room that well-instructed mothers and teachers must train the young to meet these dangers, by all needful knowledge and habits of intelligent self-control.

CHAPTER XXVIII.

FAMILY RELIGIOUS TRAINING.

There are few women who have charge of servants or of children, in the family and school, who do not suffer anxiety and perplexity, and sometimes remorse, in attempts to perform their duty as chief ministers of religion in the family state. The following suggestions may aid in diminishing these difficulties:

The main foundation of these troubles is the endless diversities of instruction as to what is right in character and conduct, and especially as to what is taught in the Bible on these points. For there are few practical questions on which persons of equal intelligence and moral worth are not in antagonism as to what *is* the right; and all the Christian sects are in equal controversy as to what are the teachings of the Bible. And yet every housekeeper, every mother, and every teacher, practically, must decide these questions for herself and her dependants, when, in the kitchen, nursery, and school-room she teaches what actions and feelings are right or wrong, or when she decides to what religious denomination she, and those she can influence, shall belong.

There is one consoling consideration in view of these conflicting opinions, and that is, that nothing tends more directly to cultivate both the intellect and moral feelings, than the study, reflection, and discussion resulting from this trying dilemma. For, were every human being infallibly directed by a superior mind as to every step and every decision, it would greatly diminish mental effort, and the moral discipline of life. All would remain as mere children, guided and upheld at every step. Instead of this, the whole moral and intellectual world is kept vigorous, earnest, and bright by conflict and discussion, while many moral virtues are cultivated by this turmoil.

The difficulties thus encountered may be much reduced

by gaining clear ideas as to *what it is* which constitutes voluntary action *right*. To settle this more clearly, we introduce again a portion of Chapter XXV., with additional considerations. The definition of *right*, in its widest use, is "any rule or method which will *best* accomplish any plan or design." It is a fact, also, that there is a created intuitive belief in all rational minds that happiness-making on the largest scale possible is the end or purpose for which all things are made.

This is proved by the fact that whenever men perceive that a given course will secure the most and the best good for both the individual and for society, all decide that it is *right*. The main difficulty is in discovering what *is* the best for all concerned.

There are two ways in which mankind learn this. The first is, by the trial of experience. Man learns "to know good and evil" by good lost or gained, and evil suffered. This experimenting has been going on in all ages, each generation gaining by the experience of the past. The other mode is, by revelations from God made in human language, and to be interpreted by the common rules of the language employed.

But one distinction is very important, and that is, the two relations in which an action is to be judged as right, viz., first, with reference to the action as best for all concerned, and next in reference to the motive or intention of the actor. For it is best and right that every mind should choose what it believes to be right; and thus it often happens that the same action is right as to motive or intention, and wrong as to actual result. So, also, an action may be right in tendency and result, while it is wrong as to motive. There is often much confusion from not recognizing this distinction.

There are many cases where experience will not avail in deciding what is best for all, especially in reference to our prospects after death, and our relations and duties toward our Creator. For all this we are dependent on revelations made in human language, to be interpreted by the rules of language. And as almost all words have more than one literal meaning, and are also used sometimes in a literal, and sometimes in a figurative sense, the chief labor in gaining God's teaching is in applying rightly the laws of language.

One difficulty in this attempt is the fact that the true interpretation of language depends greatly on the habits of thought, the prejudices of education, and the influence of excited feelings and wishes. So strong are these influences in the common affairs of life, that it has been a maxim of courts that a man is not qualified to testify where his own interests are concerned. And in all daily affairs, men always make allowances for deviation from a true judgment in what greatly interests the feelings. This accounts for the fact that such a variety of interpretations are put on the plain and natural meaning of the Bible, when such a meaning controverts favorite opinions or interferes with important plans or hopes. It is not because it is difficult to interpret the Bible correctly by the proper use of those rules men employ in daily life; it is because men's feelings, prejudices, and wishes interfere. No less is it the case that the bias of feeling constantly sways the judgment of men in deciding what is right and best, where experience and reason are the chief guides.

Another embarrassment in gaining the true teachings of the Bible is the fact that the doctrines of churches and creeds have consisted extensively of philosophical theories to explain the *how* and the *why* of the facts made known by revelation; and men have been educated to believe that these theories should be accepted as authoritative, the same as the revealed facts, and thus feeling and prejudice interfere. For example, that the sacrifice and death of Jesus Christ was needful to secure redemption to our race from sin and its penalties, is the revealed fact. *Why* it was needed, and *how* it avails to save men, is a question which men have invented various theories to answer and explain, and belief in these theories has been deemed as sacred and obligatory as if they were matters of revelation.

Another, and the chief difficulty, is the fact that the great mass, even of educated minds, have never been trained to use the rules of language in the interpretation of the Bible as they do in common life. Although it is the great and distinctive principle of Protestantism that every man is to form his own creed, and to interpret the Bible for himself, responsible not to man but to God alone, the common people have not been trained properly to use this right and privilege. And this is not because it is not as easy and practical a matter as any other duty requiring intellectual culture, practical exercises, and an honest desire for the truth. In consequence of this, much that is only figurative in the Bible has been received as literal, and repellent doctrines thus established.

It is probable that no one thing could so effectually promote unity of opinion among churches, and consequent harmony of action, as the proper training of the common people in the nursery and school-room to use the laws of language with the Bible as they do in common life. Such training would also bring confidence and peace to minds so extensively perplexed by supposed contradictions as to its teachings. It was by this method that the writer overcame difficulties, and gained such confidence and peace as can be secured in no other way. Without stating the results of her own efforts in interpreting the Bible, a few examples will follow, to illustrate the position that any woman of ordinary capacity can find relief and comfort by the same method.

We will take, first, the great question of this life. What are our dangers in the future life, and what must we do to be saved from them?

The following is a brief statement of the views of mankind on this question. Among the heathen, especially among the wisest and best, it was held that the virtuous would fare better after death than the wicked. The seventy-third Psalm shows in most terrific language the misery of the wicked, and as clearly the blessedness of the righteous at death, as believed by the Jews in all ages.

Among Christian nations, a large class have no definite opinions on this question, but by their practice assume that there is no danger at all, and so give all their thoughts and aims to the things of this life.

A large class who profess to obtain their opinions from

the Bible hold that, either at death or at some period after, all mankind will be forever good and happy in heaven.

Another large class hold that a portion of mankind will, at death, go to everlasting misery, to be tormented with literal fire and brimstone, and that all the rest will finally go to heaven; but previously the good must suffer temporary punishment for sins committed here—this period of suffering being more or less diminished by penances, and by the sacrifices and good works of Jesus Christ and the good on earth.

Another class believe that at death every human being passes directly to perfect happiness in heaven, or to dreadful sufferings in hell which are never to end. One part of this class hold that the punishment is literally existing forever in fire and brimstone, and the other part hold that the suffering will be the natural result of an endless character that insures misery, and that the language of the Bible expresses this figuratively.

Finally, another class hold that, in the life to come, happiness and misery depend on *character;* that a portion of our race in this life forms one that insures immediate and endless happiness at death; that another portion form a character that involves great suffering after death; and that in *some* cases this character is perpetuated forever, involving consequent endless suffering. But they claim that the Bible nowhere teaches that with *all* mankind character is fixed at death. Instead of this, what intervenes between death and the final day, when the righteous and wicked are to be reclothed in bodies and forever separated, is left in wise darkness.

But the most striking fact in these diverse opinions is, that Christian sects all agree that the number who will escape from whatever dangers there may be, depends upon the self-denying labor and sacrifices of the followers of Jesus Christ.

In view of these facts, the first duty of every housekeeper, of every mother, and of every teacher, is to decide which of these views as to the dangers awaiting us all at death are taught by Jesus Christ and his apostles. For if it be true that scholars, children, and servants must be trained to self-sacrifice and self-denying labor, in order to save themselves and their fellow-men from dreadful risks and dangers in the life to come, all the practical duties of daily life will be diverse from the methods pursued by those who believe in no such dangers.

To illustrate this, suppose several families recently settled near a deep, unexplored wood in a new country. The children ramble in its shades, and every day find new beauties and curiosities to attract them farther into its reserves. On a certain day a man arrives from a distant place, all torn and bleeding in efforts to reach them. He tells them that there is a frightful ravine in the unexplored depths; that pleasant but slippery paths lead to it; that it is the resort of fierce and cruel animals, which come forth and roam through its beautiful shades, and that there is no safety but in keeping the children from entering these dangerous woods.

Now these points would be clear to common sense: first, that the man, though an entire stranger, is a benevolent person, because he evidently has suffered severely to save; next, that he tells what he believes is the truth, or he would not encounter this suffering; and lastly, as he says he has long lived in that vicinity, that he has had the means of knowing the truth, and his representations are to be received as true.

Suppose, then, one family have perfect faith in this messenger, they will use every possible precaution to avoid the dangers revealed. Suppose another family is skeptical about the danger, and yet has some fear it may be true, they would use some care, and yet not be so anxious and earnest as the family which had perfect faith. Suppose another family to have no belief at all as to the danger, they would allow their children to roam as before, and give no care or thought to the matter. This illustrates the position that belief in danger modifies all rules of duty, and that faith is proved by men's conduct or works.

In like manner faith in Jesus Christ, who came in suffering and sorrow to tell of dangers in the unseen world, is proved by the way men live. If they have perfect faith in the dangers he reveals, then the most earnest efforts to save themselves and their fellow-men from ignorance and sin will follow. If they have little faith, they will make less exertions; if they have no fears for the future life, all their plans will terminate in gaining the good things of this life for themselves and those they love, sure that all the rest of mankind will be happy when they die, and that their troubles here will only serve to make rest and enjoyment the greater in the coming life.

The following is the method by which any woman may decide what is truth on this great question, so as to be at rest.

It is first assumed that the Bible is written for the common people, and is to be interpreted by the rules of language men employ in common life, which, briefly, are these:

The first is, all expressions are literal when they do not contradict the known nature of things, or known facts, or the known opinions of the writer; in which latter case they usually are figurative, but have as definite a meaning as if literal. For example, "everlasting" and "forever" mean "time without end," unless contrary to known facts, or the known nature of things, or the known opinions of the writer. So "punishment" *always* signifies "pain consequent either on violating a natural or some instituted law."

The second rule is, when any expression has several significations, that is to be taken as the right one which has *the most* evidence in its favor. Let any woman of ordinary ability and education apply these rules to the texts on this subject, and she will find little difficulty in deciding what the Bible teaches as the dangers of the future life.

Another example will be given on a subject which causes great anxiety and perplexity, and which may be relieved by the same method. The question is, Why does a Being of infinite power, wisdom, and goodness allow the dreadful miseries that oppress mankind, and, still more, why will he allow sin and suffering to reach through eternal ages? Many suppose that revelation gives no reply to this longing inquiry.

But when we take the language of the Bible in its common and literal sense, we find a satisfactory answer. For *perfect wisdom* is "that which chooses the *best* means for the *best* ends," and *perfect benevolence* is "that which seeks to make the most possible happiness with the least possible suffering." Therefore, when God reveals himself as perfect in wisdom and goodness, it is the same as saying that he has done, and will do, *all in his power* to save from sin and suffering. Almighty power does not signify power to work contradictions or absurdities; and all theologians teach that there is a limitation of power in the *nature of things*. Thus some say God can not forgive sin without an atonement; others, that he can not lie; others, that he "can not govern the stars by the ten commandments, nor free agents by the attraction of gravity." And God says of his people Israel, "What *could* I have done that I have not done" to secure their obedience.

God's inability to save *all* is expressly stated when he declares that he is "not willing that any should perish." The only proof of want of power to do something is to *will* it done, and yet it remains undone. And God declares that he is not willing to have any one perish. Still more effectively is this proved by his suffering and that of his dear Son, when Christ came. No sane mind ever suffers pain to gain an end when it could be gained without suffering; and the revelation of God as having suffered so greatly, is the highest proof that can be given that his power is limited in controlling free agents by the very nature of free agency. In his hour of extremity, our Lord prayed, "*If it be possible*, remove this cup;" thus indicating that almighty power signifies power to do all possible things, and that some things are *not* possible even to God.

The first question being settled, that there are *dangers* to be met after death, the next is, "What must we do to be saved?"

Here the Christian churches are divided, and on a fundamental point, which briefly is this: One class claims that God has the power to create minds so that, without any previous knowledge or training, they shall not only know what is right, but have a controlling principle that in all cases will secure right choice, and that the minds of all angels and of our first parents were made on this pattern. But owing to Adam's sin, all infants are born without this perfect organization, and so depraved that eternal sin and suffering in hell is the portion of all who are not regenerated before they die, while there is no *certain* way revealed by which parents can insure this boon for all their offspring.

The other class claim that the assumption that God can, or ever did, create minds on this pattern, is a theological theory for which no evidence exists in revelation or in nature; that it destroys the evidence of the benevolence of God, making him prefer the sin and suffering of infants, when he has power to make them with such minds. They claim also that if a holy mind consists in a controlling purpose or choice to do right, that it is a contradiction in terms to say that a free agent can be created with such a purpose or choice. For the distinctive feature of a free agent is intellect to perceive right and wrong, and power to choose in either of two courses; and choice can not be created. It is also objected that by this theory the chief aim of an educator is not so much to teach what is right and wrong, and secure motives and training to induce such habits of obedience to God's laws as eventually will secure a controlling purpose of obedience, but rather to employ means by which God shall regenerate the depraved mind.

Let it be particularly noticed that these two classes do not differ as to the *facts* revealed. Both recognize the fact taught, as much by experience as by revelation, that every child has such a nature as insures the constant violation of natural law, while it is entirely destitute of a controlling principle of love to God and man. They differ mainly as to a theory of accounting for this fact. One teaches that it is because the mind at birth is ignorant, undeveloped, and untrained; the other teaches that it is owing to an imperfect constitutional nature, for which God or Adam, or both, are responsible.

Every woman must examine and decide for herself on which of these systems she will train her family. In this attempt women have one advantage, and that is, they are not so liable to embarrassment and prejudice as they would be were they, as are most of their religious teachers, trained in systematic theology.

The writer has had an experience in both methods, which

may have some influence in regard to belief in the teachings of the Bible as to the dreadful dangers to be met in the life to come. This was the mainspring of feeling and effort in her father, who trained a large family to believe and to feel that the great object of life should be *to save as many as possible from eternal ruin.* Wealth, honor, power, and every earthly good, in his mind, was as the dust of the balance compared with this overmastering passion. It was this dreadful danger to herself, and to those she loved best, that changed a frolicsome, hopeful, light-hearted girl to a serious, hard-working woman as nothing else could have done. It was this that stimulated a mind whose natural tendency was to works of taste, light literature, and fun, to anxious investigation in theology, metaphysics, and Biblical science.

And the results in family and personal training are equally manifest in the history of Christian sects. It is those which are most deeply convinced of dreadful dangers in the life to come which have been most advanced in mental development, and in benevolent labor and self-sacrifice. Such heroic suffering and devotion to the best interests of humanity have never been witnessed on a large scale, except in denominations whose fundamental and motive power is belief in dreadful dangers to be encountered after death. The great difficulty in many of these denominations has been a theological theory as to the created constitution of mind, which tended to lessen hope and exertion in that training by which escape from these dangers is most readily and happily secured.

The course here suggested does not imply independent investigation, without aid from men of learning and piety. Every doctrine of theology, and every antagonistic mode of Biblical interpretation, has been sustained by such men. But with a reference Bible and Concordance, any woman of ordinary capacity can collect all that the Bible contains on a given topic, and form a decision as to which view has the most evidence in its favor. Then she can learn what has been offered both for and against this view. This having been done with a prayerful spirit, the result will rarely fail in bringing satisfaction and peace; while both intellectually and morally such exercises will have an elevating tendency.

CHAPTER XXIX.

THE CARE OF SERVANTS.

In the chapter on the *Right Use of Time and Property*, the important explanation was made of the great law of love to God and to our neighbor, which includes in its aim and spirit all other laws. The distinction is there exhibited between instinctive *emotional* love, caused by agreeable qualities in persons and things, and the *voluntary* love which is "good-will" toward God and man on the best and most extensive scale. This love is identified in the great command itself by the expression "as thyself." For the love of self is not pleasure created by our own agreeable qualities. It rather is the all-controlling desire to make self happy. For this end we are required to obey the laws of God, and thus secure the best and highest happiness both to ourselves and to our neighbors.

In addition to this supreme law, made clear both by the intuitive principle of mind and in the revealed laws of the Old Testament, we have the teachings of Jesus Christ as to the character of God as a loving Father to all his creatures. And, what is especially to be regarded in estimating the obligations of a housekeeper to her servants, we are taught that our heavenly Father feels the most care and interest in those of his children who are the most ignorant, the most neglected, and the most sinful. As the loving parent gives the most thought and tender care to the most feeble and imperfect child, so the Father of All most anxiously cares for the weak, the ignorant, and the wandering of mankind.

Few of Christ's professed followers at the present day realize what obligations they assume when they prepare large houses and establishments, which bring the most neglected members of society under their care as members of the family state.

Did they understand the sacred obligations thus assumed

to train the humble members of their family with the care and Christian love taught by both the precept and example of our Divine Lord, it is probable most would reduce their style of living, so that their own children, with one or two of God's most neglected ones, would embrace all for whom they would dare to assume such obligations.

The preceding presents the general principles to guide a housekeeper as to her duty in the care of servants. The following will suggest important details and considerations. Those in quotation-marks are from Mrs. Stowe's "House and Home Papers."

"Although in earlier ages the highest-born, wealthiest, and proudest ladies were skilled in the simple labors of the household, the advance of society toward luxury has changed all this, especially in lands of aristocracy and classes; and at the present time America is the only country where there is a class of women who may be described as *ladies* who do their own work. By a lady we mean a woman of education, cultivation, and refinement, of liberal tastes and ideas, who, without any very material additions or changes, would be recognized as a lady in any circle of the Old World or the New.

"The existence of such a class is a fact peculiar to American society, a plain result of the new principles involved in the doctrine of universal equality.

"When the colonists first came to this country, of however mixed ingredients their ranks might have been composed, and however imbued with the spirit of feudal and aristocratic ideas, the discipline of the wilderness soon brought them to a democratic level; the gentleman felled the wood for his log-cabin side by side with the plowman, and thews and sinews rose in the market. 'A man was deemed honorable in proportion as he lifted his hand upon the high trees of the forest.' So in the interior domestic circle, mistress and maid, living in a log-cabin together, became companions, and sometimes the maid, as the one well trained in domestic labor, took precedence of the mistress. It also became natural and unavoidable that children should begin to work as early as they were capable of it.

"The result was a generation of intelligent people brought

up to labor from necessity, but devoting to the problem of labor the acuteness of a disciplined brain. The mistress, outdone in sinews and muscles by her maid, kept her superiority by skill and contrivance. If she could not lift a pail of water, she could invent methods which made lifting the pail unnecessary; if she could not take a hundred steps without weariness, she could make twenty answer the purpose of a hundred.

"Then were to be seen families of daughters, handsome, strong women, rising each day to their indoor work with cheerful alertness—one to sweep the room, another to make the fire, while a third prepared the breakfast for the father and brothers who were going out to manly labor: and they chatted meanwhile of books, studies, embroidery; discussed the last new poem, or some historical topic started by graver reading, or perhaps a rural ball that was to come off next week. They spun with the book tied to the distaff; they wove; they did all manner of fine needle-work; they made lace, painted flowers, and, in short, in the boundless consciousness of activity, invention, and perfect health, set themselves to any work of which they had ever read or thought. A bride in those days was married with sheets and table-cloths of her own weaving, with counterpanes and toilet-covers wrought in divers embroidery by her own and her sisters' hands. The amount of fancy-work done in our days by girls who have nothing else to do will not equal what was done by those who performed, in addition, the whole work of the family.

"In those former days most women were in good health, debility and disease being the exception. Then, too, was seen the economy of daylight and its pleasures. They were used to early rising, and would not lie in bed if they could. Long years of practice made them familiar with the shortest, neatest, most expeditious method of doing every household office, so that really, for the greater part of the time in the house, there seemed, to a looker-on, to be nothing to do. They rose in the morning and dispatched husband, father, and brothers to the farm or wood-lot; went sociably about, chatting with each other, skimmed the milk, made the butter, and turned the cheeses. The forenoon was long; all the so-called morning work over, they had leisure for an hour's sewing or reading before it was time to start the dinner preparations. By two o'clock the house-work was done, and they had the long afternoon for books, needle-work, or drawing—for perhaps there was one with a gift at her pencil. Perhaps one read aloud while others sewed, and managed in that way to keep up a great deal of reading.

"It has been remarked in our armies that the men of cultivation, though bred in delicate and refined spheres, can bear up under the hardships of camp-life better and longer than rough laborers. The reason is, that an educated mind knows how to use and save its body, to work it and spare it, as an uneducated mind can not; and so the college-bred youth brings himself safely through fatigues which kill the unreflective laborer.

"Cultivated, intelligent women, who are brought up to do the work of their own families, are labor-saving institutions. They make the head save the wear of the muscles. By forethought, contrivance, system, and arrangement, they lessen the amount to be done, and do it with less expense of time and strength than others. The old New England motto, *Get your work done up in the forenoon*, applied to an amount of work which would keep the most common Irish servant toiling from daylight to sunset.

"Those remarkable women of old, in a measure, were made by circumstances. There were, comparatively speaking, no servants to be had, and so children were trained to habits of industry and mechanical adroitness from the cradle, and every household process was reduced to the very minimum of labor. Every step required in a process was counted, every movement calculated; and she who took ten steps when one would do, lost her reputation for 'faculty.' Certainly such an early drill was of use in developing the health and the bodily powers, as well as in giving precision to the practical mental faculties. All household economies were arranged with equal niceness in those thoughtful minds. A trained housekeeper knew just how many sticks of hickory of a certain size were required to heat her oven, and how many of each different kind of wood. She knew by a sort of intuition just what kinds of food would yield the most palatable nutriment with the least outlay of accessories in cooking. She knew to a minute the time when each article must go into and be withdrawn from her oven; and if she could only lie in her chamber and direct, she could guide an intelligent child through the processes with mathematical certainty.

"Now, if every young woman learned to do house-work, and cultivated her practical faculties in early life, she would, in the first place, be much more likely to keep her servants; and, in the second place, if she lost them temporarily, would avoid all that wear and tear of the nervous system which comes from constant ill-success in those departments on which family health and temper mainly depend. This is one of the peculiarities of our American life which require a peculiar training. Why not face it sensibly?

"Our land abounds in motorpathic institutions, to which women are sent, at a great expense, to have hired operators stretch and exercise their inactive muscles. They lie for hours to have their feet twigged, their arms flexed, and all the different muscles of the body worked for them, because they are so flaccid and torpid that the powers of life do not go on. Would it not be quite as cheerful, and a less expensive process, if young girls from early life developed the muscles in sweeping, dusting, starching, ironing, and all the multiplied domestic processes which our grandmothers knew of? Does it not seem poor economy to pay servants for letting our muscles grow feeble, and then to pay operators to exercise them for us? I will venture to say that our grandmothers in a week went over every movement that any gymnast has invented, and went over them to some productive purpose too.

"The first business of a housekeeper in America is that of a teacher. She can have a good table only by having practical knowledge, and tact in imparting it. If she understands her business practically and experimentally, her eye detects at once the weak spot; it requires only a little tact, some patience, some clearness in giving directions, and all comes right.

"If we carry a watch to a watch-maker, and undertake to show him how to regulate the machinery, he laughs and goes on his own way; but if a brother-machinist makes suggestions, he listens respectfully. So, when a woman who knows nothing of woman's work undertakes to instruct one who knows more than she does, she makes no impression; but a woman who has been trained experimentally, and shows she understands the matter thoroughly, is listened to with respect.

"Let a woman make her own bread for one month, and, simple as the process seems, it will take as long as that to get a thorough knowledge of all the possibilities in the case; but after that, she will be able to command good bread by the aid of all sorts of servants; in other words, will be a thoroughly-prepared teacher of bread-making.

"Good servants do not often come to us; they must be *made* by patience and training; and if a girl has a good disposition, and a reasonable degree of handiness, and the housekeeper understands her profession, a good servant may be made out of an indifferent one. Some of the best girls have been those who came directly from the ship, with no preparation but docility and some natural quickness. The hardest cases to be managed are not of those who have been taught nothing, but of those who have been taught wrongly—who come self-opinionated, with ways which are distasteful, and contrary to the genius of one's housekeeping. Such require that their mistress shall understand at least so much of the actual conduct of affairs as to prove to the servant that there are better ways than those in which she has been trained.

"Domestic service is the great problem of life here in America; the happiness of families, their thrift, well-being, and comfort, are more affected by this than by any one thing else. The modern girls, as they have been brought up, can not perform the labor of their own families as in those simpler, old-fashioned days; and what is worse, they have no practical skill with which to instruct servants, who come to us, as a class, raw and untrained. In the present state of prices, the board of a domestic costs as much as her wages, and the waste she makes is a more serious matter still."

It is sometimes urged against domestics that they exact exorbitant wages. But what is the rule of rectitude on this subject? Is it not the universal law of labor and of trade that an article is to be valued according to its scarcity and the demand? When wheat is scarce, the farmer raises his price; and when a mechanic offers services difficult to be obtained, he makes a corresponding increase of price. And why is it not right for domestics to act according to a rule allowed to be correct in reference to all other trades and professions? It is a fact that really good domestic service must continue to increase in value just in proportion as this country waxes rich and prosperous; thus making the proportion of those who wish to hire labor relatively greater, and the number of those willing to go to service less.

Money enables the rich to gain many advantages which those of more limited circumstances can not secure. One of these is, securing good servants by offering high wages; and this, as the scarcity of this class increases, will serve constantly to raise the price of service. It is right for domestics to charge the market value, and this value is always decided by the scarcity of the article and the amount of demand. Right views of this subject will sometimes serve to diminish hard feelings toward those who would otherwise be wrongfully regarded as unreasonable and exacting.

Another complaint against servants is that of instability and discontent, leading to perpetual change. But in reference to this, let a mother or daughter conceive of their own circumstances as so changed that the daughter must go out to service. Suppose a place is engaged, and it is then found that she must sleep in a comfortless garret; and that, when a new domestic comes—perhaps a coarse and dirty foreigner—she must share her bed with her. Another place is offered, where she can have a comfortable room and an agreeable room-mate; in such a case, would not both mother and daughter think it right to change?

Or suppose, on trial, it was found that the lady of the house was fretful or exacting, and hard to please, or that her children were so ungoverned as to be perpetual vexations; or that the work was so heavy that no time was allowed for relaxation and the care of a wardrobe; and another place offers where these evils can be escaped, would not mother and daughter here think it right to change? And is it not right for domestics, as well as their employers, to seek places where they can be most comfortable?

In some cases, this instability and love of change would be remedied if employers would take more pains to make a residence with them agreeable, and to attach servants to the family by feelings of gratitude and affection. There are ladies, even where well-qualified domestics are most rare, who seldom find any trouble in keeping good and steady ones. And the reason is that their servants know they can not better their condition by any change within reach. It is not merely by giving them comfortable rooms, and good food, and presents, and privileges, that the attachment of domestic servants is secured; it is by the manifestation of a friendly and benevolent interest in their comfort and improvement. This is exhibited in bearing patiently with their faults; in kindly teaching them how to improve; in showing them how to make and take proper care of their clothes; in guarding their health; in teaching them to read, if necessary, and supplying them with proper books; and, in short, by endeavoring, so far as may be, to supply the place of parents. It is seldom that such a course would fail to secure steady service, and such affection and gratitude that even higher wages would be ineffectual to tempt them away. There would probably be some cases of ungrateful returns, but there is no doubt that the course indicated, if generally pursued, would very much lessen the evil in question.

When servants are forward and bold in manners and disrespectful in address, they may be considerately taught that those who are among the best-bred and genteel have courteous and respectful manners and language to all they meet; while many who have wealth are regarded as vulgar, because they exhibit rude and disrespectful manners. The very terms *gentleman* and *gentlewoman* indicate the refinement and delicacy of address which distinguishes the high-bred from the coarse and vulgar.

In regard to appropriate dress, in most cases it is difficult for an employer to interfere *directly* with comments or advice. The most successful mode is to offer some service in mending or making a wardrobe, and when a confidence in the kindness of feeling is thus gained, remarks and suggestions will generally be properly received, and new views of propriety and economy can be imparted. The knowledge which is so important to every woman, contained in the chapter on *Clothing*, is as much needed in the kitchen as in the parlor. In some cases it may be well for an employer who, from appearances, anticipates difficulty of this kind, in making the preliminary contract or agreement, to state that she wishes to have the room, person, and dress of her servants kept neat and in order, and that she expects to remind them of their duty in this particular if it is neglected. Domestic servants are very apt to neglect the care of their own chambers and clothing; and such habits have a most pernicious influence on their well-being, and on that of their children, in future domestic life. An employer, then, is bound to exercise a parental care over them in these respects.

There is one great mistake, not unfrequently made, in the management both of domestics and of children, and that is, in supposing that the way to cure defects is by finding fault as each failing occurs. But instead of this being true, in many cases the directly opposite course is the best; while in all instances much good judgment is required in order to decide when to notice faults and when to let them pass unnoticed. There are some minds very sensitive, easily discouraged, and infirm of purpose. Such persons, when they have formed habits of negligence, haste, and awkwardness, often need expressions of sympathy and encouragement rather than reproof. They have usually been found fault with so much that they have become either hardened or desponding; and it is often the case that a few words of commendation will awaken fresh efforts and renewed hope. In almost every case, words of kindness, confidence, and encouragement should be mingled with the needful admonitions or reproof.

It is a good rule, in reference to this point, to *forewarn* instead of finding fault. Thus, when a thing has been done wrong, let it pass unnoticed till it is to be done again; and then a simple request to have it done in the right way will secure quite as much, and probably more, willing effort, than a reproof administered for neglect. Some persons seem to take it for granted that young and inexperienced minds are bound to have all the forethought and discretion of mature persons, and freely express wonder and disgust when mishaps occur for want of these traits. But it would be far better to save from mistake or forgetfulness by previous caution and care on the part of those who have gained experience and forethought; and thus many occasions of complaint and ill-humor will be avoided.

Those who fill the places of heads of families are not very apt to think how painful it is to be chided for neglect of duty, or for faults of character. If they would sometimes imagine themselves in the place of those whom they control, with some person daily administering reproof to them in the same *tone and style* as they employ to those who are under them, it might serve as a useful check to their chidings. It is often the case that persons who are most strict and exacting, and least able to make allowances and receive palliations, are themselves peculiarly sensitive to any thing which implies that they are in fault. By such, the spirit implied in the Divine petition, "Forgive us our trespasses as we forgive those who trespass against us," needs especially to be cherished.

One other consideration is very important. There is no duty more binding on Christians than that of patience and meekness under provocations and disappointment. Now the tendency of every sensitive mind, when thwarted in its wishes, is to complain and find fault, and that often in tones of fretfulness or anger. But there are few servants who have not heard enough of the Bible to know that angry or fretful fault-finding from the mistress of a family, when her work is not done to suit her, is not in agreement with the precepts of Christ. They notice and feel the inconsistency; and every woman, when she gives way to feelings of anger and impatience at the faults of those around her, lowers herself in their respect; while her own conscience, unless very much blinded, can not but suffer a wound.

"We can not in this country maintain to any great extent large retinues of servants. Even with ample fortunes, they are forbidden by the general character of society here, which makes them cumbrous and difficult to manage. Every mistress of a family knows that her cares increase with every additional servant. Trained housekeepers, such as regulate the complicated establishments of the Old World, form a class that are not, and from the nature of the case never will be, found in any great numbers in this country. All such women, as a general thing, are keeping, and prefer to keep, houses of their own.

"A moderate style of housekeeping, small, compact, and simple domestic establishments, must necessarily be the general order of life in America. So many openings of profit are to be found in this country, that domestic service necessarily wants the permanence which forms so agreeable a feature of it in the Old World.

"Again, American women must not try with three servants to carry on life in the style which in the Old World requires sixteen. They must thoroughly understand, and be prepared *to teach*, every branch of housekeeping; they must study to make domestic service desirable, by treating their servants in a way to lead them to respect themselves, and to feel themselves respected; and there will gradually be evolved from the present confusion a solution of the domestic problem which shall be adapted to the life of a new and growing world."

It is sometimes the case that the constant change of domestics, and the liability thus to have dishonest ones, makes it needful to keep stores under lock and key. This measure is often very offensive to those who are hired, as it is regarded by them as an evidence both of *closeness* and of *suspicion* of their honesty.

In such cases it is a good plan, when first making an agreement with a domestic, to state the case in this way: that you have had dishonest persons in the family, and that when theft is committed, it is always a cause of disquiet to *honest* persons, because it exposes them to suspicion. You can then state your reasons as twofold: one to protect yourself from pilfering when you take entire strangers, and the other is to protect honest persons from being suspected. When the matter is thus presented at first hiring a person, no offense will be taken afterward.

There is one rule which every housekeeper will find of incalculable value, not only in the case of domestics, but in the management of children, and that is, never to find fault *at the time that a wrong thing is done.* Wait until you are unexcited yourself, and until the vexation of the offender is also past, and then, when there is danger of a similar offense, *forewarn*, and point out the evils already done for want of proper care in this respect.

Success in the management of domestics very much depends upon the *manners* of a housekeeper toward them. And here two extremes are to be avoided. One is a severe and imperious mode of giving orders and finding fault, which is inconsistent both with lady-like good breeding and with a truly amiable character. Few domestics, especially American domestics, will long submit to it, and many a good one has been lost, simply by the influence of this unfortunate manner. The other extreme is apt to result from the great difficulty of retaining good domestics. In cases where this is experienced, there is a liability of becoming so fearful of displeasing one who is found to be good, that, imperceptibly, the relation is changed, and the domestic becomes the mistress. A housekeeper thus described this change in one whom she hired: "The first year she was an excellent servant; the second year she was a kind mistress; the third year she was an intolerable tyrant!"

There is no domestic so good that she will not be injured by perceiving that, through dependence upon her, and a fear of losing her services, the mistress of the family gives up her proper authority and control.

The happy medium is secured by a course of real kindness in manner and treatment, attended with the manifestation of a calm determination that the plans and will of the housekeeper, and not of the domestic, shall control the family arrangements.

When a good domestic first begins to insist that her views

and notions shall be regarded rather than those of the housekeeper, a kind but firm stand must be taken. A frank conversation should be sought at a time when nothing has occurred to ruffle the temper on either side. Then the housekeeper can inquire what would be the view taken of this matter in case the domestic herself should become a housekeeper and hire a person to help her; and when the matter is set before her mind in this light, let the "golden rule" be applied, and ask her whether she is not disposed to render to her present employer what she herself would ask from a domestic in similar circumstances.

Much trouble of this kind is saved by hiring persons on trial, in order to ascertain whether they are willing and able to do the work of the family in the manner which the housekeeper wishes; and in this case some member of the family can go around for a day or two, and show how every thing is to be done.

There is no department of domestic life where a woman's temper and patience are so sorely tried as in the incompetence and constant changes of domestics; and therefore there is no place where a reasonable and Christian woman will be more watchful, careful, and conscientious.

The cultivation of *patience* will be much promoted by keeping in mind these considerations in reference to the incompetence and other failings of those who are hired.

In the first place, consider that the great object of life to us is not enjoyment, but the formation of a right character; that such a character can not be formed except by discipline, and that the trials and difficulties of domestic life, if met in a proper spirit and manner, will in the end prove blessings rather than evils, by securing a measure of elevation, dignity, patience, self-control, and benevolence, that could be gained by no other methods. The comfort gained by these virtues, and the rewards they bring, both in this and in a future life, are a thousand-fold richer than the easy, indolent life of indulgence which we should choose for ourselves.

In the next place, instead of allowing the mind to dwell on the faults of those who minister to our comfort and convenience, cultivate a habit of making every possible benevolent allowance and palliation. Say to yourself, "Poor girl! she has never been instructed either by parents or employers. Nobody has felt any interest in the formation of her habits, or kindly sought to rectify her faults. Why should I expect her to do those things well which no one has taken any care to teach her? She has no parent or friend now to aid her but myself. Let me bear her faults patiently, and kindly try to cure them."

If a woman will cultivate the spirit expressed in such language, if she will benevolently seek the best good of those she employs, if she will interest herself in giving them instruction if they need it, and good books to read if they are already qualified to understand them, if she will manifest a desire to have them made comfortable in the kitchen and in their chambers, she certainly will receive her reward, and that in many ways. She will be improving her own character, she will set a good example to her family, and, in the end, she will do something, and in some cases much, to improve the character and services of those whom she hires. And the good done in this way goes down from generation to generation, and goes also into the eternal world, to be known and rejoiced in when every earthly good has come to an end.

In some portions of our country, the great influx of foreigners of another language and another faith, and the ready entrance they find as domestics into American families, impose peculiar trials and peculiar duties on American housekeepers. In reference to such, it is no less our interest than our duty to cultivate a spirit of kindness, patience, and sympathy.

Especially should this be manifested in reference to their religion. However wrong, or however pernicious we may regard their system of faith, we should remember that they have been trained to believe that it is what God commands them to obey; and so long as they do believe this, we should respect them for their conscientious scruples, and not try to tempt them to do what they suppose to be wrong. If we lead an ignorant and feeble mind to do what it believes to be wrong in regard to the most sacred of all duties, those owed to God, how can we expect them to be faithful to us?

The only lawful way to benefit those whom we regard as in an error is, not to tempt them to do what they believe to be wrong, but to give them the light of knowledge, so that they may be qualified to judge for themselves. And the way to make them willing to receive this light is to be kind to them. We should take care that their feelings and prejudices should in no way be abused, and that they be treated as we should wish to be if thrown as strangers into a strange land, among a people of different customs and faith, and away from parents, home, and friends.

Remember that our Master who is in heaven especially claims to be the God of the widow, the fatherless, and *the stranger*, and has commanded, "If a stranger sojourn with you in your land, ye shall not vex him; but the stranger that dwelleth among you shall be unto you as one born among you, and *thou shalt love him as thyself.*"

Mrs. Stowe says: "We are far from recommending any controversial interference with the religious faith of our servants. It is far better to incite them to be good Christians in their own way, than to run the risk of shaking their faith in all religion by pointing out to them what seem to us the errors of that in which they have been educated. The general purity of life and propriety of demeanor of so many thousands of undefended young girls cast yearly upon our shores, with no home but their church, and no shield but their religion, are a sufficient proof that this religion exerts an influence over them not to be lightly trifled with. But there is a real unity even in opposite Christian forms; and the Roman Catholic servant and the Protestant mistress, if alike possessed by the spirit of Christ, and striving to conform to the Golden Rule, can not help being one in heart, though one go to mass and the other to meeting."

To this testimony of her sister the author adds some results of her observations as a resident or visitor among a wide circle of personal and family friends. The Christian care exercised by the Catholic priesthood over family servants deserves grateful notice, while the pure and wise instructions contained in the manuals of devotion used at public and private worship by this class, in many respects, are a model of excellence. As one illustration of the good fruits, the author, for a portion of each of the last ten years, has boarded in the family of her physician, Dr. G. H. Taylor. Here not less than twelve Irish Catholic girls usually frequent the Sunday early mass when most people are asleep. In this family neither her trunk, drawers, or door were ever locked, and yet never an article has been lost or stolen. And among her many friends it is this class who, with occasional exceptions, have been unsurpassed in faithful and affectionate service.

True, much has been owing to the happy management and wise care of Christian housekeepers, who in the life to come will reap the rewards of their faithful labors. A time is coming when American housekeepers will better understand their high privileges as chief ministers of the family state. Then it will no longer be a cause of discontent that a well-trained and faithful servant is withdrawn to bless another family, or to rear one of her own. Rather it will be seen that the Christian woman's kitchen is a training-school of good servants, where ignorant heathen come to be guided heavenward, and prepared to rear healthful and Christian families of their own. Then the young daughters will aid the mother in this Home Mission, and, by imparting their acquired advantages to Christ's neglected ones, will learn with thankfulness how much "more blessed it is to give than to receive."

CHAPTER XXX.

DOMESTIC AMUSEMENTS AND SOCIAL DUTIES.

Whenever the laws of body and mind are properly understood, it will be allowed that every person needs some kind of recreation; and that, by seeking it, the body is strengthened, the mind is invigorated, and all our duties are more cheerfully and successfully performed.

Children, whose bodies are rapidly growing and whose nervous system is tender and excitable, need much more amusement than persons of mature age. Persons, also, who are oppressed with great responsibilities and duties, or who are taxed by great intellectual or moral excitement, need recreations which physically exercise and draw off the mind from absorbing interests. Unfortunately, such persons are those who least resort to amusements; while the idle, gay, and thoughtless seek those which are not needed, and for which useful occupation would be a most benefical substitute.

As the only legitimate object of amusement is to prepare mind and body for the proper discharge of duty, the protracting of such as interfere with regular employments, or induce excessive fatigue, or weary the mind, or invade the proper hours for repose, must be sinful.

In deciding what should be selected, and what avoided, the following are guiding principles: In the first place, no amusements which inflict needless pain should ever be allowed. All tricks which cause fright or vexation, and all sports which involve suffering to animals, should be utterly forbidden. Hunting and fishing, for mere sport, can never be justified. If a man can convince his children that he follows these pursuits to gain food or health, and not for amusement, his example may not be very injurious. But when children see grown persons kill and frighten animals for sport, habits of cruelty, rather than feelings of tenderness and benevolence, are cultivated.

In the next place, we should seek no recreations which endanger life, or interfere with important duties. As the legitimate object of amusements is to promote health and prepare for some serious duties, selecting those which have a directly opposite tendency can not be justified. Of course, if a person feels that the previous day's diversion has shortened the hours of needful repose, or induced a lassitude of mind or body, instead of invigorating them, it is certain that an evil has been done which should never be repeated.

Another rule which has been extensively adopted in the religious world is, to avoid those amusements which experience has shown to be so exciting, and connected with so many temptations, as to be pernicious in tendency, both to the individual and to the community. It is on this ground that horse-racing and circus-riding have been excluded. Not because there is any thing positively wrong in having men and horses run and perform feats of agility, or in persons looking on for the diversion; but because experience has shown so many evils connected with these recreations, that they should be relinquished until properly regulated. So with theatres. The enacting of characters and the amusement thus afforded in themselves may be harmless, and possibly, in certain cases, might be useful; but experience has shown so many evils to result from this source, that it has been deemed wrong to patronize it till these evils are removed.

Under the same head comes dancing, in the estimation of the great majority of the religious world. Still, there are many intelligent, excellent, and conscientious persons who hold a contrary opinion. Such maintain that it is an innocent and healthful amusement, tending to promote ease of manners, cheerfulness, social affection, and health of mind and body; that evils are involved only in its excess; that, like food, study, or religious excitement, it is only wrong when not properly regulated; and that if serious and intelligent people would strive to regulate, rather than banish, this amusement, much more good would be secured.

On the other side, it is objected, not that dancing is a sin, in itself considered, for it was once a part of sacred worship; not that it would be objectionable, if it were properly regulated; not that it does not tend, when used in a proper manner, to health of body and mind, to grace of manners, and to social enjoyment: all these things are conceded. But it is objected to, on the same ground as horse-racing and theatrical entertainments; that we are to look at amusements as they are, and not as they might be. Horse-races might be so managed as not to involve cruelty, gambling, drunkenness, and other vices. And so might theatres. And if serious and intelligent persons undertook to regulate them, perhaps they would be somewhat raised from the depths to which they have sunk. But with the weak sense of moral obligation existing in the mass of society, and the imperfect ideas mankind have of the proper use of amusements, and the little self-control which men or women or children practice, these will not, in fact, be thus regulated.

And dancing is believed to be liable to the same objections. As this recreation is actually conducted, it does not tend to produce health of body or mind, but directly the contrary. If young and old went out to dance together in open air, as the French peasants do, it would be a very different sort of amusement from that which often is witnessed in a room furnished with many lights and filled with guests—both destroying the healthful part of the atmosphere, where the young collect, in their tightest dresses, to protract for several hours a kind of physical exertion which is not habitual to them. During this process, the blood is made to circulate more swiftly than usual, in circumstances where it is less perfectly oxygenized than health requires; the pores of the skin are excited by heat and exercise; the stomach is loaded with indigestible articles, and the quiet needful to digestion withheld; the diversion is protracted beyond the usual hour for repose; and then, when the skin is made the most highly susceptible to damps and miasms, the company pass from a warm room to the cold night-air. It is probable that no single amusement can be pointed out combining so many injurious particulars as this, which is so often defended as a healthful one. Even if parents who train their children to dance can keep them from public balls, (which is seldom the case,) dancing, as ordinarily conducted in private parlors, in most cases is subject to nearly the same mischievous influences.

The spirit of Christ is that of self-denying benevolence; and his great aim, by his teachings and example, was to train his followers to avoid all that should lead to sin, especially in regard to the weaker ones of his family. Yet he made wine at a wedding, attended a social feast on the Sabbath,* reproved excess of strictness in Sabbath-keeping generally, and forbade no safe and innocent enjoyment. In following his example, the rulers of the family, then, will introduce the most highly exciting amusements only in circumstances where there are such strong principles and habits of self-control that the enjoyment will not involve sin in the actor or needless temptation to the weak.

The course pursued by our Puritan ancestors, in the period succeeding their first perils amidst sickness and savages, is an example that may safely be practiced at the present day. The young of both sexes were educated together in the higher branches, in country academies; and very often the closing exercises were theatricals, in which the pupils were performers, and their pastors, elders, and parents, the audience. So at social gatherings, the dance was introduced before minister and wife, with smiling approval. The roaring fires and broad chimneys provided pure air, and the nine o'clock bell ended the festivities that gave new vigor and zest to life, while the dawn of the next day's light saw all at their posts of duty, with heartier strength and blither spirits.

No indecent or unhealthful costumes offended the eye, no half-naked dancers of dubious morality were sustained in a life of dangerous excitement, by the money of Christian people, for the mere amusement of their night hours. No shivering drivers were deprived of comfort and sleep, to carry home the midnight followers of fashion; nor was the quiet and comfort of servants in hundreds of dwellings invaded

* Luke xvi. In reading this passage, please notice what kind of guests are to be invited to the feast that Jesus Christ recommends.

for the mere amusement of their superiors in education and advantages. The command "we that are strong, ought to bear the infirmities of the weak, and not to please ourselves," was in those days not reversed. Had the drama and the dance continued to be regulated by the rules of temperance, health, and Christian benevolence, as in the days of our forefathers, they would not have been so generally banished from the religious world. And the question is now being discussed, whether they can be so regulated at the present time as not to violate the laws either of health or benevolence.*

In regard to home amusements, card-playing is now indulged in by many conscientious families from which it formerly was excluded, and for these reasons: it is claimed that this is a quiet home amusement, which unites pleasantly the aged with the young; that it is not now employed in respectable society for gambling, as it formerly was; that to some young minds it is a peculiarly fascinating game, and should be first practiced under the parental care, till the excitement of novelty is passed, thus rendering the danger to children less when going into the world; and, finally, that habits of self-control in exciting circumstances may and should be thus cultivated in the safety of home. Many parents who have taken this course with their sons in early life believe that it has proved rather a course of safety than of danger. Still, as there is great diversity of opinion among persons of equal worth and intelligence, a mutual spirit of candor and courtesy should be practiced. The sneer at bigotry and narrowness of views, on one side, and the uncharitable implication of want of piety, or sense, on the other, are equally ill-bred and unchristian. Truth on this subject is best promoted, not by ill-natured crimination and rebuke, but by calm reason, generous candor, forbearance, and kindness.

* Fanny Kemble Butler remarked to the writer that she regarded theatres wrong, chiefly because of the injury involved to the actors. Can a Christian mother contribute money to support young women in a profession from which she would protect her own daughter, as from degradation, and that, too, simply for the amusement of herself and family? Would this be following the self-sacrificing benevolence of Christ and his apostles?

There is another species of amusement, which a large portion of the religious world formerly put under the same condemnation as the preceding. This is novel-reading. The confusion and difference of opinion on this subject have arisen from a want of clear and definite distinctions. Now, as it is impossible to define what are novels and what are not, so as to include one class of fictitious writings and exclude every other, it is impossible to lay down any rule respecting them. The discussion, in fact, turns on the use of those works of imagination which belong to the class of fictitious narratives. That this species of reading is not only lawful, but necessary and useful, is settled by divine examples, in the parables and allegories of Scripture. Of course, the question must be, what kind of fabulous writings must be avoided, and what allowed.

In deciding this, no specific rules can be given: but it must be a matter to be regulated by the nature and circumstances of each case. No works of fiction which tend to throw the allurements of taste and genius around vice and crime should ever be tolerated; and all that tend to give false views of life and duty should also be banished. Of those which are written for mere amusement, presenting scenes and events that are interesting, and exciting and having no bad moral influence, much must depend on the character and circumstances of the reader. Some minds are torpid and phlegmatic, and need to have the imagination stimulated: such would be benefited by this kind of reading. Others have quick and active imaginations, and would be as much injured by excess. Some persons are often so engaged in absorbing interest, that any thing innocent, which will for a short time draw off the mind, is of the nature of a medicine; and in such cases this kind of reading is useful.

There is need, also, that some men should keep a supervision of the current literature of the day, as guardians, to warn others of danger. For this purpose, it is more suitable for editors, clergymen, and teachers to read indiscriminately, than for any other class of persons; for they are the guardians of the public weal in matters of literature, and should be prepared to advise parents and young persons of the evils in one direction, and of the good in another. In doing this, however, they are bound to go on the same principles which regulate physicians when they visit infected districts—using every precaution to prevent injury to themselves; having as little to do with pernicious exposures as a benevolent regard to others will allow; and faithfully employing all the knowledge and opportunities thus gained for warning and preserving others. There is much danger, in taking this course, that men will seek the excitement of the imagination for the mere pleasure it affords, under the plea of preparing to serve the public, when this is neither the aim nor the result.

In regard to the use of such works by the young, as a general rule, they ought not to be allowed to any except those of a dull and phlegmatic temperament, until the solid parts of education are secured and a taste for more elevated reading is acquired. If these stimulating condiments in literature be freely used in youth, all relish for more solid reading will in a majority of cases be destroyed. If parents succeed in securing habits of cheerful and implicit obedience, it will be very easy to regulate this matter, by prohibiting the reading of any story-book until the consent of the parent is obtained.

The most successful mode of forming a taste for suitable reading, is for parents to select interesting works of history and travels, with maps and pictures suited to the age and attainments of the young, and spend an hour or two each day or evening in aiming to make truth as interesting as fiction. Whoever has once tried this method will find that the uninjured mind of childhood is better satisfied with what they know is true, when wisely presented, than with the most exciting novels, which they know are false.

Perhaps there has been some just ground of objection to the course often pursued by parents in neglecting to provide suitable and agreeable substitutes for the amusements denied. But there is a great abundance of safe, healthful, and delightful recreations, which all parents may secure for their children. Some of these will here be pointed out.

One of the most useful and important is the cultivation

of flowers and fruits. This, especially for the daughters of a family, is greatly promotive of health and amusement. Many young ladies, whose habits are now so formed that they can never be induced to a course of active domestic exercise so long as their parents are able to hire domestic service, may yet be led to an employment which will tend to secure health and vigor of constitution, by fruits and flowers.

It would be a most desirable improvement, if all schools for young women could be furnished with suitable grounds and instruments for the cultivation of fruits and flowers, and every inducement offered to engage the pupils in this pursuit. No father who wishes to have his daughters grow up to be healthful women can take a surer method to secure this end. Let him set apart a portion of his ground for fruits and flowers, and see that the soil is well prepared and dug over, and all the rest may be committed to the care of the children. These would need to be provided with a light hoe and rake, a dibble or garden trowel, a watering-pot, and means and opportunities for securing seeds, roots, bulbs, buds, and grafts, all which might be done at a trifling expense. Then, with proper encouragement and by the aid of a few intelligible and practical directions, every man who has even half an acre could secure a small Eden around his premises.

In pursuing this amusement children can also be led to acquire many useful habits. Early rising would, in many cases, be thus secured; and if they were required to keep their walks and borders free from weeds and rubbish, habits of order and neatness would be induced. Benevolent and social feelings could also be cultivated, by influencing children to share their fruits and flowers with friends and neighbors, as well as to distribute roots and seeds to those who have not the means of procuring them. A woman or a child, by giving seeds or slips or roots to a washerwoman, or a farmer's boy, thus inciting them to love and cultivate fruits and flowers, awakens a new and refining source of enjoyment in minds which have few resources more elevated than mere physical enjoyments. Our Saviour directs us, in making feasts, to call, not the rich, who can recompense again, but the poor, who can make no returns. So children should be taught to dispense their little treasures not alone to companions and friends, who will probably return similar favors, but to those who have no means of making any return. If the rich, who acquire a love for the enjoyments of taste and have the means to gratify it, would aim to extend among the poor the cheap and simple enjoyment of fruits and flowers, our country would soon literally "blossom as the rose."

If the ladies of a neighborhood would unite small contributions, and send a list of flower-seeds and roots to some respectable and honest florist, who would not be likely to turn them off with trash, they could divide these among themselves and their poor neighbors, so as to secure an abundant variety at a very small expense. A bag of flower-seeds, which can be obtained at wholesale for four cents, would abundantly supply a whole neighborhood; and, by the gathering of seeds in the autumn, could be perpetuated.

Another very elevating and delightful recreation for the young is found in *music*. Here the writer would protest against the practice, common in many families, of having the daughters learn to play on the piano, whether they have a taste and an ear for music or not. A young lady who does not sing well, and has no great fondness for music, does nothing but waste time, money, and patience in learning to play on the piano. But all children can be taught to sing in early childhood, if the scientific mode of teaching music in schools could be more widely introduced, as it is in Prussia, Germany, and Switzerland. Then young children could read and sing music as easily as they can read language; and might take any tune, dividing themselves into bands, and sing off at sight the endless variety of music which is prepared. And if parents of wealth would take pains to have teachers qualified for the purpose, who should teach all the young children in the community, much would be done for the happiness and elevation of the rising generation. This is an element of education which we are glad to know is, year by year, more extensively and carefully cultivated; and it is not only a means of culture, but also an amusement, which children relish in the highest degree; and which they can enjoy at home, in the fields, and in visits abroad.

Another domestic amusement is the collecting of shells, plants, and specimens in geology and mineralogy, for the formation of cabinets. If intelligent parents would procure the simpler works which have been prepared for the young, and study them with their children, a taste for such recreations would soon be developed. The writer has seen young boys of eight and ten years of age gathering and cleaning shells from rivers, and collecting plants and mineralogical specimens, with a delight bordering on ecstasy; and there are few, if any, who by proper influences would not find this a source of ceaseless delight and improvement.

Another resource for family diversion is to be found in the various games played by children, and in which the joining of older members of the family is always a great advantage to both parties, especially those in the open air.

All medical men unite in declaring that nothing is more beneficial to health than hearty laughter; and surely our benevolent Creator would not have provided risibles, and made it a source of health and enjoyment to use them, if it were a sin so to do. There has been a tendency to asceticism on this subject, which needs to be removed. Such commands as forbid *foolish* laughing and jesting, "*which are not convenient*," and which forbid all idle words and vain conversation, can not apply to any thing except what is foolish, vain, and useless. But jokes, laughter, and sports, when used in such a degree as tends only to promote health and happiness, are neither vain, foolish, or "not convenient." It is the excess of these things, and not the moderate use of them, which Scripture forbids. The prevailing temper of the mind should be serious, yet cheerful; and there are times when relaxation and laughter are not only proper, but necessary and right for all. There is nothing better for this end than that parents and older persons should join in the sports of childhood. Mature minds can always make such diversions more entertaining to children, and can exert a healthful moral influence over their minds; and at the same time can gain exercise and amusement for themselves. How lamentable that so many fathers, who could be thus useful and happy with their children, throw away such opportunities, and wear out soul and body in the pursuit of gain or fame!

Another resource for children is the exercise of mechanical skill. Fathers, by providing tools for their boys, and showing them how to make wheelbarrows, carts, sleds, and various other articles, contribute both to the physical, moral, and social improvement of their children. And in regard to little daughters, much more can be done in this way than many would imagine. The writer, blessed with the example of a most ingenious and industrious mother, had not only learned before the age of twelve to make dolls, of various sorts and sizes, but to cut and fit and sew every article that belongs to a doll's wardrobe. This, which was done for mere amusement, secured such a facility in mechanical pursuits, that ever afterward the cutting and fitting of any article of dress, for either sex, was accomplished with entire ease.

When a little girl begins to sew, her mother can promise her a small bed and pillow, as soon as she has sewed a patch quilt for them; and then a bedstead, as soon as she has sewed the sheets and cases for pillows; and then a large doll to dress, as soon as she has made the under-garments; and thus go on till the whole contents of the baby-house are earned by the needle and skill of its little owner. Thus the task of learning to sew will become a pleasure; and every new toy will be earned by useful exertion. A little girl can be taught, by the aid of patterns prepared for the purpose, to cut and fit all articles necessary for her doll. She can also be provided with a little wash-tub and irons, and thus keep in proper order a complete miniature domestic establishment.

Besides these recreations, there are the enjoyments secured in walking, riding, visiting, and many other employments which need not be recounted. Children, if trained to be healthful and industrious, will never fail to discover resources of amusement; while their guardians should lend their aid to guide and restrain them from excess.

There is need of a very great change of opinion and practice in this nation, in regard to the subject of social and domestic duties. Many sensible and conscientious men spend all their time abroad in business, except perhaps an hour or so at night, when they are so fatigued as to be unfitted for any social or intellectual enjoyment. And some of the most conscientious men in the country will add to their professional business public or benevolent enterprises, which demand time, effort, and money; and then excuse themselves for neglecting all care of their children, and efforts for their own intellectual improvement, or for the improvement of their families, by the plea that they have no time for it.

All this arises from the want of correct notions of the binding obligation of our social and domestic duties. The main object of life is not to secure the various gratifications of appetite or taste, but to form such a character, for ourselves and others, as will secure the greatest amount of present and future happiness. It is of far more consequence, then, that parents should be intelligent, social, affectionate, and agreeable at home and to their friends, than that they should earn money enough to live in a large house and have handsome furniture. It is far more needful for children that a father should attend to the formation of their character and habits, and aid in developing their social, intellectual, and moral nature, than it is that he should earn money to furnish them with handsome clothes and a variety of tempting food.

It will be wise for those parents who find little time to attend to their children, or to seek amusement and enjoyment in the domestic and social circle, because their time is so much occupied with public cares or benevolent objects, to inquire whether their first duty is not to train up their own families to be useful members of society. A man who neglects the mind and morals of his children to take care of the public, is in great danger of coming under a similar condemnation to that of him who, neglecting to provide for his own household, has "denied the faith, and is worse than an infidel."

There are husbands and fathers who conscientiously subtract time from their business to spend at home, in reading with their wives and children, and in domestic amusements which at once refresh and improve. The children of such parents will grow up with a love of home and kindred which will be the greatest safeguard against future temptations, as well as the purest source of earthly enjoyment.

There are families, also, who make it a definite object to keep up family attachments after the children are scattered abroad, and in some cases secure the means for doing this by saving money which would otherwise have been spent for superfluities of food or dress. Some families have adopted, for this end, a practice which, if widely imitated, would be productive of much enjoyment. The method is this: On the first day of each month, some member of the family, at each extreme point of dispersion, takes a folio sheet, and fills a part of a page. This is sealed and mailed to the next family, who read it, add another contribution, and then mail it to the next. Thus the family circular, once a month, goes from each extreme to all the members of a widely-dispersed family, and each member becomes a sharer in the joys, sorrows, plans, and pursuits of all the rest. At the same time, frequent family meetings are sought; and the expense thus incurred is cheerfully met by retrenchments in other directions. The sacrifice of some unnecessary physical indulgence will often purchase many social and domestic enjoyments, a thousand times more elevating and delightful than the retrenched luxury.

There is no social duty which the Supreme Lawgiver more strenuously urges than hospitality and kindness to strangers, who are classed with the widow and the fatherless as the special objects of Divine tenderness. There are some reasons why this duty peculiarly demands attention from the American people.

Reverses of fortune, in this land, are so frequent and unexpected, and the habits of the people are so migratory, that there are very many in every part of the country who, having seen all their temporal plans and hopes crushed, are now pining among strangers, bereft of wonted comforts, without friends, and without the sympathy and society so needful to wounded spirits. Such, too frequently, sojourn long and lonely, with no comforter but Him who "knoweth the heart of a stranger."

Whenever, therefore, new-comers enter a community, inquiry should immediately be made as to whether they have friends or associates, to render sympathy and kind attentions; and, when there is any need for it, the ministries of kind neighborliness should immediately be offered. And it should be remembered that the first days of a stranger's sojourn are the most dreary, and that civility and kindness are doubled in value by being offered at an early period.

In social gatherings the claims of the stranger are too apt to be forgotten; especially in cases where there are no peculiar attractions of personal appearance, or talents, or high standing. Such an one should be treated with attention, *because* he is a stranger; and when communities learn to act more from principle, and less from selfish impulse, on this subject, the sacred claims of the stranger will be less frequently forgotten.

The most agreeable hospitality to visitors who become inmates of a family, is that which puts them entirely at ease. This can never be the case where the guest perceives that the order of family arrangement is essentially altered, and that time, comfort, and convenience are sacrificed for his accommodation.

Offering the best to visitors, showing a polite regard to every wish expressed, and giving precedence to them, in all matters of comfort and convenience, can be easily combined with the easy freedom which makes the stranger feel as if at home; and this is the perfection of hospitable entertainment.

CHAPTER XXXI.

LAWS OF HEALTH AND HAPPINESS.

IT is hoped a day will come when these laws of God will be put on tablets in school-rooms and houses, as are the ten commandments in our churches, and that all children will be trained fully to understand them, and then to commit them to memory.

Laws of Health for the Bones.

Exercise daily in pure air, because it nourishes and gives strength to the bones. Do not habitually keep the spine out of its natural position, either when sleeping or sitting, because deformity and disease are thus induced. Never compress the chest or ribs, because it diminishes chest breathing, and thus lessens the needful amount of nourishing oxygen; and for the same reason, support all clothing from the shoulders, because any pressure on the hips and abdomen lessens abdominal breathing.

Never wear high heels, because it tends to produce internal displacement, to distort the foot, the spine, and the ankles, causes corns and bunions, and makes a graceful walk impossible. An unfailing cure for corns and bunions is once a week to soak the foot half an hour in four quarts of quite warm water, in which is dissolved a bit of soda the size of a large walnut. Three or four times will relieve and probably cure.

Laws of Health for the Muscles.

Supply pure blood and healthful food, because these are indispensable to their health and strength. Exercise all the muscles, so as to secure the healthful development of all, and avoid weakening them by excessive exercise. Change inactive habits not suddenly, but by a gradual increase of exercise. When too weak to exercise, employ an operator to increase the flow of blood to the muscles by pressure and rubbing. Never compress any of the muscles by tight clothing, because it diminishes the flow of blood and thus of nutriment. As pure air and light cause increase of strength, let all exercise be by daylight. Avoid increase of exercise when the air is impure, as it usually is in night-gatherings.

Laws of Health for the Lungs.

It is proved by many experiments that a full-grown person vitiates a hogshead of air every hour; therefore, so ventilate every room that each inmate shall have the needful pure air at this rate, especially by night. Take care so to dress, to sit, and to lie, that the lungs shall not be compressed, and thus be deprived of the needful nourishing oxygen.

Laws of Health for the Digestive Organs.

Supply every part of the body with its peculiar nutriment; nitrogen for muscle, phosphorus for brain and nerves, carbon for the lungs, and silica, iron, etc., for other parts. Let the proportions follow the example given in wheat, milk, and eggs, which have all the elements needed and in proper proportions. According to this rule, use unbolted flour rather than superfine. In selecting food, have reference to age, climate, and state of the health. Meals should be at least five hours apart, that the stomach may rest. Do not eat between meals, as it mixes partly digested food with the new supply, and impedes digestion. Do not eat too much, because it impedes digestion, and overtaxes, and thus weakens, the organs that must throw off the excess. Eat only to satisfy hunger, and not to qualify the palate after hunger is satisfied. Do not eat a great variety, because digestion is easier and more perfect with but few articles. Let there be a variety which is successive, and not at one meal.

Do not require children to eat what they do not love, because food which is relished is better digested and more healthful. If very thirsty, drink water abundantly before eating, but sparingly at meals—only one tumbler or cup. Very hot food or drink debilitates the nerves of the teeth and stomach. Very cold water, or ice, after a full meal, interferes with digestion.

Avoid stimulating drinks, or use them very weak. A *gradual* diminution of strength will modify the taste, so that a weak dilution will be relished as much, or more, than a strong. Drink only pure water; filter impure water through sand and powdered charcoal. Free drinking of pure cold water between meals tends to purify the blood and strengthen the nervous system.

All the yeast-powders for raising bread are not so healthful as hop-yeast; and those recommended by Liebig & Hosford *do not* restore several important elements lost by bolting.

Laws of Health for the Skin.

Wash the whole body either morning or night; because its capillaries contain more blood and nerve matter than all the rest of the body; because air and light cleanse and nourish them; and because when in full health the skin throws off more than half the refuse of the body, which, if not thus expelled, goes to the lungs, or bowels, or kidneys to be expelled, often causing disease. Bath-rooms are a luxury; but a wet towel, and a screen for privacy, are equally useful. Chilling the skin closes its pores, causing colds, diarrhœa, or catarrh. Immediate and free perspiration is the safest remedy. Rely on bathing, exercise, pure air, and proper food, rather than on warm clothing and warm rooms. But persons weakened by age or nervous debility must wear more clothing than others, and bathe in a warm room, or, better, by an open fire. Any diminution of clothing should be made in the morning, when the body is most vigorous. As the body radiates its heat to adjacent cold walls, be careful to avoid sitting near them, except when well protected. Many take colds or rheumatism by sitting near church or other cold walls. Taking air and sun baths tend to strengthen the nerves, and thus the whole body. Avoid a continuous current of air on any part of the body, as the withdrawal of heat causes disease in the part thus chilled.

Expose bed-clothing and garments worn next the skin to fresh air, which removes the exhalations of the skin that otherwise would be re-absorbed. Straw and hair mattresses, and cotton comforters, should also be aired occasionally. The white dust thrown out by beating them is the scales and other refuse matter from the skin.

In epidemics, nourishing food and cleansing the skin lessens danger.

Laws of Health for the Brain and Nerves.

Healthful food, a clean skin, and daily exercise in the open air, are indispensable. Take seven or eight hours of sleep by night, and not by day; and when taxed by great care, labor, or sorrow, sleep as much as you can, for thus the brain and nerves recover strength.

Always have some time each day devoted to some amusement, and this out-of-doors if practicable. Laughter is a very healthful exercise.

Have system and order in your employments, and let there be variety, so that no one set of nerves be wearied and another set unemployed.

Let the intellect and feelings be engaged in safe and worthy objects, and so exercise all the faculties as to secure a well-balanced mind in a healthful body. In all cases of disease, trust more to obedience to these rules than to medicines, which should be rarely used.

Laws of Health for the Teeth, Eyes, and Hair.

Never sleep till the teeth are cleaned with pure water, a brush, and a piece of thread or a tooth-pick to remove what lodges between the teeth. It would be well to do this after each meal. Avoid very hot food as causing decayed teeth. No tooth-powder is needed if these directions are obeyed.

Accustom the eyes *gradually* to as much light as they can bear without pain. Light is healthful, especially to the eyes, and dark rooms make weak eyes. If the eyes are weak from excessive use, continue to use them, but only a little at a time, with intervals of rest; for eyes, like all the rest of the body, grow weak by disuse. Always shade weak eyes from brilliant lights, especially when reading. For inflamed eyes or eyelids, do not use what others recommend, but consult a physician; as a remedy for one may be injurious for another case. Gentle rubbing around and over the eyes draws the blood there, and tends to increase strength. Do it only for two minutes at a time, three or four times a day. Bathing the eyes in cold water strengthens their nerves.

Never use hair mixtures until some chemist has tested them and assures you there is no *lead* in them. Many persons have had paralysis and other evils by using hair mixtures containing lead to restore the color. Brushing and washing the skin of the hair, and thus bringing the blood to nourish its roots, is a safe and sure method, and those mixtures that seem to do good are efficacious chiefly because the directions always require rubbing and cleansing the skin of the hair.

Remember that these laws of health are laws of God, and that when you disobey them you sin against your heavenly Father, who loves you, and is grieved when you injure your own soul and body. Therefore pray to be enabled to obey yourselves, and to teach these his laws to all under your care, both by precept and example.

CHAPTER XXXII.

COMFORT FOR A DISCOURAGED HOUSEKEEPER.

THERE is no doubt of the fact, that American housekeepers have far greater trials and difficulties to meet than those of any other nation. And it is probable that many of those who may read over the methods of thrift and economy adopted by some of the best housekeepers in our land, and detailed in this work, will with a sigh exclaim, that it is *impossible* for them even to attempt any such plans.

Others may be stimulated by the advice and examples presented, and may start off with much hope and courage, to carry out a plan of great excellence and appropriateness, and, after trying a while, will become discouraged by the thousand obstacles in their way, and give up in despair.

A still greater number will like their own way best, and think it is folly to attempt to change.

For those who wish they *could* become systematic, neat, and thorough housekeepers, and would like to follow out successfully the suggestions found in this work, and for those who have tried, or will try, and find themselves baffled and discouraged, these words of comfort are offered.

Perhaps you find yourself encompassed by such sort of trials as these: Your house is inconvenient, or destitute of those facilities for doing work well which you need, and you can not command the means to supply these deficiencies. Your domestics are so imperfectly qualified that they never can do any thing *just right*, unless you stand by and attend to every thing yourself, and you can not be present in parlor, nursery, and kitchen all at once. Perhaps you are frequently left without any cook, or without a chamber-maid, and sometimes without any hands but your own to do the work, and there is constant jostling and change from this cause. And perhaps you can not get supplies, either from garden or market, such as you need, and all your calculations fail in that direction.

And perhaps your children are sickly, and rob you of rest by night, or your health is so poor that you feel no energy or spirits to make exertions. And perhaps you never have had any training in domestic affairs, and can not understand how to work yourself, nor how to direct others. And when you go for aid to experienced housekeepers, or cookery-books, you are met by such sort of directions as these: "Take a *pinch* of this, and a *little* of that, and *considerable* of the other, and cook them till they are done *about right*." And when you can not succeed in following such indefinite instructions, you find your neighbors and husband wondering how it is that, when you have one, two, or three domestics, there should be so much difficulty about housekeeping, and such constant trouble, and miscalculation, and mistake. And then, perhaps, you lose your patience and your temper, and blame others, and others blame you, and so every thing seems to be in a snarl.

Now the first thing to be said for your comfort is, that you *really have* great trials to meet; trials that entitle you to pity and sympathy, while it is the fault of others more than your own that you are in this very painful and difficult situation. You have been as cruelly treated as the Israelites were by Pharaoh, when he demanded bricks without furnishing the means to make them.

You are like a young, inexperienced lad who is required to superintend all the complicated machinery of a manufactory which he never was trained to understand, and on penalty of losing reputation, health, and all he values most.

Neither your parents, teachers, or husband have *trained* you for the place you fill, nor furnished you with the knowledge or assistance needed to enable you to meet all the complicated and untried duties of your lot. A young woman who has never had the care of a child, never done housework, never learned the numberless processes that are indispensable to keep domestic affairs in regular order, never done any thing but attend to books, drawing, and music at school, and visiting and company after she left school—such an one is as unprepared to take charge of a nursery, kitchen, and family establishment, as she is to take charge of *a man-of-war.* And the chief blame rests with those who placed her *so unprepared* in such trying circumstances. Therefore, you have a right to feel that a large part of these evils are more your misfortune than your fault, and that they entitle you to sympathy rather than blame.

The next word of comfort is, the assurance that you *can* do *every one* of your duties, and do them well, and the following is the method by which you can do it. In the first place, make up your mind that it never is your duty to do any thing more than you *can*, or in any better manner than the best you can. And whenever you have done the best you can, you have done *well;* and it is all that man *should* require, and certainly all that your heavenly Father *does* require.

The next thing is, for you to make out an inventory of all the things that need to be done in your whole establishment. Then calculate what things you find you *can not* do, and strike them off the list, as what are not among your *duties.* Of those that remain, select a certain number that you think you can do *exactly as they need to be done*, and among these be sure that you put the making of *good bread.* This every housekeeper can do, if she will only determine to do it.

Make a selection of certain things that you will *persevere* in having done *as well as they can be done*, and let these be only so many as you feel sure you can succeed in attempting. Then make up your mind that all the rest must go along as they do, until you get more time, strength, and experience, to increase the list of things that you determine shall always be well done.

By this course you will have the comfort of feeling that in *some* respects you are as good a housekeeper as you can be, while there will be a cheering progress in gaining on all that portion of your affairs that are left at loose ends. You will be able to measure a gradual advance, and be encouraged by success. Many housekeepers fail entirely by expecting to do *every thing well at first*, when neither their knowledge or strength is adequate, and so they fail everywhere, and finally give up in despair.

Are you not only a housekeeper, but a *mother?* Oh, sacred and beautiful name! how many cares and responsibilities are associated with it! And how many elevating and sublime anticipations and hopes are given to inspire and to cheer! You are training young minds whose plastic texture will receive and retain every impression you make; who will imitate your feelings, tastes, habits, and opinions; and who will transmit what they receive from you to their children, to pass again to the next generation, and then to the next, until *a whole nation* may possibly receive its character and destiny from your hands! No imperial queen ever stood in a more sublime and responsible position than you now occupy in the eye of Him who reads the end from the beginning, and who is appointing all the trials and discipline of your lot, not for purposes which are visible to your limited ken, but in view of all the consequences that are to result from the character which you form, and are to transmit to your posterity!

And you who never are to bear a mother's name, but must toil for the children of others with little earthly honor or reward, remember that the blessed Lord "took upon himself the form of a servant;" that he came "not to be ministered to, but to minister;" that those who voluntarily take the lowest place are most likely to stand highest at last; that all sincere service is accepted and precious; and that our labors in this life are to bear their fruits through everlasting ages.

Remember that you have a Father in heaven who sympathizes in all your cares, pities your griefs, makes allowances for your defects, and is endeavoring by trials, as well as by blessings, to fit you for the right fulfillment of your high and holy calling.

But the heaviest care and sorrow that ever oppress a woman who, as housekeeper, has the control of children and servants, are her responsibilities as to the eternal destiny of those guided by her teachings and example. Our cruel war took thousands of our noblest youth to terrible sufferings in prisons and battle-fields, and to a torturing death. Multitudes of these sacrificed their all to save their country as really as did our Lord when he suffered for the whole world. And yet many of these martyred heroes gave no evidence of that change which their bereaved parents were trained to believe could alone save their beloved ones from everlasting misery. How many mothers have hid in silent anguish this never-healed wound—this crushing sorrow!

The most available remedy for such distress is much that is suggested in Chapters XXV. and XXVIII.; and the following queries may aid in obtaining the true teachings of the Bible on these momentous questions:

Are the definitions given in those chapters of the words *right*, *righteous*, *love*, *faith*, and *repentance*, in reference to future eternal safety, sustained by common use and by our dictionaries? What texts illustrate the distinction between *right* as to motives, or intention and *right* as to resulting consequences?

What texts show that wrong actions, owing to mistaken opinions as to what is right, do not necessarily destroy evidence of a righteous or virtuous character?

What texts show that the righteous character which secures eternal safety consists, not chiefly in emotional love to God, but rather in a controlling principle of obedience to his will, as manifested in both his natural and revealed laws?

What texts show that at some future period (it may be millions of ages hence) there will be a final separation of the righteous and the wicked?

Are there any texts which show that in the intervening ages there will be no improvement of character for those who fail in this life? and are there any which show that there may be for some, if not for all?

Are there any texts which show that the character of every human being is fixed at death?

Are there any texts which show that some of mankind will be forever sinful, and forever separated from the righteous?

Are there any texts which show that all mankind will finally become righteous, and thus forever happy?

When all the texts in the Bible on these questions are collected and arranged, when applying the rules of interpretation, these considerations are to be noticed:

1. That the word "Hades," in many cases, is translated "Hell," when its proper translation is "the place of departed spirits." The story of Dives and Lazarus, and of the repentant thief, can be properly explained only by ascertaining the meaning the Jews attached to the words Hades and Paradise; for Christ, of course, expected them to be thus understood.

Again, the meaning of many texts depends on the subject before the mind of the speaker. Thus when Christ replied to the question, "Are there few that be saved?" did he refer to all beings in the whole universe, or to the present world, and to that present time when "the righteous" were comparatively a small portion of mankind?

Again, much that relates to the spirit-world can not be fully taught or comprehended. St. Paul says that, when caught up into the third heaven, he saw, not, as in our translation, things not "lawful" to utter, but, in the original Greek, "impossible" to utter.

Again, the results thus gained from the Bible should be considered in connection with the analogies of nature and God's providence in regard to the continued development of mind and character, which in this life has so short and imperfect a period, and in most cases so many and great disadvantages.

In completing such an investigation, much time and mental effort may be required, but is there any employment of time and intellect so important as this end?

In offering these suggestions, the author may refer to her own extended observation of the results of *religious* educational training in the family, as witnessed in the diverse sects with which she has mingled, whether Catholic, Protestant, or Jewish; for she counts excellent and intelligent friends in *all.*

She finds all united in the belief of *a future life* in which the character formed in this life controls the eternal well-being; so that those who are trained to truth, justice, and mercy will be forever happier than those who grow up in sin and wickedness.

She finds that the right education of children and servants is more and more an object of care and effort; and that, as the consequence, the world is growing better rather than worse.

And finally, she rejoices in the increasingly open avenues to useful and remunerating occupations for women, enabling them to establish *homes of their own*, where, if not as the natural mother, yet as a Christ-mother, they may take in neglected ones, and train future mothers, teachers, and missionaries for the world.

20*

NOTE A.

VIEWS OF MEDICAL WRITERS

THE American Woman's Educational Association has for its object "the establishment of institutions having *endowed* departments supporting ladies of superior character and education who shall add to a collegiate course both scientific and practical training, in all relating to the distinctive duties of woman as housekeeper, wife, mother, nurse of infants and the sick, trainer of servants, and chief religious minister of the family state." As Secretary of this Association, the author requested the views of Mrs. Dr. Gleason, of the Elmira Water-cure, on the topics that follow. This lady, as wife, mother, and highly-educated physician, during over twenty years has had patients of her own sex, probably counting by thousands, and has often, by request, lectured to graduating classes in the Ingham University, the Elmira College, and other popular institutions for women. The following are extracts from her reply:

Treatment of Pelvic Diseases.

"The pelvic organs, when diseased, all have so many symptoms in common, that it requires not only good anatomical, pathological, and physiological knowledge, but close and well-cultivated diagnostic powers to decide *which* organ is diseased, and *how* it is diseased. For example, sometimes a displacement of the uterus will cause a sense of weight, dragging, and throbbing, accompanied by pain in the back and in front of the hips. But inflammation, ulceration, and induration of this organ will produce precisely the same results; and sometimes *mere nervous debility* in these parts will induce these symptoms, especially when the imagination is excited in reference to the subject. It also is often the case that extreme prolapsus occurs *in which there is no pain at all.*

"So also disease of the urinary cyst is indicated by symptoms precisely similar to those which mark the disease of the adjacent organ. These organs lying in close proximity, and supplied with nerves from the same source, would necessarily sympathize, and show disease by similar symptoms. Just as in the toothache, many a one has been unable to point out the diseased tooth. How much more difficulty exists in a case where most women are profoundly ignorant on the subject!

"It has become a very common notion that when any local displacement of the pelvic organs occurs, a woman must cease to use her arms, cease to exercise vigorously, and keep herself on the bed much of her time. All which, in most cases, is exactly the three things which she ought not to do. And thus it is that, when from want of fresh air and exercise, and from the many pernicious practices that debilitate the female constitution, the pelvic organs indicate debility, and these nerves begin to ache. Immediately a harness is put on for local support, and the bed becomes the constant resort; and thus the muscular debility and nervous irritability are increased. And yet, all that is needed is fresh air, exercise, simple diet, and *proper* mental occupation.

"In this condition, perhaps, resort is had to some ignorant or inexperienced practitioner, who has some patent supporter to sell, or who has some secret and wonderful method of curing such diseases. Then commences, in many cases, a kind of local treatment most trying to the feelings, *which is but seldom required*, and which, in a majority of cases, results in no benefit.

"Many a one has recited to me the mental and physical suffering she has endured for months in such a course of treatment, and all to no purpose. A touching case of this kind recently occurred, in the case of a beautiful young lady who was a listener to a course of lectures on the pelvis and its diseases, given by me to the graduating class of a female seminary. At the close she came to me, and, with tearful eyes and a quivering lip, said, 'I see now why all I have suffered in body and mind is worse than useless. I see now that I have never had the disease for which I have been treated.'

"Woman's trusting, confiding nature is beautiful; but oh, how much it needs to be protected by an intelligence on such subjects that will enable her properly to exercise her own judgment! And surely, in such cases, above all others, a woman should be sure that her medical adviser has had a proper education, and possesses a well-established moral character.

Effects of Imagination in Reference to these Diseases.

"Besides the evils of misunderstanding and mistreating these affections, we have a host of evils from the effects of imagination. Multitudes of women, who hear terrific accounts of the nature of these complaints, and of the treatment that is inevitable, have their imagination so excited that aches and pains that are really trifling become magnified into all the symptoms of the dreaded evil. They betake themselves to bed, become more and more nervous as they give up air, exercise, and occupation, and thus drag out a useless life, a burden to themselves and to their families. Again and again I have had such cases brought to me, where for years they could not leave their beds or walk at all, when I had nothing to do but *make them understand their own organism*, and convince them that they needed little else except to get up and *go to work*, in order to be healthy women. It is such cases that furnish a large portion of the 'wonderful cures' that attract patients into the hands of poorly-qualified practitioners.

"It is probable that thousands of women who are suffering from pain in the back and pelvic evils, and who either will soon be invalids or imagine themselves so, could be relieved entirely by obeying these directions:

"Wash the whole person, on rising, in cool water, and, if nervous or debilitated, by a fire; dress loosely, and let *all* the weight of clothing rest on the shoulders; sleep in a well-ventilated room; exercise the muscles a great deal, especially those of the arms and trunk, taking care to lie down and rest as soon as fatigue is felt; eat simple food, at regular hours; pursue useful employments, with intervals of social and healthful amusement; sleep enough, and at the proper hours; and sit often in the sun.

Peculiar Instruction needed by Young Children.

"Through information gained from my husband, from other physicians, from teachers, from medical writers, and from the reports of insane hospitals, it has become clear to my mind that there are secret and terrific causes preying extensively upon the health and nervous energy of childhood and youth of both sexes such as did not formerly exist, and such as demand new efforts to eradicate and prevent.

"Parents and teachers all over the land need to be made aware that a secret vice is becoming frequent among children of both sexes that is taught by servants and communicated by children at school. Indeed, it may result from accident or disease, with an innocent unconsciousness of the evil done, on the part of the child, while the practice may thus ignorantly be perpetuated to maturity. This practice leads to diseases of the most horrible description, to mania, and to fatuity. Death and the mad-house are the last resort of these most miserable victims.

"To protect childhood and youth from this, it is not only needful to cultivate purity of mind and personal modesty, but to teach them while quite young that any fingering of the parts referred to involves terrible penalties. No such explicit information should be given as would tempt the incautious curiosity of childhood, but the child should be impressed with a sense of guilt and awful punishment as connected with *any thing* of this kind, that would instantly recur to mind, if led by accident or instruction to this vice.

"In regard to those who have already become victims, to a greater or less degree, to this vice, one caution is very important. Medical writers and others who have attempted to guard the young in this direction have painted not only the danger but the wickedness of this practice in such strong colors that, when a young person first discovers the nature of a practice that has been indulged with little conception of the danger or wrong, overaction on the fears and the conscience is not unfrequently the result. Such horror and despair sometimes ensue as almost paralyze any effort on the part of medical advisers to remedy the evil.

"In all such cases, it is safest and best to assume that the sin is one of ignorance, and that the cure is almost certain, if the directions given are strictly obeyed. Unstimulating diet, a great deal of exercise in the open air, daily ablution of the whole person, control of the imagination, and occupation of the mind in useful pursuits, will usually remedy the evil, after its nature is understood."

[A lady, after reading the above, stated that within the last year a little boy under her care, of very delicate mind and susceptible temperament, was sent to the country to a private boarding-school, under the care of a most excellent gentleman and his wife, who were eminently faithful, so far as they knew how to be. The child staid only six weeks, and returned sick, depressed, and with a burden on his mind that could not be discovered. After learning that he would not be sent back, he revealed the shocking story, and also the fact that the boys had threatened to kill him if he ever told any one.

Another lady, after reading this article, related a similar story of a large and highly respected boarding-school for boys, and gave several mournful incidents to show the effects of such evils on the health of the pupils. Parents whose young sons are at boarding-school *can not* be too much alarmed on this subject.]

Instructions at a more Mature Age.

"You wish my views and experience in reference to instructions that should be communicated to the young, on such topics, at a more mature age.

"The terrible effects I have seen from *simple ignorance*, both on individual and domestic happiness, convince me that a great work is to be attempted in this direction. More than half the cases of extreme suffering which have come under my care could have been saved, had the course that is aimed at by you and your associates have been secured by them. I have been called repeatedly to lecture to young ladies, near the close of a school education, on subjects so important to their future health and happiness, and I never found the least difficulty, either on their part or my own.

"When the proper discriminations are made between *true* delicacy and propriety, and a fastidious and mawkish imitation of them, there is no difficulty in making them understood and appreciated. I have found, on such occasions, if a person was present known to be wanting in purity and delicacy, it was such only who made very offensive protestations against the course pursued in such instructions.

"In reference to *social* as well as secret vices of this description, it seems to me the protection of ignorance should be preserved as long as possible, and yet so that, when such knowledge dawns, there shall immediately recur the needful impression of danger and sin. These duties belong especially to parents and teachers; and the circulation of books and papers with the gross and pernicious information that many have recommended and practiced involves, as it seems to me, most hazardous results.

"The implanted principles which establish the family state are connected with the highest rewards when rightly regulated, and with most dreadful penalties when perverted or abused. And the prosperity of individuals, of families, and of nations, for this life and the life to come, depends more on the proper control and regulation of these principles than on any other social or moral duty.

"And yet there is no point of morals and religion so widely abused and so fruitful of misery and sin as much that is connected with these principles. Instead of being regulated by correct knowledge and well-formed habits of thought and action, all seems left to the mistakes of ignorance or the control of worldly fashion.

"One cause of this state of things is want of consistent rules and customs as to what constitutes *true modesty*. These are all dependent on a general principle of physiology either rarely recognized or inconsistently regarded. The principle is this:

"When the mind directs thought and volition toward any organ of the body the blood and nervous fluid tend to that organ. Thus, when the brain is used, or the eye, or the hand, the nervous fluid and blood tend to the organ to stimulate its action. If this stimulation is too frequent, or too long continued, or produced by unnatural methods, then debility or disease are the result. The capillaries of the misused organ become engorged, producing temporary or chronic inflammation or congestion.

"The same is true of those organs consecrated to marriage. Excess or unnatural abuse causes an engorgement of the capillaries, and then a resulting increase of excitement, and to a degree that sometimes baffles all efforts at self-control.

"It is owing to this physiological principle that the rules of personal modesty, of decorum, and of propriety in social intercourse have been established.

"On the principle above stated these sensibilities demand the control of the *thoughts*. For this reason it is that certain topics which lead to such thoughts are excluded from general conversation, or, if they are alluded to, are veiled in expressions that children do not understand. It is for this cause that novels, poetry, and pictures which direct the imagination to such topics are deemed objectionable, especially for the young.

"It is owing to this physiological fact that Jesus Christ declares that the guilt of adultery commences in the indulgence of the thoughts.

"Marriage is not allowable until there has been due instruction and a habit formed of regulating these sensibilities by rules of modesty, decency, and propriety, and also *knowledge* imparted as to the dangers consequent on neglecting these rules. And here is the place where the customs and practices of society are most inconsistent, false, and destructive to health and morals. For in one direction there is excessive and dangerous laxness, and in another false and dangerous strictness and fastidiousness.

"The rule to guide is this, that whenever health, life, or duty demand it, all connected with these topics should be spoken of and done without restraint or embarrassment; but when there are no such demands, they are to be excluded. Thus all these topics are spoken of plainly in the Bible and read in public worship, and also in medical, surgical, and hospital practice; and it is deemed false modesty and false delicacy to express opposition or disapproval. But when there are no such demands to serve health or life, or to protect from future dangers, conversation, poetry, jokes, or coarse expressions on such topics are vulgar, indecent, and sinful.

"Direct violation of these rules are now pervading not only our popular amusements, our poetry, and novels, but extensively the weekly and daily press is every day drawing attention to topics dangerous and forbidden except for necessary instruction and warning. The Bible as read in families and churches comes with solemn simplicity as instruction from God, and sins of all kinds are made known for warning and instruction. Very different in style and influence are the details of vices and crimes presented daily in newspapers, magazines, poetry, and novels.

"It would seem as if the Prince of Darkness had sent forth his minions to hide all that knowledge that would save from sin and suffering, and to expose all that tempts to danger and sin.

"In addition to the dangers of our popular literature, there is a wide-spread assumption that such is the constitution of man, that the unsullied purity of thought and conduct demanded of the weaker sex is not to be expected or scarcely required of the stronger. This pernicious opinion is not unfrequently implied in medical writers, especially those residing in the centres of European licentiousness.

"Therefore it is very important for parents to know, in the first place, that constitutional diversities exist, involving more temptations to some than to others; and in the next place, that *every* child is so organized, that strict obedience to the laws of health, knowledge of danger from uncontrolled thoughts, useful occupation, and suitable moral and religious training, will secure the regulation of ordinary temptations, and self-control under extraordinary ones. Where in maturity this has not been the case, it has been owing to excess either in forbidden or in legal indulgence.

"There is nothing more difficult than to change customs and prejudices, especially in matters of delicacy and propriety. And it is woman more than man who has controlling influence in these respects. Whatever the cultivated and conscientious women of our country decide *ought* to be done, and will *use their influence* to have done, will surely be accomplished.

"The evils here indicated can never be appreciated until mothers and teachers gain that knowledge of the construction of the body and the dangers connected with the duties of the family state, which now is confined to the medical profession, while physicians, by the false customs and false modesty of women, are constrained to a dangerous reticence.

"I believe that the method proposed by your Association, of securing by endowments well-qualified ladies whose *official* duty it shall be to train the young to be healthy, and to communicate all the knowledge that will fit them to fulfill healthfully and happily all their future duties and relations, will, so far as it is carried out, effectually remedy the evils, and secure the benefits designed.

"Oh, that all parents and teachers who are to train the *next* generation could be made to understand these intimations, and save their daughters from the abounding anguish which has come upon such multitudes of those now upon the stage! Very truly yours, R. B. GLEASON."

These views of Mrs. Dr. Gleason are in accordance with those of the most influential, learned, and benevolent medical men.

Dr. George T. Elliott, late President of the New York County Medical Society, says of *muscular exercise* (or, as Mrs. Gleason would say, "getting up and going to work"): "If this were properly carried out, the local treatment now so much in vogue, and the ever-ready resort to the speculum, might commonly be dispensed with."

Dr. Thomas suggests similar views in an address before the Medical Society of New York County, in which he speaks of "the wonderful improvement exerted on cases *which have long resisted local means*, by sea-bathing, or a few months passed in the country. He also says: "The fact is notorious that the local treatment of these diseases is not as successful as we could wish;" and of uterine injections he says: "My impression is, they have done, and are going to do, *a great deal of harm. I see no necessity for them.*"

Dr. Peasely, of New York City, says: "Medical applications to the uterus are *often* used in conditions not justifying them."

The senior editor of the *Pacific Medical Journal* says: "It is hoped that the fashion of women having recourse to local treatment has passed to its culmination. The highest authorities have taken the back course, and condemn their own uterine surgery in some respects."

The editor of the *Medical Record*, of New York City, says: "In a majority of cases the speculum is used only because it is the fashion. The natural tendency of this is certainly *demoralizing*."

Dr. George H. Taylor, author of an original work on diseases of women, says: "A large portion of the women treated by me for pelvic disease would, in certain stages, be cured by loose dresses supported from the shoulders, domestic exercise, and proper diet. And the *Movement Cure*, to a great extent, consists of exercises that would in many cases be as successful, and more useful, if performed in domestic labor. Moreover, in my experience, not more than one case in twenty of cures by movements requires either local examination or local treatment. A large portion of my patients could, by obeying my directions, cure themselves at home."

Most medical men now agree that the modes of dress, and the excessive mental taxation of schools, unaccompanied by the healthful domestic labor of former days, largely account for the prevalence of diseases among young girls which formerly were confined to married women, and also for the alarming increase of such diseases.

INDEX.

INDEX.

LOSSING'S FIELD-BOOK OF THE REVOLUTION. Pictorial Field-Book of the Revolution; or, Illustrations, by Pen and Pencil, of the History, Biography, Scenery, Relics, and Traditions of the War for Independence. By BENSON J. LOSSING. 2 vols., 8vo, Cloth, $14 00; Sheep, $15 00; Half Calf, $18 00; Full Turkey Morocco, $22 00.

LOSSING'S FIELD-BOOK OF THE WAR OF 1812. Pictorial Field-Book of the War of 1812; or, Illustrations, by Pen and Pencil, of the History, Biography, Scenery, Relics, and Traditions of the Last War for American Independence. By BENSON J. LOSSING. With several hundred Engravings on Wood, by Lossing and Barritt, chiefly from Original Sketches by the Author. 1088 pages, 8vo, Cloth, $7 00; Sheep, $8 50; Half Calf, $10 00.

ALFORD'S GREEK TESTAMENT. The Greek Testament: with a critically revised Text; a Digest of Various Readings; Marginal References to Verbal and Idiomatic Usage; Prolegomena; and a Critical and Exegetical Commentary. For the Use of Theological Students and Ministers. By HENRY ALFORD, D.D., Dean of Canterbury. Vol. I., containing the Four Gospels. 944 pages, 8vo, Cloth, $6 00; Sheep, $6 50.

ABBOTT'S FREDERICK THE GREAT. The History of Frederick the Second, called Frederick the Great. By JOHN S. C. ABBOTT. Elegantly Illustrated. 8vo, Cloth, $5 00.

ABBOTT'S HISTORY OF THE FRENCH REVOLUTION. The French Revolution of 1789, as viewed in the Light of Republican Institutions. By JOHN S. C. ABBOTT. With 100 Engravings. 8vo, Cloth, $5 00.

ABBOTT'S NAPOLEON BONAPARTE. The History of Napoleon Bonaparte. By JOHN S. C. ABBOTT. With Maps, Woodcuts, and Portraits on Steel. 2 vols., 8vo, Cloth, $10 00.

ABBOTT'S NAPOLEON AT ST. HELENA; or, Interesting Anecdotes and Remarkable Conversations of the Emperor during the Five and a Half Years of his Captivity. Collected from the Memorials of Las Casas, O'Meara, Montholon, Antommarchi, and others. By JOHN S. C. ABBOTT. With Illustrations. 8vo, Cloth, $5 00.

ADDISON'S COMPLETE WORKS. The Works of Joseph Addison, embracing the whole of the "Spectator." Complete in 3 vols., 8vo, Cloth, $6 00.

ALCOCK'S JAPAN. The Capital of the Tycoon: a Narrative of a Three Years' Residence in Japan. By Sir RUTHERFORD ALCOCK, K.C.B., Her Majesty's Envoy Extraordinary and Minister Plenipotentiary in Japan. With Maps and Engravings. 2 vols., 12mo, Cloth, $3 50.

ALISON'S HISTORY OF EUROPE. FIRST SERIES: From the Commencement of the French Revolution, in 1789, to the Restoration of the Bourbons, in 1815. [In addition to the Notes on Chapter LXXVI., which correct the errors of the original work concerning the United States, a copious Analytical Index has been appended to this American edition.] SECOND SERIES: From the Fall of Napoleon, in 1815, to the Accession of Louis Napoleon, in 1852. 8 vols., 8vo, Cloth, $16 00.

BALDWIN'S PRE-HISTORIC NATIONS. Pre-Historic Nations; or, Inquiries concerning some of the Great Peoples and Civilizations of Antiquity, and their Probable Relation to a still Older Civilization of the Ethiopians or Cushites of Arabia. By JOHN D. BALDWIN, Member of the American Oriental Society. 12mo, Cloth, $1 75.

BARTH'S NORTH AND CENTRAL AFRICA. Travels and Discoveries in North and Central Africa: being a Journal of an Expedition undertaken under the Auspices of H. B. M.'s Government, in the Years 1849–1855. By HENRY BARTH, Ph.D., D.C.L. Illustrated. 3 vols., 8vo, Cloth, $12 00.

HENRY WARD BEECHER'S SERMONS. Sermons by HENRY WARD BEECHER, Plymouth Church, Brooklyn. Selected from Published and Unpublished Discourses, and Revised by their Author. With Steel Portrait. Complete in 2 vols., 8vo, Cloth, $5 00.

LYMAN BEECHER'S AUTOBIOGRAPHY, &c. Autobiography, Correspondence, &c., of Lyman Beecher, D.D. Edited by his Son, CHARLES BEECHER. With Three Steel Portraits, and Engravings on Wood. In 2 vols., 12mo, Cloth, $5 00.

BOSWELL'S JOHNSON. The Life of Samuel Johnson, LL.D. Including a Journey to the Hebrides. By JAMES BOSWELL, Esq. A New Edition, with numerous Additions and Notes. By JOHN WILSON CROKER, LL.D., F.R.S. Portrait of Boswell. 2 vols., 8vo, Cloth, $4 00.

DRAPER'S CIVIL WAR. History of the American Civil War. By JOHN W. DRAPER, M.D., LL.D., Professor of Chemistry and Physiology in the University of New York. In Three Vols. 8vo, Cloth, $3 50 per vol.

DRAPER'S INTELLECTUAL DEVELOPMENT OF EUROPE. A History of the Intellectual Development of Europe. By JOHN W. DRAPER, M.D., LL.D., Professor of Chemistry and Physiology in the University of New York. 8vo, Cloth, $5 00.

DRAPER'S AMERICAN CIVIL POLICY. Thoughts on the Future Civil Policy of America. By JOHN W. DRAPER, M.D., LL.D., Professor of Chemistry and Physiology in the University of New York. Crown 8vo, Cloth, $2 50.

DU CHAILLU'S AFRICA. Explorations and Adventures in Equatorial Africa: with Accounts of the Manners and Customs of the People, and of the Chase of the Gorilla, the Crocodile, Leopard, Elephant, Hippopotamus, and other Animals. By PAUL B. DU CHAILLU. Numerous Illustrations. 8vo, Cloth, $5 00.

BELLOWS'S OLD WORLD. The Old World in its New Face: Impressions of Europe in 1867-1868. By HENRY W. BELLOWS. 2 vols., 12mo, Cloth, $3 50.

BRODHEAD'S HISTORY OF NEW YORK. History of the State of New York. By JOHN ROMEYN BRODHEAD. 1609-1691. 2 vols. 8vo, Cloth, $3 00 per vol.

BROUGHAM'S AUTOBIOGRAPHY. Life and Times of HENRY, LORD BROUGHAM. Written by Himself. In Three Volumes. 12mo, Cloth, $2 00 per vol.

BULWER'S PROSE WORKS. Miscellaneous Prose Works of Edward Bulwer, Lord Lytton. 2 vols., 12mo, Cloth, $3 50.

BULWER'S HORACE. The Odes and Epodes of Horace. A Metrical Translation into English. With Introduction and Commentaries. By LORD LYTTON. With Latin Text from the Editions of Orelli, Macleane, and Yonge. 12mo, Cloth, $1 75.

BULWER'S KING ARTHUR. A Poem. By EARL LYTTON. New Edition. 12mo, Cloth, $1 75.

BURNS'S LIFE AND WORKS. The Life and Works of Robert Burns. Edited by ROBERT CHAMBERS. 4 vols., 12mo, Cloth, $6 00.

REINDEER, DOGS, AND SNOW-SHOES. A Journal of Siberian Travel and Explorations made in the Years 1865-'67. By RICHARD J. BUSH, late of the Russo-American Telegraph Expedition. Illustrated. Crown 8vo, Cloth, $3 00.

CARLYLE'S FREDERICK THE GREAT. History of Friedrich II., called Frederick the Great. By THOMAS CARLYLE. Portraits, Maps, Plans, &c. 6 vols., 12mo, Cloth, $12 00.

CARLYLE'S FRENCH REVOLUTION. History of the French Revolution. Newly Revised by the Author, with Index, &c. 2 vols., 12mo, Cloth, $3 50.

CARLYLE'S OLIVER CROMWELL. Letters and Speeches of Oliver Cromwell. With Elucidations and Connecting Narrative. 2 vols., 12mo, Cloth, $3 50.

CHALMERS'S POSTHUMOUS WORKS. The Posthumous Works of Dr. Chalmers. Edited by his Son-in-Law, Rev. WILLIAM HANNA, LL.D. Complete in 9 vols., 12mo, Cloth, $13 50.

COLERIDGE'S COMPLETE WORKS. The Complete Works of Samuel Taylor Coleridge. With an Introductory Essay upon his Philosophical and Theological Opinions. Edited by Professor SHEDD. Complete in Seven Vols. With a fine Portrait. Small 8vo, Cloth, $10 50.

DOOLITTLE'S CHINA. Social Life of the Chinese: with some Account of their Religious, Governmental, Educational, and Business Customs and Opinions. With special but not exclusive Reference to Fuhchau. By Rev. JUSTUS DOOLITTLE, Fourteen Years Member of the Fuhchau Mission of the American Board. Illustrated with more than 150 characteristic Engravings on Wood. 2 vols., 12mo, Cloth, $5 00.

GIBBON'S ROME. History of the Decline and Fall of the Roman Empire. By EDWARD GIBBON. With Notes by Rev. H. H. MILMAN and M. GUIZOT. A new cheap Edition. To which is added a complete Index of the whole Work, and a Portrait of the Author. 6 vols., 12mo, Cloth, $9 00.

HAZEN'S SCHOOL AND ARMY IN GERMANY AND FRANCE. The School and the Army in Germany and France, with a Diary of Siege Life at Versailles. By Brevet Major-General W. B. HAZEN, U.S.A., Colonel Sixth Infantry. Crown 8vo, Cloth, $2 50.

HARPER'S NEW CLASSICAL LIBRARY. Literal Translations.
The following Volumes are now ready. Portraits. 12mo, Cloth, $1 50 each.
Cæsar.—Virgil.—Sallust.—Horace.—Cicero's Orations.—Cicero's Offices, &c.—Cicero on Oratory and Orators.—Tacitus (2 vols.).—Terence.—Sophocles.—Juvenal.—Xenophon.—Homer's Iliad.—Homer's Odyssey.—Herodotus.—Demosthenes.—Thucydides.—Æschylus.—Euripides (2 vols.).—Livy (2 vols.).

DAVIS'S CARTHAGE. Carthage and her Remains: being an Account of the Excavations and Researches on the Site of the Phœnician Metropolis in Africa and other adjacent Places. Conducted under the Auspices of Her Majesty's Government. By Dr. Davis, F.R.G.S. Profusely Illustrated with Maps, Woodcuts, Chromo-Lithographs, &c. 8vo, Cloth, $4 00.

EDGEWORTH'S (Miss) NOVELS. With Engravings. 10 vols., 12mo, Cloth, $15 00.

GROTE'S HISTORY OF GREECE. 12 vols., 12mo, Cloth, $18 00.

HELPS'S SPANISH CONQUEST. The Spanish Conquest in America, and its Relation to the History of Slavery and to the Government of Colonies. By Arthur Helps. 4 vols., 12mo, Cloth, $6 00.

HALE'S (Mrs.) WOMAN'S RECORD. Woman's Record; or, Biographical Sketches of all Distinguished Women, from the Creation to the Present Time. Arranged in Four Eras, with Selections from Female Writers of each Era. By Mrs. Sarah Josepha Hale. Illustrated with more than 200 Portraits. 8vo, Cloth, $5 00.

HALL'S ARCTIC RESEARCHES. Arctic Researches and Life among the Esquimaux: being the Narrative of an Expedition in Search of Sir John Franklin, in the Years 1860, 1861, and 1862. By Charles Francis Hall. With Maps and 100 Illustrations. The Illustrations are from Original Drawings by Charles Parsons, Henry L. Stephens, Solomon Eytinge, W. S. L. Jewett, and Granville Perkins, after Sketches by Captain Hall. 8vo, Cloth, $5 00.

HALLAM'S CONSTITUTIONAL HISTORY OF ENGLAND, from the Accession of Henry VII. to the Death of George II. 8vo, Cloth, $2 00.

HALLAM'S LITERATURE. Introduction to the Literature of Europe during the Fifteenth, Sixteenth, and Seventeenth Centuries. By Henry Hallam. 2 vols., 8vo, Cloth, $4 00.

HALLAM'S MIDDLE AGES. State of Europe during the Middle Ages. By Henry Hallam. 8vo, Cloth, $2 00.

HILDRETH'S HISTORY OF THE UNITED STATES. First Series: From the First Settlement of the Country to the Adoption of the Federal Constitution. Second Series: From the Adoption of the Federal Constitution to the End of the Sixteenth Congress. 6 vols., 8vo, Cloth, $18 00.

HUME'S HISTORY OF ENGLAND. History of England, from the Invasion of Julius Cæsar to the Abdication of James II., 1688. By David Hume. A new Edition, with the Author's last Corrections and Improvements. To which is Prefixed a short Account of his Life, written by Himself. With a Portrait of the Author. 6 vols., 12mo, Cloth, $9 00.

JAY'S WORKS. Complete Works of Rev. William Jay: comprising his Sermons, Family Discourses, Morning and Evening Exercises for every Day in the Year, Family Prayers, &c. Author's enlarged Edition, revised. 3 vols., 8vo, Cloth, $6 00.

JEFFERSON'S DOMESTIC LIFE. The Domestic Life of Thomas Jefferson: compiled from Family Letters and Reminiscences by his Great-Granddaughter, Sarah N. Randolph. With Illustrations. Crown 8vo, Illuminated Cloth, Beveled Edges, $2 50.

JOHNSON'S COMPLETE WORKS. The Works of Samuel Johnson, LL.D. With an Essay on his Life and Genius, by Arthur Murphy, Esq. Portrait of Johnson. 2 vols., 8vo, Cloth, $4 00.

KINGLAKE'S CRIMEAN WAR. The Invasion of the Crimea, and an Account of its Progress down to the Death of Lord Raglan. By Alexander William Kinglake. With Maps and Plans. Two Vols. ready. 12mo, Cloth, $2 00 per vol.

KINGSLEY'S WEST INDIES. At Last: A Christmas in the West Indies. By Charles Kingsley. Illustrated. 12mo, Cloth, $1 50.

KRUMMACHER'S DAVID, KING OF ISRAEL. **David, the King of Israel: a Portrait drawn from Bible History and the Book of Psalms. By** FREDERICK WILLIAM KRUMMACHER, D.D., Author of "Elijah the Tishbite," &c. Translated under the express Sanction of the Author by the Rev. M. G. EASTON, M.A. With a Letter from Dr. Krummacher to his American Readers, and a Portrait. 12mo, Cloth, $1 75.

LAMB'S COMPLETE WORKS. The Works of Charles Lamb. Comprising his Letters, Poems, Essays of Elia, Essays upon Shakspeare, Hogarth, &c., and a Sketch of his Life, with the Final Memorials, by T. NOON TALFOURD. Portrait. 2 vols., 12mo, Cloth, $3 00.

LIVINGSTONE'S SOUTH AFRICA. Missionary Travels and Researches in South Africa; including a Sketch of Sixteen Years' Residence in the Interior of Africa, and a Journey from the Cape of Good Hope to Loando on the West Coast; thence across the Continent, down the River Zambesi, to the Eastern Ocean. By DAVID LIVINGSTONE, LL.D., D.C.L. With Portrait, Maps by Arrowsmith, and numerous Illustrations. 8vo, Cloth, $4 50.

LIVINGSTONES' ZAMBESI. Narrative of an Expedition to the Zambesi and its Tributaries, and of the Discovery of the Lakes Shirwa and Nyassa. 1858-1864. By DAVID and CHARLES LIVINGSTONE. With Map and Illustrations. 8vo, Cloth, $5 00.

M'CLINTOCK & STRONG'S CYCLOPÆDIA. Cyclopædia of Biblical, Theological, and Ecclesiastical Literature. Prepared by the Rev. JOHN M'CLINTOCK, D.D., and JAMES STRONG, S.T.D. 4 *vols. now ready.* Royal 8vo. Price per vol., Cloth, $5 00; Sheep, $6 00; Half Morocco, $8 00.

MARCY'S ARMY LIFE ON THE BORDER. Thirty Years of Army Life on the Border. Comprising Descriptions of the Indian Nomads of the Plains; Explorations of New Territory; a Trip across the Rocky Mountains in the Winter; Descriptions of the Habits of Different Animals found in the West, and the Methods of Hunting them; with Incidents in the Life of Different Frontier Men, &c., &c. By Brevet Brigadier-General R. B. MARCY, U.S.A., Author of "The Prairie Traveller." With numerous Illustrations. 8vo, Cloth, Beveled Edges, $3 00.

MACAULAY'S HISTORY OF ENGLAND. The History of England from the Accession of James II. By THOMAS BABINGTON MACAULAY. With an Original Portrait of the Author. 5 vols., 8vo, Cloth, $10 00; 12mo, Cloth, $7 50.

MOSHEIM'S ECCLESIASTICAL HISTORY, Ancient and Modern; in which the Rise, Progress, and Variation of Church Power are considered in their Connection with the State of Learning and Philosophy, and the Political History of Europe during that Period. Translated, with Notes, &c., by A. MACLAINE, D.D. A new Edition, continued to 1826, by C. COOTE, LL.D. 2 vols., 8vo, Cloth, $4 00.

NEVIUS'S CHINA. China and the Chinese: a General Description of the Country and its Inhabitants; its Civilization and Form of Government; its Religious and Social Institutions; its Intercourse with other Nations; and its Present Condition and Prospects. By the Rev. JOHN L. NEVIUS, Ten Years a Missionary in China. With a Map and Illustrations. 12mo, Cloth, $1 75.

THE DESERT OF THE EXODUS. Journeys on Foot in the Wilderness of the Forty Years' Wanderings; undertaken in connection with the Ordnance Survey of Sinai and the Palestine Exploration Fund. By E. H. PALMER, M.A., Lord Almoner's Professor of Arabic, and Fellow of St. John's College, Cambridge. With Maps and numerous Illustrations from Photographs and Drawings taken on the spot by the Sinai Survey Expedition and C. F. Tyrwhitt Drake. Crown 8vo, Cloth, $3 00.

OLIPHANT'S CHINA AND JAPAN. Narrative of the Earl of Elgin's Mission to China and Japan, in the Years 1857, '58, '59. By LAURENCE OLIPHANT, Private Secretary to Lord Elgin. Illustrations. 8vo, Cloth, $3 50.

OLIPHANT'S (MRS.) LIFE OF EDWARD IRVING. The Life of Edward Irving, Minister of the National Scotch Church, London. Illustrated by his Journals and Correspondence. By MRS. OLIPHANT. Portrait. 8vo, Cloth, $3 50.

RAWLINSON'S MANUAL OF ANCIENT HISTORY. A Manual of Ancient History, from the Earliest Times to the Fall of the Western Empire. Comprising the History of Chaldæa, Assyria, Media, Babylonia, Lydia, Phœnicia, Syria, Judæa, Egypt, Carthage, Persia, Greece, Macedonia, Parthia, and Rome. By GEORGE RAWLINSON, M.A., Camden Professor of Ancient History in the University of Oxford. 12mo, Cloth, $2 50.

RECLUS'S THE EARTH. The Earth: a Descriptive History of the Phenomena and Life of the Globe. By Elisée Reclus. Translated by the late B. B. Woodward, and Edited by Henry Woodward. With 234 Maps and Illustrations, and 23 Page Maps printed in Colors. 8vo, Cloth, $5 00.

POETS OF THE NINETEENTH CENTURY. The Poets of the Nineteenth Century. Selected and Edited by the Rev. Robert Aris Willmott. With English and American Additions, arranged by Evert A. Duyckinck, Editor of "Cyclopædia of American Literature." Comprising Selections from the Greatest Authors of the Age. Superbly Illustrated with 141 Engravings from Designs by the most Eminent Artists. In elegant small 4to form, printed on Superfine Tinted Paper, richly bound in extra Cloth, Beveled, Gilt Edges, $5 00; Half Calf, $5 50; Full Turkey Morocco, $9 00.

SHAKSPEARE. The Dramatic Works of William Shakspeare, with the Corrections and Illustrations of Dr. Johnson, G. Steevens, and others. Revised by Isaac Reed. Engravings. 6 vols., Royal 12mo, Cloth, $9 00.

SMILES'S LIFE OF THE STEPHENSONS. The Life of George Stephenson, and of his Son, Robert Stephenson; comprising, also, a History of the Invention and Introduction of the Railway Locomotive. By Samuel Smiles, Author of "Self-Help," &c. With Steel Portraits and numerous Illustrations. 8vo, Cloth, $3 00.

SMILES'S HISTORY OF THE HUGUENOTS. The Huguenots: their Settlements, Churches, and Industries in England and Ireland. By Samuel Smiles. With an Appendix relating to the Huguenots in America. Crown 8vo, Cloth, $1 75.

SPEKE'S AFRICA. Journal of the Discovery of the Source of the Nile. By Captain John Hanning Speke, Captain H. M. Indian Army, Fellow and Gold Medalist of the Royal Geographical Society, Hon. Corresponding Member and Gold Medalist of the French Geographical Society, &c. With Maps and Portraits and numerous Illustrations, chiefly from Drawings by Captain Grant. 8vo, Cloth, uniform with Livingstone, Barth, Burton, &c., $4 00.

STRICKLAND'S (Miss) QUEENS OF SCOTLAND. Lives of the Queens of Scotland and English Princesses connected with the Regal Succession of Great Britain. By Agnes Strickland. 8 vols., 12mo, Cloth, $12 00.

THE STUDENT'S SERIES.

France. Engravings. 12mo, Cloth, $2 00.
Gibbon. Engravings. 12mo, Cloth, $2 00.
Greece. Engravings. 12mo, Cloth, $2 00.
Hume. Engravings. 12mo, Cloth, $2 00.
Rome. By Liddell. Engravings. 12mo, Cloth, $2 00.
Old Testament History. Engravings. 12mo, Cloth, $2 00.
New Testament History. Engravings. 12mo, Cloth, $2 00.
Strickland's Queens of England. Abridged. Engravings. 12mo, Cloth, $2 00.
Ancient History of the East. 12mo, Cloth, $2 00.
Hallam's Middle Ages. 12mo, Cloth, $2 00.
Lyell's Elements of Geology. 12mo, Cloth, $2 00.

TENNYSON'S COMPLETE POEMS. The Complete Poems of Alfred Tennyson, Poet Laureate. With numerous Illustrations by Eminent Artists, and Three Characteristic Portraits. 8vo, Paper, 75 cents; Cloth, $1 25.

THOMSON'S LAND AND THE BOOK. The Land and the Book; or, Biblical Illustrations drawn from the Manners and Customs, the Scenes and the Scenery of the Holy Land. By W. M. Thomson, D.D., Twenty-five Years a Missionary of the A.B.C.F.M. in Syria and Palestine. With two elaborate Maps of Palestine, an accurate Plan of Jerusalem, and several hundred Engravings, representing the Scenery, Topography, and Productions of the Holy Land, and the Costumes, Manners, and Habits of the People. 2 large 12mo vols., Cloth, $5 00.

TYERMAN'S WESLEY. The Life and Times of the Rev. John Wesley, M. A., Founder of the Methodists. By the Rev. Luke Tyerman, Author of "The Life of Rev. Samuel Wesley." Portraits. 3 vols., Crown 8vo, Cloth, $7 50.

VÁMBÉRY'S CENTRAL ASIA. Travels in Central Asia. Being the Account of a Journey from Teheran across the Turkoman Desert, on the Eastern Shore of the Caspian, to Khiva, Bokhara, and Samarcand, performed in the Year 1863. By Arminius Vámbéry, Member of the Hungarian Academy of Pesth, by whom he was sent on this Scientific Mission. With Map and Woodcuts. 8vo, Cloth, $4 50.

WOOD'S HOMES WITHOUT HANDS. Homes Without Hands: being a Description of the Habitations of Animals, classed according to their Principle of Construction. By J. G. Wood, M.A., F.L.S. With about 140 Illustrations. 8vo, Cloth, Beveled Edges, $4 50.

www.ingramcontent.com/pod-product-compliance
Lightning Source LLC
LaVergne TN
LVHW020921110826
845150LV00004B/728